Anna-Maria Sonnemann
Language Families in Contact

Language Contact
and Bilingualism

Editor
Yaron Matras

Volume 24

Anna-Maria Sonnemann

Language Families in Contact

The Mutual Impact of Slavic and Romani

ISBN 978-3-11-163175-2
e-ISBN (PDF) 978-3-11-075617-3
e-ISBN (EPUB) 978-3-11-075624-1
ISSN 2190-698X

Library of Congress Control Number: 2022943008

Bibliographic information published by the Deutsche Nationalbibliothek
The Deutsche Nationalbibliothek lists this publication in the Deutsche Nationalbibliografie;
detailed bibliographic data are available on the internet at http://dnb.dnb.de.

© 2024 Walter de Gruyter GmbH, Berlin/Boston
This volume is text- and page-identical with the hardback published in 2022.
Cover image: Anette Linnea Rasmus/Fotolia
Typesetting: Integra Software Services Pvt. Ltd.

www.degruyter.com

This book is dedicated to my parents.

Acknowledgements

Writing this book – which is based on my Habilitation thesis accepted by the Faculty of Arts and Humanities of the University of Cologne in October 2021 – would not have been possible without the professional and emotional support of many people.

First and foremost, I am enormously grateful to Yaron Matras for his invitation to publish the manuscript in the *Language Contact and Bilingualism* series at De Gruyter Mouton, for having been a great advisor over several years and for his appreciation of my work.

Very warm thanks go to my teachers of Romani Martin Gális and Iveta Kokyová and my long-standing mentors, supervisors and friends Sebastian Kempgen and Daniel Bunčić.

I want to thank Kirstin Börgen and Birgit Sievert for the very professional and kind cooperation during the process of preparing the manuscript for print, as well as the two anonymous reviewers for their incredibly thorough revision of the manuscript and countless valuable hints which definitely helped to improve the quality of the book.

The questions and comments of Viktor Elšík, Mirjana Mirić, Nikola Rašić and all the participants of the *International Conference of Romani Linguistics* 2020 and 2021 have been very helpful, just like the discussions with and hints by Norbert Boretzky, Christian Sappok, Manfred Krug, Achim Rabus, Nicolas Jansens, Birgit Hellwig and Eugen Hill.

Finally, but very importantly, I want to thank my parents Gudrun (†) and Herbert Meyer, my husband Till Sonnemann and his parents Gyburg and Jürgen, my life-coaches Luka Kadović and Andrew Woods with Olina as well as my wonderful (former) colleagues in Bamberg and Cologne for always believing in me.

Bamberg, July 2022

Contents

Acknowledgements —— VII

List of figures —— XIII

List of tables —— XV

Abbreviations —— XVII

1	**Introduction** —— 1	
1.1	History of research on Slavic–Romani language contact —— 5	
1.2	Sources for the study of Slavic–Romani language contact —— 7	
1.3	Aim of the book and structure of the chapters —— 12	

2   **Two language families in contact? On the status of Slavic and Romani** —— 16
2.1   The Slavic languages as a language family —— 16
2.2   Romani as a language family? —— 17
2.2.1   Romani dialect classifications —— 18
2.2.2   The dialectological approach in question —— 20

3   **Examining contact phenomena through a contemporary lens** —— 26
3.1   A pragmatic-functional approach to language contact —— 26
3.2   The linguistic repertoire —— 27
3.3   The bilingual mode —— 28
3.4   The link to borrowing and other language contact phenomena —— 29
3.5   A contemporary definition of language contact —— 31

4   **The structural impact of Slavic on Romani** —— 33
4.1   Phonetics and phonology —— 33
4.2   Nominal morphology —— 37
4.2.1   Inflectional endings and word formation affixes —— 37
4.2.2   Case —— 38
4.2.3   Articles —— 41
4.2.4   Comparison —— 42
4.2.5   Indefinites —— 43
4.2.6   Interrogatives —— 45
4.2.7   Possessives, personal pronouns and demonstratives —— 46

4.3	Verbal morphology —— 46	
4.3.1	Tense —— 47	
4.3.2	The "new infinitive" —— 48	
4.3.3	Voice and reflexivity —— 50	
4.3.4	Modality —— 51	
4.3.5	The conditional —— 53	
4.3.6	Renarrative and evidentiality —— 53	
4.3.7	Imperative, optative and jussive —— 54	
4.4	Syntax —— 54	
4.4.1	Prepositions and conjunctions —— 55	
4.4.2	Object doubling —— 58	
4.4.3	Conditional sentences —— 59	
4.4.4	Negation —— 60	
4.4.5	Word order —— 60	
4.4.6	Zero copula —— 62	
4.5	Discourse markers —— 63	
4.6	Summary —— 64	
5	**Slavic verbal prefixes in Romani – figures, forms and functions —— 67**	
5.1	Aspect and aktionsart in Slavic and Romani —— 68	
5.1.1	Aspect and aktionsart in Romani —— 69	
5.1.2	Aspect and aktionsart in Slavic —— 70	
5.2	Analysis of the RMS database data —— 71	
5.2.1	Methodological procedure —— 71	
5.2.2	Results —— 72	
5.3	Functions of the Slavic verbal prefixes in Romani —— 76	
5.3.1	Group 1: Varieties in contact with South Slavic —— 76	
5.3.2	Group 2: Varieties in contact with Czech and Slovak —— 79	
5.3.3	Group 3: Varieties in contact with East Slavic and Polish —— 80	
5.4	Discussion —— 86	
5.5	Contact-linguistic classification —— 87	
5.6	Summary —— 90	
6	**Lexical borrowings from Slavic in Romani —— 92**	
6.1	Slavic lexical elements in Romani —— 93	
6.1.1	Nouns —— 95	
6.1.2	Verbs —— 96	
6.1.3	Adjectives —— 96	

6.1.4	Adverbs and particles —— 97	
6.1.5	Quantifiers and numerals —— 100	
6.1.6	Lexical calquing —— 102	
6.2	Lexical borrowings in two Romani varieties in Poland —— 103	
6.2.1	Creation of the corpus —— 104	
6.2.2	Parts of speech —— 105	
6.2.3	Semantic fields —— 107	
6.2.4	Morphological integration —— 108	
6.2.5	Diachronic comparison —— 109	
6.3	Summary —— 112	
7	**Romani borrowings in diastratic varieties of Slavic —— 114**	
7.1	Romani borrowings in diastratic varieties —— 115	
7.2	Slavic argots with a Romani component —— 118	
7.2.1	Bosnian / Croatian / Serbian: Šatrovački —— 118	
7.2.2	Bulgarian: Čalgădžijski ezik —— 120	
7.2.3	Czech: Světská hantýrka —— 120	
7.2.4	Polish argots —— 122	
7.2.5	Russian and Ukrainian argots —— 122	
7.3	Romani lexicon in Slavic argots, youth slangs and colloquial varieties —— 123	
7.3.1	Bosnian / Croatian / Serbian —— 124	
7.3.2	Bulgarian —— 127	
7.3.3	Czech —— 129	
7.3.4	Polish —— 132	
7.3.5	Russian —— 133	
7.3.6	Ukrainian —— 135	
7.3.7	The most frequent Romisms in Slavic diastratic varieties overall —— 136	
7.4	Summary —— 137	
8	**Writing Romani with 'Slavic' alphabets —— 139**	
8.1	The role of literacy in Romani culture —— 140	
8.1.1	Romani culture as an oral culture? —— 140	
8.1.2	Possibilities of writing Romani —— 142	
8.2	Creating an alphabet for Romani in eight Slavic-speaking countries —— 144	
8.2.1	Theoretical background —— 144	

8.2.2 Orthographic projects for Romani in Slavophone countries —— 147
8.3 Summary —— 161

9 Conclusion —— 165

Appendix 1 (chapter 6): Alphabetical list of analyzed words —— 171

Appendix 2 (chapter 7): Romani borrowings in diastratic varieties of Slavic —— 193

References —— 219

Subject index —— 241

Language index —— 245

List of figures

Fig. 1　Estimated percentage share of Roma in total population by country and Roma population in absolute numbers (status: 2010) —— 1
Fig. 2　Extract from the RMS sample RUS-003 —— 8
Fig. 3　Localization of the analyzed RMS samples —— 12
Fig. 4　The main dialects of Romani in Europe —— 21
Fig. 5　Borrowing of Slavic prepositions into Romani —— 55
Fig. 6　Borrowing of Slavic conjunctions into Romani —— 57
Fig. 7　Two table excerpts from the samples from Russia —— 72
Fig. 8　Non-prefixed and prefixed Slavic verbs and independent Slavic prefixes —— 73
Fig. 9　Percentage of Slavic independent prefixes —— 75
Fig. 10　Borrowing of Slavic temporal and phasal adverbs in Romani —— 97
Fig. 11　Borrowing of Slavic local adverbs in Romani —— 98
Fig. 12　Borrowing of Slavic focus particles and intensifiers in Romani —— 99
Fig. 13　Evidence for Romisms in the *Hrvatski nacionalni korpus* —— 126
Fig. 14　Evidence for Romisms in the Czech national corpus —— 132
Fig. 15　Evidence for Romisms in the NKRJa —— 135
Fig. 16　Demeter and Demeter's (1990) alphabet in the Cyrillic original and Latin transliteration —— 150
Fig. 17　"Overview of the Romani, Latin and Cyrillic script" —— 155

List of tables

Tab. 1	Metadata for the RMS samples involving Slavic contact languages —— 8
Tab. 2	Comparison of Standard Czech and Standard Slovak —— 22
Tab. 3	Overview of Ammon's algorithm —— 23
Tab. 4	Comparison of Kalajdži and East Finnish Romani —— 24
Tab. 5	Aktionsart integration —— 89
Tab. 6	Texts used for the corpus —— 104
Tab. 7	Borrowings and codeswitches according to parts of speech —— 106
Tab. 8	Polish words in Rozwadowski (1936) in comparison with the contemporary corpus —— 110
Tab. 9	Polish words in Ficowski (1956) in comparison with the contemporary corpus —— 111
Tab. 10	Overview of the orthographic projects —— 162

Abbreviations

ABL	ablative
ACC	accusative
ADJ	adjective
ADV	adverb
ART	article
CAUS	causative
COMP	complementizer
COND	conditional
DAT	dative
DIM	diminutive
F	feminine
FUT	future
GEN	genitive
IMP	imperative
INF	infinitive
INS	instrumental
IPF	imperfect
IPFV	imperfective
LOC	locative
M	masculine
N	neuter
NEG	negation
OBJ	object
OBL	oblique
PASS	passive
PFV	perfective
PL	plural
PREF	prefix
PRF	perfect
PRS	present
PST	past
PTCP	participle
REFL	reflexive
SBJ	subject
SG	singular
V	verb

1 Introduction

Romani, the language of the Roma, Sinti, Kalé, Manuša and other European people groups should be of relevance for Slavicists as well as the Slavic languages for Romologists, because the contact occurring between their respective languages is, so to speak, the case of language contact *par excellence* in Eastern Europe. Native speakers of Slavic languages and native speakers of Romani live in close proximity in Eastern, South-Eastern and Central Eastern Europe.

According to censuses and estimates, the Slavic-speaking countries with the largest number of Roma currently living there are Bulgaria, Slovakia and Serbia (cf. Fig. 1 below). However, due to a lack of data, it is practically impossible to give

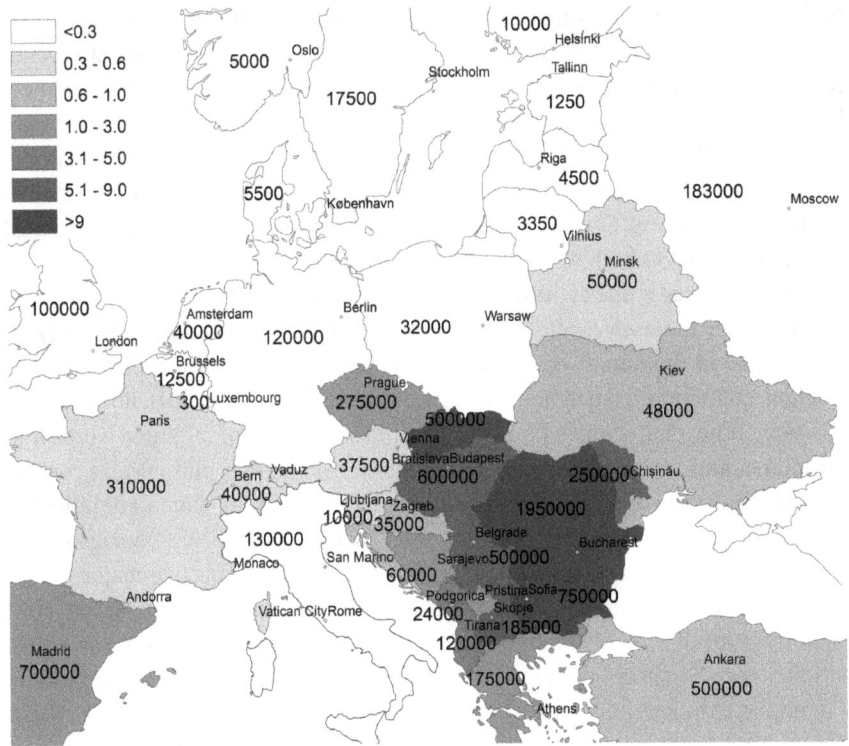

Fig. 1: Estimated percentage share of Roma in total population by country and Roma population in absolute numbers (status: 2010).[1]

---

1 Map: Till Sonnemann 2022; sources: Berlin-Institut für Bevölkerung und Entwicklung; www.perepis2002.ru; https://2001.ukrcensus.gov.ua, https://minorityrights.org; https://coe.int.

https://doi.org/10.1515/9783110756173-001

realistic numbers about the Roma population (not only) in Slavic-speaking countries. Even where nation and ethnicity are asked for in censuses, as for example in Poland's latest census from 2021, the results are not reliable, because many Roma do not identify themselves as such officially for fear of discrimination. The most conservative estimates put the number of Roma living in Europe at 3.5 million (Matras 2002: 238), but the actual figure is probably much higher. According to the *Berlin-Institut für Bevölkerung und Entwicklung* ('Berlin Institute for Population and Development'), the country with the largest Roma population in Europe is Romania, with 1.95 million, which is almost 10% of the country's total population. 500,000 or more Roma live in Bulgaria, Spain, Hungary, Slovakia, Serbia and Turkey, and between 100,000 and 400,000 in France, North Macedonia, Greece, Italy, Germany and the United Kingdom. According to official figures from 2001 and 2002, there are 182,766 Roma living in Russia (www.perepis2002.ru), and 47,600 in Ukraine (https://2001.ukrcensus.gov.ua); the actual numbers are, again, probably much higher. It is important to note, though, that the number of Roma does not equal the number of Romani speakers. In Romania for instance, but also in Hungary and elsewhere, many Roma speak Romanian, and there are more Roma than Romani speakers in other countries as well. Outside Europe, there are large Roma communities in the USA, Canada, Brazil, Argentina and Australia, among others. Correspondingly, Romani thus represents one of the largest minority languages both within Europe and worldwide.

The language is one of the most important factors in the construction of Roma identity; they themselves refer to it as *romanes* (in different variants), literally 'in the manner of the Roma', or *romani čhib* 'Roma language', from which the term *Romani*, commonly used in linguistics, is derived (Matras 2014: 101). Romani is, at the same time, characterized by a remarkably stable core of inherited words and structures and by, in part, massive influences from earlier and current contact languages. To this day, apart from very young children, all Roma are bilingual and often master other regional languages in addition to the language of the majority society (Matras and Adamou 2020: 329). The respective majority language is usually acquired in infancy after the acquisition of Romani, at the latest with the start of school attendance. Studies on first and second language acquisition among Roma children in Slavophone countries are still limited in number (cf. e.g. Kyuchukov 1999 for Bulgaria and Kyuchukov, de Villiers and Takahesu Tabori 2017 for Slovakia). Bilingualism among the Roma is – typical for minority languages worldwide – unidirectional, which means that the Roma learn the majority language of their respective country, but Romani is learned only in exceptional cases as a second language (Matras 2020: 59). The following excerpt from a narration about stealing a bride from a Ukrainian Romni shall serve as an illustration for the so-called *bilingual mode* (Grosjean 1989, 2001; Matras

2020: 110) which is the default mode of communication among Roma. In this case, the speaker switches freely between Romani, Russian and Ukrainian (the latter two are marked in italics).

(1) a. *Značit*, dro veš keras bjau. Terno, terni. *Kolys', tak.* (Gimpeny)
 b. Bjau baro. *Nu kak, vsë,* aj si do foro
 c. *hėto zavedujuščyj tam xata [g]de samolëty,*
 d. nasaro aj baro manuš, lestero njina nej, jov barvalo.
 e. *I esli tahda... a?*
 f. [Interviewer:] Terno manuš?
 g. *No* dro berša, *let tridcat pjat', let tridcat pjat' emu tam, nu do soroka, tak vot,*
 h. a je ternji, džal pala romeste pal e čhaveste, pal o rom,
 i. phenel *ax intjerjesno var*kjedy, *esli* koneste *motocykl*os kaj *est'* kasa,
 j. oo kada baro manuš barvalo, a leste *matocykl*o kaj *est'* kasa,
 k. *ja poedu posmotrju cyganskuju svad'bu, intjeresno, poedu,*
 l. huuj jov tradel *motocykl*osa.
 m. Oj! *Je* bravinta adoj, *vsë, pjaški,* tradel ko Roma dro veš, te dikhel.
 n. *Pritradel,* oooj romale! Romale! Raj baro tradel,
 o. hej, manuš baro, foroste, len... len čhuven pal o skamind, len, dikhen,
 p. *vstrečajtes',* čhuven les pal o skamind.
 q. *Davaj huljaj, pij, huljaj.*
 r. *A* i terni lel rjumki *tak dve,* pro šero čhuvel,
 s. ternji, šukar, bravinta si, *krasavica,*
 t. *i pošla v pljas, pljasatj,* rjumki duj bravintasa,
 u. čhuvel pro šero *i pošla v pljas.* [...]

 a. 'So, we have a wedding in a forest. Groom, bride. *Some time ago, yes.*
 b. A big wedding. *What of it, that's all,* and in the town there is
 c. *it is the director of the house where there are planes,*
 d. some kind of important man, he has nobody, he is rich.
 e. *And if so... what?*
 f. [Interviewer:] A young man?
 g. *Well,* in years, *thirty-five, thirty-five years old, well, not more than forty, there you go,*
 h. and there is the bride, she is getting married to a boy, to a man,
 i. she says *oh, that's interesting* sometimes, *if* someone has a *motorbike* and *there is* a luggage box,
 j. ooh this important man is rich, and he has a *motorbike* and *there is* a luggage box,
 k. *I'll go and see a Gypsy wedding, interesting, I will go,*

l. hoo, he rides a *motorbike*.
m. *Oh! There is* vodka there, *everything, drinks*, he goes to the Roma into the forest, to have a look.
n. He arrives, heeey Roma! Roma! A gentleman is coming,
o. hey, a gentleman, from the town, take... take a seat at the table, take a seat, have a look,
p. *introduce yourselves*, take a seat at the table.
q. *Come on, enjoy yourself, drink, enjoy yourself.*
r. *And* the bride, she takes *two* of these shot glasses and puts them on her head,
s. young, pretty, vodka is poured, *a real beauty*,
t. *and she went dancing, to dance*, with two shots of vodka,
u. she puts them on her head *and goes dancing*. [...]
(UKR-020, sample transcription, slightly modified)

The frequent use of the bilingual mode shall however not detract from the important fact that – apart from the special case of para-Romani – Romani is fully developed and not a deficient language. Yet it is not a state language, but a diaspora language that is spread over territories inhabited by many other peoples and nations. Halwachs (rombase.uni-graz.at) describes it as a "heterogeneous cluster of varieties without any homogenising standard". Romani is primarily used in the private, family environment for communication with other Roma and thus fulfills a basilectal function. Recently it has also been used across groups for communication between Roma activists of different origins. The respective majority language is used for all communication with non-Roma (*gadže* in Romani, English spelling *Gadje*) in various areas of public life such as administration, schools or media and thus fulfills an acrolectal function. In North Macedonia, it is an official language, government documents are produced in it, it is used at conferences and for literature. Intermediate forms can occur in semi-public spheres such as in communication at work or with acquaintances outside the family (mesolectal function). Especially in the Balkans, Romani has numerous mesolectal functions, often in parallel with other minority languages such as Turkish or Albanian (Matras 2002: 238; Halwachs, Klinge and Schrammel-Leber 2013: 18–19). In this way, loyalty and emotional connection to one's own language are closely coupled with pragmatic openness to communication outside the community (Matras 2014: 105). The importance of Romani for the construction of one's own identity in distinction to the world of the Gadje cannot be overestimated, and, of course, it also fulfills the purpose of a 'secret language' to a certain extent. It is in no small part this aspect of the "secret" and "exotic" that has made Romani so interesting for linguists for centuries.

Historically Slavic languages have been in contact with Romani since the fourteenth century and affected it considerably, both on the lexical and on the structural level. For example, the Romani varieties spoken in Russia today show influences not only from the current contact language Russian, but also from West and South Slavic languages from earlier contact situations. All Romani varieties in Europe have been influenced by the South Slavic languages in the Balkans, but the most balkanized are, of course, the dialects of those speakers who have remained in that region until today. Moreover, given the long history of language contact between the Slavic languages and Romani, as well as the similarities among the Slavic languages, it is not always possible to identify the Slavic source language that a given contact feature originated from. The analysis must also take into account that spoken varieties of Slavic play and have played a greater role than did the standard languages, since communication between the Slavic and Romani-speaking populations was exclusively oral for centuries. The influence of standard Slavic languages has been growing only in the last few decades with the increase of schooling and literacy among the Roma.

The dialect groups influenced by the Slavic languages are mainly the Northwestern, Northern Central, Southern Central, and South Balkan I dialects, as well as some Vlax dialects, but Slavic influence can be found in Romani varieties all over the world (cf. e.g. Hancock 1983 for Romani in Texas), beyond current nation-states with an official Slavic language. Thus, for example, the very name of the *Mečkar* of Albania is Slavic ('bear-trainer') (anonymous reviewer; cf. also Chapter 6.1). The extent of Slavic impact on Romani can differ significantly and depends on various factors such as the way of life of the community in question, the degree of the group's integration into the majority society, and the duration of sedentariness. The so-called Vlax dialects generally show much less Slavic influence than non-Vlax dialects but have many elements from Romanian.

1.1 History of research on Slavic–Romani language contact

Already 150 years ago, Romani aroused the interest of scholars in Slavic studies: Franz Miklosich (1813–1891) was not only the first Slavicist, but also one of the first in general to deal scientifically with Romani. His interest in the Roma and their language was probably aroused around 1847 in connection with his Sanskrit studies (Neweklowsky 2015: 208). From 1872 to 1880, he wrote twelve treatises on the language, history, fairy tales, and songs of the Roma, as well as on the term 'Gypsy' under the title *Ueber die Mundarten und die Wanderungen der Zigeuner Europa's* ('On the dialects and migrations of the Gypsies of Europe') in the *Denkschriften der Philosophisch-Historischen Klasse der Akademie der Wissen-*

schaften zu Wien. He devoted the most space to the language, and his treatise *Die slavischen Elemente in den Mundarten der Zigeuner* ('The Slavic elements in the dialects of the Gypsies') from 1872 is particularly interesting in the context of the present book. It contains a collection of Romani words that were borrowed from a Slavic language or in the borrowing of which a Slavic language played the mediating role. In addition, there are four other linguistic papers by Miklosich from the period 1874–1878 – *Beiträge zur Kenntniss der Zigeunermundarten* ('Contributions to the knowledge of the Gypsy dialects') –, including *Zigeunerische Elemente in den Gaunersprachen Europas* ('Gypsy elements in the cants of Europe') from 1876.

Miklosich studied the historical phonetics, morphology and syntax of various Romani varieties in the Habsburg Monarchy and was a pioneer of Romani dialect classification. In addition, he researched various loanword strata, especially from Greek and Slavic, and found that the dialects of most Roma groups contained numerous words of Slavic origin, e.g. *vodros* 'bed', *dosta* 'enough', *čelo* 'whole', *kralis* 'king', *stanja* 'stable', or *zelano* 'green'. He also took the trouble to learn the language, which few had done before him (Hancock 1988: 189; Matras 2002: 218; Boretzky and Igla 2004: 5; Matras 2014: 113). By comparing the Romani dialects known to him and examining historical sources, Miklosich succeeded in reconstructing the migration route of the Roma through Europe and thus continued the work of August Pott (1802–1887), who is considered the "father of modern Romani linguistics". The most detailed overview of Miklosich's research on Romani is given by Neweklowsky (2015: 206–210). Also, after Miklosich, there were several other Slavicists who focused their research on Romani: These include Jan M. Rozwadowski (1867–1935, a Polish linguist and professor at the Jagiellonian University in Cracow), who wrote the *Wörterbuch der Zigeuner von Zakopane* ('Dictionary of the Gypsies of Zakopane', cf. Rozwadowski 1936), and Edward Klich (1878–1939, professor of Slavic studies at the University of Poznań), whose romological essays were republished as a compilation only a few years ago in the volume *O polszczyźnie i cygańszczyźnie* ('On the Polish language and the Gypsy language', cf. Klich [1927] 2011). In addition, Norbert Boretzky (*1935, a Slavicist and later professor of comparative linguistics at the University of Bochum) deserves special mention, whose extremely extensive œuvre on Romani and the language contacts between Slavic and Romani will be referred to many times in this work. Marcel Courthiade (1953–2021), who was one of the most well-known Romologists worldwide, first studied Polish and South Slavic languages before turning to Romani. Victor Friedman (*1949) is equally a specialist in Slavic languages and in Romani, with a focus on the Balkan region. Given the fact that Romani has been in contact with all Slavic languages without exception, in some cases for centuries, it stands to reason that the Slavistic gaze has turned to it from the very beginning, and should continue to do so.

1.2 Sources for the study of Slavic–Romani language contact

The largest and most important data source for Romani is the RMS (Romani Morpho-Syntax) Database. It was founded under the leadership of Yaron Matras and Viktor Elšík and is freely accessible at the following address: http://romani.humanities.manchester.ac.uk/rms. For a detailed introduction to its background and features (given the technical state of the art at that time), see Matras, White and Elšík (2009). The work on the database began in 1998 with the aim of creating an electronic resource that would bundle linguistic data and metadata in the form of answers to analytical questions, make them publicly available and enable searches within entire samples. A declared goal is also the usability for contact-linguistic questions. In the metadata, information on country, dialect name, location and contact languages is given for each sample; the contact languages are divided into old, recent and current ones. An old L2 is one that has had a long-lasting, significant influence on an earlier stage of the variety in question, and older speakers may still be aware of it, but it is no longer actively used in the speech community. A recent L2 is only actively spoken by the parents' and / or grandparents' generation or by the first immigrant generation of a community, but no longer by the younger generation. A current L2 is the main contact language of the entire community in everyday interactions with non-Roma and is actively spoken by all members (Matras and Adamou 2020: 334–335).

The data were collected over many years of field research by a large team led by Yaron Matras and Viktor Elšík. All samples are based on the same elicitation questionnaire, which has been translated into many languages. The elicitation technique takes advantage of the already mentioned multilingualism of the Roma, whereby the respective majority language can easily be used for elicitation. Even though this type of language data collection also has disadvantages,[2] the RMS Database has the inestimable value of providing one and the same word or construction in a total of 122 different samples, each with about 1100 words, phrases and sentences, such that it enables one to comprehensively and systematically compare language data that does not exist anywhere else for Romani. The following excerpt from the sample RUS-003 from Russia in Fig. 2 may serve as an illustration:

---

[2] Since these are translations and not free text production, there is a risk of influence from the elicitation language, cf. for example the case of demonstrative pronouns in chapter 4.2.3, footnote 8. Moreover, the elicited utterances consist only of single words, phrases and sentences, but open interviews do exist for some samples.

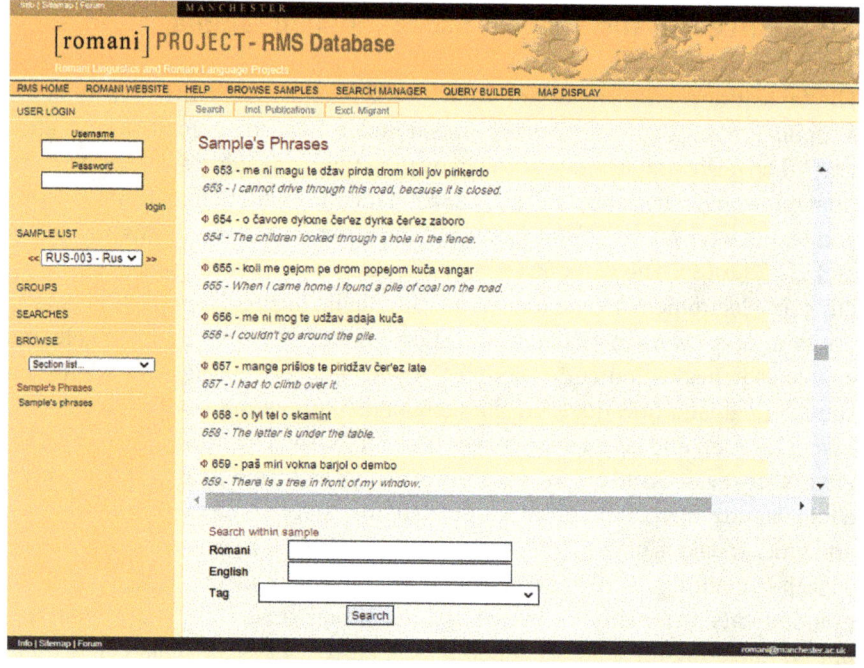

Fig. 2: Extract from the RMS sample RUS-003.

Of the total of 122 samples in the RMS Database, 84 are relevant for the present book, due to the Slavic contact language(s) involved. These are shown in the following overview table (Tab. 1). The Slavic contact languages are printed in bold and the abbreviations of the languages follow the principle of ISO 639-1 (https://en.wikipedia.org/wiki/List_of_ISO_639-1_codes).

Tab. 1: Metadata for the RMS samples involving Slavic contact languages.

Country	Dialect information			Contact languages		
	Sample reference	Dialect name	Location	Current	Recent	Old
Bulgaria	BG-001	Velingrad Yerli	Velingrad	**bg**, tr	–	el
	BG-007	Kalajdži	Dolni Čiflik	**bg**, tr	–	–
	BG-008	Kalburdžu	Sindel	**bg**	tr	–
	BG-009	Kalajdži	Pčelnik, N. Šipka	**bg**, tr	–	–
	BG-010	Muzikantska Roma	Sliven	**bg**	tr	el

Tab. 1 (continued)

Country	Sample reference	Dialect name	Location	Current	Recent	Old
	BG-011	Goli Cigani/ Nange Roma	Sliven	**bg**	tr	–
	BG-012	Rešitari/Čergari	Velingrad	**bg**	tr	–
	BG-013	Kalajdži	Malo Konare	**bg**	tr	el
	BG-014	Kalajdži	Vălči Dol	**bg**	tr	el
	BG-015	Xoraxani	Kaspičan	**bg**	tr	el
	BG-016	Kalajdži	Montana	**bg**	tr	el
	BG-023	Xoraxani	Šumen	**bg**	tr	el
	BG-024	Sofia Erli	Sofia	**bg**	–	el
	BG-045	Sindel	Sindel	**bg**, tr	–	–
	BG-052	Burgudži (-Parpuli)	Dălgopol	**bg**	–	tr
Croatia	HR-001	Gurbet	Čakovec	**hr**, de	–	ro
	HR-002	Čurjarja Arilje	Zagreb	**hr**, de	–	ro
	HR-003	Manuša Čurjarja	Istria	he	–	–
Czech Republic	CZ-001 (migr)[3]	Czech Vlax	Rakovník	**cs**, hu, **sk**	–	ro
Estonia	EST-008 (migr)	Lotfitka/ Estonska Roma	Pärnu	et, **ru**	lv	de, **pl**
	EST-009 (migr)	Lotfitka/ Estonska Roma	Pärnu	et, **ru**	lv	de, **pl**
	EST-010 (migr)	Lotfitka/ Estonska Roma	Paide	et, **ru**	lv	de, **pl**
Latvia	LV-005	Čuxny	Riga	de, lv, **ru**	–	–
	LV-006	Lotfitka	Riga	lv, **ru**	–	–
Lithuania	LT-005	Lithuanian Romani	Šiauliai	lt, **ru**	**pl**	–
	LT-007	Lithuanian Romani	Šiauliai	lt, **ru**	–	–
	LT-008	Lithuanian Romani	Troškūnai	lt, **pl**, **ru**	–	–
	LT-009	Polska Roma	Vilnius	lt, **pl**, **ru**	–	–

---

3 The tag *migr* on some samples stands for 'migrant dialect' (for details, cf. Matras 2002: 194).

Tab. 1 (continued)

Country	Dialect information			Contact languages		
	Sample reference	Dialect name	Location	Current	Recent	Old
Moldova	MD-001	Laješa/Kišinevcy	Chișinău	ro, ru	–	–
	MD-006	Čurari	Dondușeni > Chișinău	ro, ru	–	–
	MD-007	Laeši Kurteja	Zîrnești	ro, ru	–	–
North Macedonia	MK-001	Gurbet	Skopje	mk	sr, tr	ro
	MK-002	Arli	Skopje	mk	sr, tr	el
	MK-003	Arli	Skopje/Šutka	mk	tr	el
	MK-004	Kovački	Kumanovo	mk	–	el
	MK-005	Arli (Gautnikane)	Kumanovo	mk	–	el
	MK-012	Kovački	Skopje	mk	tr	el
Poland	PL-003	Polska Roma	Pabianice, Łódź	pl	de	–
	PL-007	Bergitka	Kraków	pl	–	–
	PL-014	Polish Xaladytka	Ełk	de, pl, ru	–	el, lt
	PL-015	Polish Xaladytka	Mazury	de, pl, sv	–	–
	PL-018	Polska Roma	Łódź	de, pl	–	–
	PL-019	Polska Roma	Zielona Góra	pl	–	el
Romania	RO-004	Ursari	Maglavit	ro	bg	–
	RO-006	Spoitori	Pitești	ro	bg	el
	RO-016	Spoitari	Călărași	ro	bg	–
Russia	RUS-003	Russian Roma	Jaroslavl'	ru	–	–
	RUS-005 (migr)	Lovari Čokeši	Moskva	ru	–	ro
	RUS-006	North Russian	Nižniy Novgorod	ru	–	–
	RUS-008	North Russian	Ekaterinburg	ru	–	–
	RUS-011 (migr)	Crimean	Kuban	ru	–	–
Serbia, Montenegro, Kosovo	YU-002	Gurbetsky	Deronje	sr	–	–
	YU-004	Gurbet/Rabešte	Aleksandrovo	sr	–	–
	YU-007	Bačkačjke	Čurug	sr	–	–
	YU-008	Čhurarja	Žabljak	sr	–	–
	YU-009	Katolikurja	Novi Bečej	sr	–	–
	YU-010	Kalderaš	Šid	sr	–	–
	YU-011	Arli	Beočin	sr	–	tr

1.2 Sources for the study of Slavic–Romani language contact

Tab. 1 (continued)

Country	Sample reference	Dialect name	Location	Current	Recent	Old
	YU-012	Bugurdži Arli	Beočin	sr	–	sq, tr
	YU-014	Arli	Zrenjanin	sr	–	ro, tr
	YU-015 (migr)	Lovari	Debeljača	sr	–	hu, ro
	YU-016	Kosovan Arli	Gnjilane	sr	–	tr
	YU-017	Gurbet	Budva	sr	–	ro
	YU-018	Kosovan	Prizren	de, sr	–	–
Slovakia	SK-002	East Slovak	Zborov, Šariš	cs	sk	hu
	SK-011	East Slovak	Krompachy, Šariš	cs	sk	hu
	SK-016	West Slovak	Čáry, Záhorie	cs	sk	hu
	SK-027	Eastern Rumungro	Klenovec, Gemer	sk	–	hu
	SK-031	Central Slovak	Šumiac, Horehronie	sk	–	hu
	SK-052	Central Rumungro	Litava	sk	–	hu
	SK-059	Western Rumungro	Diakovce, Žitný ostrov	hu, sk	–	–
Slovenia	SLO-001	Prekmurski	Gornji Slaveči	sl	hu	–
Ukraine	UKR-001	Crimean	Xarkiv	ru, uk	tr	–
	UKR-003	Servi (Xaladytka)	Kyjiv	ru, uk	–	ro
	UKR-004	Servi	Kyjiv	ru, uk	–	–
	UKR-007	Kišinjovcy	Kyjiv	ro, ru, uk	–	ro
	UKR-008	Kubanski Servi	Donec'k area	ru, uk	–	–
	UKR-010	Xandžari	Kyjiv	ru, uk	–	–
	UKR-011 (migr)	Šanxajcy	Odesa	ru, uk	–	–
	UKR-015	Kylmyš	Odesa	ro, ru, uk	–	–
	UKR-016	Kubanska Vlaxurja	Odesa	ru, uk	–	–
	UKR-018	Servy-Nakhale	Odesa	ru	–	–
	UKR-019	Plaščuny	Donec'k > Merefa	ru, uk	–	ro
	UKR-020	Gimpeny	Kyjiv area	ru, uk	–	–

The following map (Fig. 3) once again illustrates the regional distribution of dialects from the samples:

Fig. 3: Localization of the analyzed RMS samples (based on maps in Matras 2002: 10 and Boretzky and Igla 2004).

In addition to the RMS Database, written and oral texts in the form of fairy tales, stories, poems, dictionaries and grammars, political and journalistic texts, teaching materials, television and radio broadcasts, YouTube videos, chats in online forums etc. can be used as a corpus for linguistic studies of Romani and will feature in the present book.

1.3 Aim of the book and structure of the chapters

This book is both a compilation of four studies that have already been published and have been revised and / or translated into English for this purpose and of five

1.3 Aim of the book and structure of the chapters

hitherto unpublished chapters. What they all have in common is their focus on Slavic–Romani language contact.

A basic idea of the book is the following: Romani linguistics traditionally speaks of Romani *dialects* and, since the nineteenth century, there have been different approaches taken to classifying these dialects. The most widespread classification differentiates between four metagroups – Balkan, Vlax, Northern and Central – with further subdivisions within each (cf. e.g. Matras 2002; Boretzky and Igla 2004). In a very recent publication, however, Elšík and Beníšek (2020: 391) question this division and the term *dialect* itself for a description of Romani. The Slavic languages, on the other hand, are generally considered to be a *language family* consisting of individual *languages* (cf. e.g. Comrie and Corbett 2006; Sussex and Cubberley 2006) with different degrees of standardization. Thus, if we speak in more traditional terms, the present book is about a language family (Slavic) in contact with a group of dialects (Romani); if we follow the observation of Elšík and Beníšek (2020), however, the book is in fact about two language families in contact. In either case the object of research comprises two structurally similar, large linguistic entities, and the status of the respective contact pairs is fairly uniform. This idea is elaborated upon in the next chapter (Chapter 2).

It is followed by a theoretical chapter (Chapter 3) that deals with the contemporary state of the art in contact linguistics and introduces Matras' (2020) pragmatic-functional approach to language contact. Though the book takes a comparative approach to different pairs of related languages, it offers a unique opportunity to examine the repetition (or not) of similar types of contact phenomena ranging from the replication of linguistic matter through to convergence and contact induced grammaticalization, as well as various hierarchies of borrowability, which can all, in turn, be viewed in light of a contemporary theory.

Chapter 4 gives a comprehensive overview of the impact of Slavic on various Romani varieties on the levels of phonetics and phonology, morphology of the noun, morphology of the verb and syntax. The study is based on comprehensive international research literature as well as data from the RMS Database. This chapter corresponds to Sections 9.3–9.6 of Meyer (2020a), contributed to *The Palgrave Handbook of Romani Language and Linguistics*, ed. by Yaron Matras and Anton Tenser, with a couple of adaptations and additions.

As the field of aspect and aktionsart turned out to be particularly interesting, it is examined in more detail in Chapter 5. The aim of this chapter is to assess the proliferation of Slavic prefixing in various Romani dialects in contact with Slavic languages, to identify the functions of the prefixes and to explain the outcomes. The central question is whether or not Slavic aspect as a grammatical category in the sense of Breu (2007) has been adopted by Romani dialects. To answer this question, 76 samples from the RMS Database, existing research literature on individual Romani dialects and a written text corpus are analyzed. This chapter is an English translation of Sonnemann (2022), published in German in *Die Welt der Slaven* 67(1).

Chapter 6 provides an overview of lexical borrowings and loan translations from Slavic in Romani in general and then devotes itself in more depth to the study of Slavic lexical borrowings and one-word codeswitches in the Polska and Bergitka Romani dialects in Poland. It is examined as to which word types and semantic fields are influenced by Polish and how Polish lexis is integrated morphologically. Comparisons are made with Rozwadowski's dictionary of 1936 for the Bergitka dialect and with Papusza's poems, published in Ficowski (1956), for the dialect of the Polska Roma. This chapter is a revised version of Meyer (2018), published in *Anzeiger für Slavische Philologie* XLVI, and Section 9.2 of Meyer (2020a).

In Chapter 7, the situation is reversed: Romani is now examined as the donor language and the Slavic languages as the recipient languages with a focus on the lexicon. On the basis of historical works on Slavic argots, print and online dictionaries on modern youth slangs and colloquial varieties, as well as corpus analyses, the aim of this chapter is to work out which lexical borrowings from Romani existed in historical Slavic argots and which of these have 'made it' into modern Slavic youth slangs, possibly even into the general colloquial varieties. Between the languages studied – Bulgarian, Bosnian / Croatian / Serbian, Czech, Polish, Russian and Ukrainian, plus some insights into Slovak, Macedonian and Slovene – there are remarkable differences.

Chapter 8 deals with different approaches to writing Romani varieties in Slavic-speaking countries. Although there have been various attempts worldwide to establish and introduce a standardized spelling for Romani, there is now a clear tendency away from international and towards national and regional approaches. Eleven such attempts from eight Slavic countries are presented and analyzed on the basis of Smalley's (1964) and Coulmas' (1989) theories on the writing of hitherto unwritten languages. The questions to be answered are: Which alphabet and orthography served as templates for the projects? What solutions were found to represent the phonetic and phonological peculiarities of Romani by recourse to solutions from Slavic languages? Which orthographic principles were used as a basis? And: Have the proposals made been accepted by the language community in question? This chapter is a revised version of Meyer (2019), published in the anthology *Slavic alphabets and identities*, ed. by Sebastian Kempgen and Vittorio S. Tomelleri.

Finally, in Chapter 9, the findings of the individual chapters are summarized and suggestions for further research are made. The concluding questions are: What can be learned from this language contact situation? Does it behave uniformly or are there areal patterns? And: How do the findings fit the current discussion on language contact, grammaticalization and areal typology?

Chapters 1–3, 7 and 9 have not been published in any form before.

2 Two language families in contact? On the status of Slavic and Romani

Romani linguistics traditionally speaks of Romani as a *language* that is divided into *dialects* (four metagroups with further subdivisions), but this view has recently been questioned. The Slavic languages, on the other hand, are generally considered to be a *language family* consisting of individual *languages*. However, one may wonder whether these divergent approaches are justified, or if Romani and Slavic should not rather be treated as very similar phenomena in this respect. Thus, the central questions of this chapter are: What is a language family, what is a language, what is a dialect, and where do Romani and the Slavic languages belong within this framework?

2.1 The Slavic languages as a language family

The terminology of how to refer to the Slavic languages in their entirety varies in the Slavistic and typological literature. Kortmann and van der Auwera (2011: xv) and Sussex and Cubberley (2006: xvii, 1–2, 13) refer to them as a "language family", Hansen (2011: 97) and Comrie and Corbett (1993: 1–2) both as a "branch of the Indo-European [language] family" and as a "family" in its own right, due to different understandings of the notion "language family". This points out the necessity of differentiating between language families in a narrower and in a broader sense, as Bussmann (1996: 643–644) does:

> Language family. Group of languages that are genetically related, i.e. can be traced to a common *proto-language*. The ordering of languages into a common language family is usually based on phonological, morphological, and lexical correspondences that stem from the protolanguage. The use of the term 'language family' is not always the same; in its broader sense (also *phylum*), it refers to the largest spectrum of languages for which a genetic relationship can be demonstrated, e.g. the *Indo-European languages*; in its narrower sense (also *branch*), it refers to languages which are more closely related, e.g. the *Germanic languages*.

Following Bussmann, the Slavic languages would be a language family in the narrower sense, Indo-European a language family in the broader sense. In the tradition of family metaphors in linguistics dating back to August Schleicher, the Slavic languages would be the "branches" of a "family tree" or the "daughter languages" of a "parent language":

> The main metaphor that is used to explain the historical relationships is that of the language family, or family tree. [...] Within the Indo-European family, Proto-Indo-European is the parent language, and Latin, Greek, Sanskrit and others are the daughter languages. In a large family, it will be necessary to distinguish various 'branches', each of which may contain several languages, or 'subfamilies' of languages. This way of talking must not be taken too literally. [...] Since the 19th century, other classificatory terms have come into use. *Family* is still used as a general term for any group of languages where there is a likelihood of a historical relationship.
> (Crystal 2010: 302)

Ross (2006: 500) groups the Slavic and Baltic languages into a Balto-Slavic family:

> In her study of worldwide typological diversity, Nichols (1992: 24–25) adopted the units 'family' and 'stock'. The family she defined as a group with about the time depth of one of the older branches of Indo-European (2500–4000 years, e.g. Iranian, Balto-Slavic), recognizable by inspection when regular correspondences between word forms and morpheme paradigms are displayed. The stock is the deepest phylogenetic node at which a protolanguage is reconstructable by the comparative method (5000–8000 years, e.g. Indo-European, Austronesian). Nichols (1997) adds the 'quasi-stock' [...]. This approach lacks quantitative support, but it has the advantage that groups of languages under comparison meet the same methodological requirement.

We will not pursue the question of the existence of a Balto-Slavic unit here, which is discussed elsewhere (for a summary of the discussion see Schmalstieg 2014). In the present work we will use the term *language family* (in the narrower sense) for the Slavic languages, which are part of the Indo-European language family (in the wider sense) – just like Indo-Aryan Romani. More important than terminology, it is undisputed that the modern Slavic languages are closely related to each other and go back to Proto-Slavic as a common origin. The Slavic language family includes the Slavic standard languages Russian, Ukrainian, Belarusian (with some caveats in terms of status), Polish, Czech, Slovak, Slovene, Bulgarian, Macedonian, Croatian, Serbian, Bosnian (Wingender 2003, 2013, 2014); the Slavic micro-languages that do not fulfill all criteria of a standard language, such as the two Sorbian languages, Molise Slavic, Kashubian, Burgenland Croatian etc. (Duličenko 1981, 2006); 'extinct' Slavic varieties such as Slovincian, Pomeranian, Polabian; and, of course, Church Slavonic in its different redactions.

2.2 Romani as a language family?

Unlike the Slavic languages, Romani has usually been considered a dialect group with great interdialectal variance. Evidence for this variance exists in the innumerable differences in the form of semantically equivalent words and morphemes: for example, the adjective *tikno* 'small' from Proto-Romani has been replaced by other forms in some dialects (*churdo, buko, besko, bita, čepo* etc.) and, in all others, there are differences in the phonological form of the cognates (*tiknu, tino, tinjo, t'ikno, čikno, čikono, cikno, cəkno, cigno, cino, sikno* etc.; Elšík and Beníšek 2020: 390). Moreover, there are numerous interdialectal differences in terms of the sound system, grammar and lexicon:

> To name just a few examples, some dialects – but not others – possess: vowel harmony; a definite article; postpositions; vigesimal numerals; a T–V distinction in reference to the addressee; polysemy of the meanings 'yesterday' and 'tomorrow'; and many more.
>
> Despite cross-dialect[al] differences, all Romani dialects share a structural core, which, apart from linguistic universals, consists of a number of language-specific typological features, such as the existence of [distinctive aspirated] plosives, inflectional classes in nouns, subject cross-reference on verbs, as well as of at most several dozen cognate words and morphemes, such as reflexes of the etymon *dikh-* 'to see; to look'. [. . .] On the other hand, numerous structural linguistic features are widespread but not universal in Romani, as they are lacking in a few dialects. (Elšík and Beníšek 2020: 390)

In order to subdivide this diversity, which still maintains a common structural core, many attempts at dialect classification have been made in the history of Romani studies.

2.2.1 Romani dialect classifications

Of the numerous dialect classifications existing today, Paspati's (1870) attempt is the oldest, followed by that of Franz Miklosich (1872–80, III. Abhandlung). Miklosich's approach significantly influenced later dialect classifications. It is not based on language-internal, but on contact-related developments or isoglosses and distinguishes 13 Romani dialects on this basis. His proposal was followed by numerous other attempts for classification in the following decades, among them the long-prevailing division into Vlax and non-Vlax dialects according to Gilliat-Smith (1915–16; cf. in detail on criteria and models of dialect classification Hancock 1988; Bakker 1999: 173–180; Matras 2002: 214–237; Boretzky 2002: 938; Boretzky and Igla 2004: 18–26; Matras 2013: 201–206; Elšík and Beníšek 2020). All traditional classifications share historical relatedness as the main criterion. Matras (2005: 7) proposes a new, rather typological approach:

> According to this model, relations between dialects are not absolute, based on 'genetic' criteria, but relative: dialects are more closely, or more remotely, related to other dialects, depending on the number of relevant features that they share. The structural features that distinguish dialects are a result of processes of change and innovation that spread from one community to another. The outcome of these changes can be plotted on a map in the form

of isoglosses. Dialects thus form a geographical continuum which reflects the historical spread of structural innovations (as well as the clustering of archaisms) in time and space.

This so-called *geographical diffusion approach* (cf. also Matras 2002: 236, 2005: 9–10) also implies that some differences between dialects are more, and others less, relevant for classification (e.g., on the one hand, occasional archaisms that do not form a coherent pattern or, on the other hand, very widespread features).

A very rough division can be made between a southern and a northern group. The belt separating them, consisting of the central dialects, reflects the historical border region between the Habsburg monarchy and the Ottoman Empire in the sixteenth and seventeenth centuries. New words and structures that emerged at that time in one of the two areas could not migrate to the other. Exceptions to this are the dialects of those Roma whose migratory movements took their own course; these are mainly the dialects of the Vlax Roma who migrated in the eighteenth century from the Balkans, Ukraine and Central Europe westward to Serbia, Bosnia and Croatia and southward to Bulgaria, Macedonia, Greece, Turkey and Hungary. These Roma formed their own closed communities in their destination regions parallel to the already existing Roma populations and retained their own varieties of the language. Further special migratory movements concerned the German Roma or Sinti, who followed German colonists in the direction of Russia, Hungary and Romania. In the nineteenth century, due to the abolition of slavery in Romania, there was a period of high migration from Transylvania to other regions of Europe. Groups such as the Kalderaša and Lovara (both belonging to the Vlax Roma) settled in this way throughout Europe and today form large communities in Moscow, Stockholm, Frankfurt, Vienna, Paris and London (cf. Matras 2014: 116–118).

A finer division of the dialect groups results in four main or meta-groups with further subdivisions: the Balkan, Vlax, Northern and Central dialects (cf. Bakker and Matras 1997; Boretzky and Igla 2004).[4]

The Romani dialects of the southern Balkans are called the *Balkan* group. They are additionally divided into a more conservative southern (*South Balkan I*) and a more innovative northern (*South Balkan II*) subgroup. The former includes the Arli / Arlije of Greece, Albania, North Macedonia, Serbia and Kosovo, the Erli of Sofia and the dialects of Prilep and Prizren. The latter originated in northeastern Bulgaria and includes the Kalajdži, Bugurdži and Drindari dialects. Greek and Turkish influences are characteristic of the Balkan group. A large cohort of the speakers are Muslims. The Balkan group also includes the Ursari and Crimean Roma, but they belong to the Roma who left the Balkans before or during Ottoman rule.

---

[4] As examples of individual dialects, only those will be mentioned here that were or are in contact with Slavic languages.

The largest and most well-researched group is *Vlax* Romani, which must have emerged on Romanian-speaking territory and shows many Romanian influences. This group is also divided into a southern and a northern variety. *South Vlax* is documented mainly for migrant groups outside Romania; this includes Gurbet, spoken mainly by the Christian Roma population in the Western Balkans. *North Vlax* includes the very well documented Kelderaš or Kaldaraš dialect, as well as Lovari, which shows strong Hungarian influences.

The *Central* dialects, which are also influenced by Hungarian, are divided into two groups as well: The *Northern Central* group includes Bohemian Romani, now extinct, West Slovak Romani and East Slovak Romani. The latter is also predominant in the Czech Republic today, due to the immigration of East Slovak Roma to Bohemia and Moravia after World War II. Northern Central dialects are also spoken in southern Poland, Moravia and western Ukraine. The *Southern Central* dialects are further divided into Rumungro, spoken in Slovakia and Hungary, and Vend, which includes Prekmurje, spoken in northern Slovenia.

The term *Northern* group includes a number of smaller groups and individual dialects spoken not only in northern Europe, but also in western and southern Europe. Central among these are the closely related Sinti-Manuš dialects, which show a strong German influence. Within the Northern group, as well, two subgroups can be identified: a northwestern and a northeastern one. The latter extends across Poland, the Baltic States and northern Russia, the best documented of which is North Russian or Xaladytka Romani.

Two other quite isolated dialect groups are Abruzzo / Calabrian Romani in Italy and Croatian Romani, which is spoken today only in Slovenia and not in Croatia itself. British and Iberian Romani are extinct, remnants of which can still be found in the so-called *Para-Romani*[5] varieties Angloromani and Caló.

Figure 4 shows the main Romani dialects in Europe with their respective localization on the map.

2.2.2 The dialectological approach in question

Elšík and Beníšek (2020: 399–408), in their very recent publication on the subject, create a taxonomy of twelve dialect groups, among which are dialects or languages that are firmly established in research (North and South Balkan,

---

[5] Para-Romani is characterized by a combination of majority language structures with Romani lexis and a few Romani grammatical structures. It is not relevant for the contact situation with Slavic.

Fig. 4: The main dialects of Romani in Europe (map from Matras 2002: 10).

North and Southern Central Romani, Vlax) as well as those that have been seen as transitional dialects or as belonging to the previously assumed dialect groups. However, very interestingly, they question not only the traditional fourfold division, but also the use of the term *dialect* in Romani studies in general:

> [. . .] it has hardly been considered in Romani linguistics to conceive of Romani as a subgroup of closely related languages, rather than a single language, and to reserve the term *dialects* for those Romani varieties that have a reasonable degree of structural similarity and mutual intelligibility. (Nevertheless, the plural term Romani *languages* is often encountered outside of specialist circles.) (Elšík and Beníšek 2020: 391)

The question is: Can Romani indeed be seen as a language family rather than as a dialect group? In order to speak of Romani *languages*, it would have to be shown that the *distance* between the varieties is significant enough to justify such a labelling. Reliable data on distance or mutual intelligibility, respectively, are lacking – we prefer the term *distance* to *intelligibility* based on the arguments in Bunčić (to appear: 20) –, but Elšík and Beníšek (2020: 391) demonstrate with an example just how large the distance between two Romani varieties can actually be:

> It is certainly not the case that all Romani dialects are inherently mutually intelligible, though we are unaware of any empirical studies on this issue. Consider, for example, such a basic sentence as 'all my children are still small': Can a speaker from Kaspichan, Bulgaria,

who says *epci me xurde thaa čikone*, possibly understand a speaker from Helsinki, Finland, who says *sāre mo kenti āxena panna peska*, and vice versa? [...] The mutual intelligibility of Romani dialects is restricted especially due to lexical borrowing (cf. Boretzky 1999, p. 71) from different contact languages (e.g. *epci* 'all' and *thaa* 'still' from Turkish in the Kaspichan example vs. *panna* 'still' from Greek and *kenti* 'children' and *peska* 'small' from Low German in the Helsinki example) and reductive sound changes in some dialects (e.g. *zabaj* < *giljabani* 'she sang' in a Bulgarian variety of Romani, cf. Angăčev 2008, p. 75; Elšík 2008, p. 214), though other types of innovations, too, certainly play a role.

Following the model of Elšík and Beníšek, let us now pick one Romani sample from Bulgaria and one from Finland and compare a small text sample with respect to distance according to Ammon's (1995) method. There is extensive literature on the question of measuring distance between varieties (cf. Casad 1992; Dunn 2021 and many more), but for a first impression, Ammon's simple but ingenious approach is absolutely sufficient. It has also been applied several times by Bunčić (2008, 2015, to appear) to Slavic languages (see below). Ammon proposes a simple test which allows a distinction to be made between high, medium and low similarity. For this test, a text is used that has been translated as literally as possible into the language of comparison. For each word occurring in the two texts, it must be decided whether or not it is identical or at least cognate to its equivalent in the translation. Tab. 2 shows an example from Bunčić (to appear); the unmarked words are completely identical, the italicized ones are cognates and the bold ones are completely different from one another:

Tab. 2: Comparison of Standard Czech and Standard Slovak.

Standard Czech	Standard Slovak
Bylo horké redakční léto, kdy se nic, ale **zhola** *nic neděje, kdy se* **nedělá** *politika a kdy není* ani *žádná evropská situace*; a *přece* i v *tuto* dobu *čtenáři novin, ležící* v agónii nudy na *březích vod* **nebo** v *řídkém stínu stromů*, zdemoralizovaní **vedrem**, *přírodou, venkovským* **klidem** a *vůbec* zdravým a prostým *životem* na *dovolené, čekají* s denně *zkla-mávanou nadějí, že aspoň v těch novinách bude něco nového a osvěžujícího, nějaká* vražda **nebo válka nebo** *zemětřesení, zkrátka Něco*; a *když* to tam *není, tlukou* novinami a **roztrpčeně** *prohlašují, že v těch* novinách *nic*, ale *docela* Nic *není* a že *vůbec nestojí* za *čtení* a že už to *nebudou odebírat*.	*Bolo horúce redakčné leto, keď sa nič*, ale **úplne** *nič nedeje, keď sa* **nerobí** *politika a keď nie je* ani *žiadna európska situácia*; a *predsa* i v *túto* dobu *čitatelia novín, ležiaci* v agónii nudy na *brehoch vôd* **alebo** v *riedkom tieni stromov*, zdemoralizovaní **páľavou**, *prírodou, vonkajším* **pokojom** a *vôbec* zdravým a prostým *životom* na *dovolenke, čakajú* s *dennou sklamávajúcou nádejou, že aspoň v tých novinách bude niečo nového a osviežujúceho, nejaká* vražda **alebo vojna alebo** *zemetrasenie, skratka Niečo*; a *keď'to* tam *nie je, tlčú* novinami a **rozpačito** *vyhlasujú, že v tých* novinách *nič*, ale *celkom Nič nie je* a že *vôbec nestoja* za *čítanie* a že už to *nebudú odoberať*.

In this example, the number of completely identical words is less than 50%, but almost all of the words are recognizable as cognates. One can speak of great similarity (i.e. minor distance) between the varieties if more than half of the words are completely identical, of low similarity (i.e. major distance) if more than half of the words are completely different. In the present case, there is medium similarity – since both Czech and Slovak are undoubtedly fully developed standard varieties, which is to say, we are dealing here with *Ausbau*-languages.[6] For Ammon's test, no evaluation of massive parallel corpora is needed; as a rule, even with very short texts, it becomes clear very quickly to which category a pair of varieties belongs. While in a case of high similarity between two varieties, the affiliation to the same language is automatically given, and in a case of low similarity, they are per se different languages, the assignment in a case of medium similarity depends on sociolinguistic criteria like standardization (Ammon 1995: 1–11; Bunčić 2015, 30–32). The scheme in Tab. 3 is based on Bunčić (to appear):

Tab. 3: Overview of Ammon's algorithm.

	High similarity	Medium similarity	Low similarity
Identical words	> 50%	< 50%	
Cognate words		> 50%	< 50%
Standard variety (overlying)	same language (pluricentric lang.)	different language (*Ausbau*-language)	different language (distinct language)
Nonstandard variety (overlaid/nonoverlaid)	same language (dialect, sociolect etc.)		different language (different variety)

Let us now apply this method to two Romani varieties from Finland and Bulgaria as in Elšík and Beníšek's example. The following text sample (Tab. 4) consists of 15 literally translated sentences with the same amount of words each from the RMS Database for East Finnish Romani (FIN-002, recorded in Lahti, 100 km Northeast of Helsinki) and Kalajdži (BG-007, recorded in Dolni Čiflik, 30 km South of Varna and 60 km East of Kaspičan). Spelling is not taken into account, only pronunciation, cf. the respective audio files in the RMS Database. Here also applies: the unmarked words are completely identical, the italicized ones are cognates and the bold ones are completely different from one another.

---

6 *Ausbau*-languages are not necessarily to be considered as separate languages due to the rather small linguistic distance to their neighboring varieties, but as a result of their use for high literature, science, administration etc., they nevertheless take the position of standard languages (Kloss 1976).

Tab. 4: Comparison of Kalajdži and East Finnish Romani.

No.	RMS entry no.	Kalajdži (BG-007)	East Finnish Romani (FIN-002)	English
1	351	von akana amenge anen čorbava	jōn ānena amenge kān khāpen	They bring us soup now.
2	352	me dikhav tu	me dikkā tūt	I see you.
3	359	xurdalen aven kate! ka dav tume khajči!	aven dāri valapi[!] me tā tumenge tārta[!]	Children, come here! I will give you something!
4	377	xalav ke vasta tate pəesa!	hou tukko vast tatte panjaha	Wash your hands with warm water!
5	386	kaja angrusti si kerdi galbenostar	tauva angrusti hin čerte čonatika	This ring is made of gold.
6	393	ka pašljav mange akana soske sem čhindo	me jā kān pahhuvel me som činnime	I am going to sleep now because I'm tired.
7	403	me phaglem i čaša	me suntom pah rōki	I broke the cup.
8	409	predi te avav adathe živijsaravas but dur adathar	vahka me aijommas pūruvel tāri me āhtommas tūral	Before I came to live here, I lived far away from here.
9	410	voj gelitar peske sabaxle	joi lāhtytīlo ta tīves	She left this morning.
10	414	vov in pokindjas khančik ando xoremakos	jou na resatas sici dōri pār	He didn't pay for anything in the pub.
11	445	vov kindjas peske neve pate te džal ando foros	jou činjas neve kōla at jou vojula jal fōros	He bought new clothes so that he could go into town.
12	448	vov avilo pres januari	jō aulo vetresko tīja	He arrived in January.
13	449	voj pučljas ma so te kerel za da te kerel po but love	joi puhtas manna sō mōn mostulas sērel at lelas kutti til kuruha	She asked me what to do to earn some more money.
14	482	ašundem kadava katar məndrə duj phrala	me khunjommas totta mo tuie phēnenna	I heard about it from my two brothers.
15	516	voj in mangelas khančik piimaske	joi na kamjas pil či	She didn't want to drink anything.

Out of 90 words, 50 are neither identical nor cognates, which is 56%. Thus, Kalajdži and East Finnish Romani clearly have a low degree of similarity. This is crucial, because according to Ammon's model, they must be seen as different languages based on this count.

Making such distance measurements on a larger scale for other combinations of Romani varieties would certainly be a worthwhile enterprise for future research. For our purposes here, one example shall suffice to demonstrate how large the distance between two Romani varieties can be. It proves what Elšík and Beníšek (2020: 418) have observed and described:

> Though all Romani dialects share a structural core, the degree of cross-dialect variation within Romani is remarkable and often entails a lack of inherent inter-dialect intelligibility. Romani exhibits intricate patterns of cross-dialect variation, especially due to a complex interplay between geographical and migration-induced (sub-ethnic) dimensions of linguistic variation.

As a consequence, in terms of distance, the Romani varieties are comparable with the Slavic languages and it would be justified to speak of Romani *languages* rather than *dialects*. However, what is also crucial is that their degree of standardization is significantly lower than that of the Slavic standard languages. Questions of standardization and the tendency away from an international standard of Romani – which was not successful beyond a relatively small circle of Romani activists and intellectuals – toward different regional or national standards will be discussed in detail in Chapter 8. Hereinafter, we are going to speak mostly of Romani *varieties* (instead of *languages* or *dialects*) to use a term as neutral as possible.

The point that was to be made in this chapter is: Although the Slavic languages are self-evidently treated as a language family and Romani has traditionally been treated as one language divided into many dialects, and although several Slavic languages are standard languages whereas Romani is not (neither as a whole nor its single varieties), on the structural level, we are in fact dealing with the same phenomenon. Against this background, it seems justified to speak of a Slavic and a Romani language family and of two language families in contact. The various outcomes of the contact between these two language families shall be treated in the following chapters.

3 Examining contact phenomena through a contemporary lens

3.1 A pragmatic-functional approach to language contact

The theoretical basis of this book is the pragmatic-functional approach to language contact by Yaron Matras, as presented in Matras (2020). This chapter seeks to provide an introduction to this approach and to take a contemporary look at central concepts and theories of contact linguistics.

Why is a new theory of language contact necessary at all? In fact, Matras does not want to present a theory in the narrow sense, but rather a new, integrated theoretical framework for language contact that is embedded in a modern understanding of language and communication. He seeks to integrate individual-synchronic approaches to bilingualism with structural-diachronic approaches to contact-induced language change, which have usually been looked at separately (Matras 2020: 3–4). The pragmatic-functional approach aligns with and builds upon the pioneering works of Haugen (1950, [1953] 1969) and Weinreich (1953); the diachronic perspective of Thomason and Kaufman (1988) and Thomason (2001); the Matrix Language Frame (MLF) by Myers-Scotton (1993, 2002, 2006) and many other influential contributions to contact linguistics. Beyond that, in recent years, concepts such as translanguaging (Li Wei 2018) have increasingly questioned the strict boundaries between languages in the brain of a multilingual speaker and explored the multimodal representation of communicative repertoires. It is thus Matras' motivation to integrate all of these into a theoretical framework

> that can allow us to approach language contact phenomena in a holistic way and to explain how communicative interaction in what we perceive to be multilingual settings can shape the choices that users make and the way they manage their repertoire of linguistic structures.
> (Matras 2020: 335)

The pragmatic-functional approach to language contact seeks a) to bring together synchronic and diachronic aspects of language contact, b) to overcome the understanding of languages as separate systems and return to a view in line with Weinreich (1953: 1), who once emphasized that "language-using individuals are [. . .] the locals of contact", c) to create a typologically oriented framework of language contact based on the assumption "that the language faculty is stratified and that the hierarchical behavior of categories will reflect this stratification"; and d) to adopt a functionalist perspective that views language as a social activity and communication as being goal-driven (Matras 2020: 3)

3.2 The linguistic repertoire

A key term in the pragmatic-functional approach is *repertoire*, which counts among the basic concepts of sociolinguistics. Gumperz (1972: 20) defined it as "the totality of linguistic resources (i.e., including both invariant forms and variables) available to members of particular communities" and later, influenced by Hymes, reformulated it once again as "the totality of distinct language varieties, dialects and styles employed by a community" (Gumperz 1982; cf. also Blommaert and Backus 2013: 11). For a monolingual person, this means being able to use a stylistic variant appropriate to a given context from a complex stylistic repertoire that is fully available to him or her at any time. The same is true for a multilingual person, except that here the repertoire is even more diverse and also includes structures that we would ascribe to different 'languages'. However, the notion of 'language' is inconvenient in this context, because it suggests that we are talking about two separate systems that can temporarily be 'switched on' or 'switched off', which is not the case. Rather, they are permanently 'switched on' and available in their entirety, so a speaker can access his or her complete repertoire at any time. This view is supported by some recent psycho- and neurolinguistic work, e.g. Loebell and Bock (2003), Thierry and Wu (2007), Kroll et al. (2008). Just as with monolingual speakers, elements of the repertoire (word forms, phonological rules, constructions) are gradually associated with certain social activities, topics or people during language acquisition, and mature speakers can select the forms and structures appropriate to the context at any given time. This also means that in certain contexts 'mixing' and 'switching' languages is absolutely appropriate and accepted (cf. Matras 2020: 5). Matras follows Jørgensen's (2008: 163) polylingualism norm of human linguistic behavior here:

> Language users employ whatever linguistic features are at their disposal to achieve their communicative aims as best they can, regardless of how well they know the involved languages; this entails that the language users may know – and use – the fact that some of the features are perceived by some speakers as not belonging together.

In Jørgensen's (2008: 167) understanding, speakers use "features [that] belong together in sets which are called specific languages such as Danish and Turkish" rather than structures. 'Language' understood as an entity in itself is thus merely a theoretical construct, it should rather be regarded as a contract between people. According to Matras (2020: 5), three factors play a role in communication in a multilingual situation: adherence to certain linguistic rules and routines and a consistent selection of forms; a desire to make full use of the available possibilities to express oneself; and keeping the selection mechanism as simple as possible.

Another important aspect of the pragmatic-functional approach is that different linguistic components react differently to the pressure they are exposed to when a multilingual repertoire has to be managed. Matras (2020: 335–336) speaks of different grammatical or structural *categories* (e.g. nouns, pronouns, discourse markers, inflection markers etc.) that can be imagined as different layers that are to different extents prone to change through contact. Structural categories are "triggers of mental processing operations that allow interlocutors (speaker and listener) to share and transfer knowledge" and have "semantic-pragmatic functions that are inherent to their meaning and which pertain to their role in processing knowledge". These functions must be taken into consideration when trying to make sense of the choices that speakers make in communication.

3.3 The bilingual mode

Already two decades before Jørgensen, Grosjean (1989) warned: "Neurolinguists, beware! The bilingual is not two monolinguals in one person". Throughout his work, Grosjean repeatedly emphasized that languages are not separate in the mind of a bilingual speaker and that a bilingual speaker is not to be seen as the sum of two complete or incomplete monolinguals. Rather, he or she has a special linguistic configuration. To provide a better understanding of the situation of a bilingual, Grosjean (1989: 6) draws on the metaphor of a hurdler:

> The high hurdler blends two types of competencies, that of high jumping and that of sprinting. When compared individually with the sprinter or the high jumper, the hurdler meets neither level of competence, and yet when taken as a whole the hurdler is an athlete in his or her own right.

Like the high hurdler, the bilingual is an integrated whole, a special kind of speaker and hearer. He or she has developed competencies exactly to an extent that is needed for his or her communication. Since the needs and domains of applying the two 'languages' are usually very different, also different competencies are acquired. The bilingual rarely masters all registers of both 'languages' in the same comprehensiveness, but rather domain-specifically. Notably, also Grosjean already used the term *repertoire* in the context of his understanding of multilingualism.

The introductory chapter to this book presented a narration by a Romani speaker from Ukraine in the bilingual mode. She used this mode of communication because, in her estimation, her interlocutor was linguistically capable of following her narrative and this mode is both most adequate for what she wished to express and the path of least resistance. In a different context, such as an official, institutional one, her choice would very surely have been different. This is an insightful example from Matras' (2020: 341) description of the creative exploitation of the linguistic repertoire:

> Rather than simply block or shut off complete linguistic 'systems', in conversations with other multilingual individuals they will exploit subtle nuances in meaning differences, evoke context-specific associations by selecting words that are associated with those contexts, authenticate the replication of those words by copying their original phonology, and even draw on the contrast of languages to structure the internal cohesion of the discourse and to navigate sequences in the interaction. This ability is tightly linked to the degree of linguistic maturity and the ability to take conversational risks for the sake of creating special conversational effects.

Grosjean (1989: 8–9) speaks of a continuum in the speech of bilinguals: One end represents the monolingual mode that is used for communication with monolingual speakers; the other end represents the bilingual mode, which is used for communication with other bilingual speakers and in which mixing and switching is fully accepted and widespread. In between, there are many gradations. It also depends on the bilingual individual as to how he or she moves along the continuum: Someone who deals with language consciously and puristically such as a teacher or a poet might rarely communicate in the bilingual mode, while someone who lives in a closely tied bilingual community where mixing is the norm may be in the bilingual mode most of the time. The latter is also true for the vast majority of Romani communities, where the bilingual mode is the default; but, at the same time, it does not shake the ethnic identity of the Roma. The community pressure is high enough to disfavor complete linguistic assimilation (cf. Matras 2020: 145).

3.4 The link to borrowing and other language contact phenomena

What is compelling about the pragmatic-functional approach is that it establishes a link between synchronic, individual multilingualism and diachronic, societal contact-induced change, which have usually been presented as separate phenomena in previous contact linguistics works. In fact, however, they are closely related, because language change occurs when a particular linguistic pattern spreads and takes hold in a significant part of the speech community:

> Thus, an inserted word-form from another language may become a loanword, collective language-learning may show substrate influences in phonology (as well as in other domains of structure), the morpho-syntactic constructions of languages in bilingual communities may undergo convergence, and discourse markers from one language may be borrowed into another language. Contact-induced language change is thus ultimately the product of

> innovations that individual multilingual speakers introduce into discourse in a multilingual setting. (Matras 2020: 6; cf. also Myers-Scotton 1993)

Within his framework, Matras (2020: 338) defines *borrowing* as "the lifting of constraints around the inhibition of a particular structure, and its generalisations as employable in principle in all interaction settings and routines." The term *borrowing* was first used by Whitney (1881: 10), and already Haugen (1950: 211) pointed out its problematic nature:

> The metaphor implied is certainly absurd, since the borrowing takes place without the lender's consent or even awareness, and the borrower is under no obligation to repay the loan. One might as well call it stealing, were it not that the owner is deprived of nothing and feels no urge to recover his goods.

Johanson (2002) prefers to speak of *copying*, Matras (2020) of *replication*, but to avoid confusion, we will stick with the traditional term *borrowing*.

In line with Myers-Scotton (1993), Matras' framework and other recent contact linguistic works, we assume a codeswitching-borrowing continuum. There is thus no structural distinction between codeswitching and borrowing, but only a difference in usage conventions. Especially with multilingual speakers who are in the bilingual mode, it is often very difficult to make a distinction between the two poles. With monolingual speakers, borrowings are much easier to identify as such. Characteristics that may give an indication of one or the other are: stylistic vs. default use, core vocabulary vs. grammatical operations, singular vs. regular occurrence, and structural integration vs. non-integration (Matras and Adamou 2021: 240).

The *borrowability* (i.e. the susceptibility to borrowing) of structural categories is dealt with in detail in Matras (2007) and Matras (2020: 165–178) and will be elaborated on for Romani in Chapter 4. In the domain of the lexicon (cf. Chapter 6 for more details), mainly items that are associated with the world of the majority society, such as commerce, religion, administration and technology are prone to borrowing, whereas words for the more intimate areas of the body, the family, emotions and space are borrowed much less frequently. This leads to a compartmentalization and differing degrees of borrowability (cf. Matras 2020: 188).

Already Haugen (1950) distinguished between what is nowadays called *matter* (MAT) and *pattern* (PAT) *borrowing* (Matras and Sakel 2007), using the terms *importation of forms* and *calques* (elsewhere also: *convergence*). Sakel (2007: 15) defines the two kinds of borrowing as follows:

> MAT and PAT denote the two basic ways in which elements can be borrowed from one language into another. We speak of MAT-borrowing when morphological material and its phonological shape from one language is replicated in another language. PAT describes the case where only the patterns of the other language are replicated, i.e. the organization, distribution and mapping of grammatical or semantic meaning, while the form itself is not

borrowed. In many cases of MAT-borrowing, also the function of the borrowed element is taken over, that is MAT and PAT are combined.

Heine and Kuteva (2003, 2005) go one step further by asserting that language contact may not only be the reason for transfer or replication of linguistic matter or patterns, but that it can also lead to *contact-induced grammaticalization*, i.e. cause internal changes in a language. Pattern borrowing and contact-induced grammaticalization can be difficult to distinguish (cf. for details Gast and van der Auwera 2012: 381–382).

Matter borrowings are much easier to detect than pattern borrowings. The reasons that are usually named for matter borrowing are *gaps* in the recipient language and the *prestige* of the donor language. In the pragmatic-functional approach – where the term is generally avoided – gaps should not, however, be understood as deficiencies, "but rather as speakers' attempt[s] to avail themselves of their full inventory of linguistic resources, at all times and in all contexts of interaction" (Matras 2020: 162). The prestige hypothesis should be interpreted in a way that bilingual speakers associate certain elements from their repertoire with certain contexts of use and that these elements are activated in corresponding conversational contexts – for example, in the case of a minority language like Romani, the language of the regionally or locally dominant population is automatically activated when the topic is school or another official institution. Often 'prestige loans' have equivalents in the recipient language, but these are not complete equivalents in the pragmatic sense (Matras 2020: 162). There is a third motivation for borrowing (*cognitive pressure*), which involves language processing in the brain: In the course of repertoire management, a bilingual speaker would want to keep the 'boundary' between his two 'languages' as low as possible in order to reduce his cognitive effort. As a consequence, a phenomenon occurs, which Salmons (1990) calls *convergence* and Matras (already 1998a: 291) *fusion* – in Romani, for example, fusion happens in the domain of discourse markers or (in certain varieties) in the domain of of aspect / aktionsart marking:

> Fusion is the non-separation of languages for a particular category. It can also be seen as the structural 'devolution' of certain functions to the contact language, or alternatively as the wholesale adoption of markers belonging to a particular category. It is thus qualitatively and quantitatively different from 'borrowing' in the conventional or superordinate sense.
> (Matras 2002: 212)

3.5 A contemporary definition of language contact

The following chapters which are going to deal with different aspects of language contact between Slavic and Romani are based on this functional-pragmatic approach. Since the communication between Roma usually takes place in the bilingual mode, it is also of great importance to understand Grosjean's approach and not to label the speech of multilinguals as chaotic or deficient. Matras' holistic model looks beyond the traditional formal view of separate 'languages' or 'language systems' and views a multilingual speaker as always having an integrated, complete repertoire of forms at his or her disposal and (consciously or unconsciously) choosing adequate elements from this repertoire according to the current context. The concrete choice made in each case can be located on the broad spectrum between the monolingual and the bilingual mode. The choice is thus not random, but goal-driven and functional, and the sense of which mode is appropriate in a particular situation must be acquired by every bilingual speaker in the course of his or her linguistic biography, just as do – or rather in addition to – the stylistic variants that a monolingual speaker acquires in the course of his or her linguistic biography. In this vein, phenomena of *language contact* are nothing more or less than "the outcome of function-driven choices through which speakers licence themselves [. . .] to select a structure (word-form, construction, meaning, phonological features, etc.) [. . .]" (Matras 2020: 337). Against this background, language contact phenomena should not be viewed negatively as *interfering with* communication, as has been the case for a long time, but as *enabling* communication. The fact that certain structural categories are more susceptible to contact-induced change than others is not accidental in the context of this framework, but rather related to the function of those categories (cf. Matras 2020: 7–8).

4 The structural impact of Slavic on Romani

> Romani provides an excellent sample of structural borrowing due to intense contacts, unidirectional bilingualism, the prevalence of the bilingual mode in conversation, lax normative control over language use, and a variety of languages with which the dialects of Romani are and have been in contact. (Matras 2020: 223)

In this sense, the present chapter aims to provide a comprehensive overview of Slavic influences on the phonology, morphology and syntax of Romani. Of course, not all varieties can be covered to the same extent in a survey presentation, nor is data available on all varieties to the same extent; much of the research to date has been on the Balkan dialects, North Russian Romani in Russia, and the Northern Central dialect in Slovakia and the Czech Republic. However, supplemented by existing research on other varieties and our own analyses of the RMS Database, a good overall picture of the results of language contact between Romani and South, East and West Slavic languages alike is obtained.

4.1 Phonetics and phonology

Phonology can be said to occupy an ambivalent position somewhere in between matter and pattern replication, because, compared to other forms of structural borrowing, the production of phonological forms is, in addition, physiologically constrained. This makes phonology even more prone to 'interference' phenomena than other levels of language. In the context of Matras' (2020) pragmatic-functional approach, borrowing and convergence in phonology is explained as follows:

> From the point of view of handling the multilingual repertoire, there is a functional motivation favouring consistency in the types and points of articulation as well as the distribution rules of allophonic variation and suprasegmentals, regardless of the speech situation in which language users find themselves. This motivation exerts pressure toward convergence of the two phonological 'systems' in the speaker's repertoire. At the same time, social norms, awareness of identity, and loyalty toward the group associated with the home language may counteract levelling within the phonological repertoire by demanding conformity to the established pronunciation norms. The process of phonological borrowing is therefore usually an outcome of compromises between these two pressures.
>
> (Matras 2020: 245–246)

In the contact situation of Slavic–Romani, we can witness the replication of Slavic phonemes in loanwords, the convergence of phoneme systems and the substitution of phonemes in loanwords through inherited sounds[7] (Matras 2020: 244).

To start with, many phonological features characteristic of the Slavic contact languages have been adopted into Romani, of which only a selection can be presented here. Of course, numerous foreign sounds have been taken over along with word forms, like /š':/ from Russian into Crimean Romani: ščaveli < ščavel' 'sorrel', boršči < boršč 'borscht' (Toropov and Gumeroglyj 2013: 218). Matras (2020: 245) calls this 'authentication'. More interesting are those sounds that spread beyond loan words into the inherited lexicon, leading to an enrichment of the sound inventory of different Romani varieties. For example, in Poland, /l/ has been substituted by the semi-vowel /w/ in the environment before all vowels except /i/, e.g. love > łowe [woˈvɛ] 'money' (Matras 2002: 50; Meyer 2017: 148). In some varieties, such as Croatian Gurbet (HR-001) and the variety of the Ruska Roma (RUS-003), /l/ has undergone strong velarization. The alternation of /x/ and /h/ is also a contact phenomenon: in Kosovan and Macedonian Arli and Bugurdži, /h/ is lost due to Macedonian, Albanian and Turkish influence (e.g. haljovel > aljovel 'to understand', Friedman 2000), whereas, in Romani varieties under Polish and Russian influence, /h/ and /x/ merge into /x/ (Matras 2002: 52; Elšík, Hübschmannová and Šebková. 1999: 296). In northeastern varieties, we also often find that /i/ or /e/ has been replaced by the central vowel /ɨ/ as a result of contact with Russian, Ukrainian and Polish (Matras 2002: 59; Barannikov 1931a: 4, 1933/34: 37). In Gurbet, Bohemian Romani and other varieties, a syllabic /r/ has developed by analogy to the same sound in Serbian and Czech, e.g. berš > brš (Kopernicki 1889: 125; Matras 2002: 60). Syllabic /r/ and /l/ are also frequently found in Croatia and North Macedonia, e.g. in the variety of the Manuše Čurjarja (HR-003) and Arli (MK-002). In the Balkans, the vowel phonemes have not been noticeably modified with the exception of the spread of the central vowel /ə/, which exists in Bulgarian and Albanian, into the regional Romani varieties and even beyond loan words, e.g. aver > javər (Boretzky and Igla 1999: 712). The RMS Database contains numerous examples of a stressed central vowel in Romani varieties in Bulgaria (BG-001, BG-007, BG-008 etc.), e.g. [brəˈʃənt] 'rain' in Rešitari / Čergari, spoken in Velingrad (BG-012, 91). In sum, the borrowing of phonological features along with word-forms from a Slavic contact language into Romani often triggers or accelerates convergence, "with new phonemes diffusing 'backwards' to substitute inherited phonemes in selected words" (Matras 2020: 244).

In situations of prolonged bilingualism as in the case of the Roma, speakers may also adjust inherited phonemes to match phonemes of the contact language,

---

[7] This third aspect will be addressed in Chapter 7.

"seeking here too the advantages of not having to maintain a context-oriented separation of sound inventories within their bilingual linguistic repertoire" (Matras 2020: 244). This leads to an approximation or convergence of phoneme systems. When multilingual speakers perceive similarities between two sounds from their different 'languages', one sound is allowed to represent the other. For example, the aspirated consonants /pʰ/, /tʰ/, /kʰ/, /tʃʰ/, which are a very characteristic inherited feature of Romani, do not exist in the Slavic contact languages. Therefore, in Romani varieties in Poland and Russia, aspiration converges with the velar fricative, "which is the nearest point of articulation and is also the sound used by speakers of Polish and Russian to render the glottal fricative [h] in foreign words" (Matras 2020: 244). This results in a fricativization of the aspirated consonants to [px], [tx], [kx], [tʃx] in these varieties (cf. also Chapter 8).

Phonological rules may also undergo convergence (Matras 2020: 250): A widespread contact phenomenon in Romani is the devoicing of stops in word-final position, as in Russian, Polish, Czech and Slovak – for example, the pronunciation of *dad* as [dat] or *pandž* as [panč]. This is a tendency that can be found in many varieties influenced by European languages (Matras 2002: 54; Puscher 2005: 17; Meyer 2017: 148; Beníšek 2017: 33). In southeastern Europe, varieties in contact with Romanian and Bosnian / Croatian / Serbian have kept their final voiced consonants, whereas some varieties in contact with Bulgarian and Macedonian have not (Boretzky and Igla 1999: 713; Minkov 1997: 60).

Loanwords may not only 'import' phonological material, but can also have an impact on syllable and stress structures (Matras 2020: 247). The inherited word stress in Romani is on the final segment before inflectional endings, as in *čhavó*, *raklí*, *romanés*. One of the most striking contact-induced changes is the shift of stress to the penultimate or initial syllable in western and central European varieties (Matras 2002: 205, 2020: 251). A hub of this development is found in the varieties influenced by Slovak and its surrounding languages, because standard Slovak has initial stress and the East Slovak varieties, as well as Polish, have penultimate stress (Matras 2002: 64; Elšík, Hübschmannová and Šebková 1999: 307; Beníšek 2017: 52). This affects not only borrowed, but also inherited words, such as *čiriklo* 'bird' in West Slovak Romani (Kalina 1882: 8). However, some varieties have kept their conservative stress pattern even under Slavic influence, for example Kosovan Gurbet (Leggio 2011: 61), varieties in Bulgaria (BG-001–052), North Macedonia (MK-001–012) and Slovenia (SLO-001), or exhibit considerable variation, as in Prilep Arli in North Macedonia (Boretzky 1999: 36). In loan words, usually the stress pattern of the Slavic donor language is adopted.

A secondary development that accompanies the shift of stress is the acquisition of vowel length in Romani (Matras 2020: 251). Among the Slavic standard languages, Czech, Slovak, Bosnian / Croatian / Serbian and partially also Slovene maintain a phonological difference between long and short vowels. As a consequence, distinctive vowel length – independent of stress – has become an areal contact phenomenon for Romani varieties as well, sometimes merely phonetically, sometimes phonologically, as Beníšek (2013: 48, 2017: 42–46) attests for Serednye Romani in Western Ukraine and Wagner (2012: 27) for North West Lovari Romani. Beníšek (2017: 43) names the minimal pairs *bar* 'stone' vs. *bār* 'fence', *phariľa* 'it cracked' vs. *phāriľa* 'it became heavy; she became pregnant', *čaladenca* 'with the touched ones' vs. *čalādenca* 'with families' and *zarazinel* '(s)he infects' vs. *zarāzinel* '(s)he shakes'. (For East and West Slovak Romani, cf. Kalina 1882: 8; Rácová and Horecký 2000: 23; Elšík, Hübschmannová and Šebková 1999: 309).

A very characteristic phonetic feature of Russian is vowel reduction in unstressed position, which has, however, been transferred into native Romani words only in very rare cases, such as Lovari Čokeši (Moscow) *žjuvalo* [ʒʲuˈvałə] 'full of fleas' (RUS-005, 38) or *varekoti* [ˈvarɪkatʲi] 'some' (RUS-005, 400). Of course, it regularly appears in Russian loans such as North Russian Romani *pogoda* [paˈgodə] 'weather' (RUS-006, 79).

Finally, under Slavic influence, some Romani varieties tend to adopt the rules of consonant palatalization in the environment of front vowels (Matras 2020: 250). As Barannikov (1931a: 21) has already noted, "the influence of Ukrain[ian] and Russian phonetics accounts [...] for the extensive use of palatal[ized] sounds that occur not only in recent borrowings, but also in ancient Gypsy words". The palatalization of consonants before front vowels with phonemic status is typical of Russian, but to a lesser extent also of other Slavic languages. This has been transferred to the northeastern varieties of Romani; North Russian Romani, for instance, contains 17 palatalized consonant phonemes (Matras 2002: 58, cf. also Eloeva and Rusakov 1990: 11–13), and also Romani varieties in contact with Ukrainian are affected (Barannikov 1931a: 3; Semiletko 2008: 362; Beníšek 2013; Toropov and Gumeroglyj 2013: 210). The affricates /č/ and /dž/ have a palatalized pronunciation in all Romani varieties of the Baltic group, triggered by Russian, but, under Belarusian influence, they are non-palatalized in all positions except before front vowels, e.g. Belarusian-Lithuanian Romani *čororó* vs. North Russian *č'ororó* 'poor'. A second peculiarity is the shift from the palatalized dentals /d'/ and /t'/ to /dz/ and /c'/, which also corresponds with Belarusian (Čarankaŭ 1974: 38–39). The outcomes of sound changes affecting /Cj/ clusters have also been contact-induced, affecting especially verbs in the past and the mediopassive in most varieties in contact with palatalizing languages: *kerdjom > *kerd'om* > *kerdźom* 'I did', *dikhtjom > *dikht'om* > *dikhćom* 'I saw' (Matras 2002: 68). Genuine palatals are a recent phenomenon and have been acquired through contact, as in Macedonian and Montenegrin Arli and Gurbet: *kher* > *ćher* 'house', *kin-* > *ćin-* 'to buy' (Matras 2002: 49).

As a general hierarchy of changes to the inherited phonological system of Romani under the influence of its contact languages, Matras (2020: 252) has found: prosody > stress > vowel length > vowel quality > semi-vowels and liquids > complex consonants > other consonants.

4.2 Nominal morphology

The influence of Slavic languages upon Romani nominal morphology is found to varying degrees in word formation affixes and inflectional endings, the case system, the definite article, the category of comparison and in pronouns. While matter replication is predominant in the lexicon, phonetics and phonology, the levels of morphology and syntax are mostly characterized by pattern replication.

4.2.1 Inflectional endings and word formation affixes

Generally speaking, the borrowing of inflectional morphology is rare in comparison to the borrowing of derivational morphology, with the exception of plural markers which are borrowed even in contact situations without widespread bilingualism (Matras 2020: 229–230; Elšík and Matras 2006: 101). Individual Romani varieties have continuously borrowed plural endings for nouns ever since the time of Early Romani, among them *-ovi*, *-i* and *-e* (Matras 2002: 85). The plural ending *-o(v)ja* derives from Bulgarian *-ove* or Serbian *-ovi* plus the indigenous plural marker *-a*. The plural ending *-ja* is possibly a contracted form of *-o(v)ja* (Boretzky et al. 2008: 13), whereas *-ovia / -ovja* in North Central Romani of Kysuce, Turiec and Liptov is said to have been adapted from Slovak (Červenka 2004: 184). Bulgarian Romani frequently uses the Bulgarian vocative ending (Kostov 1963a: 69). The *-e* in some Balkan and Vlax varieties is either a reflex of the Greek or a loan of the South Slavic suffix *-e*. The *-i* in the Northern and Central varieties, Lovari and Taikon Kalderaš, has probably been borrowed from the North Slavic suffix *-i*, whereas, in the Southern Central varieties and elsewhere, it is not of Slavic origin (Elšík and Matras 2006: 144).

Word formation affixes are much more easily transferred than inflectional endings. Therefore, Slavic diminutive affixes as well as affixes marking feminine gender have frequently been borrowed. The diminutive suffixes *-ic(a)* and *-ka* are widely used in the Balkans and seem to be restricted to European loans (Matras 2002: 76). Ješina (1886: 18, 25) identified *-ica* already in the nineteenth century for Bohemian Romani as a marker of female gender: *lurd-ica* 'wife of a soldier' < *lurdo* 'soldier', *čor-ica* 'female thief' < *čor* 'thief'; as diminutive affixes he names *-ičkos*, *-ička* and *-inka*. In Romani varieties spoken in Russia, *-ka* serves as a suffix for female persons: *khelitor-ka* 'female dancer' < *khelitori* 'dancer', while *-ica* can be used both as a diminutive and feminine marker: *rrot-ica* 'little skirt' < *rrotja* 'skirt', *sebev-ica* 'female tailor' < *sebevo* 'tailor' (Čerenkov and Demeter 1990: 288; Tcherenkov 1999: 136). North Russian Romani additionally has *-uško* from Russian for generating affectionate forms (Wentzel 1980: 58).

Further Slavic affixes in Romani are *-izmo, -isto, -ato* and *-cija* < Russian *-izm, -ist, -at, -cija* for internationalisms (Wentzel 1980: 58) and – as an exceptional example of prefixation – *pra-* 'great-' from Slovak in East Slovak Romani: *pra-papus* 'great-grandfather' (Červenka 2004: 179). Semiletko (2008: 361) notes that the Servy and Lovari in Ukraine have the endings *-no, -kosko, -koske* and *-koski*, which probably go back to earlier contact, because similar endings were used in Ukrainian in the sixteenth and seventeenth centuries; however, he does not name any examples, and there is no evidence of these in the RMS Database. In the Eastern Už varieties, attenuative forms of qualitative adjectives can be formed with the help of the Slavic suffix *-ovist-*, e.g. *gulovisto* 'sweetish' < *gulo* 'sweet', *lolovisto* 'reddish' < *lolo* 'red' (Beníšek 2017: 176).

4.2.2 Case

In the Balkans, Romani has kept its relatively complex case system, in contrast to the other Balkan languages. Both the structure and the inventory have stayed almost untouched in the conservative Balkan varieties; only a few cases have taken over functions that are characteristic of their equivalents in other Balkan languages (Boretzky and Igla 1999: 715). A visible influence from Bulgarian is the increased use of prepositional constructions. Igla (1999: 210–212) shows for Sofia Erli that, e.g. with respect to constructions with the preposition 'without', the original case government became destabilized historically and was then overridden when the Bulgarian preposition *bez* 'without' was borrowed together with its own governmental properties.

In addition, Bulgarian Erli has a genitive periphrasis according to the Slavic model, as in the following example (inherited construction: *o čhaveskoro dat*):

(2) o   dat   k-o   čhavo   (Bulgarian Erli)
     ART   father   to-ART   boy
     bašta-ta   na   momče-to   (Bulgarian)
     father-ART   to   boy-ART
     'the boy's father' (Boretzky and Igla 1999: 716)

The preposition *ko* 'to' takes over the function of a genitive, analogous to Bulgarian *na* (Boretzky and Igla 1999: 716).

Another interesting phenomenon is the reflexive dative, which is documented e.g. for Serbian Kalderaš (Boretzky 1994: 167), Kosovan Bugurdži (Boretzky 1993: 109) and Arli in North Macedonia, Kosovo and Southern Serbia (Boretzky (1996b: 21). Boretzky (1994: 167) calls it a "dative of inner involvement", and, according to Matras (2002: 88), it "entails a benefactive reading": *džava mange* (go.1SG.PRS myself.DAT) 'I am going', *sovelas peskə* (sleep.3SG.PRF himself.DAT) 'he slept', *pijava mange kafava* (drink.1SG.PRS myself.DAT coffee.ACC) 'I am drinking coffee' and even with the copula *ine peske jek phuri* 'there once was an old woman' (see below). This is probably triggered by Bulgarian and Macedonian, because a similar phenomenon (*dativus ethicus*) is found in the Slavic languages:

(3) ine   peske   jek   phuri   (Arli)
    be.3SG.PRF her.DAT   one   old.woman
    si   bila   edna   starica   (Macedonian)
    her.DAT   be.3SG.PRF one   old.woman
    'there once was an old woman' (Boretzky 1996b: 21)

Several varieties from the RMS Database (Russian and North Russian Romani in Russia; Servi, Xandžari, Kubanska Vlaxurja, Kubanski Servi, Plaščuny and Gimpeny in Ukraine) copy from Russian the split between the marking of positive and negative possession, e.g.

(4a) late   sy   o   pšal   (North Russian Romani)
     she.LOC   be.3SG   ART   brother
     u neë   est'   brat   (Russian)
     at she.GEN be.3SG   brother
     'She has a brother.' (RUS-006, 967)

(4b) late   nane   pšal-es   (North Russian Romani)
     she.LOC   be.3SG.NEG brother-OBL
     u neë   net   brat-a   (Russian)
     at she.GEN NEG   brother-GEN
     'She does not have a brother.' (RUS-006, 973)

Concerning case use, the Northeastern group – especially Russian, Lithuanian and Latvian Romani – differs from other Romani varieties with respect to a whole range of constructions, as shown by Tenser (2016). Matras (2020: 285) speaks of a "wholesale re-mapping of the case system" due to prolonged contact with

Russian. Tenser (2016: 214) demonstrates that in the promotion of state construction (5), "North Russian Romani, in contact with Russian, has switched from using Romani Nominative to Romani Instrumental, thus extending the semantic range of Romani Instrumental under the influence of the model found in the Slavonic (Russian) model":

(5) me   ker-av   pe   dir'ektoro-sa   (North Russian Romani)
    I   do-1SG   REFL   director-INS
    me   kerdjov-av   direktoro   (Romungro)
    I   become-1SG   director.NOM
    ja   stanovlj-us'   direktor-om   (Russian)
    I   become-1SG.REFL   Direktor-INS
    'I am becoming a director.' (RUS-008: 354a)

(Cf. also Wentzel 1980: 64; Gilliat-Smith 1932: 76; Sergievskij 1931: 35; Rusakov and Abramenko 1998: 119). In (6), the Romani locative is used to match the functions of the Russian *u* + genitive construction to mark the possessor, whereas subjects in Romani are usually marked in the nominative and possessors in the oblique:

(6a) les-te   sys   raklori   i   rakloro   (North Russian Romani)
     him-LOC   was.3SG/PL   girl   and   boy
     u nego   byli   doč'   i   syn   (Russian)
     to him.GEN were   daughter and   son
     'he had a daughter and a son' (Rusakov 2004: 25; Tenser 2016: 222)

(6b) man-de   dukhal   nakh   (Lithuanian Romani)
     me-LOC   hurts   nose
     u menja   bolit   nos   (Russian)
     to me.GEN hurts   nose
     'my nose hurts' (LT-005: 982; Tenser 2016: 223)

In (7), Romani uses the unmodified oblique case to match the Russian genitive, both to mark the direct object and the subject of negative existence:

(7a) jov   dykhel   man   (Latvian Romani)
     he   sees   1SG.OBL
     on   vidit   menja   (Russian)
     he   sees   1SG.ACC
     'he sees me' (Matras 2020: 284)

(7b) man   na   sys   khere   (Latvian Romani)
     me.OBL   NEG   was.3SG   at home
     menja   ne   bylo   doma   (Russian)
     me.GEN   NEG   was.3SG.N at home
     'I was not at home' (LT-005: 333; Tenser 2016: 228)

Among the evidence of Slavic influence upon the case system of Romani are also constructions with verbs of removal plus dative (Boretzky 1994: 167 on Serbian Kalderaš), depletion of the partitive genitive in favor of the nominative (Boretzky 1993: 109) or disappearance of the genitive in favor of ablative constructions in Arli and Prilep in North Macedonia. The latter are triggered by Macedonian varieties that do not construct the old Slavic genitive with the preposition *na*, but with *od*. This *od* is has been taken over into Romani as an ablative or as a construction with the inherited preposition *(ka)tar* 'where from', which replaces the inherited genitive in a variety of contexts (Boretzky 1999: 125–126):

(8) ko drom   e   čhonestar   (Arli)
    on the way   ART   moon.ABL
    'on the way from the moon' (Boretzky 1999: 125)
    katar   e   po-tikni   bori   i   daj   (Prilep)
    from   ART   younger   daughter-in-law   ART   mother
    'the mother of the younger daughter-in-law' (Boretzky 1999: 125)

Inflectional case markers are rarely borrowed and, if so, then exclusively for the nominative. In some Romani varieties, the Greek nominative plural markers in nouns were replaced (or supplemented) by borrowings from current contact languages, e.g. *-ovi* from Bulgarian (Elšík and Matras 2006: 234–235).

4.2.3 Articles

Among the Slavic languages, only Macedonian, Bulgarian and partly the Torlak dialects of Serbian have a definite article. The marking of indefiniteness with the numeral 'one' is optional in Romani as well as in the Balkan Slavic languages and very restricted in Romani varieties outside the Balkans (Friedman 2001b: 288). Some Romani varieties under the influence of the Slavic languages without an article are in the process of losing their own definite article, notably those in Slovenia and the Northeastern dialect group (Boretzky 1999: 176; Matras 2002: 96; Elšík and Matras 2006: 184), e.g. Polska Roma *piravav dudali* instead of *piravav e dudali* 'I am opening the window' (Matras 1999c: 10). Uhlik (1951: 53) noted this loss for Bosnian Gurbet already in 1951; however, there is no evidence of this in the RMS Database. Under the influence of languages without articles, like Serbian in the Balkans, there is often uncertainty with respect to the use of the definite article, insofar as it is sometimes used where it is not justified semantically (Boretzky and Igla 1999: 714). An analysis of the RMS Database shows that, in the Romani varieties in contact with Bulgarian and Macedonian, the inherited use of the definite article has remained untouched, whereas the dialects in contact with East and West Slavic languages have partially lost it. No Romani variety from the database shows a complete loss of the definite article, but very strong reduction can be found in Lithuania, Latvia and Poland. In these varieties, the definite article is more likely to be maintained when it is part of a preposition like *ando* / *andi*, *pašo* / *paši*, *ko* / *ki*, *telo*, *palo*, *pro* or *anglo*. Some samples of these varieties, like those of Polska Roma (PL-003), Bergitka (PL-007) and East Slovak (SK-002), make frequent use of demonstrative pronouns and deictic expressions like *dava* / *da*, *kada* / *kaja* / *kała* / *kole* / *kola* etc. instead of a definite article, which has very probably been triggered by their Slavic contact languages.[8] Thus, definite articles are affected by convergence of patterns (Elšík and Matras 2006: 184).

4.2.4 Comparison

As Romani originally expressed comparative and superlative meaning through a single form (*-eder*), it can be said that the whole category of comparison has expanded under Slavic influence (Boretzky 1993: 106), following the hierarchies superlative > comparative > positive, and non-positive > positive (Elšík and Matras 2006: 149). In the Romani varieties of the Balkans, the inherited comparative form *-eder* has been largely replaced by an analytical form with the Slavic prefix *po-*, a late Balkanism, e.g. Velingrad Yerli (Bulgaria) *but* 'much' > *po-but* 'more' instead of *buteder*. Even the only suppletive comparative in Romani, *lačho* 'good' > *feder* 'better' can be replaced by the form *po-lačho* (Kostov 1963a: 86; Boretzky 1993: 107, 1999: 55; Cech and Heinschink 2001b: 355 etc.). Boretzky and Igla (1999: 717) explain this early and fundamental change in relation to the morphological transparency of the Balkan comparative formation. In some varieties in the Balkans, *po-* has both comparative and superlative meaning: *po-baro* 'bigger', *o po-baro*

---

[8] However, it cannot be excluded that this is an artefact of the character of the RMS data, which mostly stem from reverse translation elicitation. The translations of the English RMS questionnaire sentences with a definite article into the Slavic elicitation languages often contain demonstratives, which may thus trigger the use of demonstratives in the Romani translation (anonymous reviewer).

'the biggest' (Elšík and Matras 2006: 153). Where the formation of the comparative follows more complex and less transparent synthetic rules, such as in the East, West and some South Slavic languages, the Romani varieties have kept the old form *-eder* (Boretzky 1999: 55). North Russian Romani, in some cases, even borrows the Russian comparative marker *-š-*: *miro ternedyr-š-o pšal* < Russian *moj mlad-š-yj brat* 'my younger brother' (RUS-006, 621). Eastern Už Romani displays an interesting case of double marking of the comparative in the forms *horš-eder* 'worse' < Slovak *horšie* 'idem' and *chuž-eder* 'worse' < Russian *chuže* 'idem'; the positive forms **horšo* and **chužo* do not exist (Beníšek 2017: 308).

Since the settlement of the Roma in the Balkans, Romani varieties have adopted the Slavic prefix *naj-* to express superlative meaning, with either the positive or comparative form of the adjective, cf. *naj-baro* (Kosovan Arli, YU-016, 615) and *naj-baredyr* (Kalina 1882: 8; Ješina 1886: 28; Rácová 2015: 89) 'the biggest'. The order of elements in a construction with *naj-* can vary, e.g. *naj o phuro manuš* instead of *o najphuro manuš* 'the oldest man' (Velingrad Yerli, Bulgaria, BG-001, 995). In the Vlax varieties, Romanian *maj-* is used to form the superlative instead of *naj-*. Some varieties in contact with Russian in Russia and Ukraine use the Russian superlative marker *samyj* or morphologically adapted *samo*, which can be combined with both a positive (*samo baro* 'the biggest', Russian Roma, RUS-003, 615) and a comparative form (*samo feder* 'the best', Servi, Ukraine, UKR-004, 829), in rare cases even with an additional superlative marker, as in Gimpeny *samo najbaro* 'the biggest' (Ukraine, UKR-020, 615; cf. also Boretzky 1999: 55; Eloeva and Rusakov 1990: 17). The prefix *pre-*, used to construct an elative, e.g. *prelačho* 'extremely good', is also of Slavic origin; in the Vlax dialects, it has been transmitted by Romanian (Matras 2002: 203). Finally, most Romani varieties in Slovakia share the superlative prefix *neg-* or *jeg-*. While the latter might derive from the numeral *jekh* 'one', the former probably is a blend of the Hungarian superlative prefix *leg-* and the Slovak superlative prefix *naj-* (Elšík and Matas 2006: 154). In the varieties of Užhorod and Perečyn in Western Ukraine, superlatives can be empasized by *so* (or *čim*) according to the model of the Slavic contact languages, e.g. *so jegbareder* 'as big as possible, the very biggest' < Slovak *čo najväčší*, Czech *co největší*, Rusyn *što majbulšyj* 'idem' etc. (Beníšek 2017: 309–310).

For a classification of the distributional patterns of borrowed degree markers in Romani, cf. Elšík and Matras (2006: 150–154).

4.2.5 Indefinites

Most Romani varieties borrow indefinite markers, and, especially in the eastern and southeastern dialects of Romani, the system of indefinites ('any', 'some') has been renewed through borrowings as a recent contact development (Matras 2002: 115). An analysis of the RMS data shows that the richest inventories can be found in Servy / Nakhale (UKR-018) and Servi (UKR-004) in Ukraine, consisting of the East Slavic forms *-to*, *-nibud'*, *-tos'*, *-s'*, *čut'* and *ljubo*. Varieties in contact with Polish borrow *-ś*, *-kolwiek* and *byle*, e.g. Polish Xaladytka (PL-014) and Polska Roma (PL-018). Czech and Slovak influence is comparatively weak in this regard (Elšík, Hübschmannová and Šebková 1999: 350), though Rácová (2015: 90) and Lípa (1965: 34) mention *choč-* / *choc-* < *hoci-*, *malo* < *málo*, *šeli* < *šeljako*, *-si* and *ňekero* as having been borrowed into Romani varieties in contact with Slovak. The Eastern Už varieties borrow *chot'-* / *choč-* mainly from their East Slavic contact languages (Beníšek 2017: 216–218). In addition, there is an interesting blend of Romani *vare-* and Slovak *da-* to form *dare-* in some East Slovak varieties (Elšík, Hübschmannová and Šebková 1999: 349). The most common forms from South Slavic are *ne-*, *bilo-* and *svako*, as, for example, in Bačkačjke (Serbia, YU-007) and Arli (North Macedonia, MK-002), as well as *makar-* in Bosnian Gurbet and Central Slovak Romani. Boretzky and Igla (1999: 726) mention *i-*, *ma-* and *-godi / god(er)* as distributive determiners. In Arli, Prilep and Erli, there are new formations with *di-* / *de-* / *da-*, which have either been borrowed from Bulgarian *edi-* or Serbian *eda-* 'any-' (Boretzky et al. 2008: 20) or derived from *gde* / *kəde* 'where' (Boretzky 1999: 177). The indefinites *di-save* 'some' and *di-sar* 'somehow' in Kosovan Gurbet both contain the indefiniteness marker *di-* as well. The free-choice determiner *bilosafar* 'any' is composed of Slavic *bilo-*, inherited *sa* and Albanian *-far* (Leggio 2011: 83).

Very common in Romani are negative indefinite pronouns with the Slavic negative prefix *ni-* / *n'i-*, which is added to an inherited interrogative pronoun: *n'iko(n)* / *nikoj* / *nijek(h)* / *n'ič'i* 'nobody', *n'isavo* / *n'isov* / *n'isoza* 'no, none', *n'iso* 'nothing', *n'ik(h)aj* / *nigdi* 'nowhere', *nikaring* / *ni-kev* 'to nowhere', *n'ikhatar* 'from nowhere' or *n'išar* / *nisar* 'by no means' (Boretzky 1999: 68–69; Pančenko 2013: 15; Rácová 2015: 90; Beníšek 2017: 212–213); on older forms, cf. Kalina 1882: 60; Ješina 1886: 61–62; Kostov 1963a: 155. Slavic influence also strongly affects the pronouns meaning 'nothing' and 'nobody' (Boretzky 1993: 112; 1994: 171), but inherited forms can still be found in most Vlax and some Transylvanian varieties (*khonik* and *kha(n)či*), and further varieties have *či* (anonymous reviewer). The versions with dental *n-* are from Bosnian / Croatian / Serbian, those with palatalized *n'-* from later contact languages such as Russian. North Russian Romani (RUS-006, 701 and others) *-nito* is an interesting mixed form consisting of the two Slavic constituents *ni-* and *-to*. In sum,

> [t]here appear to be few absolute constraints on the borrowing of indefinite word forms. [. . .] One ontological asymmetry concerns the borrowing of indefiniteness markers rather than indefinite word-forms. [. . .] Further, dialects that borrow an indefiniteness marker in

some but not all ontological categories will usually have it in the determiner: . . . *ne-savo* 'some', or Serbian Kalderaš *ni-sar* 'in no manner' as well as *ni-sosko* 'no, none'."

(Elšík and Matras 2006: 311)

Elšík and Matras (2006: 287–294) also assert that, for whole indefinite word forms, universal and negative indefinites are generally more prone to borrowing than specific and free-choice indefinites, whereas the opposite is true for indefinite markers. A third borrowing hierarchy is thing > time > manner and person indefinites.

4.2.6 Interrogatives

In contrast to indefinites, interrogatives are much more resistant in contact situations (Matras 2020: 215). The most stable interrogative pronouns in Romani are the thing and manner interrogatives *so* 'what' and *sar* 'how'. Local interrogatives are also rarely affected by language contact. The most frequently borrowed interrogatives are temporal interrogative pronouns. Due to South Slavic influence, inherited *kana* 'when' has often been replaced by *kad(a) / ked(a) / koga* (Boretzky 1999: 67; Cech and Heinschink 2001b: 352); in Polish, Lithuanian and Estonian Romani varieties, one can also find *kiedy / kedy / kidy* < Polish *kiedy*, in varieties in Russia and Ukraine *koli* and *kala*. The quantity interrogative *skaći* 'how much' in Ukrainian Romani is a blend of inherited *kaći* and Russian *skol'ko* (Elšík and Matras 2006: 310). The person interrogative *ko(n)* 'who' is also relatively stable; only Prilep Arli and Sofia Erli have Bulgarian / Macedonian *koj* and the Central and some Balkan varieties have a reduced form *ko*, which might have developed under the influence of Slavic *k(t)o* (Boretzky 1999: 67). An interesting case is the (inseparable) blend *soza* 'which' in the Eastern Už varieties, which consists of the Romani interrogative *so* 'what' and the Slavic preposition *za* modelled on Slavic *čo / čto / ščo / co za*, e.g. *soza manuš avel?* 'what kind of man is coming?'. In Khudlovo and Serednye, *soza* has additionally taken on quality and quantity semantics usually expressed by *savo*, e.g. *soza tijro sastro?* 'what is your father-in-law like?' (Beníšek 2017: 201–203, 214–215).

In Romani, interrogatives also generally serve as relatives; only in some Bulgarian varieties they get an additional suffix *-to*, modelled on Bulgarian *kon-to* 'who', *koga-to* 'when', *soske-to* 'because' (Boretzy 1999: 68; Kostov 1963a: 97; Minkov 1997: 82).

Elšík and Matras (2006: 310) present the following borrowing hierarchy for interrogatives: time > place, quantity, cause/goal, determiner > manner, thing.

4.2.7 Possessives, personal pronouns and demonstratives

Cech and Heinschink (2001b: 352) observe that in Doljenski, the 3PL of the reflexive possessive pronoun 'his / her own' tends to be extended to all grammatical persons, a development modelled on Slovene *svoj*. Arli, spoken in the southern Balkans, exhibits unstressed, postponed pronouns used possessively as in Macedonian: *ko dad laki*, cf. Macedonian *kaj tatko-i* 'to her father' (Boretzky 1996b: 13). Furthermore, Boretzky (1999: 61) – unfortunately without providing examples – notes that the Romani varieties in the Southern Balkans have developed two sets of possessive constructions, as have Bulgarian and Macedonian: *moj(a)ta kniga* with a possessive pronoun vs. *knigata mi* with an enclitic personal pronoun, both meaning 'my book'.

Borrowing in the area of deixis and anaphoric elements is, generally speaking, relatively rarely attested (Matras 2020: 219). Language contact has also hardly affected personal and demonstrative pronouns in Romani, with only a few examples known: in Hravati / Doljenski (Slovenia), Perechyn (Ukraine) and the variety of Kumanovo (North Macedonia), the personal pronoun *oni* / *one* 'they' has been "modelled on Slavic, but drawing on inherited *on*" (Matras 2002: 209; cf. also Cech and Heinschink 2001a: 156; Boretzky et al. 2008: 16; Beníšek 2017: 189). Early Romani presumably had the pronominal forms *ov* 'he' and *on* 'they', which still exist in most varieties of southeastern and central Europe. What is remarkable in the above-named varieties (and also in Hungarian and Thracian Romani) is that plural affixes from the contact languages are copied onto the inherited plural pronominal form. Matras (2020: 223–224) enumerates three conditions for why this is possible:

> First, the accidental similarity in forms between the Romani pronouns and those of all three contact languages. [. . .] Second, the fact that the contact language shows an exclusively agglutinating formation of the plural pronoun, consisting of the singular pronoun with the addition of a plural suffix. [. . .] And third, the fact that this plural affix is identical to the general, nominal plural suffix used in the language. This makes the plural affix easily transparent and analysable. It is thus the plural affix, not the actual pronominal form of the respective contact language, that is borrowed into Romani. What we see is a fusion not of forms, but of the procedures that are used to derive the plural form from the singular forms.

Seen from this perspective, the phenomenon in Hravati / Doljenski and Kumanovo Romani is not as unusual as it might seem at first glance.

4.3 Verbal morphology

One of the most interesting and prominent contact features from Slavic in Romani is the borrowing of aspect and aktionsart prefixes; however, this topic will be omitted at this point because the entirety of Chapter 5 will be devoted to it. Other important contact-affected areas of verbal morphology are tense, the infinitive, voice and reflexivity, modality, the conditional, renarrativity / evidentiality and the imperative.

4.3.1 Tense

A contact-induced innovation in the tense system of Romani is the formation of an analytic perfect. In some Arli varieties, a new perfect construction has developed under Macedonian influence, linking the past participle with the auxiliary 'to be':

(9) sinum   tumenge   vakerdo   (Arli)
    sum   ti   rekol   (Macedonian)
    I.am   you.DAT   say.1SG.PTCP
    'I have told you' (Matras 2002: 157)

For a few situative verbs, comparable constructions can denote the present, e.g. Polska Roma and West Slovak Romani *me som bešto* 'I sit / am seated' (Matras 2002: 157). In Arli, there is a tendency to form the perfect with the auxiliary 'to be', which can lead to confusion with passive forms: *sigo sinum bisterdo* 'I have quickly forgotten' or 'I was quickly forgotten'. These forms are modelled on the intransitive verbs of movement in Macedonian like *sum dojden* 'I have come' (Boretzky 1994: 163–164). In North Russian Romani, the opposition imperfect-aorist has disappeared under Russian influence. The old aorist now serves as a general past and the imperfect as a special, rarely used aspectual form with iterative meaning, e.g. *bagand'a* 'he / she sang' (aorist; Rusakov 2001a: 314).

Apart from these developments, Slavic influence mainly affects the future and this, again, mainly in the Balkan varieties. Sepeči, Arli and Bugurdži have developed an analytic future marker *ka* (Matras 2002: 157), e.g. *ka dikhav* 'I shall see', and practically all Balkan Romani varieties have a typical Balkan future based on *kam-* 'to love, want' or, more marginally, *mang-* 'to want, demand' (Boretzky and Igla 1999: 719; Friedman 2001a: 154). According to Boretzky and Igla (1999: 718), the diversity of forms suggests that this feature has developed separately in the individual varieties. The negated form is *na / naj ka / naj te / nanaj / nane te*, modelled on Bulgarian and Macedonian *njama / nema da* (Boretzky et al. 2008: 29; Minkov 1997: 83). North Russian Romani and Ukrainian varieties have an analytic future with an auxiliary based on the Romani verb stems *l-* 'to take' or *(j)av-* 'to be, become; come': *me l-ava te bagav* or *me av-ava te bagav* < Russian *ja budu /*

stanu pet' 'I will sing' (Rusakov 2001b: 297–298; Matras 2002: 158). The simple future in North Russian Romani is also taken from Russian and involves aspect prefixes: *s-bagala* < Russian *on s-poët* 'he / she will sing.PF' instead of inherited *bagala* (Rusakov 2001a: 314). An interesting feature of all Romani varieties in contact with Ukrainian (and Russian) is a syncretism of all plural forms of the perfective past: *ame / tume / vone tjerde* < *my / vy / vony zrobyly* 'we / you.PL / they did', which is a recent pan-Ukrainian development (Tenser 2012: 44).

As for borrowed person markers in different tenses, Elšík and Matras (2006: 134) provide a detailed analysis for Slovene Romani:

> In Slovene Romani, we find borrowing of other person-number markers from [Slovene and/ or Croatian]. This is clearly the case with the perfective second-person plural suffix *-ate* [...] (e.g. *kerdž-ate* 'you did'); the non-perfective sets retain indigenous second-person plural inflections. In the first-person plural, all finite sets employ the suffix *-am-* (e.g. *ker-am* 'we do', *ker-am-a* 'we will do', *ker-am-ne* 'we are doing', and *kerdž-am* 'we did'). While *-am* is indigenous in the preterite, it is an innovation in the non-perfective sets. [...] There is some evidence [...] that the extension has been at least facilitated, if not triggered, by contact with Slavic. In both the present-subjunctive and the preterite, there is also a first-person plural variant *-amo* (e.g. *ker-amo* 'we do' and *kerdž-amo* 'we did'), which coincides with the Slovene/Croatian present inflection *-(a)mo*. Rather than being borrowed as such, the Slavic inflection has exerted formal influence on the indigenous first-person singular suffix *-am*, and triggered or facilitated the extension from the preterite into the non-perfective sets.

4.3.2 The "new infinitive"

Romani does not have an inherited infinitive; the early and very restricted use of an infinitive in modal constructions was lost completely due to contact with Iranian and the Balkan languages and was replaced by a non-factual 'that' construction (on the fate of the Indo-Aryan infinitive in Romani cf. Beníšek 2010). In later contact with infinitive languages like Slovene, Czech, Slovak and Polish, Romani has adapted a new infinitive. This new infinitive, which can be called a "debalkanization-effect", is very elaborately described in Boretzky (1996a), and already Puchmajer (1821: 18) mentioned this development for Bohemian Romani in contact with Czech. In Bohemian Romani, the infinitive is mainly used in less integrated clauses, such as in the case of serialization (example 10a), but not in modal sentences (example 10b):

(10a) De   mange   te pijel!   (Bohemian Romani)
      give.2SG.IMP me.DAT drink.INF
      'Give me (something) to drink!' (Matras 2002: 162)

(10b) Me   les   kamav   te mukav   te terd'ol.
      I   it.OBL   want.1SG.PRS   leave.INF stand.INF
      'I want to leave it standing.' (Matras 2002: 162)

Interestingly, not all Romani varieties in contact with West and East Slavic have developed a new infinitive; above all, the Vlax dialects have not, while Eastern Europe shows a rather mixed picture (Boretzky 1996a: 6).

The new infinitival form is usually introduced by the non-factual complementizer *te* (apart from in some modal constructions, Matras 2002: 162), followed by the 3SG present, e.g. *te šunel* 'to hear'. Thus, the functionality of finite forms has been extended from subjunctive constructions into the domain of an infinitive. According to Matras (2002: 161), "[t]he boundaries of this isogloss are defined by the neighbouring varieties of the North Russian Roma to the north, Welsh Romani to the west, and Piedmontese Sinti to the south, which do not show new infinitives". Consequently, the new infinitive has indeed developed only under the influence of infinitive languages, but not in all varieties in contact with such languages. For instance, the varieties of East Slovak Romani are split between those with 3SG generalization (*kamav te kerel* 'I want to do') and those with 2/3PL generalization (*kamav te keren* 'idem') (anonymous reviewer).

Concerning its functions, the new infinitive follows the respective contact languages. Among them is quasi-nominalization of the verb in the Northern Central dialects:

(11a) te   vakerel   hi   rup,   te   (Northern Central dialects)
      COMP   speak.INF   be.3SG.PRS   silver   COMP
      na   vakerel   somnakaj
      NEG   speak.INF   gold
      'to talk is silver, not to talk is gold' (Boretzky 1996a: 19)

Another function is the use as a converb of simultaneity, like in West Slovak Romani:

(11b) pale   dikhle   oda   mochtore   te džal   (West Slovak Romani)
      again   see.3PL.PAST   these   boxes   go.INF
      tele   pan'eha
      down   water.INS
      'They saw these boxes floating down the river again.' (von Sowa 1887: 165)

4.3.3 Voice and reflexivity

Early Romani had a construction made up of copula and past participle to form passives, in which both transitive and intransitive verbs could be used, for example *si kerdo* 'is done' (Matras 2002: 128). According to Boretzky (1986: 207, 1994: 165), the passive developed only on European soil. The older type used different forms of the personal pronouns, which are also used in reflexive constructions with non-third person antecedents (*man* 'me, myself', *tut* 'you, yourself' etc.), but under Slavic influence, *pe(s)* 'he / she, himself / herself' has become generalized to occur with all grammatical persons in many Romani varieties (Boretzky 1996b: 21).

For example, Romani varieties in the Balkans have three means of expressing passive meaning,[9] but, as the adaption of Bulgarian and Macedonian reflexive verbs proceeds, they are being replaced by the reflexive form (Igla 2001: 406–409). Igla and Sechidou (2012) demonstrate very elaborately how these varieties replicate the reflexive and passive verbs of Bulgarian and Greek. The fact that a construction with the particle *se* in Bulgarian can have both passive and reflexive meaning, but a construction with *pes* in Bulgarian Romani is exclusively reflexive, creates an asymmetry with the consequence that *pes* is expanded to new contexts and adopts passive meaning as well. Thus, the Bulgarian analytic passive has served as a model for the creation of an analytic passive in Bulgarian Romani. The new construction (intransitive verb plus *pes*, e.g. *margjovel pes* 'he is beaten') has spread and is replacing the old synthetic form and the old reflexive pattern. Romani varieties under Slavic influence outside the Balkans, however, use the transitive marker plus *pes*: *marel pes* 'he is beaten' (Igla and Sechidou 2012: 169, 172).

Reflexive constructions and the generalization of *pes* triggered by Slavic are also on the rise outside the Balkans. Rácová (2015: 82) gives the following examples for East Slovak Romani: *me pes khosav* < Slovak *ja se utieram* 'I am cleaning myself', *jon pes khosen* < *oni sa utierajú* 'they are cleaning themselves'. Also, under Slovak influence, some non-reflexive verbs have become reflexive: *ladžal pes* < *han'bit sa* 'to be ashamed' instead of *ladžal* (cf. also Beníšek 2017: 387–388). Evidence for Ukrainian Romani can be found in Barannikov (1931a: 21, e.g. *dikhe-pe* < Ukr. *dyvyty-sja* 'to see'), for North Russian Romani in Sergievskij (1931: 57, e.g. *morava-pe* < Russ. *moju-s'* 'I am washing myself') and Rusakov (2001a: 321).

---

9 These are: A synthetic passive form ("non-active") according to the Greek / Albanian model, the active form of the verb plus reflexive pronoun and (marginally) copula plus participle (Igla 2001: 406).

In practically all European Romani varieties, a kind of medialis construction composed of an active verb and a reflexive dative pronoun is known, which expresses that the agent fulfils an action willingly and in his own interest (cf. Sect. 4.2.2 on the *dativus ethicus*). The word *peske / penge* in such constructions shows a tendency towards generalization to other grammatical persons, just like *pes* (Šebková 1999: 159; Rácová 2015: 90).

The reflexive form can also have a modal function in impersonal dative constructions, which conforms to Balkan Slavic, Albanian and Romanian and is also contact-induced: *Na xal pes mange* < Serbian *ne jede mi se*, Bulgarian *ne mi se jade* 'I don't feel like eating' (Boretzky and Igla 1999: 722).

Lastly, Hübschmannová and Bubeník (1997: 136–144) mention what they refer to as second causative, i.e. the doubling of the semantic agentive structure according to the pattern 'to make X do Y' or 'to have Y done by X'. This feature has been lost in North Central Romani in Slovakia due to Slovak influence and is now expressed periphrastically as in Czech and Slovak:

(12a) *E sasvi (...)   kerlas   upre peskere čhas,*   (North Central
      the mother-in-law do.PST   on   her.ACC son.ACC   Romani)
      kaj   la   te   marel
      that   she.ACC COMP   beat.INF

(12b) *Macocha (...)   vyvolala   syna,*   (Slovak)
      the mother-in-law order.3SG.PFV   son.ACC
      aby   ju   zbil
      that   her.ACC beat.3SG.PFV
      'The mother-in-law made her son beat her [= the daughter-in-law]'

Slovak influence has contributed not only to the loss of the second causative, but to the loss of causatives in North Central Romani in general (anonymous reviewer).

4.3.4 Modality

The most stable modal expression in Romani is 'want', usually expressed by *kam-*, in the Balkans also *mang-* 'to want, demand' (Matras 2002: 163), with some exceptions: in Romani varieties in Croatia, a construction with Croatian *želi-* or *voli-* 'to want, love, wish' can be found: *uvek želisardam te žav ande Indija* or *uvek volisardem te džav ande Indija* 'I have always wanted to go to India' (Čurarja Arlije HR-002, 628 and Manuša Čurjarja, HR-003, 628). In Doljenski, Slovene *hoči* has been borrowed: *Hočemo da lam duj phabaja* 'We want to take two apples' (Cech and Heinschink 2001b: 357).

Negative ability ('cannot') is also relatively stable and usually constructed with inherited *našti* (Matras 2002: 163). One of the exceptions is North Russian Romani, which adapts Russian *ne (s)moč'* and inflects it like in Russian: *me ni smog te urakirav la te džal manca* 'I couldn't convince her to come with me' (RUS-003, 713).

Positive ability is more open to borrowing. Many varieties in contact with Slavic languages use Slavic *može* or the verbal stem *mog-* / *mož-* instead of inherited *šaj* (e.g. Boretzky 1999: 112 for the South Balkan varieties). Doljenski also has *lako* < Slovene *lahko*: *I brzo lende lako živinamo* 'we can also live without them' (Cech and Heinschink 2001b: 357), Serednye Romani has *honno* < Czech / Slovak / Ukrainian *hoden-* / *hodn-* 'capable, worthy' (Beníšek 2017: 409–410). Moreover, there is a tendency to differentiate between a general and a situative ability by analogy to Slavic and Greek: *šaj / ašti* vs. *džan-*, cf. Bulgarian *znaja* vs. *moga*, Russian *umet'* vs. *moč'*, Polish *potrafić* vs. *móc* etc. However, Boretzky and Igla (1999: 721) are undecided as to whether this phenomenon is inherited or due to interference.

Stems with the meaning 'to like, love' are also prone to be borrowed, for example *obič-* < Bulgarian *običam*, *voli-* < Croatian *voljeti*, *lub-* < Polish *lubić* and *ljub-* < Russian *ljubit'*. Most innovations and variations are, however, found in the area of necessity (Matras 2002: 162–163). The implicational hierarchy for modality in Romani is thus: necessity ('must') > positive ability ('can') > negative ability ('cannot') > desire ('want') (cf. also Elšík and Matras 2006: 209). The most frequently borrowed Slavic modal stems are *treb-* and *mus-* 'must', but also *mora-* 'idem', *majin-* 'idem' and the modal particles *valjazla / valjani* < Serbian *valja* 'it is necessary' and *nek(a)* 'may, shall' (Boretzky and Igla 1999: 720–721; Boretzky et al. 2008: 83; Beníšek 2017: 411–413), for example: East Slovak Romani *mušinav te džal* 'I must go' (Rácová 2015: 83), Kosovan Gurbet *mora te džav* 'idem' (Leggio 2011: 94) or Kosovan Muslimanje *treba te džav* 'I need to go' (YU-018, 634). The inflection of the Slavic contact language is retained only in the Romani varieties that borrow Serbian or Macedonian *mora-*, i.e. *moram*.1SG, *moraš*.2SG etc. (Elšík and Matras 2009: 295). Interestingly, Kosovo Bugurdži borrows just such a necessitative auxiliary with Serbian inflection, while the past is formed by means of indigenous morphology (e.g. *mora-nj-om* 'I had to'). Several Bulgarian Romani varieties borrow the impersonal necessitative auxiliary *trjabva* 'is necessary' from Bulgarian, and some of them form the past by means of indigenous morphology (e.g. Muzikantska *trjabv-as* 'was necessary'), while others borrow the past form from Bulgarian (Elšík and Matras 2006: 202). Eastern Už Romani additionally has *voľin-* 'should' < Ukrainian *voliti* 'to wish' and Polish *woleć* 'to prefer', e.g. *voľinďam te džan ke Maňa* 'we should have gone to Mania' (Beníšek 2017: 413). It is remarkable that Romani varieties show borrowed inflection with modal verbs but do not show it with borrowed lexical verbs; "[t]he conclusion appears to be that the adoption of full verb inflection is licenced by the adoption of verb inflection with borrowed modals (Mod-INFL > Lex-INFL)" (Elšík and Matras 2006: 320–321).

For a detailed description of expressions of necessity in East Slovak Romani, cf. Rácová (2015: 83). She also observes the adoption of Slovak *mať* 'to have' for modal constructions: *So majinav te kerel?* < *čo mám robiť?* 'what do I have to do?' (Some Romani varieties in contact with Slovak and Polish also borrow 'to have' in possessive constructions, e.g. *me majinav duj phenja* 'I have two sisters', PL-014, 477.) For a detailed classification of borrowings of modal expressions, cf. Elšík and Matras (2006: 209–210).

4.3.5 The conditional

In most European Romani varieties, the inherited conditional conjunction *te / ti* is stable, but a number of varieties (cf. table in Matras 2002: 156, 187) have borrowed the Slavic conditional particle *bi / by* or South Slavic *ako*. An important difference is that the latter may replace *te*, whereas the former only complements it syntagmatically (anonymous reviewer). Matras (2002: 158) explains this as follows: "Where a solid factual basis for an assertion is missing, speakers are inclined to devise new strategies to reinforce their assertive authority." Doljenski in Slovenia and Istria, for example, has copied the Slavic pattern with the result of a mixed construction of Romani *te / ti* and Slavic elements. The particle *bi* is used as a marker of unreal circumstances, followed by a truncated Romani verb: *Rado bi pe khel tuha* 'I would like to play with you' (for an elaborate description of this phenomenon in Doljenski, cf. Cech and Heinschink 2001a: 168–170, 2001b: 358–360). In addition, Macedonian Arli reflects the fourfold conditional subdivision of Macedonian (hypothetical vs. expectative and, within these, fulfillable vs. unfulfillable; Friedman 2001a: 154). For syntactic peculiarities of the conditional cf. Sect. 4.4.3., for a classification of conditional particles in Romani cf. Elšík and Matras (2006: 210).

4.3.6 Renarrative and evidentiality

In some Romani varieties in Bulgaria, e.g. in Sliven, a speaker can mark an action he or she has not witnessed personally by using the perfect form of the verb with the suffix *-li*: *Oda vakerjas mangi, či tu phirsas-li* 'he told me that you were going' (Kostov 1963: 133). This must have been influenced by the Bulgarian renarrative, a special verb form which signals that a speaker is repeating someone else's statement; however, the Bulgarian renarrative is not constructed with *li* (cf. Bulgarian *toj mi kaza če ti si hodel*). Friedman (1999: 520) assumed that the variety in Sliven "has borrowed the evidential category of Bulgarian by reinterpreting the /l/ of the *l*-participle as a particle, viz. *li*." However, in more recent works, Igla and Draganova (2006) and Friedman (2019) demonstrate that *li* as an evidential marker is not derived from the Bulgarian (and also Macedonian) *l*-form, but rather from the Slavic interrogative particle *li* which has received an additional function. This is consistent with other usages in South Slavic and elsewhere. Cf. also the general discussion about evidentiality in Romani in Matras (2002: 156) and Boretzky (1999: 85).

4.3.7 Imperative, optative and jussive

The imperative in Romani has gone through various changes, depending on the respective Slavic contact language. In the inherited construction, the verb stem (if necessary, expanded by an integration marker) serves as the imperative form: *dža-ø!* 'go.SG!', *dža-n!* 'go-2PL!', *ma dža-ø!* 'don't go.SG!', *ma dža-n!* 'don't go-2PL!'. In contact with South Slavic, *nek(a)* as a jussive or optative marker has been borrowed: *nek avel!* 'he shall come!' (Boretzky 1996b: 22). Boretzky (1993: 107) sees a possible South Slavic influence in a second, more attenuated negative imperative: *ma te džas!* < Serbian *nemoj da ideš!* 'don't go!'. The imperative in North Russian Romani is described in detail by Rusakov (2001b: 290–297). This variety borrows from Russian the analytic imperative formation along with the particles *davaj*, *-ka* and *že*: *davaj sbagas!* 'let us sing!' and transfers the Russian use of indicative forms into its own imperative paradigm: *džasa!* < *pojdëm!* 'let's go!'. Sometimes, inherited and borrowed forms are combined, as in *džan'ti!* 'come.PL in!', in which *-n-* (palatalized in the example due to regressive assimilation) is an element from Romani and *ti* (*-te*) an element from Russian (Eloeva and Rusakov 1990: 18).

4.4 Syntax

The field of syntax seems to have received the least attention from researchers in the context of Slavic–Romani language contact. In the following, I discuss prepositions and conjunctions as well as object doubling, conditional sentences and negation.

4.4.1 Prepositions and conjunctions

All Romani varieties in contact with Slavic languages have borrowed Slavic prepositions to varying degrees. An analysis of borrowed Slavic prepositions in 84 samples from the RMS Database reveals the following picture (Fig. 5):

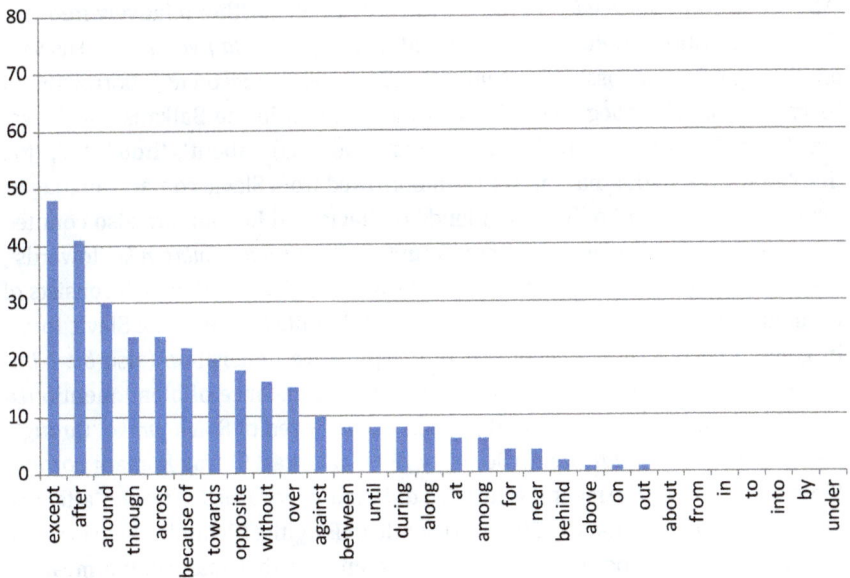

Fig. 5: Borrowing of Slavic prepositions into Romani.

The figure shows absolute numbers, which means that for 'instead of', 50 out of 84 samples show a Slavic borrowing, for 'except' 48, for 'after', 45, etc. According to this analysis, 'instead of' (*vmesto / umesto / mesta / namesto / zamiast / misti* etc.) is the most frequently borrowed Slavic preposition, cf. also Elšík and Matras (2006: 237):

> Borrowing of adpositions is the norm with the Substitutive and Exceptive case roles. [. . .] Slavic is the major source of Substitutive prepositions (e.g. *mesto, misto, vmesto, namesto, zamjast, mjesta* 'instead of'). They are found in many Northeastern, many Central, most Balkan, and many Vlax dialects, and in Slovene Romani. [. . .] Rumungro retains the form *misto* from Croatian, an old L2.

In second place is 'except' (*osven / osim / oprócz / krome / okrem* etc.), which is also affirmed by the findings of Elšík and Matras (2006: 237):

Borrowed Exceptive prepositions, including complex prepositions, are numerous. They include [...] *osven* or *s isključenie* from Bulgarian in numerous dialects of Bulgaria; *pokraj* from Macedonian in Kumanovo Arli, *osim (sem)* from Serbian in Kosovo Bugurdži, Serbian Kalderaš, and Dasikano; *okrem* and *krom'e* from Slovak and Russian, respectively, in Slovak and Lithuanian Romani; and *opruč* or *z vyn'ontkem* [sic] from Polish in the Northeastern and Central dialects of Poland.

'After' is in third place (*sled / posle / pošle / čerez* etc.). Other relatively frequent Slavic prepositions in Romani are 'around' (*okolo / dookoła / vokrug* etc.) as well as 'through' and 'across' (*kroz / prez / przez / čerez / preko* etc.). Borrowing of 'because' (*zaradi / zbog / poradi / kvôli*) is common in the Balkans and Slovakia, but rare elsewhere (Elšík and Matras 2006: 236). 'About', 'from', 'in', 'to', 'into', 'by' and 'under' have never been borrowed from Slavic contact languages, 'above', 'on' and 'out' only once. Blends of Slavic and Romani are also counted here, for example *dre kierunku / pre kierunko / dre strona / smerom ke* 'towards', *preko drom (ki) / preko puta* etc., 'opposite' and *bizo* 'without', which consists of Romani *bi* 'without', Slavic *bez* 'idem' and the definite article *o*. The Slavic forms in general frequently trigger blends of the privative preposition (also *biz / bri*) (Elšík and Matras 2006: 236). Another interesting instance of blend mentioned in the literature is *prekal* 'beyond', which is composed of Slavic *preko* 'through' and Romani *-al < perdal* 'idem' (Boretzky 1999: 118). East Slovak Romani borrows Slovak *o* to express the meaning 'after': *o duj kurke* < Slovak *o dva týždne* 'after two weeks' (Rácová and Horecký 2000: 74), while in Bergitka (Poland), there is a construction with *o* encoding comparative difference (rather than spatial meaning as in Meyer 2017: 149, anonymous reviewer), e.g. *buxlikano o duj metri* < Polish *poszerzony o dwa metry* 'extended by two meters'. Rácová and Horecký (2000: 55) also mention the adoption of Slovak *po* into East Slovak Romani with several different meanings. To what extent the case government of the Slavic languages has been incorporated into Romani along with the borrowed prepositions seems to vary (Elšík, Hübschmannová and Šebková 1999: 375), but requires further investigation.

Elšík and Matras (2006: 236) have also found evidence for the borrowing of the preposition 'with', e.g. South Slavic *s(a)*:

> Borrowed sociative (Comitative and Instrument) prepositions are well attested. [...] In Varna Bugurdži and Yerli, the use of the Bulgarian preposition is triggered by Bulgarian determiners (e.g. *s nekolko gostenca* 'with some guests'). [...] This seems to indicate that Comitative is more prone to borrowing than Instrument. Also, a specifically Comitative preposition *sos(v)e* 'together with' (from Macedonian) is borrowed into Kosovo Bugurdži.

Conjunctions are borrowed from Slavic into Romani more frequently than are prepositions, as reflected in the data below:

4.4 Syntax

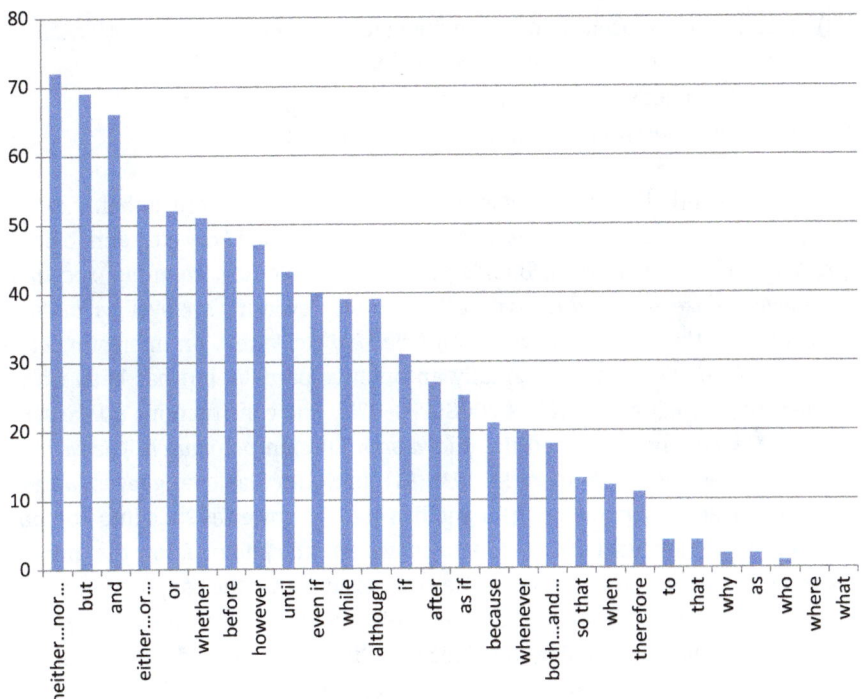

Fig. 6: Borrowing of Slavic conjunctions into Romani.

Figure 6 shows absolute numbers like Figure 5, thus the implication is that 72 of 84 samples show borrowing of 'neither...nor...', 69 of 'but', 66 of 'and', etc. The three conjunctions most frequently borrowed from Slavic are 'neither...nor...' (*ni...ni... / nito...nito... / ani...ani...* etc.), 'but' (*no / ale / ali / a / ama*) and 'and' (*a / i*). This is in line with the general observation that "at the top of the subset hierarchy for connectors are those items around which speakers must 'work hardest' in order to sustain their authority in conversation: expressions of contrast and expressions of sequentiality" (Matras 2020: 210). The borrowability hierarchy for contrast across languages is 'but' > 'or' > 'and'. 'Or' and 'and' in Romani are sometimes also retained from an older contact language (Matras 2020: 210; Elšík and Matras 2006: 185). For complex connectives, the hierarchy is 'neither – nor' > 'either – or' > 'both – and' (Elšík and Matras 2006: 186).

Almost two-thirds of the Romani varieties that have borrowed Slavic 'and' have also adopted the differentiation between adversative *a* and copulative *i* that exists in most Slavic languages. An excerpt from sample's transcription UKR-019 shall serve as an illustration:

(13) [...] Nu, var, moženav dopustim dujen te lav, kirves *i* kirva, (Plaščuny)
a moženav eščё dujen te lav, to est' duj pary moženav te lel. [...]
Well, I can, let's say, take a pair, godfather *and* godmother,
and I can take two pairs, that means I can have two pairs.

Further frequently borrowed Slavic conjunctions in Romani are 'either...or...' (*ili...ili...* / *albo...albo...* / *alebo...alebo*), 'whether' (*da li* / *czy* etc.) and 'before' (*pred(i)* / *poka* / *zanim* etc.). Blends are also possible, e.g. *kana-to* / *xoc-kana* 'whenever', *daže kana* / *daže syr* / *esli dava* etc. 'even if', *syr by* / *syr budto* / *sar bi* etc. 'as if' or *sled kana* / *posle kaj* / *sled kaj* etc. 'after'. An interesting case is Croatian *nek*, which was originally an optative particle, but has been transformed into a conjunction (Elšík 2008: 270–271). The constructions *adake syr* < Russian *tak kak* 'because' and *pal adava so* < Russian *potomu čto* / *iz-za togo, čto*, 'idem' are calques (Sergievskij 1931: 81). In South Slavic languages, *da* is a widespread factual complementizer and has been borrowed as such into Romani, for example in Doljenski *džanu, da mro čhavo ma rado imini* 'I know that my son loves me'. Cech and Heinschink (2001a: 172) assume that the conjunction *kaj* for factual complements first merged with non-factual *te* / *ti* and was then replaced by Slavic *da*. Embedded polar questions with 'if' are introduced either by inherited *te* or, under South Slavic influence, by *li*: *pušlem e maestro de li avol ko abav* 'I asked the teacher if he would come to the wedding' (Leggio 2011: 107), and, under West Slavic influence, by *či* / *čy*: *Kampel te phučel, či pes manuša prindžaren* 'it is necessary to ask if the people know each other' (Rácová 2015: 91; Matras 2002: 187). Generally speaking, the most frequently borrowed subordinating conjunctions stand for concessive or causal relations, purpose and conditionality (Matras 2020: 211).

4.4.2 Object doubling

Pronominal object doubling is a characteristic Balkan phenomenon found in Romani varieties in the Balkans and in Vlax varieties, although with different manifestations depending on the respective contact language. Object doubling is most distinctive in Macedonian, e.g. *go vidov bratot*, literally 'I saw him, the brother'; consequently, Romani varieties in contact with Macedonian are most strongly affected. However, the feature is not grammaticalized but optional and generally less widespread in Romani than in the other Balkan languages. An example from Arli (North Macedonia) is:

(14a) i   kniga   halja   la   o   her   (Arli)
       ART book.OBJ eat.3SG.PST her.OBJ ART donkey
       'The donkey ate the book.' (Boretzky and Igla 1999: 727)

Object doubling is very often used in possessive constructions with the auxiliary *si* plus accusative:

(14b) i   daj   si   la   duj   čhave   (Arli)
       ART mother.OBJ be.3SG.PRS her.OBJ two   children
       'The mother has two children.' (Friedman 2001a: 158)

In (14a), the object fronting makes the doubling highly likely if not required, in the possessive construction in (14b), the doubling is obligatory. (Cf. Boretzky 1999: 125; Boretzky and Igla 1999: 727; Friedman 2001a: 158; Matras 2002: 173–174).

4.4.3 Conditional sentences

As mentioned above, the Slavic conditional particle *bi / by* has frequently been borrowed into Romani varieties. In Bulgarian Romani, for example, *bi* can stand in front of or after the verb in a conditional sentence: *Te na phengjanasbi mange, sar bidžanavas meda?* 'if you hadn't told me, how should I have known?' (Kostov 1963a: 138). The following example from North Russian Romani combines an inherited (by means of the non-factual complementizer *te*) with a borrowed (by means of the particle *by*) formation:

(15) Me koli   te   javavas   dre Moskva   (North Russian Romani)
      I   when   COMP come.COND   in   Moscow
      to but   sykl'ovavas   by
      then much learn.COND   COMP
      'If I were in Moscow, I would learn a lot.' (Wentzel 1980: 137)

East Slovak Romani only inserts *bi* if it is not clear from the context that we are dealing with a conditional (Rácová 2015: 83) and in the Eastern Už varieties of North Central Romani, the use of *bi / bo* is also optional (Beníšek 2017: 68–70); for North Russian Romani, cf. Wentzel (1980: 137). In the Balkans, inherited *te* can be replaced by *ako* or syntagmatically complemented by *bi*, but there is also a construction with *ka*, as in *ka dikhelas* 'would see, would have seen', modelled on Greek or Macedonian (*ḱe gledaše* 'idem') (Boretzky 1999: 107). In Doljenski, conditional sentences are introduced by *ako* or *da*, as in South Slavic: *Ako bi ma ov love, me bi av but pute* 'if I had money, I would come often' or *da bi džan, kon hi li doja romni, phenave tuke* 'if I had known who that woman is, I would have told you' (Cech and Heinschink 2001b: 360).

4.4.4 Negation

Apart from the negative particle, more complex negative constructions in Romani have also been influenced by the Slavic contact languages. Already Ackerley (1941: 83), who investigated Bosnian Romani, noticed that Romani varieties tended to adopt Slavic double negation, as did Kostov (1963a: 155) for Bulgarian Romani, Beníšek (2017: 213–214) for the Eastern Už varieties and Cech and Heinschink (2001a: 170) for Doljenski in Slovenia and Istria, for example: *Nije Rajko nič mothav*, literally 'Rajko did not say nothing'. Thus, the preterit in Doljenski is negated with the Slavic copula *nije* 'is not' in combination with the Romani verb stem; instead of the participle, Romani uses the truncated verb. In Perechyn Romani, the pronominal subject may have accusative marking, "an innovation triggered by the genitive marking of the subject noun phrase in East Slavic negative constructions" (Beníšek 2017: 399), e.g. *kanake ade ňikas.*ACC *nane* 'there is nobody here now'. In the variety of Sliven (Bulgaria), *nanaj / nama* is used for negation, which usually appears in combination with *te* and reflects the Bulgarian construction *njama da* (Kostov 1963a: 155). In Macedonian Arli, *nae te* calques *nema da* as the negative future marker (anonymous reviewer). These cases of borrowed negative auxiliaries are an exception to the general observation that affirmative forms are more likely to be borrowed than negative forms (Elšík and Matras 2006: 160). Southwestern Vlax varieties have *ni* as a negator, "perhaps an original Southern Vlax innovation, which may have merged with the Slavic negators of the surrounding languages (*ne/nie*)" (Matras 2002: 189). In most varieties in Ukraine, among others, the separate imperative marker *ma* has been lost in favor of *na* for all kinds of negation (Anton Tenser, personal correspondence).

4.4.5 Word order

A final contact phenomenon concerns word order in the sentence. The conservative word order in Romani is relatively free with a certain preference for VO (e.g. *(me) dikhav o kher* 'I see the house'; Boretzky 1996c: 96) and the option of object fronting for focus. The subject can precede (contrastive-thematic order) or follow (connective-narrative order) the verb, there are no divergent rules for subordinate or interrogative clauses (Matras 2002: 167; 190). VSO is even fairly frequent, e.g. *kerel.v o manuš.*SBJ *buti.*OBJ *trin berš* 'the man works for three years' (Boretzky 1996c: 96).

The Balkan and Vlax varieties largely stick to the conservative VO pattern (cf. Boretzky 1996b: 25, 1996c: 99; Boretzky and Igla 1999: 726; Leggio 2011: 105). Boretzky (1996c: 116–117) only highlights the position of interrogatives and complementizers in interrogative sentences (16a) and subordinate clauses (16b) that can change due to the impact of colloquial Macedonian and other contact languages on the Balkans:

(16a) e   prvo   rjat   so   ka   kerel?   (Balkan)
      the   first night   what   FUT   do
      'The first night, what is he going to do?' (Boretzky 1996c: 116)

(16b) me   kana   somas   ciknoro, ...   (Balkan)
      I   when   was   small
      'When I was small, ...' (Boretzky 1996c: 116)

Romani varieties in contact with West and East Slavic languages tend to place the pronominal object before the verb, as in the following example from Bergitka in comparison with Arli (Matras and Adamou 2020: 343; cf. also Boretzky 1996c: 100, 102; Matras 2002: 168, 206):

(17a) jov   les   na   dikhla   (Bergitka)
      he   him.OBL   NEG   see.3SG.PST
      'He did not see him.' (PL-007, 353c)

(17b) ov   na   dikhlja   ole   (Arli)
      he   NEG   see.3SG.PST   him.OBL
      'idem' (MK-002, 353c)

In conservative varieties, the complementizer *te* and the verb cannot be separated – except in negative sentences –, but in Romani varieties in contact with West Slavic languages it is possible. Boretzky (1996c: 107) shows that not only personal pronouns (18a), but also several phrases (18b) can stand between *te* and the verb:

(18a) te   na   man   xudel   musatar   (Bergitka)
      COMP   NEG   me.OBL   seize.3SG.PRS   arm.ABL
      'that he does not seize me by the arm' (Boretzky 1996c: 107)

(18b) sar   te   len o benga andre jak   ispidnehas   (East Slovak)
      how   COMP them the devils in the fire push.2SG.PST
      'as if the devils had pushed them into the fire' (Boretzky 1996c: 107)

The following verb-initial word order patterns from Romani in contact with East Slavic languages would be impossible in Balkan and Vlax varieties:

(19a) doristja   jou   les   (North Russian Romani)
      catch up.3SG.PST   he   him.OBL
      'He caught up with him.' (Dobrovol'skij 1908: 2, cited in Boretzky 1996c: 102)

(19b) i   otčindja   leske   širo   (North Russian Romani)
      and cut off.3SG.PST him.DAT head
      'And he cut off his head.' (Boretzky 1996c: 102)

Generally speaking, however, Slavic impact on Romani word order seems to be relatively limited. Where it exists, it has, according to Boretzky (1996c: 199), led to more freedom without any new restrictions.

4.4.6 Zero copula

The RMS Database shows that all Romani varieties from Russia, Ukraine and Lithuania except Crimean Romani omit the copula in the present tense due to contact with Russian and partially Ukrainian, two languages with a zero / null copula. The same applies for East Slovak Romani under the influence of East Slovak, e.g. *amaro dad lačho* 'our father is good' (anonymous reviewer). The following example from Gimpeny Romani (Ukraine) shows the parallel to the structure in Russian and Ukrainian and the difference to other Romani varieties, exemplified here by Polish Xaladytka:

(20) o stulo   Ø   nevo,   a   o pato   Ø   purano   (Gimpeny)
     stul   Ø   novyj, a   krovat'   Ø   staraja   (Russian)
     krislo   Ø   nove,   a   ližko   Ø   stare   (Ukrainian)
     banko   sy nevo,   a   čhiben   isy purano   (Polish Xaladytka)
     the / this chair is new but the bed is old
     'The chair is new, but the bed is old.' (UKR-020, 612; PL-014, 612)

Like all Slavic–Romani contact phenomena in the domain of syntax, this observation would be worth further investigation.

4.5 Discourse markers

Discourse markers (fillers, tags, interjections, hesitation markers) are a very widespread phenomenon in bilingual speech and a striking example of fusion between Slavic and Romani. According to Matras (2020: 145; cf. also 1998a: 291–293), discourse particles are treated by speakers

> as an integral part of the Romani discourse. [...] This is a consequence of the acceptance of the bilingual mode in the context of Romani interaction. What is the reason behind this acceptance specifically of discourse operators? There are, I suggest, two principal motivations, which are interconnected. The first is the vulnerability of discourse operators to selection malfunctions [...]. This leads to a relatively high frequency of 'slips' or fallbacks into the pragmatically dominant language. [...] The second reason has to do with the fact that discourse operators or utterance modifiers carry out highly automated routine tasks, for which routine schemas appear to exist. [...] They are, in other words, 'pragmatically detachable' from their source language.

For example, for the Romani varieties in contact with Serbian, we find the discourse markers *pa, e, znači* and *(i) to je to* (cf. sample's transcriptions for YU-007, -009, -012, -016, -017, -018). The following excerpt from YU-016 (Kosovan Arli) shall serve as an illustration (apart from the discourse markers, it additionally contains the connectors *i* 'and' and *onda* 'then' as well as some lexical elements from Serbian):

(21) [...] *Pa* taj Bajram traje, traje dva dana. [...] (Kosovan
Sar slavinjala le *pa*, akana, nja Ramazan mesec dana i odova Arli)
postisajlo,
i akana avela Bajram i akana klanja se, klanjini pe, sabalje
džalja pe ko grobija,
onda keda aveja čhjere ačhjel ručko pe familija, *znači* mas ono i
onda ima isi men igranka.
Znači dža ki igranka i dža duj dive i onda više nane odova,
onda nakhela o Ramazani o Bajrami em sa. [...]
[...] 'Well, and Bajram lasts two days. [...]
How do we celebrate it, *well*, now, during Ramadan for a month
and that, we fast
and now Bajram is coming and we go to pay respect, in the
morning we go to the graves,

then we come home, we have dinner with the family, *that means* meat, and then we have a celebration.
That means you go to the celebration and it goes on for two days and then there is nothing more,
then Ramadan is over, Bajram and everything.' [...]

For the Romani varieties in contact with Slovak, we find the discourse markers *tak, veď, no* and the interjection *jaj!* (cf. sample's transcriptions for SK-011, -016, -031, -052). Very productive are those used in the samples from Ukraine with the contact languages Ukrainian and Russian (cf. sample's transcriptions UKR-008, -010, -011, -015, -016, -019, -020). Here, we find the fillers *vot, no, nu, da, to est', značit, kak by, dopustim*, the question tag *pravda?* and the interjections *oj!* and *davaj!*. The first part of sample UKR-008 (Kubanski Servy) will serve as an example:

(22) Amende syn kecave serbatorja sar Patradji, Kreščuno, bjav, (Kubanski
 vot kala vazden cer, xotinp...? Servy)
 Vot de save serbatorjenge.
 No, sar amen vjerujuče Roma amy... amy... serbatorja kecave,
 save de Svento Lil tčento ande Biblja,
 vot kadala serbarorja.
 Nu a kadike inkje sar bolde čauoren serbatorja. [...]
 'We have several celebrations like Easter, Christmas, weddings,
 well, when they build a house, what else...?
 Well, during some holidays.
 Well, we Roma who believe in God, we... we... those big holidays,
 that are written in the Holy Scripture, in the Bible,
 well, those holidays.
 Well and also a holiday when they baptize children.' [...]

4.6 Summary

Since the arrival of the Roma in Europe, Romani has been influenced by Slavic contact languages not only in the lexicon, but also in phonetics and phonology, morphology and syntax. The affected dialect groups are mainly the Northeast, Northern Central, Southern Central and South Balkan I, but structural borrowing from Slavic can be found in Romani dialects all over Europe. Probably, the most widespread contact phenomenon in the field of phonetics and phonology is the devoicing of stops in word-final position (in all Romani dialects except those in contact with Bosnian / Croatian / Serbian) and the shift of stress to the penultimate or initial syllable in the Central European dialects. East Slavic palatalization of front vowels has been widely transferred to the Northeast group. Furthermore, several characteristic sounds of the respective Slavic contact language(s) have been adopted into Romani, e.g. /ł/ from Polish, /ə/ from Bulgarian, /ɨ/ from Russian, Ukrainian and Polish, syllabic /r/ from South Slavic and Czech and velarized /l/ from East Slavic. From a contact linguistic point of view, phonology is generally a field where borrowings fill structural 'gaps', which happens particularly easily when the changes are merely allophonic and not phonological. This confirms Matras' (2007: 37) observation that language contact leads to an enrichment of the phonological system. Also, the examples presented here prove that new phonological features first find their way into the recipient language via loanwords and then spread beyond them. The adoption of phonological features is, on the one hand, a pragmatic advantage for speakers, but, on the other, it is also in competition with loyalty to the L1, such that the result is often a compromise in which only certain aspects of the phonological system are adapted (cf. Matras 2007: 40).

In Romani nominal morphology, the category of comparison has generally expanded under Slavic influence, and those dialects in contact with Slavic languages without an article (i.e. all but Macedonian and Bulgarian) are in the process of losing their own definite article. An interesting novelty in the Romani case system is the use of a reflexive dative, especially in the Balkan varieties in contact with South Slavic. Russian, Ukrainian and Polish have had a significant influence on the case system of Romani dialects in Russia, Ukraine and Lithuania.

Slavic aspect and aktionsart prefixes were excluded here because Chapter 5 deals with it in detail. In the tense system, the most Slavic influence can be found in the future; in the Balkans, we can also witness the development of an analytic perfect. Boretzky (1996a) has introduced the term of a 'new infinitive' that has developed in many (but not all) Romani dialects in contact with infinitive languages like Slovene, Czech, Slovak and Polish. Also, under Slavic influence, the reflexive pronoun *pe(s)* has become generalized to occur with all grammatical persons, most widely spread in the Balkans. The most stable Romani modal expressions are 'want' and 'cannot', whereas 'can', 'like / love' and especially 'must' are very open for borrowings from Slavic. Many dialects have also borrowed Slavic conditional particles. Romani under Slavic influence thus confirms many general tendencies for structural borrowability (cf. Matras 2007, 2020) but also shows some peculiarities, such as the "new infinitive" or (as Balkanisms) object doubling and renarrative / evidentiality. Matras (2007: 46) explains these tendencies in terms of the degree of a speaker's control:

[E]xternal circumstances that limit the degree of speaker control – mood and modality in general – are the most contact-sensitive. They are followed by a qualification of the internal structure of the event – aspect and aktionsart – these too being beyond the immediate control of the speaker. Only then do we find contact influence in tense, the most intimate relationship between the event and the speaker's own perspective, though it is noteworthy that in ou[r] sample it is limited to the future tense, which identifies the event as being least stable and secure from the speaker's perspective. The overall theme is therefore once again the speaker's epistemic authority; its absence or weakening correlates with high borrowability.

Beyond all that has been said, it is remarkable that most Romani varieties have survived and kept a stable core of vocabulary and grammatical structures until the present day, in spite of the strong influence exerted upon them by the Slavic (and other) majority languages surrounding them since the eleventh century.

5 Slavic verbal prefixes in Romani – figures, forms and functions

In the context of verbal morphology, it is a particularly interesting and striking phenomenon that Romani – a suffixing language without inherited verbal prefixes – has borrowed prefixes from numerous contact languages. This pertains not only to the Slavic languages, but also to German (cf. Igla 1992; Schrammel 2002, 2005; Kiefer 2010; Bodnarová and Wiedner 2015 etc.), Lithuanian (cf. Ariste 1973; Tenser 2008) and Hungarian (cf. Kiefer 2010; Bodnarová and Wiedner 2015 etc.). Slavic prefixes in Romani and the influence of Slavic aspect and aktionsart have been studied before; however, the aim and novelty of this chapter is to provide a cross-dialectal overview of the amount of Slavic prefixes and their form and function in Romani by way of a corpus study and a discussion of the existing research literature in order to provide empirical evidence for tendencies that have already been hinted at in the literature.[10] In this respect, it will address what Igla laid out as a desideratum in 1998:

> Da der Einfluß schon einer einzigen Kontaktsprache sich in unterschiedlicher Weise auswirkt, ist zunächst die detaillierte Untersuchung von einzelnen Dialekten vonnöten, bevor die Einwirkung verschiedener Sprachen mit Verbalaspekt auf das Romani umfassend und vergleichend erfaßt werden kann. ['As the influence of only a single contact language has an impact in various ways, the detailed analysis of individual dialects is needed first, before the effect on Romani of various languages with an aspect system can be comprehensively and comparatively ascertained.'] (Igla 1998: 78)

Since then, several investigations of Slavic verbal prefixes in single Romani varieties or dialect groups have been conducted. In addition, we now have enough accessible language data to venture a comparative survey. A particularity of the present chapter lies in its research perspective, in that the underlying understanding of aspect and aktionsart follows the tradition of Slavic linguistics.

The hereafter following Section 1 explains this understanding and gives an introduction to aspect and aktionsart in Slavic and in Romani. Section 2 presents the findings of a comprehensive study of Slavic verbal prefixes in 76 Romani language samples from 17 countries. The objective is to ascertain the quantity of Slavic prefixes in these varieties – both in combination with Slavic verb stems and with Romani ones. Of greatest interest are the prefixes borrowed into Romani

---

10 Cf. Matras (2002: 159): "The wholesale borrowing of the Slavic aktionsart prefix system (or Slavic aspect) is characteristic of the Northern Central and Northeastern dialects of Romani, in contact with western and eastern Slavic languages. [. . .] But there is also some infiltration of Slavic aktionsart markers as derivational prefixes into Balkan dialects of Romani." (Further: Matras 1999: 14, 2002: 202–203; Tenser 2005: 34; Matras personal correspondence.)

independently of Slavic verb stems, because they show a higher degree of autonomy and demand more abstraction from language users. Section 3 seeks to answer the question of what functions the Slavic prefixes bear out in Romani. This will be done on the basis of existing studies and the analysis of additional Romani language data (fairy tales, poems, journalistic texts, teaching materials, informational brochures and forum posts on the internet). Of central significance is the question of whether any varieties have taken over the complete aspectual system (in the understanding of the present chapter, i.e. the grammatical opposition of perfective vs. imperfective verb forms) from the respective Slavic contact language(s). Rusakov (2001a, 2004) has postulated this for North Russian Romani, and Boretzky (1989: 368) contemplated the following already three decades ago: "Es ist nicht ausgeschlossen, daß sich in Ansätzen so etwas wie der slavische Verbalaspekt [im Romani] herauszubilden beginnt." ['It cannot be ruled out that something like the Slavic verbal aspect is rudimentarily emerging [in Romani].']). The purpose of Section 4 is to integrate the observations from the previous sections into Matras' (2020) contact-linguistic model. Section 5 gives a summary of all relevant findings and perspectives for future research.

5.1 Aspect and aktionsart in Slavic and Romani

Some challenges in dealing with Slavic verbal prefixes in Romani are the enormous extent of the aspectological literature, the differing understandings of (Slavic) aspect between Slavic linguistics and Romani or general linguistics and the inconsistent terminology used. For example, a core issue in the history of aspectological research has been the question of whether "Slavic-style aspect" should be seen as grammatical (viewpoint) aspect, lexical aspect / actionality or as a category of its own. Outside of Slavic linguistics (Dahl 1985; Thieroff 1994, 1995; Bertinetto and Delfitto 2000 etc.), "Slavic-style aspect" is usually not seen as a 'prototypical' example of aspect, but as a special case, due to its derivational character that cannot be put on an equal level with the inflection-based aspectual systems of other languages. On the other hand, some Slavic or Russian linguists accept only the Slavic type as representing 'true' aspect, whereas other languages have 'merely' aktionsarten (Breu 2007: 124). To complicate matters, the aspectual systems of Slavic languages exhibit partially significant differences. Dickey (2000) thus identifies an eastern (Russian, Ukrainian, Bulgarian), a western (Czech, Slovak, Slovene) and a transitional (Polish, Serbo-Croatian) group. Very roughly speaking, the western perfective stands for totality, the eastern one for temporal definiteness; the western imperfective stands for quantitative, the eastern one for qualitative temporal indefiniteness.

The vast majority of works on Slavic verbal prefixes in Romani do not stand in the tradition of Slavic linguistics. Matras for example sees himself in the tradition of Dahl and Thieroff and uses the terms 'Slavic aspect' and 'aktionsart' synonymously (Matras 2001: 176, 2002: 158–159, 193). Slavic linguists, however, understand Slavic aspect (Russian *vid*) as a grammatical category, regardless of its derivational character, whereas the notion of aktionsarten refers to lexical-actional classes. The present study follows the functional view as presented in Breu (2007, cf. also 2000, 2009), who argues that both English, Romance and Slavic languages have a grammatical aspect opposition that exhibits many functional similarities, no matter by what formal means it may be expressed.

Against this background, the following section will give a short overview of the categories aspect and aktionsart in Romani and Slavic.

5.1.1 Aspect and aktionsart in Romani

Breu (2007: 138) differentiates between three morphosyntactic types of verbal aspect: derivational ("derivativ"), inflectional ("flexivisch") and periphrastic ("periphrastisch"). Among these, Romani patterns after the second type. It is essentially a suffixing language without any prefixes in its inherited verb morphology. The inherited TAM system in Romani consists of three dimensions: the temporal (± remote), the aspectual (± perfective) and the modal dimensions, which comprises only intentionality; everything else is indicative (cf. Matras 2002: 151). Hence, Romani expresses perfectivity morphologically just as do the Slavic languages, however, in contrast to them it does not have a marker for imperfectivity. Therefore, a negative definition of imperfectivity as the "absence of perfectivity" has proven most useful (Matras 2002: 152).

When a verb form bears a perfectivity marker, it follows the verb stem, and, if present, the loan adaptation suffix and the transitivity marker. The origin of the perfectivity marker is the Old Indo-Aryan participle affix *-ta*; in modern Romani the perfectivity markers are (depending on the variety) *-d- / -d'- / -dž-, -l- / -l'- / -j-, -t- / -t'- / -č-, -n- / -n'-, -in-* or *-il-* (Matras 2002: 138–142), as the following examples from different varieties illustrate: *ker-d'-om* 'do-PFV-1SG = I did', *beš-l-em* 'live-PFV-1SG = I lived', *su-t-em* 'sleep-PFV-1SG = I fell asleep'. The perfective is used with simple or remote past (pluperfect) tense forms and expresses completion. Even without an additional marker for tense, a perfectivity marker can establish a relation to the past. However, the perfective is not restricted to past tenses, but can also mark anticipated completion in the future or have irrealis functions (Matras 2001: 165, 2002: 151–152). Unlike the tenses, the perfective has, just like in Slavic, no deictic anchorage. It denotes a subjective perspective on the event, which is perceived by the speaker both as being completed and as a unit without internal phases (Matras 2001: 165). Non-perfective verb forms, by contrast, denote uncompleted events. They are characteristic for the present and imperfect.

Spatial relations in Romani are expressed by adverbs, e.g. *džav angle* 'I go ahead', *džav avri* 'I go outside', *džav tele* 'I go down', *džav upre* 'I go up' etc. A basic set of such adverbs can be found in all Romani varieties. Some simplex forms, by contrast, carry a spatial meaning in and of themselves and are not combined with adverbs, e.g. *iklel* 'to go out', *uštel* 'to stand up', *xulel* 'to go down'.

5.1.2 Aspect and aktionsart in Slavic

The aspectual systems of the Slavic languages differ remarkably from the aspectual system of Romani, which is inflection-based and mainly pertains to the past. According to Breu (2007: 138), the Slavic aspectual systems are of the *derivational* type, that is, the aspectual opposition is expressed through morphological means that otherwise belong to word formation, i.e. to the realm of the lexicon. The South Slavic languages also partially belong to the inflectional type (cf. Breu 2007: 140–141). The aspectual opposition in Slavic is not restricted to the past and consists of the two grammemes *perfective* and *imperfective*. Thus, an aspectual pair is a pair of verbs with the same lexical meaning but a grammatical differentiation into an imperfective and a perfective partner that together constitute a complete lexeme (Breu 2007: 138–139). The perfective aspect shows a high degree of temporal dynamics, it expresses an event in its entirety including its inherent borders (as well as, in the Eastern group, a change of situation). The imperfective aspect shows a medium or low degree of temporal dynamics and is restricted to the description of a situation without any further specification of its inherent boundaries (Breu 2007: 128, 142). In contrast to Romani, the Slavic languages possess a large repertoire of verbal prefixes that play an important role in the expression of aspect and whose functions are a subject of linguistic debates to this day. However, prefixes are not the only means of aspect modification in Slavic; stem formation suffixes are also highly productive, while suppletion plays a minor role (cf. Breu 2007: 138). From a historical perspective, the prefixes in the Slavic languages at first had lexical (spatial etc.) meanings, which became weaker over time. The prefixes underwent an actional modification and the actional meaning was 'utilized' for telicity. Finally, and as a Slavic peculiarity, a distinction of viewpoint aspect developed upon this basis as the actional meaning was generalized as an aspectual meaning (Wiemer and Seržant 2017: 265–268).

It is important to mention that, also within Slavic linguistics, there are different points of view about the question of where the boundary between the grammatical and the lexical function of a prefix has to be drawn.[11] The point of view of some aspectologists (e.g. Isačenko 1968; Zaliznjak 1977) – who accept only such aspectual pairs as have come about through suffixation, whereas prefixation, in their view, always brings about a change of the lexical meaning – has not been widely accepted in Slavic linguistics. Nevertheless, a research group around Janda has argued that Russian aspectual prefixes have not lost their lexical meaning; it only seems so because their meaning overlaps with that of the simplex verb (Janda et al. 2013). Clasmeier (2015: 38) attempts to reconcile the two perspectives by drawing a clear distinction between the diachronic and synchronic perspective.

In the present chapter, the notion of aspect – this explicitly includes that of the Slavic languages – is defined as a *grammatical* category. In other words, it always means viewpoint aspect. Thus, when we ask whether a particular Romani variety has taken over the aspectual system of its Slavic contact language(s), the grammatical status of the outcome of language contact in question has to be proven. This means that there has to be a systematic, obligatory choice between perfective and imperfective verb forms throughout the verb inventory, and it may not be a merely lexical phenomenon.

5.2 Analysis of the RMS database data

5.2.1 Methodological procedure

The present study is based on 76 samples from 17 countries. A prerequisite for the consideration of a data record is that the Romani variety in question is or has been in contact with one or more Slavic language(s) at present or at an earlier point in time. All samples were searched for prefixed and non-prefixed Slavic borrowed verbs as well as for independent Slavic verbal prefixes combined with inherited Romani verb stems. Since the RMS Database does not offer an automatic search function tailored to this purpose, this had to be carried out manually. The relevant database entries were transferred to tables like in Fig. 7 for further analysis.

The 76 samples examined comprise nearly all of the relevant samples available in the RMS Database, i.e. all those that show current or prior contact with Slavic. Four samples (PL-003, UKR-003, UKR-019, EST-005) have significant gaps and were therefore not taken into account. Since the RMS Database contains a relatively large number of samples from Bulgaria, a selection was made here in

---

[11] A summary for Russian can be found in Clasmeier (2015: 34–38).

5 Slavic verbal prefixes in Romani – figures, forms and functions

	A	B	C	D	E	F
1		RUS-003 Russian Roma	RUS-005 Lovari Čokeši	RUS-006 North Russian	RUS-008 North Russian	RUS-011 Crimean
2	157 kill	x	x	te umaras	te umares	x
3	160 understand	te poles	x	te poles	te poles	x
4	162 speak	x	x	x	x	te zbordizes
5	167 guard	te zrakoxes	x	x	x	te storožyskeres
6	168 cough	te kašlines	x	te kašlines	te kašljanes	x
7	169 count	x	x	x	te sgines	x
8	173 grab, hold	te uxtyles	x	te uxteles	te uxteles/te rikires	x
9	174 open	x	x	te otkeres	te otkeres	te phjinraves/te načinaiskeres
10	179 fly	x	x	x	l'etas	x
11	184 find	te poperes	x	x	x	x
12	185 meet	te udyloxes	x	x	te udyloxes	te kjidas amen/te raskeldjijas amen
13	188 wait	te dužakires [do-]	x	te dužakires [do-]	te dužakires	x
14	193 embrace	te obles	dosangalja	te obles pe	te obles	x
15	241 open	me otkerav	x	me otkerav	me otkerav	x
16	242 opened	me otkerdjom	x	me otkerdžom	me otkerdjom	x
17	263 shut	me zakerav	x	me zakerav	me zakerav	x

	A	B	C	D	E	F
145	662 I prefer my coffee with milk.	me pr'edpočitaju kofe budesa	x	mange ravicu miro kofe budesa	me pr'edpočitaju kofe e budesa	x
146	663 We had to wait because of the rain.	amenge prigeja pe te dužakiras pal o brišynt	x	amenge trebi te dužakiras paldava so brišynt	amenge prigeja pe te dužakires palo brišyn	x
147	665 Everybody except the grandfather left.	akramja pxuromestes sare ogyne	x	sare akramja papuste ugene	x	x
148	666 She went past the village.	joj progeja mamuj gav	x	jej progeja paš gav	jej progeja mimo gav	x
149	669 She came out of the house.	x	x	jej vygeja koerestyr	jej vygeja e koerestyr	x
150	671 Can you mend these holes with thread?	tu možyš te zasyves ada dyry txavesa?	x	možeš tu zasyves adale dyrki txavesa?	tu možeš zaštopaš adale dyry koavesa	x
151	672 This chair is made of wood.	x	x	[kerdo]	x	x
152	673 That one over there is made of metal.	x	x	a odova skerdo sastyrestyr	x	x
153	675 When I opened the door, it crawled under the bushes.	koli me otkerdjom e porta jov geradyja tel o kusty	x	koli me otkerdjom e porta jov uprastandyja dro kusty	kedy me otkerdjom e porta jov zapols talo kusty	x
154	678 Old women like to sit in front of the house and talk for hours.	o pxurja ljubinen te bešen paš o koer i te rakiren časenca	x	e pxurane džuvlja ljubinen te bešen pašo koer i te rakiren drivan but	x	phure džjuvlja dexen te bešen angal ko kher taj te zbordizen but sahatja

Fig. 7: Two table excerpts from the samples from Russia.

order to avoid an excessive imbalance. Further unequal weighting (e.g. there is only one sample each from the Czech Republic and Slovenia and none from Belarus or Bosnia) is compensated for as much as possible in the next section by using existing studies on the underrepresented countries and / or additional language data. Tokens, not types, are counted. The reference value for each set is 979, which is the total number of verb tokens in each sample (only full verbs, no modal verbs or copulae). The results are, of course, also contingent upon the nature of the database entries (e.g. multiple repetition of certain verbs) or the structure of the questionnaires. It is also important to mention that some inherited Romani verbs stem from the same Indo-European roots as do their Slavic cognates (this primarily concerns *pek-* 'bake', *pi-* 'drink' and *(d)živ-* 'live'). Therefore, they are counted as inherited and not as loans from Slavic.

5.2.2 Results

The diagram in Fig. 8 below shows the proportion of Slavic non-prefixed verb stems (orange), Slavic prefixed verb stems (orange with blue stripes) and Slavic

5.2 Analysis of the RMS database data — 73

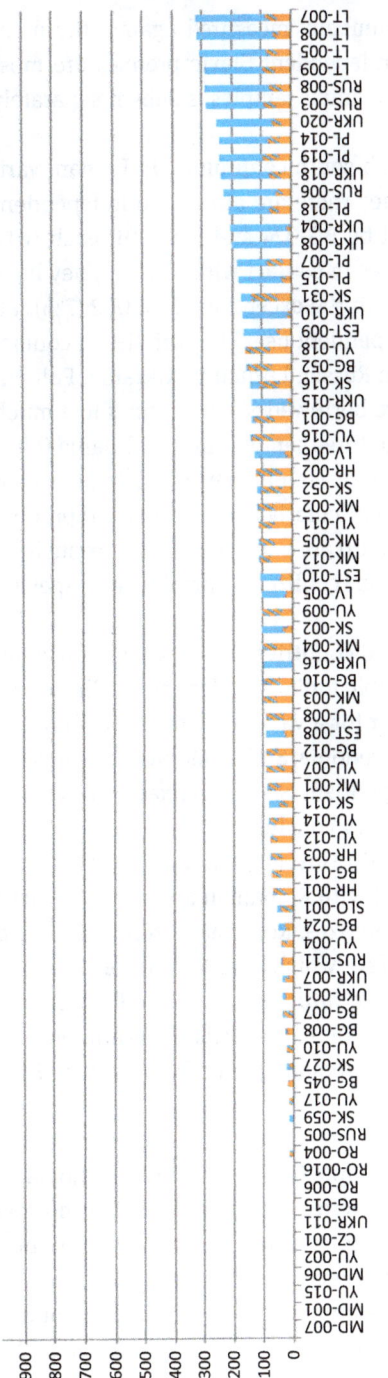

Fig. 8: Non-prefixed and prefixed Slavic verbs and independent Slavic prefixes.

independent prefixes (blue) in absolute numbers, measured against the mentioned reference value of 979. Since the independent Slavic prefixes are most interesting here, their percentage in the individual samples is shown separately in Fig. 9.

The overall picture clearly shows a north-south continuum. In Romani varieties in contact with South Slavic languages there are almost no independent Slavic prefixes; the highest values are had by BG-024 and SLO-001, each with 2%. In the lower middle field are the varieties in contact with Slovak. They have borrowed only a few Slavic prefixes and, with the exception of SK-002 (7%), all remain below 4% with respect to their independent use. The varieties in contact with Polish and the East Slavic languages in Russia, Lithuania, Ukraine, Poland, Latvia and Estonia, on the other hand, have borrowed Slavic prefixes to a much greater extent. The frontrunners are found in three samples from Lithuania (Lithuanian Romani) and one from Russia (North Russian Romani). Judging from the RMS data, independent Slavic prefixes are particularly autonomous and productive in the northeast, while prefixes in the south are borrowed almost exclusively together with Slavic verb stems. The figures thus confirm the previously suspected tendencies mentioned at the outset.

Let us take a closer look at the individual countries and language constellations. In Bulgaria, BG-024 (Sofia Erli) is notable for its 21 independent Slavic prefixes, which is a comparatively high number for a variety in contact with South Slavic languages. In the varieties of North Macedonia, Serbia, Montenegro, Kosovo and Croatia, there are practically no independent Slavic prefixes – no variety has more than two. The RMS data are not very conclusive for Slovenia because there is only one sample (SLO-001) with few (7) Slovene prefixes. The varieties in Romania are, of course, primarily in contact with Romanian and therefore have very few purely Slavic stems and no Slavic prefixes. Romanian itself is known to have a very large share of Slavic loan words – which is reflected, for example, in such Romani words as *povestizel* 'to tell' or *hranizel* 'to feed' (< Romanian *a povesti, a hrăni*) – but these are not counted here. Otherwise, the influence of Slavic upon the verb morphology in both the Romanian and the Moldovan RMS samples can be neglected.

For the Romani varieties in Slovakia, the proportion of Slavic independent prefixes is between 1% and 4%, and in one sample (SK-002, East Slovak Romani) 7%. SK-016, SK-031 and SK-052 represent varieties that have tended to borrow prefixed and non-prefixed Slavic verbs as a whole, rather than independent prefixes. The Czech sample shows no Slavic influence in verb morphology, since it is a Vlax or migrant dialect, i.e. the speakers immigrated to the Czech Republic relatively recently. Thus, in the overall comparison, Romani in Slovakia is in the lower middle field in terms of borrowed Slavic prefixes.

5.2 Analysis of the RMS database data — 75

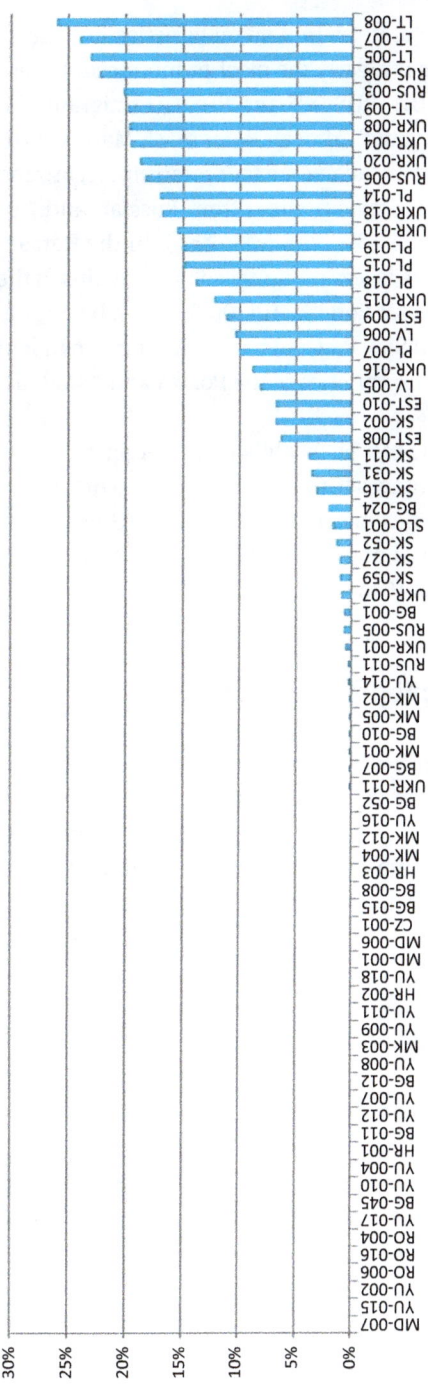

Fig. 9: Percentage of Slavic independent prefixes.

The adoption of independent Slavic prefixes in Romani varieties in Poland, Russia, Ukraine and the Baltic countries is clearly the most pronounced. Exceptions are revealed by the samples UKR-011, RUS-005 and RUS-011 (migrant dialects), UKR-001 (representing the conservative Crimean Romani, cf. Matras 2002: 6) and UKR-007 with a maximum of 1%. For each of the four forerunners, around a quarter of the verbs have independent Slavic prefixes from Russian and / or Polish (LT-008: 26%, LT-007: 24%, LT-005: 23%, RUS-008: 22%). In the Romani varieties in Estonia and Latvia, this feature is less pronounced and remains in the range of 6–11%. In Poland it is the sample for Bergitka (PL-007), which belongs to the Northern Central dialects like those in Slovakia and has the least independent Slavic prefixes, with 10%, compared to the varieties of the Polska and Xaladytka Roma with 14–17%.

Based on these results, three groups can be established: the Romani varieties in contact with the South Slavic languages (Group 1; the influence of Slovene has yet to be clarified), the Romani varieties in contact with Slovak (Group 2; the influence of Czech has yet to be clarified) and the Romani varieties in contact with Polish and the East Slavic languages (Group 3).

5.3 Functions of the Slavic verbal prefixes in Romani

In the following, we will explore which functions the Slavic verbal prefixes in Romani have. In addition, information on the varities in the countries that are poorly represented in the RMS Database is supplemented by research from other authors and, if necessary, by language data collected for this purpose from the written sources mentioned above. The analysis is organized according to the three groups just mentioned.

5.3.1 Group 1: Varieties in contact with South Slavic

There is no published research on Bosnian / Croatian / Serbian as a potential donor language for the contact phenomenon discussed here, which is why a number of primary texts are analyzed here in addition to the RMS samples.[12] As a result, it can be stated that non-prefixed and (less frequently) prefixed verbs

---

[12] Ahmeti (2003); Boretzky (1986); Djurić (1989); Haliti (2006); Jek Romni kata i Prizreno [A Romni from Prizren] (2003); Jovanović (2003); Tahirović-Sijerčić (2009); RMS Sample's Transcriptions YU-007–-009, YU-012, YU-015–-018.

from the contact languages do occur in the Romani of the region, but only very few independent prefixes. The only form that is strikingly common (especially in Ahmeti 2003; Boretzky 1993; also YU-014, 173, 902) is *do-lel*, which can have different meanings: 'to grab, clasp; touch; reach; start' (Boretzky and Igla 1994a: 75).

The Prekmurski variety in Slovenia, represented by the RMS sample SLO-001, has hardly any Slavic prefixes, which is probably due to it being under stronger Hungarian influence. In the texts by Halwachs (2002: 51–52) and Levačič (2003: 174–177), there are none at all; the examples in the RMS sample are almost exclusively limited to *po-bister-* 'to forget', which seems to have replaced the non-prefixed form (SLO-001, 780–782, 785, 875). Doljenski is significantly richer in Slavic prefixes; the analyzed texts[13] contain *do-, na-, od-, po-, pre-, s- / z-* and *za-*. Strikingly common is *od-vaker-* 'to answer' (sometimes also just 'to say') under the influence of Slovene *odgovarjati*.IPFV / *odgovoriti*.PFV. In this variety as well, *po-bister-* 'to forget' has replaced *bister-* (Cech and Heinschink 2001b: 348) and *iz-del* 'to betray' (< Slovene *izdajati*.IPFV / *izdati*.PFV) the inherited *phukavel* (Cech and Heinschink 2001a: 151). In the text corpus, the prefixes are mainly found in combination with perfective Romani verb forms and mark punctual or ingressive events (cf. also Cech and Heinschink 2001a: 149).

Findings from Bulgaria are available for West Bulgarian and East Bulgarian Romani as well as for Erli in Sofia. The most important studies on Bulgarian prefixes in Romani are by Igla (1998, various varieties) and Schrammel (2002, West Bulgarian Romani).[14] Earlier mentions of the phenomenon can be found in Kostov (1963a: 112, various varieties) and Kenrick (1969: 43, variety of Kotel, Eastern Bulgaria). Regarding East Bulgarian Romani, it can be said in advance that Slavic prefixes are entirely absent, which can be connected to the strong Turkish and weaker Slavic influence on this variety (Schrammel 2002: 71–72).

The studies cited make it clear that this is a purely lexical phenomenon and that prefix borrowing is more likely when it brings about a greater semantic difference (Igla 1998: 70). A prerequisite for prefix borrowing is (partial) semantic equivalence between the simplex verb in Romani and its Bulgarian counterpart as in *sovav – spja*.IPFV 'to sleep', *za-sovav – zaspja*.PFV / *zaspivam*.IPFV 'to fall asleep' (Igla 1998: 68).

The most common prefix is *za-* (cf. also Igla 1998: 69; Schrammel 2002: 61), followed by *iz-* and occasionally *do-, pre-, raz-* and *po-*. Igla (1998: 69) attributes the frequent use of *za-* and *iz-* to the relatively high semantic transparency and,

---

13 Cech and Heinschink (2001a); Kovačič (1999, 2003a, b); Štrukelj (1980).
14 I would like to express my gratitude to Barbara Schrammel-Leber for providing me with her unpublished dissertation at the University of Manchester.

thus, easier analyzability of these prefixes. The former is generally used with inchoative meaning in West Bulgarian Romani. Bulgarian inchoative verbs with the prefix *za-* or the construction *započna* 'to begin' + verb have been copied (Schrammel 2002: 62), e.g.:

(23) *Taman of piravdes o udar za-din-es* (Velingrad Yerli)
 just he opened the door PREF-rain-3SG.PST
 'Just as he opened the door, it began to rain.' (BG-001, 406)
 Bulgarian *Tymko kogato toj otvori vratata zavali*.

According to Schrammel (2002: 61), the other prefixes in West Bulgarian Romani have concrete or figurative spatial meaning. This applies to *iz-* (e.g. *oj iz-landə* 'she left', BG-015, 410), *pre-* (*pre-hurpinav* 'to climb over', BG-024, 657; *pre-nakhav* 'to cross', BG-024, 679, 682) and *do-* (*do-lav* 'to grab, hold', BG-024, 173). The only RMS evidence for *raz-* is *o čhave raz-čiven o kher* 'the children make the house dirty' (BG-024, 907). The meaning of *raz-čhivel* from *raz-* 'apart' and *čhivel* 'to put' may best be understood literally as 'to dismantle (the house)' in the sense of 'to leave nothing in its place, produce chaos'. Sometimes a spatial meaning is also expressed twice by a prefixed verb plus a prepositional phrase:

(24) *Me pre-nakh-lj-om upral o mostovja* (Sofia Erli)
 I PREF-go-PFV-1SG across the bridge
 'I went across the bridge.' (BG-024, 682; Schrammel 2002: 61)

In addition, prefixes have been borrowed without any change in meaning. Apart from some evidence for *po-* (cf. Schrammel 2002: 63), the most widespread case is *za-bistrav* 'to forget'. Although *bistrav* also appears in all RMS samples from Bulgaria, according to Igla (1998: 69) the prefixed form has already replaced the simplex in numerous varieties in the Southern Balkans. The equivalent in the Bulgarian and Macedonian contact languages is a prefixed verb (*zabravja, zaborava*), which, however, is synchronically not perceived as being prefixed because there is no simplex counterpart. This example shows that semantic motivation is not always necessary in order to borrow a prefix. Igla also provides several examples for 'arbitrary' prefixation, in which neither the model of the contact language is reflected nor are new regularities set up (cf. Igla 1997: 149, 1998: 70).

The varieties in Macedonia (Arli, Gurbet, Kovački) have borrowed Slavic prefixes almost exclusively together with Slavic verbs. The few exceptions found in the RMS Database again include *do-le(la) / do-la / do-ljol* in the meaning of 'to grab, hold' (MK-001, -002, -004, -005, 173) and 'to pat' (MK-001, -002, -005, 1054), derived from the simplex *lel* 'to take', as well as *do-džal* from the simplex form *džal* 'to go', surely modelled after Macedonian *(dobre)dojde*:

(25) *Ov putardzas o vudar hem do-dža kerdzas amen* (Kovački)
he opened the door and PREF-go.IMP.2SG made us
'He opened the door and welcomed us.' (MK-012, 774)

Overall, it should be noted that the prefix inventory in the Romani varieties in Bulgaria and Macedonia – just like in the other South Slavic countries – is limited, and the prefixes are a purely lexical adaptation of the aspect and aktionsart prefixes from the Slavic contact languages, i.e. they in no way amount to a grammaticalized aspectual opposition (cf. also Igla 1998: 70; Friedman 2001a: 152, 1985: 8).

5.3.2 Group 2: Varieties in contact with Czech and Slovak

In contrast to the varieties in the South Slavic area, East Slovak Romani has taken over the complete prefix inventory of its contact languages. In several publications, Rácová (1997: 85, 1999: 65, 2015: 80; Rácová and Horecký 2000: 37)[15] analyzes a large number of texts in East Slovak Romani and demonstrates that the Slovak prefixes have generally been adopted mechanically and usually have the same spatial or actional meaning as in Slovak (and Czech[16]). Some examples in Rácová (2015: 81), however, show that Slavic prefixed verbs have been analyzed with their figurative meaning and have been transferred into Romani as semi-calques using the Slavic prefix, e.g. Slovak *zniesť* 'to endure, tolerate' > Romani *z-ľidžal* 'idem', *zdať sa* 'to seem' > *z-del* 'idem' (*del* 'to give'). In general, East Slovak Romani borrows the entire prefix repertoire of Slovak and Czech.

The functional equivalents to the Slavic prefixes in the Northern Central dialects, to which East Slovak Romani belongs, are the already mentioned adverbs expressing spatial or actional meaning, e.g. *ande* 'in, into', *a(v)ri* 'out, outside', *(e)khetan(e)* 'together', *pale* 'back', *tele* 'below, down', *opre / upre* 'above, up' etc. Spatial meanings have e.g. *džal opre* 'to go up', *anel avri* 'to carry out / away', *avel pale* 'to go back'; a more abstract actional variant is *xal opre* 'to eat up' (*xal* 'to eat', *opre* 'up') (Elšík, Hübschmannová and Šebková 1999: 372; Rácová and Horecký 2000: 36–37).

---

15 Cf. on the work of Racová and Horecký the critical review by Elšík (2007).
16 For Romani in the Czech Republic, the following texts were analyzed and showed no significant differences to what is said about Slovak Romani: Baro (2003); Hejkrlíková (2019); Horváth (2006); Horvátová (2003); Kačová (2019); Pešta (2007).

A notable peculiarity is that, in East Slovak Romani, the adverb *avri* is used for loan translations of Slovak *vy-* in order to reproduce abstract meanings from Slovak using inherited means: *vyhlásiť* 'to call out' > *akharel avri* 'idem' (*akharel* 'to call'), *vypytovať sa* 'to interrogate' > *phučkerel avri* 'idem' (*phučkerel* 'to ask'), *vyzerať* 'to look (like)' > *dičhol avri* 'idem' (*dičhol* 'to see'), *vyhrať* 'to win' > *khelel avri* 'idem' (*khelel* 'to play') (examples from Rácová 2007: 131, 2015: 81).[17]

Excursion: Iterative suffixes

A special feature of the Northern Central dialects in contact with Czech and Slovak is the use of the suffix *-av-* as an iterative marker, as in *čhiv-* 'to throw' > *čhiv-av-* 'to throw repeatedly' (Bohemian Romani), according to Matras (2002: 123) "modelled on Slavic aspect distinctions".[18] What is meant is the double imperfectivization in Slovak and Czech, e.g. Slovak *chodil* 'he went' > *chodie-va-l* (go-ITER-PTC) 'he went repeatedly' > *chodie-vá-va-l* (go-ITER-ITER-PTC) 'he went (quite) repeatedly', Czech *nosil* 'he carried' > *nosí-va-l* 'he carried repeatedly' > *nosí-vá-va-l* 'he carried (quite) repeatedly'. The *-ker-* suffix has the same function as *-av-*. Both can be doubled (e.g. *phir-ker-ker-el* 'to carry repeatedly') or combined (e.g. *čhiv-av-ker-el* 'to throw repeatedly'). The use of the (inherited) suffix *-av-* could also be favored by analogy to the similar Slavic suffix *-va-*, but in the RMS corpus, *-ker-* (6 records) is more common than *-av-* (1 record).

5.3.3 Group 3: Varieties in contact with East Slavic and Polish

The Romani varieties in contact with Polish and the East Slavic languages not only have by far the greatest number of independent prefixes, but also have taken over the complete prefix inventory of the contact languages. In what follows, they will be examined in detail with all their special characteristics.

The earliest findings on prefixing in the Romani varieties of Poland come from Klich ([1927] 2011, thereafter Pobożniak 1964: 53). For Slavic prefixing in the Bergitka variety, it was not Polish, but Slovak that initially played the central role: "[. . .] nie musiały oczywiście wszystkie powstać na gruncie słowackim, ale tam się to musiało zacząć: postać taka tych prepozycji jest przecież słowacka, nie

---

[17] According to Rácová and Horecký (2000: 37), these adverbs can even develop into prefixes, as in the case of *ari-farbinel* 'to finish painting' and *ari-avel* 'to come out', but this is an incorrect interpretation of the underlying data; the statement is not applicable.

[18] Cf. also the numerous examples in Beníšek (2017: 113–116) for iteratives in Eastern Už Romani, where iterative derivation is highly productive.

polska" ['[. . .] of course, they did not all have to develop on a Slovak basis, but this is where it must have begun, because the form of these prepositions is actually Slovak, not Polish'] (Klich [1927] 2011: 38).

What functions do these prefixes perform? In his analysis of the variety of the Polska Roma, Matras (1999: 14–15) comes to the conclusion that, in most cases, we have a modification of aktionsart or of the spatial relationship, e.g. *pše-geja* '(time) passed' < *geja* 'he / she / it went', *vy-xane* 'they ate up' < *xane* 'they ate', *pod-šunenys* 'they were listening' < *šunenys* 'they heard', *do-dav* 'I add' < *dav* 'I give', *od-łeł* 'to answer the telephone' < *łeł* 'to take', *vy-geja* 'he came out' < *geja* 'he went'. The proportion of prefixes that express spatial relationships is very high in the RMS data. However, it also happens that the prefixes become productive beyond the lexical distribution in the contact languages.

A very interesting peculiarity of the Romani varieties in contact with Polish is their use of double prefixes, which are not found elsewhere. Tcherenkov and Laederich (2004: 379) present Romani *po-za-line saro* < Polish *pozabrali wszystko* 'they took all' as an example. There are four records (all from the Polska Roma variety) in the RMS Database for this phenomenon:

(26) *do-do-džal*   (Polska)
      PREF-PREF-go.INF
      'arrive, reach' (PL-014, 187)

(27) *Po-s-ked-e*   *love*
      PREF-PREF-collect-2SG.IMP   money
      'Collect the money!' (PL-015, 373)

(28) *Me   čhaj   po-s-ker-eł   kher*
      my   daughter   PREF-PREF-do-3SG.PRS   house
      'My daughter cleans the house.' (PL-015, 366)

(29) *Jov* [. . .] *jamenca   po-pšy-ker-dž-a*
      he   us   PREF-PREF-do-PFV-3SG.PST
      'He [. . .] welcomed us.' (PL-014, 774)

The discussion in the research literature on Romani varieties in Russia, especially on North Russian Romani, is the most interesting and extensive one. North Russian Romani from the Baltic group, which has an enormous number of Russian prefixes, has been investigated especially by Rusakov (Rusakov 2000, 2001 a–c, 2004; Eloeva and Rusakov 1990). There is no reference to Russian prefixes in the work on the Kalderaš in Russia (Čerenkov and Demeter 1990; Tcherenkov 1999;

Šapoval 2008a), which is not surprising, due to the conservativism of the Kaldaraš variety that belongs to the Vlax group.

Let us take a closer look at North Russian Romani. Of interest is the theory by Eloeva and Rusakov (1990: 16) that the variety is in transition to a tense-aspect system as in Russian, though this development is not yet complete. In several of his publications, Rusakov (2000: 17, 2001a: 314, 2004: 35) reproduces the example *bagal* 'to sing' as proof of this theory:

(30)   *bagand'a*.IPFV   *s-bagand'a*.PFV   (North Russian Romani)
      'he / she sang'   'he / she sang'
      bagala.IPFV   *lela te bagal*.IPFV
      'he / she sings'   'he / she will sing'
      s-bagala.PFV
      'he / she will sing'

However, he himself admits that this example is idealized, and the reality is much more complicated. In North Russian Romani, it is by no means possible to prove such an ideal usage pattern for every verb. Rusakov also refers to Boretzky (1989: 358), who speculated about the possibility of interpreting the prefix *po-* as an aspect marker, because the dictionary of Sergievskij and Barannikov usually gave a perfective Russian verb as a translation for such forms, which could mean that Slavic aspect has been introduced through these prefixes. However, he then relativizes his statement, saying that, of course, this does not yet produce a complete aspectual system like in Russian, because there are no means of creating imperfective verb forms from a perfective verb. Relying on his text corpus and a speaker survey, Rusakov (2004: 35) finds wide variation in the use of prefixed and non-prefixed verb forms and concludes that the use of prefixed verb forms to express the perfective aspect is not mandatory. From time to time, prefixed verbs are also used in imperfective contexts.

It is proven also for North Russian Romani in Estonia (Schrammel 2002: 65–66) that adding a prefix changes the lexical meaning of the verb. This mostly concerns spatial meanings, but also actionality: *za-*, for example, marks the beginning of an action (e.g. *za-sal* 'to begin laughing', *za-xačkyrel* 'to set on fire'), *u-* and *vy-*, alongside the spatial meaning 'out-', express exhaustive and egressive meaning.[19] The Russian aspectual system is therefore not systematically grammaticalized in North Russian Romani:

---

[19] Schrammel (2002: 85) provides a very good overview of all the spatial and actional prefix meanings in the Romani varieties from Russia and Bulgaria that she has examined.

Thus, it is legitimate to conclude that although North-Russian Romani has a system of borrowed prefixes used as lexical and aspectual modifiers of verbs, the role of perfectivizers is not yet fully grammaticalized [...]. [...] To conclude, contact-induced influences in the domain of aspect (at least, of the 'Slavic-style' aspect) are to a large extent restricted to both matter- and pattern-borrowing of formally transparent and functionally loaded elements [...], i.e. Aktionsarten (including telicity) rather than highly abstract aspectual oppositions, and lexically and semantically, rather than morphosyntactically determined categories.
(Arkadiev 2017: 8–9, 13; cf. also Kožanov and Arkadiev 2017: slides 24–43)

For Ukraine, there are especially three interesting recent works: Beníšek (2013, 2017) and Pančenko (2013). Pančenko (2013: 15, 22–23) identifies Slavic prefixes in Ukrainian Vlax varieties, which is rather unusual, cf. the three imperative forms Vlax *pri-le* < Russian *priberi!*, *za-le* < *zaberi!*, *u-le* < *uberi!* (all 'take / put away!') as well as the examples *ot-terel* 'to open' < *otkryt'* 'idem', *po-lel* 'to understand' < *ponimat'* 'idem', *u-marel* 'to kill' < *ubit'* 'idem', all of which can be classified as semi-calques. In Serednye Romani in Transcarpathia, there are many Slavic prefixes (Beníšek 2013: 55). The most interesting example of their use is found in *othov-*, composed of *thov-* 'put' and Slavic *od-*, whereby the consonant cluster of the original *od-thov-* has undergone assimilation. The basic meaning of 'to put aside' has shifted to 'to hide' at the expense of the inherited *garuv-* / *garav-*, which no longer exists in Serednye. The morphological pattern of the Eastern Už varieties in general, as described by Beníšek (2017: 117–124), indicates stronger influence from the East Slavic contact languages Russian and Ukrainian than from Slovak, cf. *pre-lidža-* 'to translate', composed of *lidža-* 'to carry off' and *pere-vesti* 'to translate', and *pod-l̃iker-* 'to support', composed of *l̃iker-* 'to hold, to keep' and *pod-deržat'* 'to support'. Interestingly, the Slavic prefixes *na-*, *u-*, *v-* and *vy-* have not been borrowed into these varieties. The majority of prefixes is semantically transparent, but quite a number of prefixed verbs also have rather unpredictable meanings, such as *rosker-* 'to spend (money)' < *ker-* 'to do, to make' and *zarod-* 'to earn (money)' < *rod-* 'to look, to search'.

The only work pertaining to Belarus with an analysis of the Polska and Xaladytka varieties comes from Čarankaŭ (1974: 36–37). Romani in Belarus, or the former BSSR, has (depending on the region) potentially been influenced by three contact languages: Belarusian, Russian and, in the case of older speakers and especially in the west, also Polish. Čarankaŭ describes the borrowing of the complete prefix inventory from all three contact languages as one of the most striking characteristics of these varieties, although the donor language cannot always be clearly determined. There are some cases of semi-calques, as with the prefix *pre-*, which is composed of Polish *prze-* and Belarusian *pera-* (cf. *pre-mangou* 'excuse me' < Polish *przepraszam*).

In the Romani varieties in Lithuania, Latvia and Estonia, influences in the area of prefixing are not exclusively Slavic, but the Slavic prefixes are the older ones (cf. Ariste 1969, 1973 for the Čuchny or Lotfitka variety). Later, these were complemented by Lithuanian ones in Lithuanian or Litovska Romani and by Latvian ones in Lotfitka Romani. There are more Baltic prefixes in the Latvian varieties and more Slavic prefixes in the Lithuanian ones, whereby it is not always possible to decide which Slavic contact language a prefix came from (Kožanov 2011: 311–312). Baltic and Slavic prefixes can also exist side-by-side, cf. *uš-čhakirou* and *za-čhakirou* 'to wrap up' (Russian *zavoračivat'*). Slavic prefixes can also be used according to models that are typical of Lithuanian. For Estonia, Ross (2016: 165) currently considers the influence of Russian in the field of verb prefixing to be very extensive, while the influence of Latvian prefixes is here limited in comparison to the Latvian Lotfitka Roma. Here, too, Slavic prefixes precede Latvian historically, with the greatest historical influence from Polish.

In Lithuanian Romani, just as in North Russian Romani and the variety of the Polska Roma, it is a relatively widespread phenomenon that the prefixing of Romani verb stems leads to abstract meanings for which there are no equivalents in the Slavic languages, i.e. that the prefixes become productive beyond the lexical distribution in the contact languages (Tenser 2008: 163).

Beyond this, Lithuanian Romani has a very interesting peculiarity; it is the only variety with an inherited prefix that developed through contact-induced grammaticalization: *pale-*. It corresponds to *pše-* / *piri-* from Polish *prze-* or Russian *pere-*. There is no evidence of this in the RMS Database, but Kožanov (2011: 312, 314) recorded the following attestations in Vilnius:

(31) *Pale-gij-om   pale   ulica*   (Litovska)
     PREF-go-PST.1SG   across   street
     'I went across the street.'
     Russian: *Ja perešel čerez ulicu.*

(32) *Pale-de   leske   kniška*
     PREF-give.IMP.2SG   him   book
     'Give him the book.'
     Russian: *Peredaj emu knižku.*

This finding is so interesting because it is one of the very few examples of a calqued prefix (a case of pattern borrowing) in Romani.

In three RMS records from varieties in Estonia and Lithuania, whose former contact language was Polish, there is also further evidence for double prefixes. Example (34) even exhibits a hybrid construction using a Latvian (*pa-*) and a Slavic (*za-*) prefix:

(33) *Sir-ta   u-do-lij-a   pe   krik   te džaal*   (Lotfitka)
     somehow PREF-PREF-take-3SG.PST REFL away   go.INF
     'Somehow he managed to leave [. . .]' (EST-010, 508)

(34) *Doj   pa-rakir-la   doj   pa-za-bistir-de*
     story PREF-tell-3SG.PTCP.PST.PASS story PREF-PREF-forget-3SG.PTCP.PST.PASS
     'The story was told and forgotten.' (EST-008, 780)

(35) *Jou   javja   ranjšedyr,   o-pše-gy-ji*   (Litovska)
     they came   earlier   PREF-PREF-go-PTCP.PRS.3SG
     palo   veš
     through.the   forest
     'They arrived early by taking the way through the woods.' (LT-005, 824)

Finally, Tenser (2008: 157) points out that prefixed verbs in the Northeastern dialect group (North Russian Romani, Xaladytka, Polska Roma, Litovska Roma, Lotfitka Roma) can have an additional transitivizing function. Transitivization works synthetically with the help of the suffixes *-av-* or *-kir-*, e.g. *dar-* 'to fear' > *dar-av-* 'to frighten', *rov-* 'to cry' > *rov-lja-kir-* 'to make cry'. However, analytical constructions with prefixed verbs are even more productive:

(36) *lakiro rosphenybe za-čidja*   (North Russian Romani)
     her   story   PREF-make.PFV.3SG.PST
     amen te   rovas
     us   COMP   cry.1PL
     'Her story made us cry.' (Tenser 2008: 157)

(37) *jej   čuvela   nejegus   po   skamin   sob   te*   (Lotfitka)
     she   puts   child   on   table   so.that   COMP
     po-del   la   te   po-xal
     PREF-give.3SG / INF   her   COMP   PREF-eat.3SG / INF
     'She sits the child down on the table in order to feed her.' (Tenser 2008: 157)

In addition to its extensive use of independent prefixes, Lithuanian Romani seemingly also exhibits the greatest variety in their functions, which includes all of the previously mentioned.

5.4 Discussion

Why is it that Slavic prefixes are so strongly represented in the Romani varieties from Group 3? It is very likely that the reason lies in a combination of several factors.

First of all, the lifestyle of the Roma groups certainly plays a role. The Vlax or migrant dialects have practically no Slavic prefixation – not even in the East Slavic countries, Poland and the Baltic states – due to their relatively conservative speakers who live separate from the majority society. Vlax speakers have also arrived much later into these regions, so that the contact has remained more superficial. In the Vlax varieties, the Romanian influence is known to be much stronger than the Slavic one; for migrant dialects, the duration of the language contact has been too short.

A second factor could be the time at which the adoption of Slavic prefixes into a variety began. If one looks at the older attestations and research literature on Romani in Russia, it can be seen that prefixation began very early in contact with Russian. Contact between Russian and Romani was documented already by Böthlingk (1853): "Die russischen Präpositionen [sic] kommen in Verbindung mit Verben überaus häufig vor." ['The Russian prepositions [sic] occur very often in connection with verbs.'] Gilliat-Smith (1922: 160) speaks – referring to the language data in Patkanov (1900: 55–56) – of a mass adaptation of Russian prefixes into the dialects of the Roma from Moscow and St. Petersburg.[20] Sergievskij (1931) also rates the phenomenon as very widespread.[21] The prefix inventory furthermore appears to have been large and stable for at least 150 years: Wentzel (1988: 61) and Toropov (2005: 364) each list 14 prefixes, Gilliat-Smith (1922) 16, Böthlingk (1853) at least 10. Barannikov (1931a: 21, 1933/34: 101) counts 14 Ukrainian and Russian prefixes in Ukrainian Romani dialects.[22]

---

[20] Of note is his positive assessment of this development regarding the vitality of Romani: "These formatives will doubtless be strongly disapproved of by our Romani purists. They could not be abolished without destroying the dialect, and they have in many cases been the cause of a Romani verb being preserved in common use which would otherwise have been lost." (Gilliat-Smith 1922: 160)

[21] He, too, sees this as a positive development: "Благодаря этому способу образования цыганский язык получил возможность широко использовать свой основной запас глагольных корней, не прибегая к заимствованию самых глаголов из других языков." ['Thanks to this manner of [word] formation, the Gypsy language was able to make extensive use of its main stock of verb stems without resorting to borrowing the very verbs from other languages.'] (Sergievskij 1931: 80)

[22] The literature on the other countries in Group 3 is too recent to argue on the basis of: the earliest evidence of prefixes in the Bergitka variety (Poland) comes from Klich ([1927] 2011),

A third reason for the frequent occurrence of Slavic prefixes in the Baltic countries and especially in Lithuanian Romani is most likely to be found in the multiple, mutually reinforcing influence of Polish, Russian and the Baltic languages, cf. Kožanov (2011: 311): "Особенностью префиксальных систем этих диалектов следует считать использование префиксов как славянского, так и балтийского происхождения" ['The use of prefixes of both Slavic and Baltic origin should be considered a peculiarity of the prefix systems of these dialects']. Or, in other words: on the way from the Balkans to Northeastern Europe, more prefixes were able to be "picked up".

As a fourth and quite important reason, verbal aspect is most grammaticalized in the so-called North Slavic languages and, above all, in Russian, and prefixing plays a greater role there than in the South Slavic languages, which, in turn, affects the respective contact languages.

5.5 Contact-linguistic classification

Finally, the results should be placed in a contact linguistic context. Tenser (2005: 34) explains the borrowing process in three stages using the example of Lithuanian Romani, whereby each stage requires a higher level of analysis by the speakers. The levels relate to the degree of semantic integration of the prefixes, but do not necessarily reflect the diachronic sequence of the process.

First, a Slavic verb is mechanically borrowed along with its (aspect and / or aktionsart) prefix, i.e. the prefix and the verb stem are perceived as a single unit, as in the following example from East Slovak Romani:

(38) *"No po-modlj-in tut, imar oka pes modljinel." Po-modljinda pes.* (East Slovak Romani)
"'So pray, the other one is already praying." He prayed (began to pray).'
Slovak *"No pomodli sa, druhý sa už modlí." Pomodlil sa.*
(Cech et al. 2004: 212)

This pattern exists in all three groups.

At the second level, equivalence between the two languages is established. Slavic prefixes can be isolated in the form of a semi-calque and attached to

---

Kopernicki (1930) and Rozwadowski (1936). The evidence for the variety of the Polska Roma (poems by Papusza) must have come from the same time; the poems were published by Jerzy Ficowski (1956) after the Second World War. For the Baltic countries, there is no evidence earlier than Ariste (1969: 181, 1973: 81).

Romani verb stems. The prefixes become, so to speak, more autonomous. An example of this is given by Tenser (2008: 162) for North Russian Romani:

(39) *Jov javja ke me khere te porakirel manca.* (North Russian Romani)
 'He came to my house to talk to me.'
 Russian *On prišel ko mne domoj pogovorit' so mnoj.*

In order that the form *po-rakir-* can be used in this construction, an equivalence between Romani *rakir-* and Russian *govor-* (or perhaps with older Russian *rekat'*) is established, then Romani *rakir-* can copy the semantic behavior of the Russian equivalent. Features from this level can also be found in all three groups, though least of all in Group 1. The examples of loan translations in East Slovak and Lithuanian Romani, in which the prefix itself is reproduced by inherited linguistic means, also fit in here.

At the third level, the prefixes become independent and, together with the Romani verbs, form new meanings that do not exist in the Slavic contact language(s). The complete system of Slavic aktionsart prefixes with all their concrete and abstract meanings is adopted and becomes productive beyond the distribution in the contact language. This happens to a minimal extent in Group 2 but very extensively in part of Group 3. This is an example of *fusion* (Matras 1999, 2002, 2020; cf. also Schrammel 2002; Tenser 2005, 2008) per excellence in the context of Matras' pragmatic-functional approach to contact linguistics, the definition of which shall be repeated here:

> Fusion is the non-separation of languages for a particular category. It can also be seen as the structural 'devolution' of certain functions to the contact language, or alternatively as the wholesale adoption of markers belonging to a particular category. It is thus qualitatively and quantitatively different from 'borrowing' in the conventional or superordinate sense.
> (Matras 2002: 211)

This is an attempt to explain what happens cognitively in such a language-contact situation. Applied to the case of verbal prefixes, this would mean that the two systems, i.e. the respective Romani variety and its corresponding Slavic contact language(s), are not considered to be two separate systems in the mind of an active bilingual speaker, but become inseparable; they 'merge'. With this understanding, the prefixes belonging to the respective Romani variety and to the Slavic contact language(s) likewise 'merge'. In this way, the speakers are able to reduce the cognitive effort involved in language processing. It is important for the correct understanding of the term that the 'merged' item must always be a complete class of units, such as a complete set of verbal prefixes from the contact language(s). The prerequisite for this is long-lasting, intensive contact and lively bilingualism.

In Tenser (2005: 35), the three levels just mentioned are presented in an overview with examples from North Russian Romani (Tab. 5):

Tab. 5: Aktionsart integration (Tenser 2005: 35).

Prefix	Borrowing		Calquing		Semantic integration	
	Romani stem	Russian equivalent	Romani stem	Russian equivalent	Romani stem	Russian equivalent
po-	po-dumin- 'to think'	po-dum-	po-mang- 'to ask'	po-pros-	po-dykh- 'to see'	u-vid-
pod-			pod-gij- 'to approach'	pod(o)-jti	pod-l- 'to take'	Ø-vz-
ros- (ras-)	ras-pravin- 'to fix'	ras-prav-	ros-pxen- 'to tell'	ras-skaz-	ros-suv- 'to sew'	za-š-
vy-	vy-krasin- 'to paint'	vy-kras-	vy-pi- 'to drink'	vy-p-	vy-bič h- 'to send'	ot-prav-
za-	za-stavin- 'to force'	za-stav-	za-pres- 'to pay'	za-plat-	za-xačkir- 'to burn sth.'	pod-pal-

The observation that no Romani variety – not even in Group 3 – has adopted a complete Slavic aspectual system (as a grammatical category with a systematic opposition of perfective vs. imperfective), is congruent with the fact that the borrowing of a complete grammatical category is much more complex than the adoption of aktionsart prefixes; cf. also Matras (2002: 212):

> It appears that conceptualizations in terms of specific spatial metaphors of event duration, punctuality, or outward projection of an action are easily susceptible to transfer and replication in language contact situations.

Finally, the question remains as to why, in contrast to German prefixes, like in the following example from Sinti, Slavic prefixes are not translated to a greater extent in Romani:

(40) *Pasewen je bisla pre.*   (Sinti)
      'Pay a little attention.'
      German *Passt ein bisschen auf.* (Igla 1992: 45)

Igla (1998: 67) and Kiefer (2010: 144) assume that the reason for this is the greater semantic opaqueness of the Slavic prefixes. Schrammel (2002: 71) remarks:

> I do not entirely agree with this statement in this form, since most Slavic prefixes are semantically as transparent as German half-prefixes: Slavic prefixes are quite productive as means

to express concrete spatial meanings. Also as a marker of actionality, Slavic verbal prefixes have relatively predictable effects on the meanings of verbs [. . .] and express these meanings much more consistently than German half-prefixes express actionality meanings.

However, Igla's and Schrammel's analyses do not fundamentally contradict each other. Both Schrammel and Matras (2002: 212) see two reasons for the divergent handling of German and Slavic prefixes, and the present book is in line with their view: Firstly, Slavic prefixes are always bound morphemes, while German aktionsart markers can become separated from the verb and are therefore easier to analyze (e.g. *ausgehen* 'to go out' vs. *sie geht aus* 'she goes out'). On the other hand, Slavic prefixes contain not only a relatively easy-to-analyze lexical component expressing aktionsart or actionality, but also the more complex grammatical component of aspect.

5.6 Summary

The aim of the present chapter was to substantiate the extent of Slavic prefixing in various Romani varieties by means of concrete figures and to discuss the functions of the borrowed prefixes. Primary focus was given to the question of whether any Romani varieties have systematically grammaticalized the aspectual system of their Slavic contact language(s). In order to get to the bottom of these questions, 76 samples from the RMS Database, the existing research literature on individual varieties and, where necessary, a separate text corpus were consulted.

The results of the analysis of the RMS Database show a clear North-South continuum, while the examined samples could be assigned to three groups. The varieties in contact with South Slavic (Group 1) have practically no independent Slavic prefixes, the varieties in contact with Czech and Slovak (Group 2) are in the lower middle field and the varieties in contact with Polish and East Slavic (Group 3) extensively use independent Slavic prefixes (with a few understood exceptions). Additionally, they make use of the complete prefix inventory of the contact languages, and the prefixes have a wide range of lexical-actional functions.

Special features observed in individual varieties are: very rare cases of calquing of Slavic prefixes (*pale-* in Lithuanian Romani), double prefixing in various varieties that are, or have been, in contact with Polish, iterative suffixing in East Slovak Romani and prefixes with a transitivizing function in the Northeast dialect group.

Very probably, the fact that the adoption of Slavic prefixes in Group 3 is so extensive is due to a combination of four factors: the lifestyle of the individual groups, the point in time when prefix borrowing began, the mutually reinforcing influence of several contact languages (Polish, East Slavic, Baltic) and the strong grammaticalization of verbal aspect in the so-called 'North Slavic' languages. Even within this group, however, the Slavic aspectual system has so far not been systematically grammaticalized in any Romani variety.

6 Lexical borrowings from Slavic in Romani

The impact of the Slavic languages on Romani is most obvious in the lexicon (cf. the comprehensive compilation of Slavic lexical borrowings from Slavic into Romani in Boretzky 2013). Lexical borrowings also reflect the domains of life that have been affected by contact with the respective surrounding Slavic-speaking population. However, it was already addressed in Chapter 3 that, in multilingual speech communities, it is often hard to distinguish between one-word codeswitches (also: *insertions, ad hoc borrowings* or *nonce borrowings*) and established borrowings (also: *loanwords*), and that we therefore assume a codeswitching-borrowing continuum. Spontaneous switching of a word is the starting point, which leads to an established borrowing through multiple repetition over a longer period of time by a whole group of speakers. An indication of an established borrowing can be the default (instead of stylistic) use of an item, its belonging to the core vocabulary, regular occurrence and structural integration (Matras and Adamou 2021: 240). To simplify matters, in this chapter, the term *borrowing* will be used both for established borrowings and spontaneous one-word codeswitches as well as everything in between on the codeswitching–borrowing continuum.

With regard to parts of speech, nouns are – not only in Romani – most frequently borrowed, followed by verbs and then other parts of speech (Matras 2007: 48; Tadmor 2009: 59). There are various strategies for borrowing nouns: they can be adapted to the inherited inflection patterns, they can be adopted in a simplified but unadapted form, or together with the inflection from the donor language, or a new integration strategy can be found to mark borrowings. A combination of these is also possible. Verbs are borrowed less frequently than are nouns because they are morphologically more complex and their integration requires more effort (Matras 2007: 48).

Myers-Scotton (1993: 163) further distinguishes two semantic types of borrowed word forms: The first are so-called *cultural loans*, i.e. words for concepts that did not originally exist in the target culture such as new social activities, cultural acquisitions and official institutions. The second type are *core forms*, i.e. words for concepts that have equivalents in the target culture or matrix language but are nevertheless adopted from the contact language in a situation of active bilingualism and frequent codeswitching.

The present chapter first deals with Slavic lexical borrowings in Romani in general, before turning to two specific examples for a more detailed analysis: the Polska and Bergitka varieties in Poland.

6.1 Slavic lexical elements in Romani

There are (at least) two problems that the researcher has to face when studying Slavic lexical elements in Romani: First, in the multilingual communication mode of the Roma, it is very often not possible to decide whether one is dealing with an established or a nonce borrowing, especially from the current contact language(s). To answer this question, one needs a sufficiently large and preferably diachronic data source, which is not always available. Second, it can be difficult to tell whether a lexeme originates from a current or an earlier Slavic contact language. This is especially problematic in the case of closely related Slavic languages, for example Croatian and Slovene in the case of Doljenski Romani in Slovenia (Cech and Heinschink 2002: 2). In such cases, there is nothing for it but to label the borrowing more generally as 'Slavic' or 'South Slavic'.

As mentioned above, there are different layers of loans in Romani and their analysis sheds some light on the historical migration routes of Roma through Europe. For example, the Lotfitka variety contains, alongside recent Russian borrowings, also loans from Polish as an earlier contact language, e.g. *breza* < *brzoza* 'birch tree', *venka* < *wędka* 'fishing pole', etc. (Tenser 2016: 220). North Russian Romani has *blato* < Bulgarian *blato* 'dirt, mud' and *praxo* < Bosnian / Croatian / Serbian *prah* 'dust, ashes' from its Balkan past, *vendzlo* < Polish *węzeł* 'knot' from earlier contact with Polish and, of course, many borrowings from the recent contact language, Russian (Wentzel 1980: 31–32; Gilliat-Smith 1922: 156). Furthermore, Slavic words are not restricted to Romani varieties in Slavic-speaking countries – rather, the lexicon of every Romani variety is layered according to the historical migration route of the respective group, and thus, Slavic words can 'migrate' far beyond their places of origin. For example, Matras (2010: 64) and Hancock (1983: 118) enumerate *dosta* 'enough', *kralis* 'king', *vodros* 'bed', *dzhamba* 'toad', *mačka* 'cat' etc. in Angloromani, Welsh Romani or Texan Romani, *sak(k)o* 'every' in Sinti, Finnish Romani, Mexican Vlax as well as many other early Slavic loans outside of current nation states with a Slavic majority language.

An example of a shift in meaning by analogy to a contact language is found in *šukipe* from Bulgarian Romani: this lexeme has adopted the meaning 'mainland' in addition to 'drought' due to the influence of Bulgarian *suša* (from a Slavic root meaning 'dry'), which also has both meanings (Kostov 1963a: 161). Furthermore, numerous examples show that spoken varieties of Slavic, rather than the Slavic standard languages, were the sources of borrowing, e.g. *dripes* 'clothes' and *polena* 'fields' (standard Bulgarian *drexi* and *poljana*) taken from a southeastern Bulgarian Rup variety and found in the Romani variety of the Rhodopes, Bulgaria (Igla 1997: 148–149).

Slavic languages have served not only as direct donor languages for lexical units, but also as intermediary languages. Thus, for instance, many German words like *biglajs* < *Bügeleisen* 'pressing iron' have entered East Slovak Romani via Slovak (Rácová 1997: 85). Occasionally, Romani words disappear due to Slavic influence; as an early example, Gilliat-Smith characterized the case of *musí* 'arm' from the Romani variety of St. Petersburg as follows: "*Musí* always disappears in dialects subject to Slavic influence owing to most Slavic languages using only one word to express 'arm' and 'hand'" (Gilliat-Smith 1922: 155). On the other hand, sometimes several parallel words from different languages coexist, e.g. in East Slovak Romani *svetos* < Slovak *svet* and *vilagos* < Hungarian *világ*, both meaning 'world' (Rácová 1995: 13). Furthermore, some pairs of originally synonymous words are now used with slight differences in meaning, creating variation in speech; for instance, in Serbian Kalderaš, *mlada* (a South Slavic loan) exclusively means 'bride' and the inherited *bori* means 'daughter-in-law; newly married woman' (Boretzky 1994: 181–182).

As for parts of speech, usually nouns are borrowed more often than verbs and verbs more often than adjectives. A precise count can be found in Meyer (2017) for the Polska and Bergitka varieties in Poland, in Mirić and Ćirković (2022) for Serbian Gurbet and in Boretzky (1994) for Kalderaš in Northern Serbia. The counts reveal the following (rounded) ratios of nouns to verbs to adjectives: 6:1:1 (Polska), and 6:2:1 (Bergitka), 7:5:6 (Gurbet), 7:4:1 (Kalderaš).

Romani has not only borrowed Slavic lexemes for new items and phenomena which have no inherited equivalents, such as *škola* 'school', but also replaced inherited words, e.g. East Slovak Romani *myšos* < Slovak *myš* 'mouse' and *stromos* < *strom* 'tree' (Kralčák 1999: 180). In North Russian Romani, especially the younger generation of speakers frequently replaces Romani words with Russian equivalents: *guruv* is replaced with *byko* < Russian *byk* 'ox', *ryč* with *medvedjo* < *medved'* 'bear' and *buzno* with *kozël* 'billy-goat' (Toropov 2005: 364). The question as to which semantic fields have been affected by Slavic borrowings is discussed in the following chapter for the Polska and Bergitka varieties in Poland, and there is a similar study by Boretzky (1993: 117–124) for Bugurdži in Kosovo. Both studies show that the semantic fields of nature (animals, plants, weather, landscape etc.) and dwelling (buildings, furniture, household articles) have been most strongly influenced by the Slavic contact languages (Polish and Bosnian / Croatian / Serbian, respectively). Additionally, the fields of politics and military, education, economy, the human body, religion and food have been affected in Polska and Bergitka, while Boretzky lists tools and people for Bugurdži.

Lastly, speakers' attitudes towards loan words can differ. Rácová (2000: 45) refers to Slovak Romani speakers with a high language consciousness who refuse to use Slovak words and rather rely on inherited elements to enlarge their vocabulary. Consequently, they prefer *dikhado* (< inherited *dikhel* 'to see') to *divadlos* (< Slovak *divadlo* 'theater'), *ľiľali* (< *lil* 'leaf; page') to *kňižka* (< *knižka* 'book.DIM'), or *sikhaďi* (< *sikh-* 'to learn') to *škola* 'school'. They furthermore use such mixed collocations as *vladno avrikidno manuš* 'representative of government', derived from Slovak *vládny* 'governmental', Romani *te kidel avri* 'to elect' and Romani *manuš* 'man' (Rácová and Horecký 2000: 14; Rácová 2007: 131). However, all these expressions are restricted to public writing and would rather not be used in oral communication (anonymous reviewer). Other speakers of Romani insert Slavic words into their speech freely and regard them as a natural part of their language.

6.1.1 Nouns

There is great variation with respect to whether and how borrowed Slavic nouns are adapted to Romani grammar. Unlike nonce borrowings, established borrowings are adapted to the gender system of Romani, which recognizes only two genders, in contrast to the three found in Slavic languages. Slavic masculine and neutral nouns receive – with some variance across the varieties – the Greek-derived endings *-os / -o*, *-as*, *-is / -i* or *-e* and are assigned to the class of Romani athematic masculines: *fermer-o* < Russian *fermer*.M 'farmer', *vagon-o* < Russian *vagon*.M 'waggon' and *kridl-os* < Slovak *krídl-o*.N 'wing' (Semiletko 2008: 361; Čerenkov and Demeter 1990: 291). Of special interest are masculine nouns ending in *-a*, such as Bulgarian *sădij-a* 'judge'. They are adapted to Bulgarian Romani in their original form with the feminine definite article *i*, such that the resulting form is *i sădij-a* by analogy to Bulgarian *sădij-a-ta*.ART.F 'the judge', whereas morphosyntactically, they are treated as masculines: *i sădija si lačh-o*.M 'the judge is good' (Kostov 1989: 121). Feminine nouns usually receive or keep the ending *-a*, e.g. in North Russian Romani *pušk-a* < Russian *pušk-a*.F 'cannon' (Čerenkov and Demeter 1990: 292). In Eastern Už Romani, the suffixes *-ka / -kinja* are most commonly used, e.g. *kraľis* 'king' > *kraľkiňa* 'queen' (Beníšek 2017: 169). As a basic principle, what applies to loans in Romani in general also applies to loans from Slavic:

> Loans may be assigned gender based on the natural sex of the animate noun, on the grammatical gender of the loan in the source language or the grammatical gender of the original noun which it replaces, or else on the phonological shape (usually the ending) of the loan.
> (Matras 2002: 72)

Borrowed word stems can be very productive in terms of word formation, e.g. Russian *žar* 'heat, blaze' and the adjective *žarkij* 'hot' have served as a basis for *žar-o* 'hot.ADJ', *žar-k-es* 'hot.ADV', *žar-inela* 'he heats', *žar-k-ito* 'hot-headed' and many more derivations in North Russian Romani (Toropov 2005: 363).

6.1.2 Verbs

The adaptation of Slavic verbs is also based on Greek inflectional endings that were taken over in the period of Early Romani and have stayed productive ever since (Matras 2002: 128). The most frequent suffix used for this purpose outside the Balkans is *-in-*. Moreover, there are individual deviations; for instance, nonce borrowings from Czech and Slovak in South Slovak Romani receive an additional Hungarian suffix *-ál-*: *sledov-ál-inel* 'to follow; obey' < Slovak *sledovať* / Czech *sledovat* 'to follow, observe' (Elšík 2009). The situation in the Balkans is more complex; there is great variation in the adaptation of loan verbs. The most widespread markers are *-in-* / *-an-* / *-on-*, *-iz-* / *-az-* / *-oz-*, and *-is-* / *-as-* / *-os-* (Matras 2002: 128). Vlax dialects use *-is-*, to which *-ar-* is attached for transitive verbs. Most non-Vlax varieties use *-in-* and some Bulgarian and the Bugurdži / Kovač varieties in North Macedonia use *-iz-* (Igla 1991b: 51). In North Russian Romani, there is a strong tendency not to adapt Russian loan verbs (Rusakov and Abramenko 1998: 110), however, it depends on the verb. The adapted forms *te xodines* < *xodit'* 'to go', *te dumines* < *dumat'* 'to think', and *te kupines* < *kupit'* 'to buy' are more common than their non-adapted alternatives, probably because these verbs are particularly frequent and have existed in this variety for a long time (Eloeva and Rusakov 1990: 28). For an overview of the semantic fields associated with (South) Slavic loan verbs in Serbian Bugurdži, cf. also Boretzky (1993: 124–127).

6.1.3 Adjectives

Boretzky (1994: 175, 1993: 116–117) notes that only very few adjectives have been borrowed into the Balkan Romani varieties that he investigated. Nor is a preference for particular semantic groups noticeable, except that three color terms have been borrowed from South Slavic: *kafeno* 'brown', *zeleno* 'green' and *zlatno* 'gold'. One of the most frequently borrowed Slavic adjectives in Romani is *drugo* < *drugi* 'another, the other', replacing inherited *(j)aver* (Boretzky 1999: 69). Borrowed adjectives are assigned to an inflectional class characterized by the gender-indifferent ending *-o* in the nominative singular; this is recorded e.g. for North Russian Romani (Eloeva and Rusakov 1990: 21), West Bulgarian Romani (Minkov 1997: 74), Arli in North Macedonia (Friedman 2001a: 153), East Slovak Romani (Rácová 2015: 88) and the Eastern Už varieties (Beníšek 2017: 173). The plural and oblique endings also seem to be largely uniform (*-a* and / or *-on(e)-*; cf. e.g. Boretzky 1993: 117 on Kosovan Bugurdži). A frequently used strategy is to retain inflection on adjectives from the contact language, as in Serbian Kalderaš but *dosadn-i si le* 'they are very bothersome' (Matras 2002: 95; Boretzky 1994: 48) where the Serbian plural inflectional ending *-i* is kept.

6.1.4 Adverbs and particles

The majority of adverbs and particles in Romani have been taken from contact languages. Phasal adverbs are always European loans, they are high – but not the highest, compared to connectors and discourse markers – on the scale of likelihood of borrowing (Matras 2020: 213). The following diagram shows the wide variety of Slavic temporal and phasal adverbs in Romani from our own analysis of the RMS Database. The aim was to find out how often a borrowed Slavic form or a hybrid form is used to express these categories. The result is shown in Fig. 10 (just like Figs. 5 and 6, the following figures show absolute numbers):

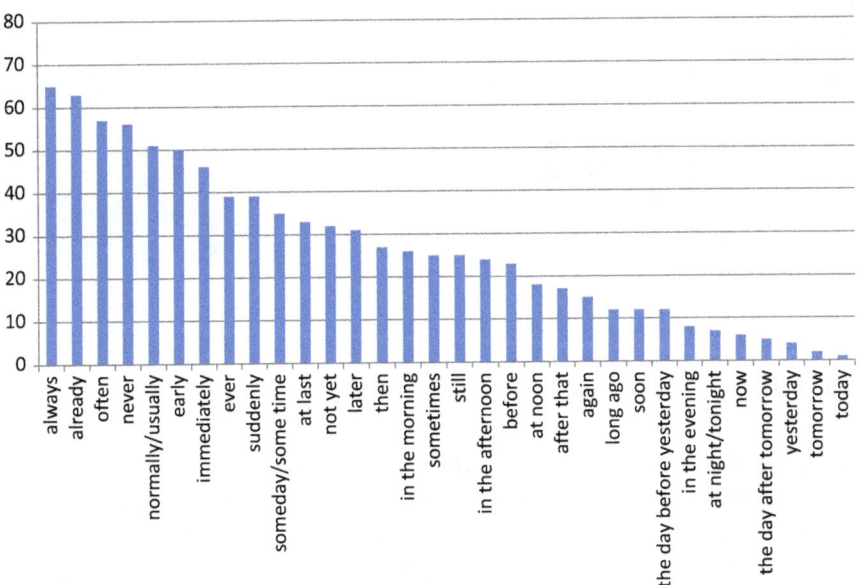

Fig. 10: Borrowing of Slavic temporal and phasal adverbs in Romani.

At the top of the frequency scale are 'always' (*vinagi / uvek / zawsze / vsegda* etc.), 'already' (*veče / već / już / uže* etc.), 'often' (*často / często / často / stalno* etc.) and 'never' (*nikoga / nikad / nigdy / nikda* etc.); the adverbs 'today' and 'tomorrow', on the other hand, are almost never borrowed from Slavic.

The range of local adverbs from Slavic is much smaller; it consists only of 'left' (*naljavo* / *nal(j)evo* / *(v)levo* etc.), 'direct' (*(na)pravo* / *preko* / *direktno* / *rovno* / *prosto* / *bezpośrednio* / *prjamo* etc.), 'nowhere' (*njakăde* / *nigde* / *nigdzie* etc.), 'somewhere' (*negde* / *gde-nibud'* etc.) and 'outside' (*na zewnątrz* and the blend *pe ulica* < Russian *na ulice*). Adverbs with the meanings 'back', 'here' and 'there' are never borrowed from Slavic (Fig. 11).

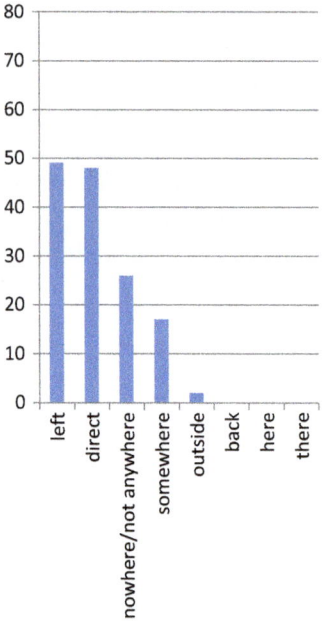

Fig. 11: Borrowing of Slavic local adverbs in Romani.

Focus particles, which distinguish discrete information units, are, like phasal adverbs, very often European loans in Romani; thus they are also high on the scale of likelihood of borrowing and support the thesis that contrast favors borrowability (Matras 2020: 213; Elšík and Matras 2006: 185). The adjective 'same', e.g. South Slavic *isto*, can be considered functionally related to focus particles "in its implicit reference to other members of a presupposed set" (Matras 2020: 214). The implicational hierarchy for borrowing according to Elšík and Matras (2006: 185) is 'only' > 'even' > 'too'. Among the focus particles and intensifiers, 'neither' (usually in blends with inherited *na*: *ni na* / *tože na* / *isto na* / *też na* etc.), 'also / too / as well' (*săšto* / *tože* / *isto* / *t(i)ež* etc.) and 'only' (*samo* / *tol'ko* / *tylko* etc.) have most frequently been borrowed from Slavic; 'very' and 'so' bring up the rear end of the scale (Fig. 12).

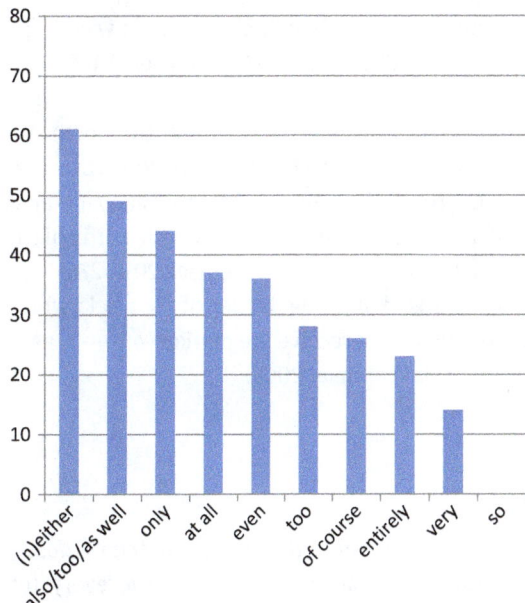

Fig. 12: Borrowing of Slavic focus particles and intensifiers in Romani.

Another interesting form noted by Elšík, Hübschmannová and Šebková (1999: 339) is *inakšie* 'else, otherwise' which has been borrowed as *inakšeder* in East Slovak Romani (cf. also Beníšek 2017: 231–232). It contains both the Romani comparative marker *-eder* and the Slovak comparative marker *-š-*, but is in fact a sham comparative because it is synonymous with the positive *inak*. Interrogative sentences are introduced by the Slavic particle *či / čy*, which introduces polar (or yes–no) questions, e.g. East Slovak Romani *Či na oj odi ehas so mange iľas ka romňa?* 'Was it not her who took my wife away?' (Rácová 2015: 92). For further examples of adverbs and particles, cf. Cech and Heinschink (2001b: 353) for Doljenski in Slovenia, Rácová (2015: 92) for East Slovak Romani, Boretzky (1993: 115, 1994: 174) for Kalderaš and Bugurdži in Kosovo and Serbia and the second part of this chapter on the Polska and Bergitka varieties in Poland.

Svako / vsjako / vseko / sjako / sako / seko 'every' is the most frequently borrowed distributive determiner; it exists in the majority of Romani varieties, alongside North Slavic *každo / kažno* in Polish, Lithuanian and Crimean Romani (Elšík and Matras 2006: 288, 291).

Apart from the negative indefinite pronouns with the Slavic negative prefix *ni- / n'i-* that have been mentioned in chapter 4, Romani has also frequently taken over whole Slavic negative pronouns in numerous regional varieties, for example *nic / n'ic / nič / n'ič / n'iš(t) / ništa / ništo* 'nothing', *nikdy / nigdy / n'igda / nikoga /*

nikəde / nikad 'never', *nigde* 'nowhere', *niko(j)* 'nobody', *nikako* 'in no way' (Lípa 1965: 34; Rácová 2015: 90; Boretzky 1994: 171, 1999: 68–69; Beníšek 2013, 2017: 215–216; Elšík and Matras 2006: 278).

When adverbs are derived from Slavic adjectives, they receive their own suffixes, usually the Romani adverb derivational suffix *-es* (Lithuanian Romani *ran-es* < Polish *rano* 'early', LT-005, 770) or *-ones* (East Slovak Romani *všeobecn-ones* < Slovak *všeobecne* 'omnipresent'); the latter goes back to the oblique suffix of the athematic sub-class of adjectives *-on-* (cf. Rácová 2015: 91; Beníšek 2017: 276–277). A related phenomenon is found in adverbs expressing the day of the week, which in East Slovak and Northeast Romani also often receive the marker *-on-* + *-e*, as in *vtork-one* 'on Tuesday', *piatk-one* 'on Friday' (Tenser 2005: 14).

6.1.5 Quantifiers and numerals

Popular Slavic quantifiers are *celo / calo* 'whole', *dosta / dostatǎčno / dosć / dovoljno* 'enough', *para* 'some, a couple of' and *s(v)ako / každo / kažno* 'every' (cf. Beníšek 2013: 52, 2017: 223–224, 274; Boretzky 1993: 111–112). There are also many borrowed forms of the indefinite paucal quantifier, for example *biľa / ščeblo / šťipka / troška / krapinka* from dialectal Slovak and Czech in North Central Romani (anonymous reviewer), a lot of mixed forms like *harica / nabutkica / kicy-nibud'*, and the Eastern Už varieties use *kapka*, lit. 'drop(let)' (diminutive *kapkica* 'a little bit') for this purpose (Beníšek 2013: 52, 2017: 272). Of special interest is the idiom *svako drom* 'every time', which is composed of Slavic *svako* and Romani *drom* 'way; time' (cf. Leggio 2011: 83). *Drom* is a calque from Slavic *put / pǎt*, also meaning both 'way' and 'time'. Western Rumungro has the pronoun *sogodi* 'every, each, all' instead of *savoro*, containing the Slovak suffix *-god* (SK-059, 569, 583). It might seem surprising that Romani – in company with many other languages, in fact – borrows numerals. According to Matras (2020: 217),

> [t]he borrowing of numerals is [...] not 'gap-filling'; it is another one of those instances where participation in an activity context that is associated with a particular language leads to a generalisation of the relevant word-form from that language. [...] Romani speakers [...] generally use numerals from the majority language when citing dates, a task that is performed primarily in the context of official institutions. In some situations, the sociolinguistic specialisation of loan-numerals for institutional use will lead to a generalisation of loans for the more abstract numerals, those that are beyond everyday counting abilities and are primarily in use in abstract, formal, and institutional-bound calculations.

Numbers are another example of fusion in the contact situation of Romani–Slavic. Remarkably, Romani mainly borrows higher cardinal numbers, but also lower ordinal numbers, from its Slavic contact languages. Most frequent is *prvo*, *pervo, peršo* etc. 'first' (which can also be part of a compound ordinal, e.g. Russian Romani *deš-u-prvo* 'eleventh'). Only a few varieties, among them Russian Romani, Sofia Erli, Yerli and Varna Kalajdži, have borrowed *vtoro* 'second' from a Slavic contact language (Elšík and Matras 2006: 172; Matras 2020: 219). The most frequent Slavic numeral is 'thousand', e.g. *tysjača* in Lithuanian Romani (LT-005, 476; LT-007, 476) and North Russian Romani (RUS-008, 476), *tysiące* in Lithuanian Romani and the variety of the Polska Roma (LT-008, 476; LT-009, 476) and *tišic* in East Slovak Romani (SK-002, 476). In the Eastern Už varieties, the expressions *perširaz* 'for the first time' and *posľedno raz* 'for the last time' are borrowed from the Slavic contact languages, as well as the distributive particle *po*, e.g. *po jekh* 'one each, one at a time', *po duj* 'two each, two at a time' etc. (Beníšek 2017: 265–266).

Elšík and Matras (2006: 170–171) have closely examined Romani varieties from Slovenia and Slovakia in terms of numerals and have found that:

> Slovene Romani retains the indigenous '1' through '4', and only some speakers also '20'; all other cardinals are from Slovene. Numerous varieties of Slovak Romani have only retained low unit numerals (e.g. '1' through '4' in Balog, or '1' through '6' in Zbojné); all others are borrowed from Slovak. In other dialects, there appears to be an arithmetic limit on non-fused numerals, irrespective of whether they are simple or compound. Thus, the Northern Central varieties of Podhradie and Švedlár use old (indigenous or Greek) numerals up to '29', while all higher numerals are Hungarian or Slovak, respectively. The Slovak Romani variety of Pribylina illustrates a combination of both principles: in addition to the (simple or compound) old numerals up to '29', there are also pre-Slovak forms for the simple order numerals '100' and '1000' (the latter a loan from Hungarian, the previous contact language). Numeral fusion may be, of course, gradual. Thus, Slovak Romani of the Humenné region has only old forms for '1' through '6', both old and Slovak forms for '7' through '10', '20', '100' and '1000', and only Slovak forms for all other cardinals.

The following excerpt from an interview with a speaker of Central Slovak Romani shall serve as a closing example. Here, the lower cardinal number 'one' is given in Romani, whereas the ordinal number 'eighth' (morphologically adapted) and the higher cardinal numbers 'sixteen' and 'four hundred seventy-seven' (not morphologically adapted) are given in Slovak:

(41)   Jaj, vičinav man Jana, phirav andi *osmo* trjeda, avla mange   (Central
        šestnásť rokou, [. . .]   Slovak)
        Well, my name is Jana, I go to the *eighth* class, I'll turn *sixteen*
        soon. [. . .]
        Bešen adaj *štyristo sedemdesiatsedem* roma, bešas andi *jekh* osada. [. . .]
        Four hundred seventy-seven Roma live here, we live in *one* settlement. [. . .]
        (SK-031, Sample's Transcriptions)

6.1.6 Lexical calquing

Another method used to create new words and phrases on the basis of Slavic contact languages is pattern borrowing (also: lexical calquing or loan translation). Among the earliest evidence of calques in Romani are attestations recorded in Petulengro's (1915: 68) notes on Drindari in northeastern Bulgaria, but it is for East Slovak Romani that they have been researched most thoroughly. Written texts by Romani writers and activists include forms like *maškarthemutno* < Slovak *medzinárodný* 'international' or *bikherengro* < Slovak *bezdomovec* 'homeless' (Rácová and Horecký 2000: 14; Rácová 2007: 133). Similar phenomena are documented for Macedonian Romani: *maškarthemutno* (anonymous reviewer) and North Russian Romani: *vybut'aker'iben* < Russian *vyrabotka* 'elaboration' or *dorak'ir'iben* < *dogovor* 'contract' (Wentzel 1980: 32). These are hybrid formations between calqued and directly borrowed language material. Slovak influence in East Slovak Romani is also visible in the copying of reduplicative constructions, which are used to mark duration or intensity. Reduplication takes place in different ways, among others in combination with *sar* 'how' (*marel sar marel* < Slovak *bije ako bije* 'he beats and beats = he beats for a long time'; Rácová 2015: 84) or *so* 'what' (*berš so berš* < *rok čo rok* 'year after year'; Rácová and Samko 2015: 177). Adjectives are rarely reduplicated, but constructions such as *šukar prešukar* < *krásny prekrásny* 'extremely beautiful' are possible (Rácová and Samko 2015: 170).

There are countless further instances of calques from Slavic constructions, but only a few shall be named here: the inherited syntactic model for 'What is your name?' is the structurally New Indo-Aryan construction *Sa / Savo hin tiro lav?* (Rácová 2015: 92; anonymous reviewer). Among the new constructions that have developed under Slavic influence is *Sar pes vičines?*:

(42) Sar   pes   vičines?   (Romani)
     Jak   se   jmenuješ?   (Czech)
     Ako   sa   menuješ / voláš?   (Slovak)
     Jak   się   nazywasz?   (Polish)
     how   REFL   call.2SG.PRS

A similar example for calquing is that of *Keci ori?* 'What time is it?' (Miltner 1965: 107; Rácová 2015: 92–93). In addition, a few very characteristic Russian constructions have been calqued in North Russian Romani, among them the construction for 'to marry':

(43a) Sr'edn'e   phen   vygeja   pale   rakleste   (North Russian
      second   sister   went.out   behind   fellow.LOC   Romani)
      pale   rom.
      behind   man

(43b) Drugaja   sestra   vyšla   za   muž   za   molodogo   čeloveka
      second   sister   went.out behind   man   behind   young.ACC   man.ACC
      'The second sister has married a fellow.'

Eastern Už Romani calques and expands structures based on Slovak *málo-kto* and Ukrainian *malo xto* 'hardly anybody' (Beníšek 2017: 207):

(44a) menk   ritkan   ko   tut   dela   cigarekľa   (Eastern Už)
      still   rarely   who   you.ACC   give.FUT.3SG   cigarette
      'Hardly anybody will give you even a cigarette.'

(44b) ov   ritkan   kan'   arakhel   varesij   buvťori
      he   rarely   when   finds   some   job.DIM
      'He hardly ever finds some good job.'

(44c) ode   phares   ko   pomožinla
      there   hard.ADV   who   help.FUT.3SG
      'Hardly anybody will help there.'

6.2 Lexical borrowings in two Romani varieties in Poland

After this general overview, in the following, two Romani varieties will be examined in more detail with regard to the lexical borrowings from their current Slavic contact language – Polish. For this purpose, a text corpus consisting of oral and written texts in the two largest Romani varieties in Poland (Polska and Bergitka) was analyzed to answer the following questions: What is the proportion of Polish borrowings in the lexicon, which semantic fields and parts of speech are affected, and to what extent are the borrowings adapted to the morphological structures of Romani? For an additional diachronic perspective – which, however, does not claim to be representative –, the contemporary Polish borrowings in the Bergitka variety will be compared with the older Polish borrowings as compiled in Rozwadowski (1936), the Polish borrowings in the Polska variety correspondingly with those from the poems of the famous poet Papusza, collected by Ficowski (1956).

6.2.1 Creation of the corpus

Due to the lack of comparable contemporary language data from the other Romani varieties in Poland (i.e. Xaladytka Roma, Sasytka Roma, Kalderaša, Lovara), the corpus is limited to the varieties of the Polska and Bergitka Roma. The collection of more recent language data for the other varieties and, ideally, their incorporation into the RMS Database, is a desideratum for future linguistic fieldwork. Important criteria in the creation of the corpus were: contemporary text material (the oldest text dates back to 1993), comparability of the texts in both varieties and inclusion of both spoken (elicited) and written language. Except for the poems, all pairs of texts are translations of the same original text into the two varieties, which makes them well suited for comparison. The following texts have been chosen for the analysis (Tab. 6):[23]

Tab. 6: Texts used for the corpus.

Type of text	Polska Roma	Bergitka Roma
Comic	Gierliński 2006 [Gier1]	Bladycz 2006 [Bla]
Information brochure	Milewski 2012 [Mil1]	Milewski 2012 [Mil2]
School primer	Gierliński 2007 [Gier2]	Gierliński 2008 [Gier3]
Poetry	Dębicki 1993 [Dęb]	Mirga 1994; Mirga 2006 [Mir]
Transcribed elicited utterances	RMS samples PL-018, -019	RMS samples PL-007

A complete list of the analyzed words can be found in Appendix 1.

The percentage of Polish lexemes in the Polska and Bergitka varieties based on a corpus of 4,000 lemmas (nouns, verbs and adjectives as the most frequent autosemantic parts of speech) very similar to this one was already calculated in Meyer (2017: 149). It showed that in the Bergitka variety, Polish borrowings account for 21.5% of the lexicon, while in the Polska variety they account for 12.5%. The difference can be explained primarily by the better integration of the Bergitka Roma into the Polish majority society. Considering the percentage of Polish borrowings in each text type individually, it is striking that the proportion is much higher in spoken than in written language. A particularly high proportion of Polish borrowings can also be found in the information brochure (especially in the Bergitka version) because of the large number of cultural loans from the area of school and other social institutions, for which Romani does not have inherited words or equivalents from earlier contact languages. The comics and school

---

[23] Part of the corpus texts was kindly provided by the Roma Documentation Center in Legnica and the Ethnographic Museum in Tarnów.

primers range in the middle, while the poems have the smallest proportion of Polish borrowings. The reason is that Romani writers deal very consciously with language and avoid foreign elements as much as possible, particularly when the poems deal with their own history, culture and identity, as these do.

6.2.2 Parts of speech

For this part of the analysis, the number of corpus texts a word (type) or part of speech appears in is counted. The most frequent nouns of Polish origin in the variety of the Polska Roma are *litera* 'letter', *kolega / koleżanka* 'friend' and *nauczyciel(ka)* 'teacher', the most frequent verb is *te musineł < musieć* 'to have to', followed by *te pomoginel* 'to help', *te moginel < móc* 'to be able' and *te myślinel* 'to think'.[24] The most common adjectives and lexical adverbs are *ceło / cało < cały* 'whole'[25] and *miło < miły* 'dear'. Furthermore, there are 10 conjunctions, 7 prepositions and numerous adverbs among the borrowings and switches: *może* 'maybe', *często* 'often', *tylko* 'only', *nigdy* 'never', *też* 'also', *bardzo* 'very' etc.; *czy* is widespread as well, both as an interrogative particle and meaning 'if, whether'. Most of the borrowed lexemes are nouns (213 / 241[26]), followed by verbs (40 / 54), adjectives and lexical adverbs (40 / 47), conjunctions, prepositions and grammatical adverbs (32 / 35). The relevant collocations are expressions of time and place, e.g. *o siódmej* 'at seven', *po drodze* 'on the way' and *w ciągu* 'in the course (of)'. It is assumed that lexemes that occur in several corpus texts are better established in the variety in question.

The most frequent Polish nouns in the Bergitka Roma variety are *n(i)ebo(s)* 'sky' and *szkoła* 'school', the most frequent verb is also *te musineł* 'to have to', followed by *te pomożinel / pomaginel* 'to help' and *te (na)pisynel* 'to write'. Among the adjectives and lexical adverbs, *cało / ceło* 'whole' has been found to be the most frequent. Again, the numerical difference between nouns and verbs is considerable: the corpus contains 290 nouns, 94 verbs, 52 adjectives and lexical adverbs and 31 further adverbs, conjunctions, prepositions, and numerals. The relevant collo-

---

24 It is worth mentioning in this context that "the only known word-form borrowing in Romani with the meaning of possession is the Polish verb *ma-*, borrowed into Polish Romani (*majinav* 'I have')" (Matras 2020: 225).
25 The form *ceło* could be older (South Slavic), unquestionably Polish is the form *cało*.
26 The two different figures stand for the two different samples for the varieties of the Polska Roma in the RMS Database. The first figure always refers to sample PL-018, the second to PL-019. A comparison of the two samples also shows that the use of Polish lexemes in Romani speech can vary among individual speakers.

cations are *na zewnątrz* 'outside' and terms for the days of the week, e.g. *w piątek* 'am Freitag'.

Table 7 shows an overview of the results:

Tab. 7: Borrowings and codeswitches according to parts of speech.

	Nouns	Verbs	Adjectives, lexical adverbs	Conjunctions, prepositions, further adverbs	Σ
Polska Roma	213 / 241 (Ø 64%)	40 / 59 (Ø 14%)	40 / 47 (Ø 12%)	32 / 35 (Ø 10%)	325 / 382
Bergitka Roma	290 (62%)	94 (20%)	52 (11%)	31 (7%)	467

The large number of borrowed nouns can be explained by their referential function: Nouns cover the most differentiated area with respect to the denomination of concepts and objects (Matras 2020: 181) and are most easily integrated into the system of the recipient language. Closed word classes like conjunctions are on the other end of the scale, and it takes much longer for them to find their way into another language:

> [...] coordinating conjunctions (and other discourse markers) and partly word order rules are likely to undergo convergence with a dominant contact language after several generations. [...] With the adoption of Polish items the dialect also adopts the Polish coordinative configuration, for example a three term additive-contrastive continuum with Polish *i* 'and' (addition), *a* 'and however' (semantic opposition), and *ale* 'but' (denial of expectation).
> (Matras 1999c: 16)

It is not surprising that the most frequently borrowed verb is *te musineł* 'to have to', because Romani often borrows modal verbs and particles from its contact languages and obligation is generally on top of the borrowing hierarchy of modal expressions in Romani as shown in Chapter 4. The Polska and Bergitka varieties are no exception to this rule.

It is important to note that there is no mutual exclusivity between having a Polish or an inherited word (or a word from an earlier contact language, respectively), but that variation between the two is possible and very common. This is also typical of such active bilingual speaker communities as the Roma in Poland. Examples of variants from the corpus are *danda* vs. *zęby* 'teeth', *hudipen* vs. *więzienie* 'prison', *kher* vs. *dom* 'house', *kali* vs. *kawa* 'coffee', *foro(s)* vs. *miasto* 'town', *te leł vera* vs. *ożeninel* 'to get married' and many more. Such cases should be considered spontaneous one-word codeswitches.

6.2.3 Semantic fields

To answer the question as to which semantic fields are affected, only the nouns have been analyzed, because in many cases it is impossible to unequivocally assign the representatives of other parts of speech to a particular semantic field. Because of the high percentage of nouns within the whole borrowed lexicon, the results will still be conclusive. Here, Polska and Bergitka Romani are looked at collectively, not comparatively.

By far the largest semantic field affected by borrowing is that of nature, to which belong animals (*orło* < *orzeł* 'eagle', *wilko* < *wilk* 'wolf', *robakos* < *robak* 'worm', *mucha* 'fly' etc.), plants (*dębo* < *dąb* 'oak', *kwiatko* / *kwiat(os)* < *kwiat(ek)* 'flower', *krzak* 'bush' etc.), landscape features (*polana* 'glade', *morzo* / *morze* 'sea', *pol(i)o* < *pole* 'field' etc.), natural materials (*lodo* < *lód* 'ice', *węglo* < *węgiel* 'coal', *drewno* 'wood', *kamienios* < *kamień* 'stone' etc.) and many more (*księżyc(o)* 'moon', *pogoda* 'weather', *niebo* 'sky' etc.). This might be surprising in view of the traditional non-sedentary, close-to-nature lifestyle of the Roma, but it is by far not an exception among the Romani varieties. A number of lexemes from this semantic field do still have Romani equivalents, but the poverty of the inherited lexicon here has been proven in several studies (Matras 2002: 28). Many inherited words got lost along with the shift away from a non-sedentary lifestyle, or even earlier, being replaced by words from contact languages. With Myers-Scotton (1993), we can speak of a clear case of *core forms*.

The second largest semantic field is occupied by abstract concepts, among them many internationalisms, e.g. *sytuacja* 'situation', *problema* 'problem', *możliwość* 'possibility', *znakos* < *znak* 'sign', *temat* 'topic', *kultura* 'culture' and many more.

The third largest field is that of dwelling, with words for accommodation (*namiotis* < *namiot* 'tent', *dom(os)* < *dom* 'house', *osiedlenio* < *osiedle* 'settlement' etc.), furniture (*krzesło* 'chair', *stolikos* 'table.DIM', *mebli* < *meble* '(pieces of) furniture', *dywanos* < *dywan* 'carpet', *lampa* 'lamp' etc.), household articles (*lusterko* 'mirror.DIM', *koc* 'blanket', *filiżanka* 'cup', *talerz(o)* 'plate' etc.).

The fourth place is equally held by the fields of politics / military, education, economy and the human body, which each exhibit borrowing in equal measure. The large number of borrowings is obvious for the first three cases, because they mainly denote realia from the Polish majority culture, which means we are dealing with *cultural loans* there. The field of the human body is another example that shows how open Romani is to borrowing even when inherited words would be available. Examples are *kolano(s)* 'knee', *palco* < *palec* 'finger', *żołądko* / *żelądko* < *żołądek* 'stomach', *stopa* 'foot'. A comparison with Swadesh's reduced list of 50 words (Swadesh 1955) also shows to what extent the core vocabulary of the Polska and Bergitka Romani varieties is affected by Polish: four of Swadesh's words, 'knee', 'leaf', 'stone' and 'tooth', belonging to the semantic fields of nature and the human body, are borrowed or code-switched.

In the fifth place are religion (*ołtarzo* < *ołtarz* 'altar', *papieżo* < *papież* 'pope', *rożańcos* < *różaniec* 'rosary', *dusza* 'soul' etc.) and food (*miodo(s)* < *miód* 'honey', *orzech(o)* 'nut', *zupa* 'soup', *kawa* 'coffee' etc.). The Roma on Polish ground adopted the Catholic faith very quickly and combined it with their own traditions, so that numerous words from the semantic field of religion were borrowed from Polish.

The list of semantic fields affected by borrowing does not end here. Words for food, for days of the week, names of months and certain time units (*minuta* 'minute', *rano* 'morning', *chwila* 'moment', *przyszłość* 'future') and 'time' itself (*czasos / ćaso* < *czas*) have been taken over from Polish, as well as words for clothing (*sukienka* 'dress', *kurtka* 'jacket', *płaszczo* < *płaszcz* 'coat', *czapka* 'cap' etc.), road traffic (*ulica* 'street', *skrzyżowanie* 'crossing', *autos* < *auto* 'car', *chodnik* 'pavement' etc.) and buildings (*mosto(s) / mostis* < *most* 'bridge', *zamko(s)* < *zamek* 'castle', *rynko(s)* < *rynek* 'market place', *teatro* < *teatr* 'theater' etc.). A small number of further words belong to the semantic fields of celebration, denomination of persons, materials and objects from everyday life.

6.2.4 Morphological integration

The degree of morphological adaptation can also be a hint regarding to what degree a Polish lexeme has already been integrated into the Romani lexicon. In the area of morphological adaptation of Polish borrowings into the structures of Romani, there is a lot of variation, while a number of words also stay in their original Polish form, e.g. *rachunek* 'check'. When nouns are adopted, they have to be integrated into the Romani gender system, which only has two grammatical genders (masculine and feminine); Polish neuter nouns get a masculine ending or keep their original Polish form, e.g. *przyjęcie* 'reception', *ubezpieczenie* 'insurance', *stypendium* 'scholarship'.

Masculine nouns are adapted very often and easily and receive the ending *-o* (Polska Roma), *-os* or *-is* (Bergitka Roma) borrowed from Greek, e.g. *obozo* < *obóz* 'camp', *ołtarzo* < *ołtarz* 'altar', *kolcos* < *kolec* 'thorn', *domos* < *dom* 'house', *metalis* 'metal'. The school primer contains some unusual examples of word formation for abstract concepts in the Bergitka variety: *ćwićisagos* 'exercise', *miśliśagos* < *myślenie* 'thinking', *przyzwoliśagos* < *przyzwolenie* 'consent'. These are internal deverbal derivations by means of the Hungarian origin nominalizing suffix *-išag-* (Hungarian *-ság*; anonymous reviewer). Feminine nouns in Romani end in *-i*, however, interestingly there are only very few examples in the corpus of lexemes that have been adopted in this way. An interesting case in terms of word formation is *teści* 'mother-in-law' (PL-018, 450), as the regular Polish form would be *teściowa* but the speaker derives *teści* by using the Romani ending *-i* to create a female form of *teść* 'father-in-law'. Usually feminine nouns remain unchanged, e.g. *nauczycielka* '(female) teacher', *sytuacja* 'situation', *szkoła* 'school', *czarownica* 'witch'.

Verbs are almost always composed of a Polish stem, the morpheme *-in-* (also from Greek), which is used to mark foreign verbs in Romani, as well as the infinitive marker *te* and the infinitive ending *-eł*. In this way, they can be inflected like inherited verbs, e.g. *te pisyneł* 'to write', *te skończyneł* 'to end', *te musineł* 'to have to'. Interesting is the mixed form *te ciągnąć* 'to pull' from the Bergitka variety in PL-007, 165. Both perfective, prefixed verbs and imperfective, unprefixed verbs have been borrowed, for example, both *te malineł* and *te pomalineł* 'paint', *oszczędzineł* and *zaoszczędzineł* 'to save', *witineł* and *powitineł* 'to greet', *ćitineł* / *ćytyneł* and *przećitineł* 'to read', *pomagineł* and *pomożineł* / *pomożineł* 'to help' can be found in the corpus; however, the unprefixed imperfective forms are more frequent. Reflexive verbs receive the Romani reflexive pronoun *pe(s)* instead of Polish *się*, e.g. *te bawineł pe(s)* 'to play'. The RMS Database also includes a few Polish verbs that are not morphologically adapted to Romani at all, but this is the exception.

Adjectives receive the ending *-o* (masculine, e.g. *pogańsko* 'pagan', *swento* 'holy'), rarely the multimorphemic genitive marker *-oskro* (e.g. *orłoskro* 'eagle-') and *-i* (feminine), or stay in the Polish original; both are equally common. Adverbs can keep Polish *-o* or, more rarely, receive Romani *-es* (e.g. *łatwones* 'easily').

6.2.5 Diachronic comparison

For the variety of the Bergitka Roma, Rozwadowski's *Wörterbuch des Zigeunerdialekts von Zakopane* ['Dictionary of the Gypsy dialect from Zakopane'] (1936) is a precious historical source that can serve for comparison with the findings from the contemporary corpus (Tab. 8). For the variety of the Polska Roma, we can refer to Papusza's poems (*Pieśni Papuszy / Papušakre gila*), published by Jerzy Ficowski in 1956 (Tab. 9). Of course, these sources are very scarce and the comparison therefore does not claim to provide any significant results. However, it can give an impression of the different character of the historical and contemporary texts and the different character of the Polish lexemes within them.

Tab. 8: Polish words in Rozwadowski (1936) in comparison with the contemporary corpus.[27]

Rozwadowski (1936)	Contemporary Bergitka corpus	Original Polish word	Translation
ale	ale	ale	'but'
bankos	–	bank	'bank'
cało	cało, ceło	cały	'whole'
casos	czasos, ciasos, ćaso	czas, dial. cas	'time'
ći	czy, ci	czy, dial. cy, ći	interr. particle
xoj-	–	choć-	'some-, any-'
xolja	–	dial. hala	'mountain pasture'
jeśeńis	–	jesień	'autumn'
kaćka	–	kaczka	'duck'
karćma	–	karczma	'inn'
kf'atkos	kwiatos, kwietek	kwiat	'flower'
te klenkineł	–	klękać / klęknąć	'to kneel'
kohutos	–	kogut, dial. kohut	'rooster'
krutko	–	krótki	'short'
ława	–	ława	'bench'
l'iśćos	liść	liść	'leaf'
liskineł pes	–	dial. łyskać się	'to flash'
(m'edža)	–	(miedza, possibly South Slavic)	'balk = ridge delimiting a field'
mexos	–	mech	'moss'
m'eśonckos	–	dial. miesioncek	'moon'
mgła	–	mgła	'fog'
te myśl'ineł	te myślineł	myśleć	'to think'
mišos	myśos	mysz	'mouse'
młinos	młynos	młyn	'mill'
te obći'neł	–	obciąć	'to cut off'
płaxta	–	płachta	'sheet'
potokos	–	potok	'stream'
rakos	–	rak	'crawfish'
śadłos	–	siodło	'saddle'
samo	samo	samo	'the same'

---

[27] The word łańcos 'chain', which is not in the list but also appears in Rozwadowski (1936), is a loanword from Hungarian, not from Polish. Likewise, sługadźis 'soldier' is of unclear Slavic etymology, but certainly not derived from Polish sługa (anonymous reviewer).

6.2 Lexical borrowings in two Romani varieties in Poland — 111

Tab. 8 (continued)

Rozwadowski (1936)	Contemporary Bergitka corpus	Original Polish word	Translation
śkłos	–	szkło	'glass'
te spotkineł	te spotkineł	spotkać	'to meet'
śreńos	–	sreń / śreń dial.	'hoarfrost'
stavos	–	staw	'pond'
strixineł	–	[strzyc]	'to shear'
šogork'ini	–	[?szogorka dial.]	'sister-in-law'
zamkn'imen	–	zamknięty	'closed'
te žezineł	–	rzezać dial.	'to cut'

It can be seen from the table that 11 entries from the contemporary Bergitka Romani corpus already existed in Rozwadowski's time at the beginning of the twentieth century. On the other hand, more than half of the Polish-derived words in Rozwadowski (1936) do not occur in the contemporary corpus, among them all dialectal forms. The latter is certainly due to the fact that the texts in the modern corpus are primarily from written documents and therefore show fewer dialectal influences.

Tab. 9: Polish words in Ficowski (1956) in comparison with the contemporary corpus.[28]

Papusza (1956)	Contemporary Polska corpus	Original Polish word	Translation
ale	ale	ale	'but'
bławaty	–	bławaty	'cornflower'
čy	czi, czy	czy	'or'
dembo	dębo	dąb	'oak'
dživno	dziwno	dziwny	'strange'
gžybo	grzyb	grzyb	'mushroom'
juš/juž	już	już	'already'
kochano	–	kochany	'beloved'

---

[28] As an aside, Papusza's poems also contain some interesting words from other Slavic languages: *jołki* < Russian *ëlki* 'firs', *zelen-* < South Slavic *zelen* 'green', *mraz-* < Serbo-Croatian *mraz* 'frost', *(za)mraś-* < Serbo-Croatian *(za)mraz-* 'to freeze', *podum-* < Russian *podum-* 'to think', *sveto / sfeto* < South Slavic or Russian *svet* 'world', *nek* < Serbo-Croatian *nek* (optative particle, supported by Polish *niech*).

Tab. 9 (continued)

Papusza (1956)	Contemporary Polska corpus	Original Polish word	Translation
kołysynet	–	kołysać	'to rock'
kruko	–	kruk	'raven'
malinytko	–	malinowy	'raspberry' *(adj.)*
modro	–	modry	'cornflower-blue'
moginet	moginet	móc *(ja mogę)*	'to be able'
može	može	może	'maybe'
muśinet	musinet, muśinet	musieć	'to have to'
okrušečki	–	okruszeczki	'crumbs.DIM'
ostro	–	ostry	'sharp'
paxńiset	–	pachnąć	'to smell of'
pamieńć	–	pamięć	'memory'
pomoginet	pomoginet	pomóc *(ja pomogę)*	'to help'
potem	–	potem	'then, thereafter'
pšyšłość	przyszłość	przyszłość	'future'
ružno	–	różny	'different'
stepo	–	step	'steppe'
škoła	szkoła	szkoła	'school'
šuminet	–	szumieć	'to swoosh'
śfjećinet	[światło 'Licht']	świecić	'to shine'
tšebi	–	trzeba	'one should'
vierš(yk)	–	wiersz(yk)	'poem(.DIM)'
volinet	–	woleć	'to prefer'
vružynet	–	wróżyć	'to tell s.o.'s fortune'
vyvjurečka	–	wiewióreczka	'squirrel.DIM'
zryśćot	–	zrywać (się)	'to break, arise' (a storm)

Of the 35 Polish loanwords in Papusza's poems, 12 or 13 also appear in the modern corpus, but overall the semantic domains of the Polish borrowings in Papusza's poems are rather different from those for the modern language.

6.3 Summary

Romani is repeatedly cited as providing an example of particularly massive lexical borrowing (a very illustrative example is provided by Elšík 2009: the Selice variety in Slovakia that he investigated consists to 62.7% of loanwords, of which again 84.2% are from the current contact language, Hungarian), and the impact of the Slavic contact languages on the Romani lexicon in question is also strong – ranging from early borrowings found in Romani varieties all over the world to spontaneous switches from a current Slavic contact language. The semantic fields most influenced are nature and dwelling; the largest group of borrowings are nouns, followed by verbs, temporal and phasal adverbs and quantifiers.

With regard to the more closely investigated Polska and Bergitka Roma varieties in Poland, it was shown that, as expected, the lexical influence of Polish on Romani is very pronounced in general and that the Bergitka variety is more widely affected than is the Polska variety: the former borrows or switches more than one fifth, the latter one eighth of its lexicon from Polish. In terms of parts of speech – again unsurprisingly – most of the borrowed words are nouns, followed by verbs, adjectives, and lexical adverbs, respectively. The five semantic domains that contain the most Polish lexemes are: 1. nature; 2. abstract concepts; 3. dwelling; 4. (in equal measure) politics and military, education, economy and the human body; and 5. (in equal measure) religion and food. Noteworthy are some special cases of word formation such as *teści* and the fact that even the core Swadesh vocabulary is affected by borrowing and codeswitching. It is important to emphasize that inherited and borrowed forms often coexist. A comparison of the two samples for the Polska Roma variety also reveals that there are differences between individual speakers for numerous words.

7 Romani borrowings in diastratic varieties of Slavic

The Slavic languages primarily influence Romani and not vice versa because, as majority and state languages in the countries concerned, they are clearly the dominant ones in this contact situation. However, the reverse case, in which Romani is the donor language, also exists.

This case has two perspectives: The first concerns the situation of bi- or multilingualism among the Roma. It has been observed several times that certain forms and patterns from Romani, the L1, are transferred into the respective Slavic L2. Gjorgjević observed the following about the Roma in Serbia as early as 1903:

> Ich merke als sehr bezeichnend noch an, dass die Zigeuner, die zigeunerisch sprechen, sehr leicht nach ihrer Betonung der serbischen Worte als Zigeuner erkannt werden, indem sie den charakteristischen Akzent ihrer Sprache auf die serbische übertragen. [. . .] Ich erwähne noch, dass der Zigeunersprache eine besondere, schwere Betonungsweise eigentümlich ist, die es bewirkt, dass man redende Zigeuner leicht erkennen kann, auch wenn man sie nicht sieht. Diese Betonungsweise ist bei den Zigeunern derart eingewurzelt, dass sie sie auch, wenn sie serbisch reden, beibehalten und daran kann man auch den fliessend serbisch sprechenden Zigeuner als solchen ohne weiteres erkennen. (Gjorgjević 1903: 20–21)

['I additionally note as very indicative that the Gypsies who speak Gypsy can be very easily recognized as Gypsies due to their accentuation of the Serbian words, in that they transfer the characteristic accent of their language to Serbian. [. . .] I would also mention that the Gypsy language has a special, heavy accentuation peculiar to it, which allows one to easily recognize speaking Gypsies, even if one cannot see them. This characteristic accent is so ingrained in the Gypsies that they retain it even when they speak Serbian, and from this one can easily recognize the fluent Serbian-speaking Gypsy as such.']

Friedman (2001a: 151) notes for North Macedonia that

> for example, an ethnic Romani announcer on a Macedonian-language radio program is immediately recognizable to Macedonians as a Rom from his intonational patterns, in particular rises in pitch occurring where they would not in Macedonian.

Thus, the respective Slavic L2, when spoken by Roma, can have specific ethnolectal characteristics.[29] The only monograph to date about the influence of Romani

---

29 Two instructive examples from non-Slavic regions can be named at this point: For American English spoken by Vlax Roma, Hancock (1971, 1980) identifies a lack of contrast between /w/ and /v/, /t/ and /θ/, /d/ and /ð/, as well as idiosyncrasies in word formation. Matras (2002: 242) observes that ethnolectal German spoken by Roma and Sinti often shows de-rounding of umlauts (*gerist* < *Gerüst* 'scaffold', *bēse* < *böse* 'evil'), neutralization of the dative and accusative (*mit den Bruder*.ACC instead of *mit dem Bruder*.DAT 'with the brother', *bei die Leute*.ACC instead of *bei den*

on a Slavic L2 among Roma in a Slavic-speaking country is Bořkovcová's study *Romský etnolekt češtiny* ['The Romani ethnolect in Czech'] (2006), in which phonetic and phonological, lexical, morphological and (morpho-)syntactic peculiarities of this ethnolect are analyzed. (On the ethnolectal lexicon of Roma in the Czech Republic, cf. also Elšík 2017). This study shows that collective second-language acquisition followed by stabilization can lead to a new form of the target language, which is not substantially different from the target language in the lexicon but can differ remarkably in pattern organization. Ultimately, it is a supra-individual form of fossilization of learner varieties in the course of acquiring an L2. Such collective interlanguage characteristics are very common among linguistic minorities and are not restricted to the Roma (cf. also Matras 2020: 243, 251, 253).

These examples all concern the linguistic behavior of Roma in a context of active bi- or multilingualism. In this chapter, however, we will deal with the second perspective of Romani as the donor language in a contact situation: the influence of Romani on the language of monolingual speakers of Slavic languages. This influence exists exclusively on the level of the lexicon.

7.1 Romani borrowings in diastratic varieties

Since the prestige of the donor language plays an important role for lexical borrowing, it must be assumed that Romani is considered prestigious by certain speakers within certain registers. Although it has never been the language of the social majority or the powerful in any country, it was and still is highly regarded by some groups as a kind of 'anti-language' to express nonconformism:

> The influence of Romani on other languages is best observed in those domains of interaction with mainstream society in which the Rom had prestige: activities that questioned or challenged the norms of the establishment. The Rom have often been regarded by other marginalized groups in society as successful conspirators against social order, and as ideologically self-sufficient in the sense that they are consistent in maintaining their own internal system of loyalties, resisting external pressure to accommodate.
>
> (Matras 2002: 249; cf. also Matras 2014: 123)

Leuten.DAT 'with the people') and the use of auxiliary verbs in subordinate clauses (*er versteht mehr als er zugeben tut*, lit. 'he understands more than he does admit'). All these features can be found in German dialects as well, but not in the specific combination observed in the ethnolectal German of the Roma (and Sinti).

Activities that are negatively associated within the majority society, such as begging or distrust of others, can represent something positive in the sense of something essential for survival for people on the fringes of this society. For them, Romani can serve as a model worth imitating. Hence, according to Matras (2002: 249–250), one of the two main reasons for adopting Romani lexicon lies in the image of the Roma; Leeuwen-Turnovcová (2003: 27) speaks of a 'downward solidarization' ("Solidarisierung nach unten"). The (stereotypical) flair of freedom and rebellion against the establishment and the social mainstream emanating from the Rom has made Romani particularly attractive to young people to this day.

A second reason relates to the inherent secrecy function of slangs, the associated demarcation against the outside world and the evasion of communicative norms. This is done for example by referring to taboo areas (Matras 2002: 249–250; Leeuwen-Turnovcová 2003: 27). Lexical elements from Romani, which fall into semantic taboo areas, undoubtedly fulfill a euphemistic function (for details, cf. Burridge and Allan 1998).

Historically speaking, the path of a lexical element from Romani into another language usually begins with it being borrowed into the specialized secret vocabulary of other peripatetic groups. From there it spreads further into the in-group lexicons of the urban underworld and anti-establishment groups, then into the slang of the relatively open and socially mobile adolescents and young adults and finally into the general colloquial language. The number of lexemes is reduced with each step, so that only very few achieve a general level of awareness (Matras 1998b, 2002: 250). In this manner, the following words have made it into (British) English colloquial language: *pal* 'friend, companion' < *phral* 'brother', *lollipop* < *loli phabaj* 'red apple', *chav(vy)* as a derogatory term for young people from a lower social class < *čhavo* 'Romani boy', *cosh* 'stick; strike' and *to cosh s.o.* 'to knock s.o. over the head' < *kašt* 'tree; wood; stick'; *minge* < *mindž* as a vulgar term for the vagina (Grant 1998: 170–171; Matras 2002: 250; www.urbandictionary.com; *pal* is also common in the informal register of American English and *lollipop* is standard American English). There is also a small number of Romani words in colloquial German: Best known are *Bock* < *bokh* 'hunger' in the phrase *(keinen) Bock auf etwas haben* '(not) to be keen on sth.' and *Zaster* 'money' < *saster* 'iron, metal'. In the German word *Kaschemme*, which is originally Slavic, Romani *kačima / kirčima / karčma* etc. played an intermediary role in the borrowing process. Romani *gav* 'village' was discussed for a long time as the original word for colloquial German *Kaff* 'village', but it is more likely that *Kaff* is of Hebrew origin (Matras 1998b: 198–199, 203, 2002: 250). Through the very popular German rap song "Chabos wissen, wer der Babo ist" by the artist known as Haftbefehl (2012), *chabo* 'boy, guy' (also derived from *čhavo*) and *babo* ('boss, leader';

in Balkan Romani varieties, *baba* 'father')[30] have at least entered German youth slang, if not even the general colloquial language. *Babo* was voted Youth Word of the Year in 2013. Possibly, the colloquial phrase *du bist Zucker*, lit. 'you are sugar', meaning 'you are sweet / pretty / beautiful' can be traced back to Romani *šukar / šuker / zukker* 'beautiful' (cf. also Šapoval 2012: 535; Wolf 1956: 301). In a European comparison, Matras (2002: 249) identifies as the most frequently borrowed Romani items into substandard varieties *čor-* 'steal', *mang-* 'to beg; to demand; to ask for', *ma(n)ro* 'bread, food', *gadžo / gadži* 'non-Rom(ni); outsider, stranger' and *love* 'money'. Further items refer to the semantic areas of food, drink, people, animals and sexuality.

With respect to terminology, as already shown in Meyer (2020b: 82–83), Slavic sociolinguistics has a partially chaotic variety of terms and definitions in the field of sub- / non-standard varieties. The term *argot* is used here in line with Mokienko and Walter (2014: 2156–2157),

> um bestimmte soziale oder berufliche Abweichungen von der Allgemeinsprache zu charakterisieren (Argot der Künstler, der Musikanten, der Sportler, der Soldaten usw.), d.h. in derselben Bedeutung wie Jargon. Im engeren Verständnis bezeichnet das Argot die Sprache der sozial Unterprivilegierten sowie der kriminellen Welt [...]. Die historisch bedingte Spezifik des Terminus Argot besteht darin, dass er ebenso wie der Terminus Geheimsprache vor allem die Subsprachen abgeschlossener korporativer Verbände meint, die sich in Europa einschließlich der slavischen Länder in der Zeit des Feudalismus herausgebildet haben: der reisenden Händler, der Bettler, der Diebe usw. Das Argot entsteht als Mittel des Selbstschutzes, der Abgrenzung von der Gesellschaft und des Bewahrens von Berufsgeheimnissen.

> ['to characterize certain social or professional deviations from the general language (the argot of artists, musicians, sportsmen, soldiers etc.), i.e. in the same meaning as jargon. In a narrower understanding, argot describes the language of the socially underprivileged and the criminal world [...]. The historically determined specific character of the term argot is that, like the term secret language, it primarily refers to the sub-languages of exclusive corporative associations that emerged in Europe, including in the Slavic countries, during the time of feudalism: that of travelling merchants, beggars, thieves etc. The argot arises as a means of self-protection, demarcation against the society and the keeping of professional secrets.']

The historical component is central to the present chapter.[31] The term *slang* or *jargon*, as used here,

---

30 *Babo* also exists in the same meaning in Turkish, Bosnian and other languages. Turkish *babo* is probably the origin of *babo* in the other Balkan languages.
31 The first list of Romani words in European argots was compiled by Franz Miklosich (*Zigeunerische Elemente in den Gaunersprachen Europas* ['Gypsy elements in the cants of Europe'], 1876), but Slavic languages do not play a role in it apart from a brief mention of *ofenskij* ("afinskoe"): "Im südlichen Russland haben folgende Wörter Eingang in die Sprache, wohl der Gauner, gefunden: beng

konkurriert in vielen Untersuchungen mit dem Terminus Argot, jedoch ohne dessen diachrone Konnotationen und wird gewöhnlich in weitem Sinne als Sondersprache bestimmter durch Beruf, Stand u.a. geprägter Kreise mit speziellem Wortschatz (Jargonismen) verstanden. [...] Der Jargon verfügt im Unterschied zum Argot über einen offeneren Charakter und wird gewöhnlich in größeren vorwiegend jugendlichen Sprechergruppen verwendet, die durch gemeinsame berufliche und kulturelle Interessen, durch die Zugehörigkeit zu einem bestimmten sozialen Milieu (Wehrdienst, Studium, Saisonarbeit, Klubs usw.) verbunden sind. (Mokienko and Walter 2014: 2157)

['competes with the term argot in many studies, but without its diachronic connotations, and is usually understood in a broad sense as the special language of certain groups with a special vocabulary (jargonisms), which are characterized by occupation, status etc. [...] A jargon has a more open character than an argot and is usually used in larger, predominantly adolescent groups of speakers, which are based on common professional and cultural interests or belonging to a certain social milieu (military service, academic studies, seasonal work, clubs etc.).']

Hereinafter we are going to speak of *(historical) argots, (contemporary) youth slangs* and *colloquial languages*.

Against this background, the following questions are asked: Which Romisms are documented for Slavic argots from the end of the nineteenth to the middle of the twentieth century and which of them have been preserved in (or added to) Slavic youth slangs and colloquial languages in the 21st century? Some important studies on the historical component already exist, the results of which are to be brought together here. With regard to contemporary varieties, our own analyses were carried out with the help of corpus and (online) dictionary queries. The investigated languages are Bosnian / Croatian / Serbian and Bulgarian for South Slavic, Czech (with some remarks on Slovak) and Polish for West Slavic and Russian and Ukrainian for East Slavic.

7.2 Slavic argots with a Romani component

7.2.1 Bosnian / Croatian / Serbian: *Šatrovački*

The term *šatrovački* (*govor*) includes a whole series of historically developed sociolects from former Yugoslavia, the entire sector of the spoken, esoteric, predom-

---

Teufel; *dádos* Haupt eines Zigeunerlagers, *grássi* Buhlerinn [sic], eig. Stute, lat. lupa; *maribe* Tod, Skelett; *maribij* sterblich, smertnyj; *rom* Zigeunerknabe; *romni* Zigeunermädchen." ['In southern Russia the following words have found their way into the language, probably that of the tricksters' cant: *beng* devil; *dádos* head of a Gypsy camp, *grássi* paramour, actually mare, lat. lupa; *maribe* death, skeleton; *maribij* mortal, smertnyj; *rom* Gypsy boy; *romni* Gypsy girl.]' (Miklosich 1876: 539)

inantly lexically characterized non-standard (urban) varieties (Hinrichs 2014: 2175). Within the broad spectrum that Šatrovački represents, there is a variant with a strong Romani component, especially in Bosnia and Hercegovina:

> The Bosnian variety of Yugoslavian Šatrovački shows heavy lexical borrowing from Romani, which seems to be due to the fact that it [was] adopted by Gypsies who had shifted from Romani to Serbian, [thereby] enriching Šatrovački [with] words [from] their old mother tongue. (Boretzky and Igla 1994b: 56)

However, the circle of Šatrovački users reaches far beyond the Romani community. Its vocabulary is based on Bosnian / Croatian / Serbian, with elements from numerous neighboring languages. The fact that Šatrovački is both subject to constant change and exists in many different varieties complicates its description. The etymological origin of the term *šatrovački* goes back to *šatrōndža* 'prison', a Slavic word which, in turn, goes back to Turkish *şatranç* or *satranç* 'chess game' (the analogy lies in the form of the grid). The frequently made reference to the tents of nomadic Roma (cf. Bosnian / Croatian / Serbian *šatra*) is a folk etymology (Hinrichs 2014: 2175). The earliest and most extensive work on Romisms in Šatrovački was published by Rade Uhlik (*Ciganizmi u šatrovačkom argou* ['Gypsyisms in the Šatrovački argot'] 1954), and according to him, the Romani element is an indispensable part of Šatrovački: "[. . .] šatrovačkim govorom provejava tipičan ciganski duh, ili, kaošto neki smatraju, da je ciganski jezik nadahnut šatrovačkim duhom" ['[. . .] a typical Gypsy spirit permeates Šatrovački, or, as some believe, the Gypsy language is inspired by the spirit of Šatrovački.'] (Uhlik 1954: 6). Uhlik is also convinced that the stylistics of Šatrovački are typical of Romani. He confirms this with loan-translated phrases, e.g. *dajem vatru tabanima* < *čalavav jag e prnende* 'I propel', lit. 'I give so. fire under the feet', *ubijem džadu* < *marav drom* 'I'm on my way', lit. 'I hit the road' (the English colloquial phrase *to hit the road* is possibly of the same origin). Two layers of Romisms in Šatrovački have been identified: The older forms, e.g. *vakeriši!* 'say!', *cidel* 'to drink', *kaštrin* 'wood', mostly come from the variety of the Arlije (Uhlik calls them "Turkish Gypsies"), the newer ones from the varieties of the Gurbet ("Tent Gypsies" in Cortiade 1991: 153). The material for Uhlik's study was mainly collected in Sarajevo, Mostar and other places in Bosnia and Hercegovina, but also in Belgrade, Zagreb and elsewhere (Uhlik 1954: 7–8). Uhlik lists 113 Romani items that were borrowed into Šatrovački and partially became very productive there, Cortiade (1991), in a later work, deals with them in terms of their morphological integration.

7.2.2 Bulgarian: *Čalgădžijski ezik*

In his contribution *Ciganski dumi v bălgarskite tajni govori* ['Gypsy words in Bulgarian secret languages'] (1956), Kiril Kostov identifies only a few words from Romani in the Bulgarian colloquial language of his time and even in the "secret languages" (*tajni govori*). The only exception is the so-called *čalgădžijski* (as in Argirov 1901) or *cigularski ezik* (as in Găbjuv 1900), the secret language of musicians in Bulgaria (Kostov 1956: 411, 422). Argirov (1901) identifies a Romani origin for 79 of the 163 collected words – i.e. about one half –, followed by Turkish, Greek, Romanian, Judeo-Spanish as well as one Albanian and one Bulgarian word each. The etymology of 29 further lexemes is unclear to him. He explains the great influence of Romani as follows:

> Много силниятъ цигански елементъ и по-слабиятъ турски въ чалгѫджийския езикъ се обяснява отъ обстоятелството, че въ нашитѣ музикантски групи въ турско врѣме, па и сега, които участвуватъ на сватби и други народни тържества по градове и села, първо мѣсто завзиматъ циганитѣ, които обикновено добрѣ владѣятъ и турски.
> (Argirov 1901: 30)

> ['The very strong Gypsy element and the weaker Turkish element in *čalgădžijski ezik* can be explained by the fact that in our musicians' troops in Turkish times, and also today, who take part in weddings and other popular celebrations in towns and villages, the first place is occupied by Gypsies who usually have a good command of Turkish as well.']

A very small number of Romani words can also be found in other Bulgarian argots like *tarikatski ezik* (Angelov 2014: 2189–2193). *Tarikat* refers to a certain type of young man from the interwar period who distinguished himself through arrogance, boasting and sarcasm, a smart alec, bully and Casanova. The words in *tarakatski ezik*

> [...] have a very different meaning from that in the original languages from which they were borrowed by way of strange analogies, and their figurative uses have transformed them beyond recognition. This also applies to the typical Romany (Gypsy) words балама 'fool', баро 'important man, boss, chief', гаџе 'girlfriend/boyfriend' (cf. discussion in Kostov 1956, 414 ff.), манго 'Gypsy', абе/хабе 'bread'; as well as to other words with the typical suffix -ис/из: мариз 'beating', кериз 'steal, watch', пандиз 'prison', чорис/чоравел 'theft'.
> (Angelov 2014: 2191–2192)

This sociolect is described in more detail in Mladenov (1930, 1940).

7.2.3 Czech: *Světská hantýrka*

The *mluva světských* or *světská hantýrka* (the term *hantýrka* comes from the German verb *hantieren* 'to fiddle') plays a central role in the inflow of Romani vocabulary into Czech. Puchmajer (1821) understands the term *hantýrka* in the narrower sense as Czech thief cant ("tschechische Diebessprache"), today it is rather used in a broader sense as a generic term for various Czech argots or as a synonym for *argot*. In the Bohemian Hantýrka, Yiddish was predominant for a long time, but from the second half of the nineteenth century the influence of Romani increased strongly (Leeuwen-Turnovcová 2003: 27; Hugo 2006: 23; Elšík 2017). If Hantýrka is understood in a broader sense, the *mluva světských* is its most important representative in terms of Romisms with by far the largest share. The *světští* (*lidé*) include – historically, but also up to the present day – various Rom and non-Rom groups who work in peripatetic professions. Podzimek is the first to introduce the term in his *Slovníček "světská hantýrka"* (1937) and defines it as follows:

> K lidem „světským", tj. světem jdoucím či kočovným, počítáme loutkáře, komedianty, majetníky zábavních podniků, koňské handlíře, brusiče a tuláky. Ti vytvořili hantýrku, lišící se značně od zlodějské, zejména velikým počtem slov, přejatých z jazyka cikánského.
> (Podzimek 1937: 5; quotation from Starhon 2018: 74)

['The "světští", i.e. people who wander the world or who are nomadic, include puppeteers, comedians, owners of entertainment businesses, horse traders, tool grinders and vagabonds. They created a *hantýrka* that is very different from the thief language, especially in the large number of words that come from the Gypsy language.']

In the past, the *světští* were perceived from the outside as people who moved on the borders of social conventions. They shared this fringe zone of non-sedentary lifestyle and marginalization with the Roma, so that close contacts developed (especially in the interwar period), which are also reflected in the language. The relevant Romani varieties were Bohemian Romani and the variety of the Sinti. Already Puchmajer (1821: iv–v; cf. also Starhon 2018: 72; Elšík 2017) mentions the rudimentary knowledge of Romani by so-called *bílý Cikány* ("white Gypsies"), who probably were the ancestors of today's *světští*. The *světská hantýrka* serves as a means of belonging to a group (emblematic function), deterrence of outsiders and secrecy (cryptic function), the latter being particularly relevant in the historical context (Starhon 2018: 82). It is likely that the *světská hantýrka* was also the main source for the Romisms in the Czech criminal argots. Hugo (2006: 24) defines the proportion of Romani in it at around 35%; in the example texts from 1960 published in Starhon (2018: 76–77), it is even almost 50%.

The Slovak argots have not been researched from as early nor as extensively as have the Czech ones (Mokienko and Walter 2014: 2154–2155; Odaloš 1990) and not as much can be said about them. No Romisms are mentioned in Ondrus' study of the argot of the Slovak peripatetic craftspeople (*argot slovenských vandrovných remeslníkov*, 1978), which is probably the oldest documented Slovak argot.

7.2.4 Polish argots

Compared to Czech, there are extremely few Romisms in Polish argots. Yiddish is much more strongly represented there than Romani, followed by Russian and Ukrainian, German, Greek, Latin and French in the role of donor languages (Ułaszyn 1951: 47–48). Bierich (2008: 55) nevertheless does mention Romani as a donor language for Polish argots, but without giving examples.

7.2.5 Russian and Ukrainian argots

For Russian, Barannikov's treatise *Cyganskie ėlementy v russkom vorovskom argo* ['Gypsy elements in Russian criminal argot'] (1931b) would seem to be the most relevant work on Romisms in argots. For decades it was also treated that way, being cited again and again, and having its contents reproduced by many authors (e.g. Bondaletov 1967; Stavic'ka 2005, 98–99; Horbač 2006: 370–385). Barannikov states that the argot of the Russian criminals has a relatively large Romani component and that, from there, they found their way into other argots and even into general colloquial Russian (Barannikov 1931b: 139). Four treatises serve as the basis for his investigation: Trachtenberg (1908), Popov (1912), Potapov (1927) and an unpublished card file by Larin. In total, he cites over 200 Romani borrowings in the Russian criminal argot. For a good two decades now, however, Barannikov's theses have been heavily questioned. Bessonov (undated) and Demeter, Bessonov and Kutenkov (2000) refute many of his statements and deal very critically with the ideological background of his work. In linguistics, it is primarily Šapoval (2001a, 2007b, 2008b, 2011a, 2012 etc.) who has most thoroughly deconstructed Barannikov's thesis of the great influence of the Romani varieties of Russia on the Russian and East Slavic criminal argot as a whole:

> Весьма сложным является вопрос о мифическом влиянии цыганских диалектов России на так называемый криминальный жаргон (арго). Описания последнего, возникшие в XIX веке как любительские подражания французским и иным западноевропейским изданиям, до сих пор остаются на уровне словарей дифференциального типа, фиксирующих лексические курьезы самого разнообразного свойства. Единство объекта описания не обосновывалось ничем, кроме ощущения собирателей, присовокуплявших свои собственные находки к материалам вековой и большей давности, искаженным неоднократным и торопливым копированием. В эти сборники «товара сомнительной доброты» попадали и цыганские слова.
>
> (Šapoval 2012: 13)

['The question of the mythical influence of the Gypsy dialects of Russia on the so-called criminal jargon (argot) is very difficult. Descriptions of the latter, which arose in the 19th century as amateur imitations of French and other Western European publications, still remain at the level of differential dictionaries, cataloguing lexical curiosities of the most diverse nature. The unity of the object of description was not substantiated by anything but the perceptions of the collectors, who added their own finds to centuries-old and older materials, distorted by repeated and hasty copying. These collections of "goods of dubious quality" also included Gypsy words.']

Barannikov uncritically took over a list of Romani words from Potapov (1927), and this taken-over material was passed on in the following years, such that the majority of Romisms in more recent non-standard dictionaries can be classified at most as occasionalisms or ghost words, which have little to do with linguistic reality (Šapoval 2002: 14, 2004: 115, 2008b). According to Šapoval (2011b: 57–59), the number of Romisms is generally very limited and usually has only a local scope. Among the rare regional borrowings that have been in use for a long time are the South Russian *rakló* 'tramp, thief', *šuvaní* 'experienced Romani fortune teller', *balabás* 'bacon, pork' and, the most common one, *lové* 'money'.

7.3 Romani lexicon in Slavic argots, youth slangs and colloquial varieties

In order to answer the question of which Romani items have been borrowed into Slavic historical argots as well as into contemporary youth slangs and colloquial varieties, all available material has been evaluated: This includes treatises from the nineteenth and the first half of the twentieth century, the results of existing studies on Croatian, Bulgarian and Czech, national corpora, dictionaries on youth slangs and colloquial language from the year 2000 onwards as well as crowdsourced online dictionaries that work according to the principle of the Urban Dictionary (www.urbandictionary.com).[32] A tabular overview of all collected words can be found in Appendix 2. To begin, the six Slavic languages are examined individually, which is then followed by a comparative evaluation of the most widespread Romisms in Slavic.

---

[32] The Urban Dictionary is a crowdfunded, open online dictionary that works according to the motto "define your world", i.e. any user can enter definitions for lemmas which cannot be found in standard-language dictionaries. Compared to printed dictionaries on youth slangs, which quickly become out of date, it reflects a very up-to-date language status. Equivalents of the Urban Dictionary exist for various Slavic languages.

7.3.1 Bosnian / Croatian / Serbian

For Šatrovački, Uhlik (1954) was taken as the source and, in terms of modern youth slangs and colloquial varieties, for Bosnian the word list in *Govor grada Sarajeva i razgovorni bosanski jezik* ['Speech of the city of Sarajevo and colloquial Bosnian language'] (Halilović, Tanović and Šehović 2009), for Serbian the *Beogradski frajerski rečnik* ['Belgrade cool-guy dictionary'] (Imami 2003) and the online dictionary *Vukajlija – Rečnik slenga* ['Vukajlija – Slang dictionary'] (https://vukajlija.com) and the two studies on Croatian "The Romani groups and dialects in Croatia. With a special emphasis on the Romani borrowings in the Croatian language" (Lapov 2005) and "Words of Romani origin in the Czech and Croatian languages" (Fałowski 2013) were used.[33]

Of the 102 Romani word stems that are documented for Šatrovački, the largest part (83) no longer plays a role in the contemporary language; 19 have been preserved, four have been added. Since it is not possible – as for all historical argots – to determine the frequency of use for Šatrovački, the wealth of variants in derivation is used here as an alternative indicator for the frequent and productive use of a word. We are now going to take a closer look at the most varied of the 19 Romani lexemes that have survived to this day as well as their counterparts in Bosnian / Croatian / Serbian. The ordering is alphabetical. The first number in brackets relates to the number of derivations in the historical text corpus, the second to the number of derivations in the contemporary text corpus. If known, the word stress is also given:

bul 'ass' (7/8): continuation of the meaning 'ass' (*bulja* / *buljiška* / *bul(j)ina* etc.) is observed in addition to extension of the meaning to *buljiti* 'to shit', *buljobris* 'toilet paper' and *buljouvlakač* 'scaredy-cat';

čorel 'to steal' (8/10): no noticeable changes;

das 'non-Rom; farmer; Serb; Croat etc.' (8/1): formerly exhibiting many variants, nowadays it is hardly in use; only *dasa* '(handsome, elegant, respected) man; boyfriend' is documented;

džal / *geljom* 'to go' (21/3): historically by far the most varied Romism, e.g. *džal(d)isati* / *džalirati* 'to go, to walk', *džališka* 'pedestrian', *dodžalisati* 'to come', *džaltara* 'abhorrent woman', *gljarnica* / *gljarka* 'shoes', *gljavalica* 'leg', for the contemporary language, *giljati* 'to go' etc., *gilje* 'shoes' and *giljka* 'shoe' are still documented;

---

[33] For a thorough analysis of the accomodation of Romani loan verbs into Serbian / Croatian, cf. Vučković 2017.

7.3 Romani lexicon in Slavic argots, youth slangs and colloquial varieties — 125

džukel 'dog' (5/5): historically also documented with the meaning 'horse', currently it is also used in the form of *džukac / džukela* as a pejorative name for a person;

chal 'to eat' (8/9): extension of the meaning is observed from 'to eat' (*hal(d)isati / hal* etc.) to 'greed' and 'to steal' (*halap* 'greedy person', *halapljiv* 'greedy', *hapanje* 'theft', *hapati / hapnuti* 'to steal');

love 'money' (6/18+): extremely productive in modern colloquial language, see below;

marel 'to beat' (4/15): significant extension of the meaning is observed from 'to beat; to fight' (*marisati / marnuti* 'beat', *mara* 'fight', *omarisan* 'beaten') to the areas of theft, law enforcement, money and imprisonment (*marela* 'theft', *marisana* 'prison sentence', *marica / mariola* 'police car', *marijaš* 'money' etc.);

naj negation particle (7/2): fewer variants are documented in the contemporary language;

Rom (6/6+): many creative, expressive variants are documented for the contemporary language, see below.

Newer Romisms are various derivations of *baro paj* 'sea', lit. 'big water' < *baro pani* 'idem', *duja* 'B (school grade)' < *duj* 'two', *Gurbet* as a very pejorative name for a person < *Gurbet* 'Gurbet Rom', and *šorati* 'to piss; to fight; to beat' in a remarkably large variety of derivations < *čhorel* 'to spill; to urinate etc.'. Romani items that are relatively varied in Šatrovački with 5–7 derivations, but no longer documented for contemporary Bosnian / Croatian / Serbian, are *čalavel* 'to beat; to have sex; to cheat etc.', *chochavel* 'to lie, to cheat, to deceive', *ikhel* 'to see, to look at etc.', *koro* 'blind', *khul* 'dung, dirt' and *mothovel* 'to say'.

The dissemination of Romisms in contemporary colloquial Croatian is demonstrated in a very revealing way by Fałowski (2013): He shows that *love* 'money' not only found its way into the Croatian national corpus as one of the few Romisms there at all, but is also by far the most widespread Romism in Croatian (Fig. 13):

Fałowski himself comments:

> Romani words appear in the corpus material 584 times, out of which as many as 499 lexemes – i.e. more than 90% – are forms derived from the word *lóve/love*, which confirms the unparalleled popularity of the lexeme *lova* 'money' in colloquial language. It is also very productive, which can be corroborated by the presence in the database of derivations formed from this base: *lovaš, lovator, lovatorica, lovica*.

Lapov (2005: 86), who identifies a total of 13 Romisms in Croatian, also emphasizes *lova* as being particularly widespread in colloquial language:

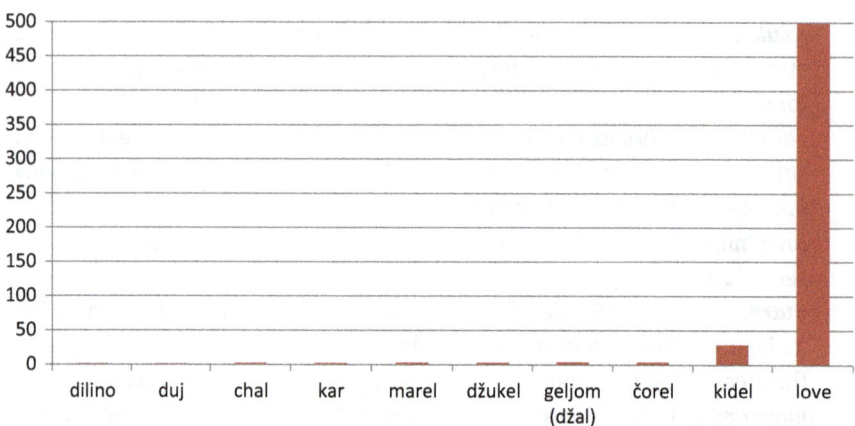

Fig. 13: Evidence for Romisms in the Hrvatski nacionalni korpus (our own presentation based on data from Fałowski 2013: 113).[34]

> It is a question of 13 basic words – verbs and nouns – which [have been] multiplied thanks to the inner productivity of the Croatian language. They are all pretty colloquial and/or slang terms, used mainly in the Croatian dialect spoken in the city of Zagreb and its surroundings. Some of them have [entered into] the local common dialectal heritage too (e.g. *hásati, gédžo*). Some others [have become] completely customary in everyday Croatian, [being] subsequently [used] in movies' subtitles, literature etc. (e.g. *lóva, lovátor, džúkac* or *džúkela*). Such terms [have] even enter[ed into] some common Croatian sayings/phrases, e.g. *lóva do króva* 'a lot of money, full of money', lit. 'money up to the roof'. Several among them are today generally employed by children or youths (e.g. *šóra, šórati, mára, márati, gíljati*). Usually, however, everybody understands these terms, even if they are not actively used by everybody!

The examined (online) dictionaries show that *love* is extremely common and productive in countless expressions, also in Serbian and Bosnian. They mention *lova / lovica / loviška* 'money', *lovočuvar* 'scrooge', *lovaš / lovator / lovan(er)* 'rich person; greedy person', *lovatorica / lovanka* 'rich woman', *lovokradica* 'female thief; woman who steals from men', *lovčuga / lovina / lovudža* 'big money'.

Especially the Romisms in youth slang (cf. vukajlija.com for Serbian) testify to linguistic wit and creativity, e.g. *Romaldinho* 'Romani boy who plays football very well', *šoroskop* 'urine analysis' or *šaje* 'no chance' as a blend of Bosnian / Croatian / Serbian *šansa* and Romani *naje*. Many also have a vulgar and / or pejorative connotation, which Lapov (2005: 86–87) also observes (for Croatian):

---

34 Translation: *dilino* 'crazy; stupid', *duj* 'two', *chal* 'to eat', *kar* 'penis', *marel* 'to beat', *džukel* 'dog', *geljom* 'I went' (*džal* 'to go'), *čorel* 'to steal', *kidel (drom)* 'to set out, to go away', *love* 'money'.

At least some of the Romani loanwords are considered to be quite vulgar, offensive, abusive or derogatory. For example, the nouns *kára*, together with its derivations, and *mindža* are commonly defined as being vulgar. The connotations of the terms *džúkela* and *džúkac* 'dog', mostly 'old, shabby dog' have brought about another meaning, namely 'man', but in the pejorative sense of 'scoundrel, bastard, ruffian, cur'. The terms *gédžo, gédža, gedžován, gadžován* have almost lost their original meaning of 'peasant' and are nowadays usually employed in the pejorative sense of 'boor, peasant, rude person, rube, cornball' and for 'Serb or Serbian peasant'.

Beyond this, some words clearly have to be classified as racist, such as the aforementioned *Gurbet* and several derivations of *Rom* on vukajlija.com.

7.3.2 Bulgarian

For the Bulgarian argots, Argirov (1901) and Kostov (1956)[35] were used as sources, for the contemporary varieties the *Rečnik na bălgarskija žargon* ['Dictionary of Bulgarian jargon'] (Armjanov 2001), the online dictionary https://bgjargon.com and the study "Semantic Processes in Lexical Adoptions from the Romani in diastratic varieties of Bulgarian" (Leschber 2002). For the first half of the twentieth century, Argirov and Kostov recorded a total of 75 Romisms; a third (25) of these have survived into modern Bulgarian, which is comparatively many. New borrowings are derivatives of *lav* 'word' (*laf* 'word; fairy tale; interesting conversation', *láfja* 'to talk'), *čhorel* 'to spill; to urinate etc.' (*šóram* 'to pee; to drink alcohol') and *Rom*. In the past quite varied but now no longer documented are derivations of *manuš* 'person; man' (*mánuk* 'Turk; lord', *mánče* 'landlord; lord', *mánuka* 'wife' etc.), *dikhel* 'to see' (*díkizi* 'eyes', *dikízim / dikízja* 'to look' etc.) and *pijel* 'to drink' (*piizán* 'drunken', *kálopis* 'wine' etc.).

Here collected are the most important words that have survived to this day, with information given on formal and derivational variants as well as on changes in meaning:

[ʔ*aver* 'second, other' (2/4): a partial shift of meaning has occurred from *avér* 'friend; professional thief' and *alavér* 'comrade' to *avér* 'friend, acquaintance; boy; man'; see below];

čorel 'to steal' (2/5): no noticeable changes;

---

35 Kostov (1956) also gives a more detailed analysis of the morphological adaptation of the Romisms to the structures of Bulgarian. In further individual studies, he examines the etymology of selected Romisms in more detail: *papín / pápinja* 'fool' (Kostov 1963b), *šošoréa* 'hare' (Kostov 1966), *me kareste* 'I don't care' and *kerisčija* 'thief' (Kostov 1974), *č(h)ang* 'leg' and *č(h)angalo* 'with long legs' (Kostov 1975).

chal 'to eat' (9/1): the wealth of forms and their semantic breadth has strongly decreased, with currently only *chabé* 'food, bread' documented; earlier *(ch)abé / abénce / abizán* 'bread', *chabésărkaf* 'mouth', *abédžij(k)a* 'baker; innkeeper' etc.;
lel 'to take' (5/2): no noticeable changes;
mangin 'possession, fortune etc.' (5/8): the wealth of forms has increased slightly; originally *mángis / mangís / mangízi* 'money', *mangízim / mangízja* 'theft';
marel 'to beat' (11/4): a decrease in the wealth of forms and a partial narrowing of the meaning are observed from originally *máris / marís / maríz* 'fight', *marizím / marízja / marizlájsvam* 'to beat', *marífčija* 'policeman', *marifčísărkaf* 'uniform' etc. to exclusively 'to beat';
mindž 'vagina' (1/10): the wealth of forms has strongly increased from exclusively *mindža* 'idem' to numerous playful, expressive variations, e.g. *mindžurija / mindžafara / mindžifurka* 'idem', *domindžos* 'miniskirt', *mindžipljaktor* 'man who has sex with many women' etc.;
phandel 'to close; to tie; to lock up' (5/11): an increase in the wealth of forms is observed within a constant semantic field comprising 'to lock up', 'detention', 'prison', e.g. *pandíz / pandís* 'prison; section', *pandízja* 'to imprison', *pandízčija* 'prisoner';
phenel 'to speak, to say' (6/2): a narrowing or change of meaning has occurred from *penizja* etc. 'to speak, to tell' to *píniz* 'joke' and *péniz* 'trick'.

Leschber's (2002) study is revealing with respect to the contemporary use of the mentioned Romisms. She presented Kostov's word list to native speakers of Bulgarian almost 50 years after it was published with the result that a large part of the words was not known by speakers of modern Bulgarian slang: accordingly, only 13 out of 73 are in use today[36] (Leschber 2002: 59). A problematic case, however, is *avér*, which is particularly emphasized in Leschber's study:

> Als interessantes Beispiel für eine Art ‚Wiederbelebung' eines Wortgebrauchs soll hier bulg. *avèr* 'Freund, Bekannter, Gefährte' dienen, das mir von einem Informanten sogar als ‚neumodisches Wort' beschrieben wurde. Es würde ‚erst seit kurzer Zeit' benutzt, wenn ‚die Bulgaren' über ‚die Roma' sprächen, und zwar genauer, über ihre Roma-Freunde. Früher habe man das Wort nicht gehört. Dann plötzlich wurde mir erklärt, dass man *avèr* im bulgarischen Fernsehen höre, und in der Zeitung lesen könne, in der Umgangssprache sei es ungebräuchlich. Dies nun stellt eine echte ‚Karriere' eines Lexems dar, das von Kostov (1956) noch dem geheimsprachlichen Wortbestand zugerechnet wurde. [...] Eine Entwicklung ist

---

[36] Namely: *aver, balama / balamurnik, barovec, gadže, kirizja / kirizim / kirizčija, levam / levkam, mangizi / mangis / mangic, mango, maris / marizim / marizja / marizčija, mekareste, mindža / mindžurija, pandiz / pandis / pandizja / pandizim / pandizen, čalnat / čaldisan / čalnosen / čalbasen*.

übrigens nicht nur für die Gebrauchssphäre des Wortes zu konstatieren, sondern auch für seine Semantik: so wurde es in Kostov (1956: 413) mit der negativ konnotierten Bedeutung 'Genosse, Berufsdieb' aufgezeichnet. Heute jedoch wird es im Bulgarischen hauptsächlich weitgehend unkonnotiert verwendet: 'Freund, Bekannter, Gefährte'; im Romani funktioniert *avèr* als Pronomen: 'anderer, der nächste, der folgende'. (Leschber 2002: 93–94)

['Bulgarian *avèr* 'friend, acquaintance, companion' shall serve here as an interesting example of a kind of 'revival' of a word's usage, which one informant even described to me as a 'new-fashioned word'. It is reportedly being used 'only as of recently' when 'the Bulgarians' talk about 'the Rom', and more precisely, about their Romani friends. Formerly the word was never heard. Then suddenly it was explained to me that you can hear *avèr* on Bulgarian television and read it in the newspaper; in colloquial language it is uncommon. This then represents a real 'career' for a lexeme, one which Kostov (1956) had ascribed to the inventory secret-language words. [. . .] Not only the sphere of use of the word has developed further, but also its semantics: it was recorded in Kostov (1956: 413) with the negatively connotated meaning 'comrade, professional thief'. Today, however, it is used in Bulgarian, for the most part, largely without any connotations: 'friend, acquaintance, companion'; in Romani, *avèr* functions as a pronoun: 'the other, another, the next, the following'.']

There is, however, another possible and even more probable etymology for *aver*:[37] It could be derived from Yiddish *chawer / chower* 'friend, comrade, mate', which goes back to Hebrew *chawer*. It was the preferred form of address among Jewish Communists and Socialist Zionists but has a less political connotation in other languages. In Austrian German, for example, *Haberer* (also *Hawerer, Hawara*) can be a friend or (booze) buddy, but also a lover or suitor (Rosten 2003: 133; Gutknecht 2010). *Haver* 'buddy, crony, dude' also exists in Hungarian. Additionally, the word could have entered via Judezmo, which also has access to Hebrew vocabulary. The loss of initial /x/ is characteristic of Macedonian, which, for speakers of Bulgarian, would give the word an additional basilectal nuance, given their attitude to Macedonian (anonymous reviewer).

Finally, it is remarkable that the Romani word *love*, which is so widespread in Bosnian / Croatian / Serbian, plays no role at all in Bulgarian, neither historically nor at present.

7.3.3 Czech

The most extensive work to cover both the historical argots and the contemporary diastratic varieties of Czech is *Slovník nespisovné češtiny* ['Dictionary of unwritten

---

[37] I want to thank the audience of the 14th International Conference of Romani Linguistics for their insightful discussion of this question.

Czech'] (Hugo 2006). It summarizes Romisms from the following works: Puchmajer (1821), Juda (1902), Bredler (1914), Rippl (1926), Nováček (1929), Oberpfalcer (1934) and Podzimek (1937). The online dictionary *Čeština 2.0 – Slovník, který tvoříte vy* ['Czech 2.0 – The dictionary created by you'] (https://cestina20.cz/slovnik) as well as the essays "Words of Romani origin in the Czech and Croatian languages" (Fałowski 2013) and "Lexikální romismy v češtině" ['Lexical Romisms in Czech'] (Elšík 2017) are used here, in addition, for the contemporary language. One problematic aspect of Hugo (2006) is, however, that it summarizes only a part of the Romisms from Podzimek (1937), where about 330 certain Romisms are listet, some with and some without a Romani etymology given by the author (anonymous reviewer; cf. also the critical remarks in Elšík 2017, section 4). Unfortunately, Podzimek's original publication was not accessible to us. Against this background, the actual number of Romisms in Czech argots has to be estimated significantly higher.

Most of the 134 Romani items – counted on the basis of the available literature – with counterparts in Czech argots no longer play a role in modern youth slang and colloquial language. 27 of them have been preserved (some being more common than others) and four have been added (*degešák* 'despicable person' < *degeš* 'riff-raff', *tátoš* 'homosexual' < *tato* 'warm; homosexual', *parno* 'crystal meth', ?*čang* 'thigh' < *čang* 'leg'). The most important Romisms still in use in Czech today are:

beng 'devil' (6/8): a narrowing of the semantic spectrum has occurred; originally 'devil', as in Romani, alongside *bengík / bengoro* 'policeman in a puppet show' and *bengores* 'evil', currently related only to the police (*bengo(š)* 'policeman', *benga (v plechu)* 'policemen (on patrol)', *bengokára* 'police car', *bengárna* 'police station');

čorel 'to steal' (14/17): no noticeable changes in meaning have occurred, while exhibiting nonce creations in youth slang, such as *čórkatlon* 'thief triathlon (= run to the swimming pool, swim, ride home on a stolen bike)';

dilino 'crazy; stupid' (4/9): a greater wealth of formal variants and hardly any semantic changes are observed; contemporary examples: *dyliňák / dyliňak / dylina / dilina* 'madman, idiot, fool', *dylinka* 'stupid young woman, fixated only on her appearance', *dylinec* 'psychiatry';

džukel 'dog' (2/13): the wealth of variants has increased, exhibiting more creative and diverse use; historically documented are only *čukl / žukl* 'dog', currently also playful, expressive derivations such as *čoklbuřt* 'cheap salami', lit. 'dog sausage', *čoklmafie* 'group of irresponsible dog owners' and *čoklvajler* 'unspecified breed of dog', but also *čokložrout* 'dog eater' as a racist description for East Asian people;

gadžo, gadži 'non-Rom(ni)' (4/6): no noteworthy changes;

7.3 Romani lexicon in Slavic argots, youth slangs and colloquial varieties — 131

chal 'to eat' (3/8): the wealth of formal variants has increased with no significant semantic expansion;

kerel 'to do, to work etc.' (5/14): a remarkable increase in the wealth of variants has occurred, in part within the newly created semantic field of tattooing: *vykérovat* 'to tattoo', *(po)kérovaný* 'tattooed', *kérka / k(h)érko* 'tattoo', *kérkař* 'tattooist (male)', *kérkarka* 'tattooist (female)', *kérkárna* 'tattoo studio' and the nonce creations *kérkonoš* 'tattooed person', *kérotoman* 'person obsessed with tattoos';

love 'money' (6/6): no noteworthy changes;

Rom (4/1+): numerous new playful and expressive nonce creations are observed, e.g. *rombudsman* 'representative for national minorities', *romofobie* 'fear of the Rom', *romotluk* 'skinhead', *romosvod* 'Romani community that serves as a scapegoat for all possible problems'.

In addition, *kulový* 'shit, shitty; I don't give a shit' < *khul* 'dung, dirt' has found its way into common colloquial language (Elšík 2017). *Phandel*, which was very productive in the argots (e.g. *p(h)andelit, p(h)anglit* 'to arrest' etc., *panglo* 'policeman') is no longer documented. Worth mentioning is also Fałowski's (2013) research in the Czech national corpus (https://korpus.cz), which, thanks to its subcorpora for spoken language (BMK, PMK, ORAL 2006, ORAL 2008), provides revealing results about present-day Romisms in Czech. 25 Romani stems are represented there: "the most widespread are continuations of the words *džukel* and *khulo*, which are not only recorded in the Prague corpus of spoken language (PMK)" (Fałowski 2013: 106). Fałowski's results can be depicted in Fig. 14.

All these results together show that Romani is very vibrant and productive in the youth slang and colloquial variety of Czech.

To get at least an impression of the contemporary situation in Slovak (although there is not sufficient data on historical argots, which makes Slovak unsuitable for the research questions of this chapter), two dictionaries were analyzed: *Slovník slovenského slangu* ['Dictionary of Slovak slang'] (Hochel 1993) and *Slovník slangu a hovorovej slovenčiny* ['Dictionary of slang and spoken Slovak'] (Oravec 2014). Both of them contain a small number of Romisms that are also listed in the attachment, namely: *bašavel / bašálel* 'excessive party', *bulo / bulko / bula* 'dull, uncouth person; villager; non-Rom', *čongáľa, čungáľa, čongála* '(long) leg', *čúro* 'knife', *degeš* 'fool; Rom, Gypsy', *dilin(k)o, dilina* 'fool, idiot', *džamore / Džamorák / džamorák* 'Rom, Gypsy', fem. *džamoráčka / Džamoráčka* (cf. also *more!*), *čokel / čoklík* '(small) dog', *kár* 'penis', *kandel* 'stench', *pangel* 'policeman' / *pangelnica* 'police station' as well as several derivations of *čor* 'thief', *čhaj* '(Romani) girl; daughter', *čhavo* '(Romani) boy; son', *čhorel* 'to urinate; to spill', *dikh!* 'look!', *gadžo* 'non-Rom', *chal* 'to eat', *kerel* 'to do' modified to 'to tattoo',

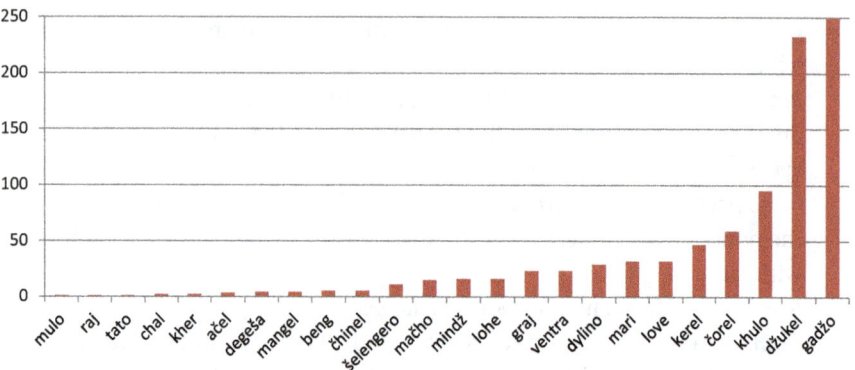

Fig. 14: Evidence for Romisms in the Czech national corpus (our own presentation, based on data from Fałowski 2013: 107–112; lohe, ventra and mari are presumably not Romani).[38]

love 'money', *marel* 'to beat' and *Rom*. Variants of *beng*, which is widespread in Czech, are not documented in the dictionaries.

7.3.4 Polish

In contrast to the languages discussed so far, Romisms are remarkably scarce in Polish, as Fałowski (2013: 96) confirms.

The following dictionaries on Polish argots were searched unsuccessfully for Romisms: Estreicher ([1903] 1979), Kurka ([1907] 1979), Ludwikowski and Walczak ([1922] 1979), Ułaszyn (1951), Budziszewska (1957) and Kania (1995). For the contemporary language, the dictionaries by Czeszewski (2001, 2006) and Lubaś (2001–2006) as well as the online dictionary *Miejski słownik slangu i mowy potocznej* ['City dictionary of slang and colloquial language'] (www.miejski.pl) were analyzed. Almost all of the few references to Romani are found in the latter. Accordingly, the most productive Romani lexeme in Polish is *čhavo* '(Romani) boy; son': The *Miejski słownik* contains the entries *czabo* 'boy' and *czawuś* 'person who shuns work and / or uses others for their own purposes' as well as *ciabar(ak)* and

---

38 Translation (excl. *lohe, ventra* and *mari*): *mulo* 'dead; ghost of a dead person', *raj* 'lord', *tato* 'warm; homosexual', *chal* 'to eat', *kher* 'house', *ačhel* 'to stay; to live', *degeša* 'riff-raff', *mangel* 'to ask for; to beg', *beng* 'devil', *čhinel* 'to cut; to write', *šelengero* 'policeman', *mačho* 'fish', *mindž* 'vagina', *graj* 'horse', *dylino* 'crazy; stupid', *love* 'money', *kerel* 'to do; to work', *čorel* 'to steal', *khulo* 'dung, dirt', *džukel* 'dog', *gadžo* 'non-Rom'.

*ciabata*³⁹ as pejorative names for a Rom. *Czaja* 'girl' is derived from Romani *čhaj* '(Romani) girl; daughter'. *Gadzio*.M and *gadzi*.F are borrowed as designations for non-Rom. *Mores* probably goes back to Romani *more!* 'Hey, dude, buddy! etc.', which is a salutation for a well-known person or a friend; however, in colloquial Polish it is used as a very derogatory, racist term for a Rom or, according to the definition in *Miejski słownik*, for a 'dark-skinned person who begs to buy cigarettes or alcohol'. *Dyk*, as an expression of surprise or fascination, could be traced back to Romani *dikh!* 'look!' and *zmarany* 'exhausted, tired' to *marel* 'to beat, to hit'.

7.3.5 Russian

The most important source for Romisms in the East Slavic languages is, in historical and contemporary terms, the *Kratkij slovar' cyganizmov v vostočnoslavjanskich jazykach* ['Short dictionary of Gypsyisms in the East Slavic languages'] (Šapoval 2012). With regard to argots, it includes the works of Dobrovol'skij (1897, 1908, 1916), Tichanov (1899), Putincev (1906), Barannikov (1931b) and Potapov (1927) and subjects all actual and apparent Romisms to a critical analysis. However, the assessment of which lemmas can securely be counted among the Romisms in Russian turns out to be extremely difficult, since the historical works are reliable to quite varying degrees, and in many cases Šapoval does not come to a conclusive judgment. Particularly problematic are for example numerals, which play a major role in Barannikov (1931b), because it is difficult to determine to what extent they were actually used in Russian argots. Each individual case was decided after carefully weighing up the sources. In addition to Šapoval (2012), the online dictionary *Slovar' molodëžnogo slenga* ['Dictionary of youth slang'] (https://teenslang.su) and the Russian National Corpus (NKRJa, http://ruscorpora.ru) were used for the contemporary language.

Of 58 Romani word stems from the historical sources, only eight are recorded for present-day Russian. *Deš* 'ten', *gras* 'horse', *pandž* 'five' and *raklo / -i* 'boy; girl' were widespread in the argots (7–10), but are no longer in use today. The nine stems still relevant today are:

balo 'pig' (3/1): an extension of the meaning has occurred from 'bacon' (*balabás / balavás*), 'sausage' (*baljásina*) to *balabás* 'food; delicacy; failure';
čhavo 'Romani boy' (2/7): a change in meaning has occurred from *č(j)ámoro* 'litterbug' to *čav* 'gopnik', a derogatory term for a (criminal) youth from a

---

39 The similar form *ciapaty* is also a racist term for a person from a Middle Eastern country or for a person with dark skin (https://www.miejski.pl/slowo-Ciapaty).

dubious background; also in use are *čávyj / čavélla / čavél(a) / čavėl(a)* 'Rom, Gypsy', always with a pejorative connotation;

džuv 'louse' (1/3): constantly occurs in *čuvák* 'boy, man, guy', with newer forms *čuvícha / čuvačók*, see below;

gilabel 'to sing; to play (an instrument)' (3/3): consistently occurs in the semantic field of music: *lábat'/ labát' / lábuchat'* 'to make music, to play (an instrument)', *lábuch* 'musician';

chal 'to eat' (5/17): the wealth of forms has greatly increased, yielding in the contemporary language *cháv(a) / chavló* 'mouth; ivories; food', *chávka / chavanína* 'food', *chavúl'nja / chávnja / chavélla* 'cafeteria, school canteen' and *(za)chávat'* 'to eat', and the range of meaning has expanded to include 'to understand, to catch on, to believe';

ladž 'shame, disgrace' (3/18): a very large variety of forms are observed from *oblažát'* 'to cheat, to defraud, to betray' and *oblážnik / -ica* 'fraud' to *lažát'* 'to make a mistake, to do sth. wrong (in general and especially while making music); to embarrass so.', *lážnja* 'nonsense, crap', *lažók / lažúk / lažák* etc. 'bad pupil', *lažóvost'* 'mess, botchery', *lažóvyj / lažëvyj / lážnyj* 'bad, deficient, unsuccessful';

love 'money' (5/14): also exhibiting a greatly increased wealth of forms, with a slight narrowing of meaning from 'money' and 'theft' to just 'money' and 'profit, income', e.g. *lavė / lavé / lav'ë / lėvė*;

mindž 'vagina' (5/2): originally *minžá* 'vagina', *menževát'sja* etc. 'to be afraid, to be cowardly', now with a narrowing of meaning to 'to be afraid, to hesitate'[40] (*menževat'sja*);

parno 'white' (3/1): most probably independent borrowing of *parn(j)ák / parnjága* '25-ruble banknote' and *párno* 'crystal meth' in different speech subcommunities (anonymous reviewer).

Additionally, there is *nané / nanė / naný* '(there are) none', which is only used in modern youth slang and not in argots. It is noteworthy that numerous Romisms occur in the NKRJa, but all of them belong to only five Romani word stems: *džuv* (*čuvák, čuvícha, čuvačók*), *chal* (*chávat', schávat', chávka, chávčik, chavál'nik, zachávat', zachávat', nachávat'sja*), *gilavel* (*lábuch, lábat'*), *ladž* (*oblažát'sja, lažanút'sja, lažát', lažóvyj, oblažát', lážnyj, lažovost', lažóvščik*) and *love* (*lavė, lėvė*) (Fig. 15).[41]

---

40 Šapoval (2012) also traces *menža / menta* 'reverse gear' and *pominžirit' / pominžirovat' / pominžurit'* 'to change' back to this source.
41 For *labúch*, cf. also Šapoval (2001a, b).

7.3 Romani lexicon in Slavic argots, youth slangs and colloquial varieties — 135

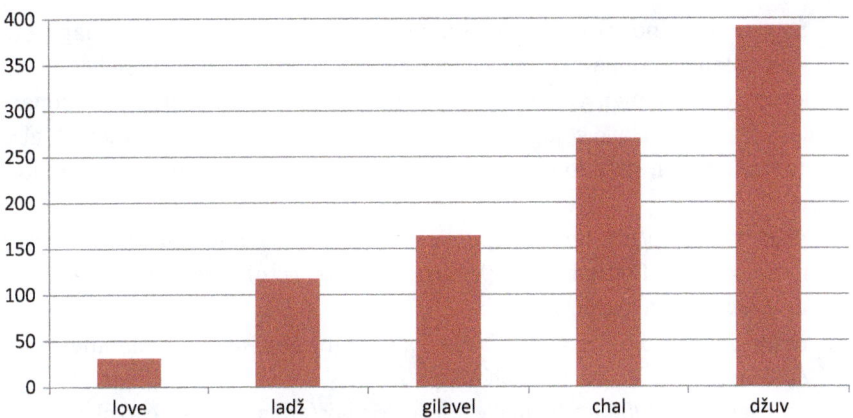

Fig. 15: Evidence for Romisms in the NKRJa (our own data).[42]

It is striking that the derivations of *ladž* and *gilabel*, which are so widespread and varied in Russian, do not play a role in any other Slavic language, apart from one known exception in Bulgarian.

Finally, the disputed etymology of *čuvák* requires more detailed explanation. While D'jačok and Šapoval (1988) have suspected that it was to be traced back to *čhavo* 'Romani boy', Šapoval (2012: 566–567) casts doubt on this explanation, partly because of the problematic use of *čhavo* for non-Roma. He offers several alternative etymologies, the most convincing of which is *džuv* 'louse' as the source, especially since there are parallel cases in Czech and Bulgarian jargons (Hübschmannová 1994: 57; Kostov 1956: 416).

7.3.6 Ukrainian

Very few Romisms have been recorded for Ukrainian argots, including those of the Lirniki and Ofeni / Afeni. Apart from *č'chája* 'girl' < *čhaj* 'idem', *rakló* 'tramp' (adj. *rakljác'kij*), *ráklyj* 'thievish' < *raklo* 'non-Romani boy' and *lav'ë* 'money' < *love* 'idem', attempts to trace words from these argots back to Romani are rejected by Šapoval (2012). In other argots, there are at least *du-dékonnyj* 'two-hryvna-' < *duj* 'two', *lačó* 'good' < *lačho* 'idem' and *maribé* 'death; skeleton' / *maribyj* 'deadly' < *maribe* 'death'.

---

[42] Translation: *love* 'money', *ladž* 'shame, disgrace', *gilavel* 'to sing; to play (an instrument)', *chal* 'to eat', *džuv* 'louse'.

Šapoval does not provide any examples for the contemporary language, but the youth slang dictionary *Peršyj slovnyk ukraïns'koho molodižnoho slenhu* ['First dictionary of Ukrainian youth slang'] (Pyrkalo 1997) and the online dictionary Myslovo (http://myslovo.com) do. Four Romani items, which, by the way, are also central in Russian, have to be particularly emphasized because of their productivity:

chal 'to eat' (0/10): literally *(po)chávaty* 'eat, chew' and *chávalo / chávka / chávčik* 'food', figuratively *(za)chávaty* 'to like', *(pro)chávaty* 'to understand' and *prochavanyj* 'experienced';

džuv 'louse' (0/6): *čuvák / čuvílo* 'boy, man, guy' and in feminine forms *čuvícha / čuváčica / čuví / čuvýrdla*;

gilabel (0/9): *(z)labáty* 'to make music, to play (an instrument); to play wrong (when making music); to work', *pidlábuvaty / pidlabáty* 'to play along', *lába / labandžós* 'music', *lábuch* 'musician (general and in restaurants)', *pidlábka* 'background musician', *lábuda* 'nonsense, nuts';

ladž 'shame, disgrace' (0/8): *láža* 'unpleasant, embarrassing situation; mistake in making music', *lažóvyj* 'uncomfortable, embarrassing; bad, inferior', *(na)lažáty* 'to do sth. wrong or embarrassing', *lažonúty* 'to deliberately do sth. bad to so.', *lažonútysja* 'to do stupid things', *oblažáty* 'to reject, to criticize', *oblažátysja* 'to be ashamed'.

Also documented for Ukrainian are: *napytysja v drabadán* 'to get very drunk' < *drab* 'drink; drug; poison', *balabás* 'head' < *balevas* 'bacon' (with an unclear change in meaning), *dik!* as an exclamation of self-praise < *dikhel* 'to look, to see', *rakló* as a term for a cheeky, indecent or clumsy person < *raklo* '(non-Romani) boy', *lindík* 'clitoris' (also in Romani) and *lavé* 'money' < *love* 'idem'.

7.3.7 The most frequent Romisms in Slavic diastratic varieties overall

For four out of the six Slavic languages (Bosnian, Croatian and Serbian are counted as one language for practical reasons) investigated here, the following lexemes from Romani have been taken over into their argots and thus count among those most widespread in Slavic in the nineteenth and first half of the twentieth century: *čorel* 'to steal', *čhavo* 'Romani boy; son', *dilino / delino* 'crazy; stupid', *džukel* 'dog', *džuv* 'louse', *gadžo / gadži* 'non-Rom(ni)', *graj / grast* 'horse' / *grasni* 'mare', *chal* 'to eat', *kalo* 'black', *kar* 'penis', *lačho* 'good, nice; right', *ma(n)(d)ro* 'bread', *mindž* 'vagina', *phandel* 'to close; to tie; to lock up' / *phandlo* 'policeman'. For four of the six Slavic languages, *chal* 'to eat' and *mindž* 'vagina' also occur in the contemporary language; due to their widespread distribution in the argots, it is not surprising that they have survived to the present day. For three out of six languages, *čorel* 'to steal', *džukel* 'dog', *gadžo / gadži* 'non-Rom(ni)', *love* 'money', *marel* 'to beat' and *Rom / Romni / Romanes* are recorded, the last three also for the argots of three languages. These results fit quite well with the observations by Matras (2002: 249) cited at the beginning on other European languages: He named *čor-, mang-, ma(n)ro, gadžo / gadži* and *love* as the most frequently borrowed Romani stems.

7.4 Summary

Of course, in the present study it was possible to record only what has been documented in writing within the past decades and it cannot be ruled out that other Romisms exist or have existed in Slavic languages beyond that. However, due to the careful evaluation of as wide a range of sources as possible and the discussion of the findings with native speakers of the respective Slavic languages, it can be assumed that the results presented here come relatively close to the linguistic reality. It has been shown that, in Russian, around a seventh, in Bosnian / Croatian / Serbian and Czech (without consideration of Podzimek 1937), around a fifth and, in Bulgarian, around a third of the Romani lexemes from the historical argots have 'survived' up to now. It is difficult to make a statement with respect to Ukrainian as there is almost no historical evidence (the same goes for Slovak), and, in Polish, Romisms are generally marginal. The extent of Romisms in the individual languages also roughly correlates with the size of the Roma population in the respective language area: As expected, a particularly large number of Romisms can be found in Czech and the South Slavic languages, while very few Romisms are documented for Polish; Russian and Ukrainian are in between. The most widespread modern Romisms already existed for the most part in the argots; they have been preserved over many decades, have undergone formal and semantic extensions and have, at the same time, 'advanced socially' from the secret languages of socially marginalized groups into the modern diastratic varieties.

For the future, it would be desirable to complete the list with data from the remaining Slavic (standard) languages, especially Macedonian and Slovene. A lot of research still has to be done on Macedonian sociolects (Mokienko and Walter 2014: 2155), for which respective dictionaries are widely missing. For a study of Macedonian argots, the works of Polenakoviḱ (1951a, 1951b, 1952) can be useful (cf. also Minova-Ǵurkova 2003: 144–145). Trenevski's (1997) jargon dictionary includes *buljar / buljaš* 'no-good, fool' and *buljaši se* 'to act like a fool' < *bul* 'butt', *domindžos* 'mini-skirt' and *domindžosana* 'girl wearing a mini-skirt' < *mindža* 'cunt', *kidavela* 'to clear off; to play truant' < *kidel (drom)* 'to set out, to go away' and *karabatka* 'penis' < *kar* 'idem'. Romisms definitely exist in contemporary colloquial Macedonian as well, e.g. *mindža* 'cunt' and *džukela* 'street dog, mutt (also as a derisive term for a person)' (anonymous reviewer), but they still need to be systematically collected and analyzed. For the *plintovska spraha* or *rokovnjak*, the argot of Slovene vagabonds, Jagić (1895: 34–35) named *bakerman* < *bakro* 'sheep' and *klavati* 'to jump' < *khelava* 'to dance; to jump'. In addition, *pošati* 'to buy' is traced back to *phučel* 'to ask (for), to demand'. For a thorough analysis, reliable dictionaries on Slovene youth slang and colloquial varieties would be necessary.

8 Writing Romani with 'Slavic' alphabets

Traditionally, Romani was passed on from generation to generation exclusively in an oral manner and the written form began to play a greater role only in the course of the twentieth century. Until about a hundred years ago, no texts written by the Roma themselves existed. The earliest attempts to find an orthography for Romani were made by non-Roma, who wrote down the language by ear and against the background of their own more familiar tongues. The first evidence of written Romani is found in England and dates back to 1547 (Bartosz 2009: 154). For several decades now, the Roma have been using their language(s) more and more naturally in writing, and today writing is by no means an exception (Matras 1999b: 97). Nevertheless, despite several attempts, no worldwide written standard for Romani has yet been established. Instead, it has been and continues to be written spontaneously, resulting in countless spelling variations; Bartosz (2004: 115) lists a dozen spellings for the collocation *romani čhib* alone: *romani czib, romani cib, romani chib, romani chiw, romani tsiw, romani tsiv, romani tscheeb, rromani chib, romani sib, romani sip, xomani ćip, romani chib, rhomani ćhib, romanyj sip, kxomani tchib*. (While some of these are different spellings of identical forms, others represent different phonological forms.) This does not even include spellings in alphabets other than Latin. This great variability, combined with a lack of a separate state territory, a central government and sufficient financial and organizational resources, is a barrier to the international implementation of a standardized orthography.

The great diversity of smaller national and regional undertakings to implement a written standard for Romani is particularly evident in the Slavic countries. In the following, eleven proposals from eight countries (Russia, Ukraine, Czech Republic, Slovakia, North Macedonia, Bulgaria, Serbia and Poland) for the creation of an alphabet and an orthography for Romani will be presented and compared according to the following questions: Which writing systems and orthographies served as models? What solutions were found to represent the phonetic peculiarities of Romani by recourse to solutions from Slavic languages and orthographies? Which orthographic principles were chosen? And: Have the proposals been accepted by the language community in question? The theoretical basis for the analysis is found in the works of Smalley (1964) and Coulmas (1989) on the creation of alphabets for hitherto unwritten languages. It will also be worked out as to which of the criteria named by Smalley and Coulmas are particularly important for Romani in Slavic-speaking countries, where either the Latin or the Cyrillic script – or both – with different orthographies are used.

First of all, however, it is important to understand what value writing has for the Roma in general and what attitudes exist among them towards writing.

8.1 The role of literacy in Romani culture

Following Ong (1982), it is very important that primarily oral cultures should in no way be regarded as primitive or deficient, but as equal to literate cultures. The problem of a – conscious or unconscious – devaluation of orality can be explained quite simply by the difficulties for a literal society to imagine how an oral culture works. It is as if one wanted to explain the meaning of 'horse' by beginning from the idea of a car (Ong 1982: 12–13). In an oral culture, sounds have a different relationship to time; they exist only for a moment and cannot be conserved. Therefore, the spoken word is of great importance, it is the most important guide to social action, just as Hebrew *dabar* means 'word' and 'event' at the same time (Ong 1982: 32).

8.1.1 Romani culture as an oral culture?

In traditional Romani culture, very often narrative and lyric forms (fairy tales, riddles, proverbs, songs etc.) are used to orally convey important information. This regulates life in the group and the part that each member plays in it. Thus, the group's cultural identity is honed and passed on from generation to generation (Toninato 2014: 46, 48). For a very long time, Romani culture has been perceived as an exclusively oral one – "nicht zuletzt deshalb, weil sich diese Zuschreibung [...] problemlos mit den essenzialistischen Meinungen über kulturelle Rückständigkeit und Anpassungsunfähigkeit verbinden liess [sic]" ['not least because this ascription [...] can be linked smoothly with essentialistic opinions about cultural backwardness and the unability to adapt.'] (Kurth 2008: 77). Both Kurth and Toninato advocate that one should not strictly separate orality and literacy, because of the countless hybrid forms:

> [T]he lack of an alphabetical writing system does not automatically imply the absence of all forms of writing, since writing is a much broader phenomenon encompassing the production and the use of graphic systems for communicative purposes. (Toninato 2014: 53)

It would be more correct to say: Communication that is based on alphabetic writing is not central to Romani culture; however, the Roma have developed their own ways of passing on information over the centuries in ways other than oral, above all using non-alphabetic graphic signs.

A historical example can be found in Piasere (1985: 162): When a group of Roma was travelling and, on their way, had nothing extraordinary to report to a following group, this was signaled by tying three bunches of herbs to a branch by the wayside or crossroads, with a small stone tied to the first bunch. In dangerous situations, for example during escape, following groups were warned by scattering the herbs on the ground in the middle of the road. Among the Slovene Roma, this way of communication is called *tragi* 'signs', often also *patrin*, the Romani word for 'leaf' (Toninato 2014: 55–59). The linguist and ethnographer Heinrich von Wlislocki[43] (1994: 142) wrote down his observations about a group of "Upper Hungarian travelling Gypsies" ("oberungarische (marmarosche) Wanderzigeuner"), whose leader wanted to communicate to the following group(s) the place where he had stayed on the Wednesday after the fifth Sunday after Whitsun: a rag was tied to a tree in the direction of travelling; it was provided with five (for the number of Sundays) stitches of red wool (the sign of the leader) lengthwise and three stitches across (for the three days of the week). Romani women in Wlislocki's times additionally used so-called *čine* signs – *čine* is the name for vagrant activities of women, such as selling small items, begging and fortune-telling –, which were written on house walls. Wlislocki (1994: 144) mentions, among others, a double cross, which means "inhumane treatment", or a double circle, which means "very good people". Both kinds of signs are closely linked with the traditional vagrant lifestyle of the Roma and are invisible to outsiders. With the increasing tendency towards a sedentary lifestyle, these forms of communication have gradually lost their importance.

Furthermore, the Roma have, at all times, been under the influence of the literary cultures surrounding them, even though the majority of them were not literate themselves (Toninato 2014: 1). If it became necessary for them, they were able to write; however, for a long time, they had restricted access to writing or deliberately avoided taking over the literacy of the majority population in order to stave off foreign influence from affecting their own culture. It was only a few decades ago that the approach of the Roma to writing began to change. Consequently, they are presently facing the dilemma of wanting to keep their own, valued culture but being less and less able to prevent themselves from omnipresent literacy, which also offers better chances for education and employment. The critical attitude of many Roma to schooling guarantees the preservation of their culture to a certain degree but, on the other hand, hinders their chances of social advancement, which brings economic independence and more integration into the society at large. It is important to understand that the transition from orality to literacy does not simply mean a change in manner of communication, rather it brings with it profound changes in social structures. Against this background,

---

[43] Tcherenkov and Laederich (2004: 571) correctly point out numerous errors in Wlislocki's works, but not explicitly in this one.

it is difficult to decide whether literacy is rather useful or harmful for the Roma. Ong (1982: 15) sums up the dilemma as follows:

> This awareness is agony for persons rooted in primary orality, who want literacy passionately but who also know very well that moving into the exciting world of literacy means leaving behind much that is exciting and deeply loved in the earlier oral world. We have to die to continue living.

8.1.2 Possibilities of writing Romani

In spite of this dilemma, the writing of Romani seems to be inexorable and has, in fact, been practiced for many decades already. Apart from letters, poetic and narrative anthologies, texts with a symbolic function such as bible translations and political publications,[44] especially online communication in Romani is gaining ground:

> The establishment of Romani-language websites and email discussion lists from around 1995 onwards has changed the face of written communication in Romani completely. It is impossible to estimate the number of Romani-language email users; the figure is definitely rising rapidly. Email has given Rom from different countries, who do not necessarily share a second language, a medium for spontaneous written communication in Romani.
> (Matras 2002: 257)

Very often and especially in online communication, Romani is scripted spontaneously by way of the alphabet and orthography known to the writer, i.e. the alphabet and orthography of the respective majority language. This is the most unsystematic, but probably the most widespread solution for writing the language.

To find a more systematic approach, attempts have been made since the 1970s to standardize Romani. At the 4th International Romani Congress in Serock near Warsaw in 1990, a proposal was submitted by the language commission of the International Romani Union (IRU)[45] for a worldwide uniform orthography on the basis of the Latin alphabet. In charge was Marcel Cortiade (Courthiade). This alphabet, consisting of the graphs ⟨a⟩, ⟨b⟩, ⟨c⟩, ⟨ć⟩, ⟨ćh⟩, ⟨d⟩, ⟨e⟩, ⟨f⟩, ⟨g⟩, ⟨h⟩, ⟨x⟩, ⟨i⟩, ⟨j⟩, ⟨k⟩, ⟨kh⟩, ⟨l⟩, ⟨m⟩, ⟨n⟩, ⟨o⟩, ⟨p⟩, ⟨r⟩, ⟨rr⟩, ⟨s⟩, ⟨ś⟩, ⟨t⟩, ⟨th⟩, ⟨u⟩, ⟨v⟩, ⟨z⟩, ⟨θ⟩, ⟨ʒ⟩, along with a system of orthographic rules, was officially accepted on April 8th, 1990, by a congregation of Roma from 20 countries. The project and its history are elaborately described in Courthiade (2012) and elsewhere. However, it is a matter of

---

[44] On text forms and motivations for writing in Romani, cf. Matras (1999b).
[45] The IRU (in Romani: *Internacionalno Romano Jekhetanibe*) was founded in 1978 during the 2nd International Romani Congress in Geneva and is the most important international union of Romani people.

some controversy: Igla (1991a: 87) criticizes especially the "abstract morphographemes" of the Warsaw alphabet (see also the criticism in Kochanowski 1995 and Friedman 1995). It has been used in practice,[46] but not as widely spread as it was hoped for by its author. Less well-known, but worth mentioning, is the attempt at standardization by the Spaniard Gitano Juan de Dios Ramirez Heredia, which has, however, not been picked up by other Roma (Matras 1997: 112). Apart from this proposal, also Kenrick (1981) and others have discussed possibilities for finding a standardized orthography for the international Romani community, however, a generally accepted solution has so far not emerged.

The only area in which a relatively uniform standard was able to be established is in linguistics. Although it has never been explicitly codified, a convention for writing Romani in linguistic works has developed over the decades. It makes use of the Latin alphabet, háčeks (in Romology: *čiriklos*, lit. 'birds') for the notation of palato-alveolar consonants (⟨š⟩, ⟨ž⟩, ⟨č⟩), the grapheme ⟨h⟩ for aspirated consonants (⟨kh⟩, ⟨ph⟩, ⟨th⟩, ⟨čh⟩) and ⟨x⟩ for the velar fricative. However, even here we find deviations from the established convention (Matras 1999a: 488, 2002: 254; Heinschink and Cech 2013: 72).

There is also an ongoing trend that leads away from an international standardization of Romani orthography towards smaller, national or regional approaches. The examples from the present chapter underline this development. Hübschmannová and Neustupný formulated a plea already in 1996 rather drastically but correctly:

> [. . .], we cannot wait for the development of an international standard of Romani lest we risk that, in the meantime, the language disappears. The international standard, if needed, can be developed alongside the pluricentric standard.

In accordance with this "pluricentric standard" (Friedman 2005: 163 calls it "polycentric"), writers of Romani often use the alphabet and orthography of the majority language in their country. Matras (1997: 114) takes it as an advantage that these projects are smaller in size and involve a manageable circle of people who support the idea and are ready to actively work on it. Although there are usually one or two people in charge, these projects are not one-man endeavors, which is beneficial to their success. Furthermore, they address the language community in their own variety and with an alphabet that can be learned without much effort due to its proximity to that of the majority language of the country.

---

[46] E.g., in Romania, where a government-supported initiative introduced the alphabet for the school curriculum in dozens of schools with a high number of Romani children (Matras 2014: 125). Furthermore, the IRU and the academic journal *Studia Romologica* (www.studiaromologica.pl) use it for international publications.

8.2 Creating an alphabet for Romani in eight Slavic-speaking countries

By the somewhat simplified formulation "creating an alphabet" we understand the introduction of a script and an orthography for a hitherto unwritten language. This implementation can stand for itself or can be part of a larger standardization process which also involves other levels of the language. Challenges and possibilities that can arise during this process are validly presented in Smalley (1964) and, based on this, in Coulmas (1989: 225–240). Hence, their findings shall serve as the theoretical basis of the later analysis.

8.2.1 Theoretical background

To Coulmas (1989: 226), a good orthography is more than a mere transcription system. Writing systems and orthographies are emotionally charged, they represent a mirror of the identity of the language community in question and possess strong symbolic power – therefore, not only linguistic, but also social aspects have to be considered. Smalley (1964) compiles a list of five criteria, which is discussed and further elaborated by Coulmas:

1. *Maximum motivation for the learner*: By this, Smalley and Coulmas refer to the above-mentioned fact that the language community has to accept the writing system, i.e. that its success does not depend on linguistic factors only. Language attitudes play an important role, especially when it comes to the imitation of or – on the contrary – demarcation against another writing system, usually that of the majority population of the country in question. It can either serve as a prestigious model worth copying or as a negative example to deviate from (Coulmas 1989: 227).

2. *Maximum representation of speech*: The idea behind this criterium is that an orthography should represent the spoken language as faithfully as possible, which, however, is not easy to apply in practice. First, the problem of language-internal variation must be solved, i.e. the question must be answered as to which variety should serve as the basis. This alone can lead to many difficulties through potential discrimination against a part of the language community (Coulmas 1989: 229). Romani is divided into a huge number of varieties worldwide, whereas none of them possesses an especially high supra-regional prestige and would therefore be more appropriate than others for the leading role. Once this difficulty is resolved, the criterion of maximum representation of the respective spoken lan-

guage can, according to Smalley (1964), best be achieved by a phonematic transcription, i.e. by the principle that every phoneme is represented by exactly one grapheme. Coulmas sees no reason to refuse this approach in general, however, he indicates that orthographies empirically move further away from simple phonematic representation over the years:

> [M]ature alphabetic orthographies encode morphological and lexical information in addition to phonemic information; and mature readers make use of this information more than they do of letter-sound correspondences. (Coulmas 1989: 230)

Therefore he – at least theoretically – pleads not only for a phonological, but also for a thorough morphological, syntactic and lexical analysis of the respective language. In practice, he is aware of the complexity of this endeavor, so a focus on phonology is justifiable to him. However, this seemingly simple solution also brings certain challenges: How, for example, should phonemes be represented for which there are no established corresponding characters in the source alphabet? With the Latin alphabet, various solutions have been found in the past, among them the adoption of signs from the International Phonetic Alphabet, letter combinations, the reinterpretation of 'superfluous' letters, letters in different sizes, sub- or superscripting, diacritic signs or different fonts (Coulmas 1989: 231).

3. *Maximum ease of learning*: This seemingly trivial postulate that an orthography should be easy to learn, at first glance, speaks for a phonematic transcription. However, it is not a trivial matter to segment phonemes correctly and then assign a grapheme to each one; some segments may be impossible to identify as separate sounds. Besides, it has to be taken into consideration that writing and reading make different demands. What eases reading can impede writing and vice versa. Accordingly, for speakers of a language with a distinctively morphological-etymological orthography, such as Polish, the different spelling of phonetically identical words such as ⟨może⟩ 'maybe' and ⟨morze⟩ 'sea' (both pronounced [ˈmɔʒɛ]) can be helpful for reading comprehension but a frequent source of errors in writing. In trying to find a compromise, Coulmas (1989: 233) eventually recommends orientation towards readers rather than writers – which would, in turn, speak against a solely phonematic orthography.

4. *Maximum transfer*: Generally, languages that have been written down for the first time only in modern times are unlikely to be widely used in written communication. As a rule, the desire to develop for them a written standard is nevertheless based on the rational idea that speakers, once they have become literate in their mother tongue, will also more easily become literate in other languages. This hope can, however, only be fulfilled when the alphabet and orthography

of the language in question show great similarity to the surrounding majority language. When it comes to the Roma, the situation is the reverse: They usually become literate in the majority language first and only later, if at all, in Romani, whereby the orthography of the majority language has an intermediary function. Direct transfer of the orthography can be warranted most easily if, in the hitherto unwritten language, the same graphic forms may represent equivalent sounds to those in the majority language. Vice versa, no graphic forms from the majority language should be used whose established sound correspondences have no counterparts in the sound system of the hitherto unwritten language. For sounds without an established representative in the alphabet of the majority language, new letters or letter combinations have to be introduced (see above). Thus, the alphabet and orthography of the surrounding majority language can serve as a basis, to be adapted as necessary (Coulmas 1989: 235).

In the case at hand, this means: When Romani is compared to its Slavic contact languages, the following special features have to be considered: Like the Slavic languages, Romani possesses five vowels: /a, e, i, o, u/, which are inherited from Indo-Aryan and can be found in all varieties. Further phonemes that exist in only some varieties such as the schwa in Bulgaria, are contact-induced. The same applies to vowel length. The diphthongs /aj, oj, ej/ do exist, but can only be found in very few inherited words. The most important peculiarity of the consonant system is the aspiration of /p, t, k, tʃ/ (/pʰ, tʰ, kʰ, tʃʰ/), an inherited feature of Romani that has been preserved in almost every variety, e.g. *phral* 'brother', *thud* 'milk', *kher* 'house', *čhaj* 'daughter'. This feature clearly identifies Romani as an Indo-Aryan language and poses a certain challenge to anyone trying to capture it in writing. The phoneme /ʒ/ is rather marginal and in most varieties limited to loan words. Many, but not all varieties palatalize consonants before front vowels, and some possess palatal phonemes such as /t͡ʃ/ and /d͡ʒ/. Some conservative varieties in south-eastern Europe have preserved two rhotic consonants: a 'rolled' /r/ and a further /r/-sound that can be pronounced [ʀ], [ɣ] or retroflex [ɽ]. Early Romani had a sonorant /ř/, which traces back to historical retroflex consonants, and, in Bulgaria's Rhodope region, such a retroflex pronunciation exists still today (Igla 1997: 152). Elsewhere, this sound has merged with the 'rolled' [r] that is typical of most Slavic languages as well, such that there is no phonemic distinction between them anymore. A further challenge is the differentiation of the closely related phonemes /h/ and /x/ as well as the question of whether to represent final devoicing in writing or not.

5. *Maximum ease of reproduction*: This last criterium is a purely technical one, but it still plays a decisive role in the process of developing orthographic norms for an unwritten language. The graphemes must be easy to write on a computer without

the need for complicated additional characters that often cannot be accessed by Romani writers on the devices available to them. Smalley's five criteria are thus, to a certain extent, in conflict with each other and cannot all be equally respected. Beyond this, much depends on the language in question. However, Coulmas emphasizes that the prestige and the acceptance of a given orthography is the decisive factor in the end: "Linguistic analysis can be of great service and should be the foundation of any new orthography[,] but it can only serve, it cannot dominate" (Coulmas 1989: 238).

8.2.2 Orthographic projects for Romani in Slavophone countries

Russia, Ukraine

In Russia, publications were created in Romani surprisingly early, and, after the foundation of the Soviet Union, a liberal nationality policy with the aim of fostering loyalty to, and identification with, the new state was introduced (Matras 2014: 123). After the October Revolution, Roma in the Soviet Union obtained the opportunity to attend school and to cultivate their language. When, in 1927, the first newspaper in Romani (*Zora*) appeared and several schools were opened where Romani children were taught by Romani teachers, it became necessary to have a means of writing down the language and to publish books and teaching materials in it (Djurić 2002: 33). From the early 1920s onwards, translations of Russian classics, the Bible, children's literature and political pamphlets were published in Romani. In the course of this development, in 1938, North Russian Romani was put into writing, as the first Romani variety in Eastern Europe, by Sergievskij and Barannikov,[47] who used the Cyrillic alphabet for this purpose. However, some very scarce notes on the matter of finding an alphabet for North Russian Romani can be found already in Sergievskij (1931: 9). The authors were aware of their pioneering work and broached the issue in the preface of their *Cygansko-russkij slovar'* ['Gypsy-Russian dictionary']:

> Цыганский язык до революции был совершенно безписьменным (каким он остается и сейчас в капиталистических странах). В нашей стране благодаря ленинско-сталинской национальной политике советской власти цыганы имеют свою письменность и литературный язык. (Sergievskij and Barannikov 1938: 3)

---

[47] Maksim Vladimirovič Sergievskij (1892–1946) was a professor of philology, specializing in Romance and other languages, among them Romani (https://ru.wikipedia.org/wiki/Сергиевский,_Максим_Владимирович). Aleksej Petrovič Barannikov (1890–1952) was a professor of philology and Indology (https://ru.wikipedia.org/wiki/Баранников,_Алексей_Петрович).

['The language of the Gypsies was completely unwritten until the Revolution (and remains so today in the capitalist countries). In our country, thanks to the Leninist-Stalinist national policy of the Soviet authorities, the Gypsies have their own writing and literary language.']

The authors chose the Russian Cyrillic alphabet as the basis, which was slightly adapted to the needs of North Russian Romani. The alphabet reads: ⟨а⟩, ⟨б⟩, ⟨в⟩, ⟨г⟩, ⟨ґ⟩, ⟨д⟩, ⟨е⟩, ⟨ё⟩, ⟨ж⟩, ⟨з⟩, ⟨и⟩, ⟨й⟩, ⟨к⟩, ⟨л⟩, ⟨м⟩, ⟨н⟩, ⟨о⟩, ⟨п⟩, ⟨р⟩, ⟨с⟩, ⟨т⟩, ⟨у⟩, ⟨ф⟩, ⟨х⟩, ⟨ц⟩, ⟨ч⟩, ⟨ш⟩, ⟨ы⟩, ⟨ь⟩, ⟨э⟩, ⟨ж⟩, ⟨я⟩ (Sergievskij and Barannikov 1938: 153). As compared to the Russian alphabet, ⟨ъ⟩ and ⟨щ⟩ are absent, while the character ⟨ґ⟩, which exists in the Ukrainian, but not the Russian, Cyrillic alphabet, has been newly introduced. It stands for the voiceless glottal fricative /h/, as in ⟨гирил⟩ [hiˈril] 'peas'. Aspirated consonants are written by means of the digraphs ⟨кх⟩, ⟨пх⟩, ⟨тх⟩, e.g. ⟨пхаро⟩ [pʰaˈrɔ] 'heavy', ⟨тхуд⟩ [tʰut] 'milk', ⟨кхэр⟩ [kʰɛr] 'house' (Sergievskij and Barannikov 1938: 154). The example ⟨тхуд⟩ [tʰut] also shows that final devoicing was not represented here in writing. If the palatalization of a consonant is not indicated contextually through the influence of the following front or palatalized vowel (⟨е⟩, ⟨и⟩, ⟨ё⟩, ⟨ю⟩, ⟨я⟩), a soft sign has to be inserted, as in ⟨бельвель⟩ [bʲelʲiˈvʲelʲ] 'wind'. If the [ʃʃ] sound happens to appear in a loan word from Russian, ⟨шш⟩ is written, as in ⟨баршшё⟩ [ˈbaršʲːjɔ] 'borscht' (the example also shows that ⟨ё⟩ does not necessarily represent a stressed vowel as in Russian) (Sergievskij and Barannikov 1938: 155).

Sergievskij and Barannikov's proposal later served as an example for other authors over many years, which hints at its having been accepted in at least parts of the language community. Among others, Machotin (1993: 5) refers to it in his dictionary and merely reintroduces ⟨ъ⟩ and ⟨щ⟩. Šapoval (2007a: 15) does the same, giving the following explanation:

> Надо сказать, что эти искусственные ограничения были отчасти воплощением теоретических принципов создателей алфавита, а отчасти были вызваны орфографической модой текущего момента (неприятие буквы Ъ в послереволюционной России). Впоследствии они не закрепились, и российские цыгане при записи своей речи на практике не отказались от букв Щ и Ъ.

> ['It must be said that these artificial limitations were partially the embodiment of the theoretical principles of the alphabet's authors, and partially they were evoked by the orthographic fashion of the day (the non-acceptance of the letter Ъ in post-revolutionary Russia). Consequently, they have not established themselves, and the Russian Gypsies have in practice not refrained from using the letters Щ and Ъ.']

Through the changes in nationality policy under Stalin, the positive developments for the Roma in the Soviet Union came to an end. Publications in Romani were forbidden and attempts to put it into writing and standardize it suspended for many years. Only in the late 1960s did the first new initiatives come to life

(Matras 2014: 124; Toninato 2014: 76). In 1990, Demeter and Demeter[48] published their Russian–Romani dictionary for the variety of the Kalderaš. According to the authors, the idea of creating an alphabet for this variety had been developing since the 1950s, but could not be published until 1990, due to the political circumstances (Demeter and Demeter 1990: 8). The authors appreciate the work of their forerunners Sergievskij and Barannikov and subscribe to it in many respects; they only replace ⟨r⟩ with ⟨ғ⟩. By doing so, they demonstrate a closer proximity to Turkic languages spoken in Russia, such as Bashkir and Kazakh, rather than to Ukrainian. Furthermore, they account for two different realizations of /r/ in their orthography, represented as ⟨р⟩ and ⟨рр⟩. Demeter and Demeter explicitly aim at maintaining a close proximity to the Russian Cyrillic orthography and place special emphasis upon the phonematic principle: "каждой фонеме (фонетическому явлению) – свой знак, с тем, чтобы один и тот же знак не служил для обозначения разных фонем" ['to each phoneme (phonetic phenomenon) its own sign, so that one and the same sign does not serve the purpose of marking different phonemes'] (Demeter and Demeter 1990: 9). Palatalized vowels can, however, be represented in two ways (which contradicts the stated principle): either as ⟨я⟩, ⟨е⟩, ⟨ё⟩, ⟨ю⟩ or as ⟨йа⟩, ⟨йе⟩, ⟨йо⟩, ⟨йу⟩. Per the request of international researchers, the authors present all entries also in Latin transliteration (see Fig. 16).

A decade later, Cvetkov (2001: 20) referred to Demeter and Demeter in his dictionary for the variety of the Russian Lovari. He adapted the orthography only insofar as the letter ⟨r'⟩ is introduced to represent /h/ and double vowels are introduced to mark vowel length, as in ⟨пативаало⟩ 'upright, honest'.

The most recent project to create an alphabet for Romani in the East Slavic area was published by Toropov and Gumeroglyj[49] (2013) and pertains to the variety of the Crimean Roma. A basic principle for the authors is the exclusive use of characters from the modern Russian-Cyrillic alphabet; at the same time, they emphasize that their orthography is something of its own:

Каждый человек, пишущий на языке крымских цыган, должен понять, что он пишет на цыганском языке, используя оригинальный цыганский алфавит, составленный из кириллических букв, со специфическими, только ему присущими, правилами алфавита и орфографии, а не записывает цыганские слова по правилам орфографии

---

48 Roman Stepanovič Demeter (1920–1989) was a Romani poet, folklorist and ethnographer with a PhD in pedagogy. His brother Petr was a composer. They come from a mixed Kalderaš-Servika Roma family (https://ru.wikipedia.org/wiki/Деметер,_Роман_Степанович).
49 Pavel Borisovič Gumeroglyj (1960–1999) was a Crimean Rom. He and the Russian Vadim Germanovič Toropov got to know each other in 1979 and discovered their common interest in the language and culture of the Crimean Roma (Toropov 2003: 3).

Цыганский алфавит / Gypsy alphabet	Страница / Page	В международной транскрипции соответствует / International transcription	Цыганский алфавит / Gypsy alphabet	Страница / Page	В международной транскрипции соответствует / International transcription	Международная транскрипция / International transcription	Страница / Page	Соответствие в цыганском алфавите / Gypsy alphabet	Международная транскрипция / International transcription	Страница / Page	Соответствие в цыганском алфавите / Gypsy alphabet
А а	21	A a	П п	114	P p	A a	233	А а	O o	259	О о
Б б	31	B b	ПХ пх	128	PH ph	B b	235	Б б	P p	260	П п
В в	42	V v	Р р	132	R r	C c	238	Ц ц	PH ph	264	ПХ пх
Г г	51	G g	РР рр	135	RR rr	Č č	239	Ч ч	R r	265	Р р
Ғ ғ	57	H h	С с	137	S s	D d	241	Д д	RR rr	266	РР рр
Д д	60	D d	Т т	148	T t	E e	—	Е е	S s	267	С с
Е е	—	ye	ТХ тх	155	TH th	F f	243	Ф ф	S š, S ś	271, 272	Ш ш
Ё ё	—	yo	У у	156	U u	G g	244	Г г	T t	273	Т т
Ж ж	70	Z ž, Z ź	Ф ф	157	F f	H h	246	Ғ ғ	TH th	275	ТХ тх
З з	72	Z z	Х х	160	X x	I i	247	И и	U u	275	У у
И и	74	I i	Ц ц	164	C c	Ï ï	248	Ы ы	V v	276	В в
Й й	76	Y y	Ч ч	166	Č č	K k	248	К к	X x	278	Х х
К к	78	K k	Ш ш	171	S š S ś	KH kh	252	КХ кх	Y y	279	Й й
КХ кх	91	KH kh	Ы ы	178	I ï	L l	253	Л л	Z z	279	З з
Л л	93	L l	Э э	179	Ə ə	M m	255	М м	Z ž, Z ź	280	Ж ж
М м	98	M m	Ю ю	179	yu	N n	258	Н н	Ə ə	281	Э э
Н н	108	N n	Я я	179	ya						
О о	112	O o									

Fig. 16: Demeter and Demeter's (1990) alphabet in the Cyrillic original and Latin transliteration.

русского языка, как это делали некоторые российские лингвисты до 1918 г. Например, цыганские слова *пхол* 'золото' и *кхам* 'солнце' в своей публикации от 1875 г., этнограф В. Х. Кондараки записал следующим образом: *холъ* 'золото' и *камъ* 'солнце' [. . .]. Буква ъ в цыганских словах в этом конкретном случае – дань русской орфографии того времени, а не обозначение какого-либо цыганского звука.

(Toropov and Gumeroglyj 2013: 202)

['Everybody who writes in the language of the Crimean Gypsies should understand that he is writing in the language of the Gypsies, using an original Gypsy alphabet, consisting of Cyrillic letters with specific alphabetic and orthographic rules inherent only to it, and that he is not writing Gypsy words according to the rules of Russian orthography, as was done by some Russian linguists until 1918. For example, the Gypsy words *phol* 'gold' and *kham* 'sun' were written by the ethnographer V. Ch. Kondaraki in his publication from 1875 as follows: *холъ* 'gold' and *камъ* 'sun' [. . .]. The letter ъ in Gypsy words is in this particular case a tribute to the Russian orthography of that time and not the denotation of any Gypsy sound.']

Abiding by this principle without the use of additional diacritic signs facilitates writing Romani on a computer (Toropov and Gumeroglyj 2013: 199). The authors suggest a combination of the phonematic and the etymological principle and emphasize the advantage of the smaller graphic inventory in the former. Final devoicing is not represented in writing, e.g. [gat] 'shirt' should be spelled ⟨гад⟩ (Toropov and Gumeroglyj 2013: 199). The greatest difficulty in the opinion of the authors is the representation of unstressed vowels. In such a case, they allow what they call etymological spelling. As an example, they present three possibilities for spelling a loan word from Tatar meaning 'work': ⟨хезмети⟩, ⟨хызмэти⟩ or ⟨хэзмэти⟩ (all with the stress on the second syllable). For a consistent spelling of the first, unstressed vowel, the authors decide for the spelling with ⟨ы⟩, appealing to the etymology of the word (Toropov and Gumeroglyj 2013: 200). The first ideas with respect to a written form of Crimean Romani can be found already in Toropov (1999). He introduces them by means of a letter, written in Romani by a Crimean Rom, which is analyzed and corrected by him according to his own ideas about Crimean Romani orthography (Toropov 1999: 16–17).

Czech Republic, Slovakia
The second oldest attempt to develop a Romani writing system in a Slavic-speaking country after Sergievskij and Barannikov (1938) dates back to the year 1969 and is based on the orthographies of Czech and Slovak. The publication of literary texts in Romani began in the region at the same time, around the end of the 1960s and the beginning of the 1970s.

In 1969, the Czechoslovak Romani organization *Svaz Cikánů-Romů* ['Society of Gypsies-Roms'] (SCR) was founded and began publishing the bulletin *Romano ľil* ['Romani letter'], which also contained texts in Romani from the third issue onwards. The chief editor, Andrej Pešta, developed an orthography for Slovak Romani (because of the numerical majority of the Slovak Roma and because all the productive Romani writers at that time used that variety in their publications), the so-called SCR orthography. The basic principles were published in the journal *Romano ľil nevo* ['New Romani letter'] (Hübschmannová 1993), and it was used, with slight modifications, in numerous Romani publications (Hübschmannová 1995: 193). The alphabet consists of the following letters: ⟨a⟩, ⟨b⟩, ⟨c⟩, ⟨č⟩, ⟨čh⟩, ⟨d⟩, ⟨ď⟩, ⟨dz⟩, ⟨dž⟩, ⟨e⟩, ⟨f⟩, ⟨g⟩, ⟨h⟩, ⟨ch⟩, ⟨i⟩, ⟨j⟩, ⟨k⟩, ⟨kh⟩, ⟨l⟩, ⟨ľ⟩, ⟨m⟩, ⟨n⟩, ⟨ň⟩, ⟨o⟩, ⟨p⟩, ⟨ph⟩, ⟨r⟩, ⟨s⟩, ⟨š⟩, ⟨t⟩, ⟨ť⟩, ⟨th⟩, ⟨u⟩, ⟨v⟩, ⟨z⟩, ⟨ž⟩. A peculiarity is found in the use of the acute: It does not, as in Czech and Slovak, represent long vowels, which originally did not exist in Romani, but the short form of a future or imperfect tense, such as ⟨kerás⟩ 'I did' – so, here, morphology is represented in writing. The palatalization of consonants is marked by a háček or an apostrophe. Final devoicing is not represented in writing, e.g. ⟨dad⟩ [dat] 'father'. The character ⟨x⟩ is to be avoided and ⟨ch⟩ written instead (Hübschmannová 1993: 197). With respect to the acceptance of the project, Hübschmannová and Neustupný (1996: 100–101) come to a positive conclusion:

> Out of 16 Romani publications launched on the territory of former Czechoslovakia so far 14 use the agreed spelling. Only one of those written in the Slovak-and-Czech variety does not adhere to its rules. Three weekend seminars have been organized so far in the 1990s to discuss matters of spelling and other issues of language. [. . .] Overall we can say that

[...] spelling in journals and other publications has been unified to a remarkable extent. In particular, the use of y has virtually been eliminated and palatalization has systematically been marked with the 'hook'. However, deviations appear. Editors do not always correct the spelling.

The orthography was taken over with only minimal changes for the *Romsko-český a česko-romský kapesní slovník* ['Romani–Czech and Czech–Romani pocket dictionary'] (Hübschmannová, Šebková and Žigová 1991), which was published in the year of the breakup of Czechoslovakia. In the years after the political turnover, a uniform version of Romani was fostered through journals and books, and the number of publications in Romani was on the rise. However, the spelling developed in a manner that Hübschmannová (1995: 196) calls "trial and error", rather than through language planning. Some authors applied the SCR orthography, others spelled Romani spontaneously by ear. In the face of these developments, Hübschmannová and Neustupný (1996) plead for a "postmodern" and "polycentric" approach to writing Romani, based on already existing written texts and accepting variation. They are convinced that variation does not necessarily lead to difficulties in understanding but is rather beneficial to the acceptance of the endeavor by the language community. The call for unification takes a back seat. Matras (1999b: 99) views this "trial and error" principle as the simple result of pragmatical necessity, rather than as a symbolic, elitist project.

A few years later, the need for a more uniform orthography for Romani seemingly arose in former Czechoslovakia once again, because the first and, so far, only system of rules for writing Romani developed in independent Slovakia was published in 2006, written by a large collective of authors around Milena Hübschmannová,[50] titled *Pravidlá rómskeho pravopisu* ['The rules of Romani orthography']. It is the wish of the authors that their work may contribute to the preservation of the cultural and linguistic heritage of the Roma (Hübschmannová et al. 2006: 9). It is supposed to be a useful aid both to philologists and non-philologists alike and was developed on the basis of the variety of Romani spoken by 80% of the Romani population in Slovakia (Hübschmannová et al. 2006: 8) – i.e. the Northern Central dialect. The alphabet is, of course, Latin-based and consists of the following letters: ⟨a⟩, ⟨b⟩, ⟨c⟩, ⟨č⟩, ⟨čh⟩, ⟨d⟩, ⟨ď⟩, ⟨dz⟩, ⟨dž⟩, ⟨e⟩, ⟨f⟩, ⟨g⟩, ⟨h⟩, ⟨ch⟩, ⟨i⟩, ⟨j⟩, ⟨k⟩, ⟨kh⟩, ⟨l⟩, ⟨ľ⟩, ⟨m⟩, ⟨n⟩, ⟨ň⟩, ⟨o⟩, ⟨p⟩, ⟨ph⟩, ⟨r⟩, ⟨s⟩, ⟨š⟩, ⟨t⟩, ⟨ť⟩, ⟨th⟩, ⟨u⟩, ⟨v⟩, ⟨z⟩, ⟨ž⟩. Loan words and proper names can also contain ⟨q⟩, ⟨w⟩, ⟨x⟩ or ⟨y⟩ (Hübschmannová et al. 2006: 18). The authors rely on the phonematic prin-

---

[50] Milena Hübschmannová (1933–2005), an Indologist from Prague, is presumed to have been the founder of Romani studies in Czechoslovakia. Although she was not a Romni herself, she spoke Romani fluently and was awarded many prizes for her commitment in matters of the Roma (https://en.wikipedia.org/wiki/Milena_Hübschmannová).

ciple, which is, however, in special cases complemented by the morphological, etymological and the so-called interdialectal principles (for explanations, cf. Hübschmannová et al. 2006: 19–20). In this project, there is also only one ⟨r⟩-type character, which corresponds to the Slovak /r/, and aspirated consonants are indicated by a following ⟨h⟩: ⟨čhon⟩ [t͡ʃʰɔn] 'moon', ⟨kham⟩ [kʰam] 'sun', ⟨phuv⟩ [pʰuf] 'earth', ⟨thud⟩ [tʰut] 'milk'. Final devoicing is not represented in writing. Palatalized consonants are marked with a *haček* or a stroke, respectively.

(North) Macedonia
Romani has been used in Macedonia in a written form since at least the 1960s, and the first to conduct the experiment of creating an alphabet for Romani in Macedonia were Jusuf and Kepeski.[51] In 1973, they composed a bilingual (Romani and Macedonian) grammar based on the two varieties Arli and Džambazi, which was, however, only published in 1980. At the same time, they introduced an orthography for these varieties based on the Latin (!) alphabet, which they justify as follows:

> Авторите на оваа книга беа во дилема кои знаци да ги земат за обележување на гласовите што се слушаат кај Ромите во нашата земја; најпосле се решија за латиницата, бидејќи има Роми и во европски земји каде што народите со кои живеат се служат со латиница. (Kepeski and Jusuf 1980: 19)

> ['The authors of this book found themselves in the dilemma of which characters they should use to mark the sounds heard among the Roma in our country. In the end, they decided on the Latin script, as there are Roma also in European countries in which the people they live with use the Latin script.']

Arli is, still today, the variety spoken by the majority of Roma in Macedonia, as well as in Serbia and Kosovo (this is the region Kepeski and Jusuf refer to), and that which the Romani literature in the area is based on. For some sounds from this variety, which have no counterparts in Latin, special characters had to be found, or Cyrillic letters had to be used: for example, the schwa is represented as ⟨ä⟩. Friedman (1985) comments that "the choice of yet another separate letter for Romani is not without justification", yet points to the fact that the schwa sound is so rare in the respective varieties that it was not really necessary to introduce a special character for it. He concludes: "The problem of [the] schwa in Romani dialects and the literary standard is thus clearly in need of further

---

51 Šaip Jusuf (ca. 1933–2010) was a Rom from Skopje and a sports teacher with a diploma from the University of Belgrade (https://de.wikipedia.org/wiki/Šaip_Jusuf). Krume Kepeski (1909–1988), a non-Rom, was a linguist and professor at the pedagogical academy of Skopje (https://de.wikipedia.org/wiki/Krume_Kepeski).

elucidation" (Friedman 1985). Kepeski and Jusuf's Romani alphabet consists of 32 characters (see Fig. 17). Macedonian influence is visible in the letter combinations ⟨kj⟩ (cf. Mac. ⟨ќ⟩) and ⟨gj⟩ (cf. Mac. ⟨ѓ⟩), which is also commented on by Friedman (1985: 58):

> According to RG [*Romani Gramatika*, A.-M. S.], the Romani sounds are closer to the Macedonian sounds represented by the Cyrillic letters ќ, ѓ than they are to the Serbo-Croatian sounds represented by the Cyrillic ћ, ђ and the Latin ć, đ. It is certainly the case that in the pronunciation of palatal or palatalized stops or affricates the various dialects of Romani often agree most closely with the pronunciation of the non-Romani languages or dialects with which they are in closest contact [...]. The dialects of RG are typical in this respect.

Sibilants are written with a háček and final devoicing is not represented in writing. As is often the case, a difference between ⟨x⟩ and ⟨h⟩ is made, but "Jusuf and Kepeski (1980) fail to make the distinction in practice, using both ⟨x⟩ and ⟨h⟩ in the same roots, e.g. *xiv, hiv* 'hole', *xhor* 'depth' but *horadaripe* 'deepening' [...]" (Friedman 1995: 182). The aspirated consonants are, surprisingly, not explicitly named in the overview (cf. Fig. 17), but, elsewhere in the text, one can find the explanation that they are represented using a following ⟨h⟩ in Latin and ⟨x'⟩ in Cyrillic, e.g. ⟨than⟩/⟨тх'ан⟩ 'place', ⟨kham⟩/⟨кх'ам⟩ 'sun', ⟨čhaj⟩/⟨чх'ај⟩ 'girl', ⟨phen⟩/⟨пх'ен⟩ 'sister' (Kepeski and Jusuf 1980: 23). /h/ is also represented with ⟨x'⟩ in the Cyrillic version, e.g. ⟨hava⟩/⟨х'ава⟩ 'to eat' (Kepeski and Jusuf 1980: 23). There is one grapheme for the velar (Latin ⟨x⟩ and Cyrillic ⟨x⟩) and one for the glottal fricative (Latin ⟨h⟩, Cyrillic ⟨x'⟩).

Friedman (1985: 59) also mentions that, in Kepeski and Jusuf's system of rules, both ⟨lj⟩ and ⟨l⟩ can occur before front vowels, such that one can find both the spelling ⟨ljil⟩ and ⟨lil⟩ for 'book', to name just one example. According to him, a clear decision should be made here if [lj] and [l] are to be seen as corresponding to separate phonemes. With respect to voicing, Friedman (1985: 59) attests to the authors' relatively consistent approach:

> The orthography in RG is generally consistent in portraying underlying voiced and voiceless consonants in environments of neutralization, as indicated in the examples just given, although no explicit rules are stated, and occasional slips do occur, e.g. the spelling of *dat* for *dad*.

As in most Macedonian varieties of Romani, there is only one /r/, so no differentiation in writing is necessary here. The alphabet is used, among others, in the *Makedonsko–romski i Romsko–makedonski rečnik* ['Macedonian–Romani and Romani–Macedonian dictionary'] by Petrovski and Veličkovski (1998).

In 1992, a year after Macedonia attained independence from Yugoslavia, a conference was held in Skopje with the aim of standardizing Romani and intro-

8.2 Creating an alphabet for Romani in eight Slavic-speaking countries — 155

PASAKJERDO DIKKJERIBA KO ROMANO-LATINSKO THAJ KIRILSKO HRAMONDO			НАПОРЕДЕН ПРЕГЛЕД НА РОМСКОТО, ЛАТИНСКОТО И КИРИЛСКОТО ПИСМО		
romani	latinica		ромско	латиница	кирилица
A, a	A, a	A, а	A, a	A, a	А, а
Ä, ä	–, –	–, –	Ä, ä	–, –	–, –
B, b	B, b	Б, б	B, b	B, b	Б, б
C, c	C, c	Ц, ц	C, c	C, c	Ц, ц
Č, č	Č, č	Ч, ч	Č, č	Č, č	Ч, ч
Kj, kj (Ć, ć)	Kj, kj	Ќ, ќ	Kj, kj	Kj, kj	Ќ, ќ
D, d	D, d	Д, д	D, d	D, d	Д, д
Gj, gj (Đ, đ)	Gj, gj	Ѓ, ѓ	Gj, gj	Gj, gj	Ѓ, ѓ
Dž, dž	Dž, dž	Џ, џ	Dž, dž	Dž, dž	Џ, џ
E, e	E, e	Е, е	E, e	E, e	Е, е
F, f	F, f	Ф, ф	F, f	F, f	Ф, ф
G, g	G, g	Г, г	G, g	G, g	Г, г
H, h	H, h	–, –	H, h	H, h	–, –
X, x	X' x'	Х, х	X, x	X, x	Х, х
I, i	I, i	И, и	I, i	I, i	И, и
J, j	J, j	J, j	J, j	J, j	J, j
K, k	K, k	К, к	K, k	K, k	К, к
L, l	L, l	Л, л	L, l	L, l	Л, л
Lj, lj	Lj, lj	Љ, љ	Lj, lj	Lj, lj	Љ, љ
M, m	M, m	М, м	M, m	M, m	М, м
N, n	N, n	Н, н	N, n	N, n	Н, н
Nj, nj	Nj, nj	Њ, њ	Nj, nj	Nj, nj	Њ, њ
O, o	O, o	О, о	O, o	O, o	О, о
P, p	P, p	П, п	P, p	P, p	П, п
R, r	R, r	Р, р	R, r	R, r	Р, р
S, s	S, s	С, с	S, s	S, s	С, с
Š, š	Š, š	Ш, ш	Š, š	Š, š	Ш, ш
T, t	T, t	Т, т	T, t	T, t	Т, т
U, u	U, u	У, у	U, u	U, u	У, у
V, v	V, v	В, в	V, v	V, v	В, в
Z, z	Z, z	З, з	Z, z	Z, z	З, з
Ž, ž	Ž, ž	Ж, ж	Ž, ž	Ž, ž	Ж, ж

Fig. 17: "Overview of the Romani, Latin and Cyrillic script" (Kepeski and Jusuf 1980: 20–21).

ducing the language as a subject in Macedonian schools (Friedman 1995: 179).⁵²
In this connection, Kurth (2008: 55) affirms that the standardization of Romani
has made steady progress since the *Romani Gramatika*:

> Die Konferenz von 1992 trug trotz Versuchen von politischer Instrumentalisierung durch alle Fraktionen dazu bei, die absolute Notwendigkeit einer konsistenten Orthographie aufzuzeigen. Die Einführung des Romischen als Unterrichtssprache auf der Grundstufe wird einen grossen [sic] Einfluss auf den Kodifikationsprozess ausüben, und zwar über die Grenzen Makedoniens hinaus.

> ['The conference of 1992, in spite of attempts at political instrumentalization from all fractions, contributed to demonstrating the absolute necessity of a consistent orthography. The introduction of Romani as a language of instruction on a basic level will have a great influence on the codification process, even beyond the borders of Macedonia.']

One of the results was a new proposal for an orthography, which took away some of the scope that Kepeski and Jusuf had left available to writers and strove for more uniformity and stricter rules. The new proposal allowed for Romani in Macedonia to be written both with Latin and with Cyrillic letters: ⟨a⟩, ⟨b⟩, ⟨c⟩, ⟨č⟩, ⟨čh⟩, ⟨d⟩, ⟨dž⟩, ⟨e⟩, ⟨f⟩, ⟨g⟩, ⟨h⟩, ⟨i⟩, ⟨j⟩, ⟨k⟩, ⟨kh⟩, ⟨l⟩, ⟨m⟩, ⟨n⟩, ⟨o⟩, ⟨p⟩, ⟨ph⟩, ⟨r⟩, ⟨s⟩, ⟨š⟩, ⟨t⟩, ⟨th⟩, ⟨u⟩, ⟨v⟩, ⟨ž⟩ and ⟨а⟩, ⟨б⟩, ⟨ц⟩, ⟨ч⟩, ⟨чх⟩, ⟨д⟩, ⟨џ⟩, ⟨е⟩, ⟨ф⟩, ⟨г⟩, ⟨х⟩, ⟨и⟩, ⟨ј⟩, ⟨к⟩, ⟨кх⟩, ⟨л⟩, ⟨м⟩, ⟨н⟩, ⟨о⟩, ⟨п⟩, ⟨пх⟩, ⟨р⟩, ⟨с⟩, ⟨ш⟩, ⟨т⟩, ⟨тх⟩, ⟨у⟩, ⟨в⟩, ⟨з⟩, ⟨ж⟩.⁵³ Also in Macedonia, activists involved in the standardization of Romani have spoken out against an internationally normed orthography and prefer to follow the trend of regional or national orthographies. Although some publications in Macedonia have been published in Cortiade's orthography, the conference participants agreed on the practice of taking spontaneously produced Romani texts as a model, as had been done in Czechoslovakia. This concerns, among others, the use of ⟨dž⟩ instead of ⟨ʒ⟩ for /d͡ʒ/. Cortiade's acute for marking sibilants was also rejected in favor of a háček (Friedman 1995: 181–182). This orthography, in contrast to that of Kepeski and Jusuf (1980), does not contain a character for the representation of the schwa: "In the rare instances of schwa in the Arlija dialect, the corresponding form in Džambaz or some other Romani dialect with a different vowel will be taken as the literary norm", says the document (Friedman 1995: 183). A number of grade school textbooks and other children's literature that have been published for teaching Romani as a language of study in North Macedonia for the most part follow the 1992 orthography (anonymous reviewer). In spite of

---

52 The conference and its final document are elaborately presented in Friedman (1995). Furthermore, according to Kyuchukov (2009: 60), a second conference was held in Skopje in 2006, with Romani participants from Macedonia, Serbia, Bosnia and Bulgaria, who discussed the standardization of Romani on a regional level.

53 The ordering of the Cyrillic letters follows the Latin alphabet here.

all efforts to orthographize and standardize Romani in Macedonia, Friedman (2005: 171) concludes:

> Aside from the orthography conference of 1992, norm selection is progressing in Macedonia de facto rather than de jure. In this sense, the process of Romani standardization in Macedonia is following patterns seen for Romani in other countries which is to say that consensus is emerging through usage.

Bulgaria

Romani literature in Bulgaria began to develop already in the 1950s (Toninato 2014: 82), while the first bilingual Bulgarian–Romani reader for children, entitled *Romano ABC lil*, was published in 1993 (Kyuchukov 2009: 56). Beyond this, the Romani books that have been published for use at Bulgarian universities play an important role in the process of standardizing an orthography for Romani in the country (Kyuchukov 2009: 63–64).

Probably the majority of publications on Romani in Bulgaria were penned by Xristo Kjučukov,[54] so it is not surprising that both proposals for a Bulgarian Romani orthography were devised by him, each in cooperation with a different researcher. The first orthography, from the 1990s (Kjučukov and Yanakiev 1996; cf. also the summary in Kyuchukov 2009: 58), is notable insofar as it is based on the Latin script and, additionally, on English orthography. To represent the schwa, the character ⟨w⟩ was chosen, and prejotated vowels are written with a ⟨y⟩: ⟨ya⟩, ⟨ye⟩, ⟨yo⟩, ⟨yu⟩. Aspirated sibilants are written as digraphs with an ⟨h⟩: ⟨chh⟩, ⟨kh⟩, ⟨ph⟩, ⟨th⟩. This orthography, although designed for the Roma in Bulgaria, makes a very international impression due to the influence of English orthography and, thus, clearly delimits itself from the Bulgarian Cyrillic alphabet.

In the year 2000, a new proposal for a Romani orthography was made in Bulgaria (Hancock and Kjučukov 2000), which takes over many elements from the first version, but also makes some changes: the schwa is now represented as ⟨y⟩ and prejotated vowels are indicated with ⟨j⟩ instead of ⟨y⟩: ⟨ja⟩, ⟨je⟩, ⟨jo⟩, ⟨ju⟩. The English influence is reduced in that aspirated sibilants are now written with a háček (⟨š⟩, ⟨č⟩, ⟨ž⟩, ⟨dž⟩), as in earlier works by Hancock, with an international orientation (cf. also the summary in Kyuchukov 2009: 58–59). It is difficult to ascertain the extent to which the two projects have been applied in practice beyond Kjučukov's own publications.

---

54 Xristo S. Kjučukov, born in 1962 in Provadija as Xjusein Selimov Kjučukov, is a specialist in Romani linguistics and education. He holds a PhD in General Linguistics from the University of Amsterdam and other academic titles (https://bg.wikipedia.org/wiki/Христо_Кючуков).

Poland

The first known written Romani texts produced by Polish Roma date back to the poet Bronisława Wajs, known as Papusza (1910?–1987). Her poems were published by Jerzy Ficowski, both in Romani and Polish editions, at the beginning of the 1950s. Papusza's original spelling is spontaneous and intuitive. Until not long ago, only few Roma in Poland saw the necessity of using their language in a written form; it was only within a short time span, in 2007 and 2008, that a number of publications were released in Romani, in which the problem of orthography was resolved in very different ways.

In the course of this development, Adam Bartosz[55] (2009) published the first systematic proposal for a Romani orthography in Poland. The project is called *Pisownia sulejowska* 'Sulejów orthography' after the place where the people involved in the project first gathered. Bartosz, who was in charge, describes it as the Polish reply to Hübschmannová's proposals for the Czech Republic and Slovakia (Bartosz 2009: 158–159). He emphasizes (Bartosz 2009: 164–165) that the *Pisownia sulejowska* is to be seen as a draft and a basis for discussion, not as a finalized system of rules. It is based on the main varieties of Romani that are spoken in Poland, and the influence of Polish orthography is clearly visible. Bartosz (2009: 160–161) justifies this as follows:

> Pojawiła się potrzeba ujednolicenia zapisu, ale próby nawiązania do wcześniej ustalonych zasad napotkały niemały opór zainteresowanych. [...] Nie ma bowiem szansy na wprowadzenie w najbliższym czasie instytucjonalnych form nauczania pisowni romskiej (brak nauczycieli, systemu nauczania, zapotrzebowania samego środowiska na takie nauczanie etc.). W takiej sytuacji należy się zdecydować na zastosowanie pisowni w oparciu o alfabet polski.

> ['The necessity of unifying the orthography arose, but attempts to rely on earlier defined rules evoked resistance among the people involved. [...] Namely, there is no chance of introducing institutionalized forms of teaching a writing system for Romani in the foreseeable future (lack of teachers, lack of an education system, the need even for an environment for such a form of education etc.). In such a situation, it is necessary to decide for the use of a script on the basis of the Polish alphabet.']

The orthography accommodates the tendencies that can be seen in spontaneous Romani text production in Poland. It consists of the following characters: ⟨a⟩, ⟨b⟩, ⟨c⟩, ⟨ćh⟩, ⟨d⟩, ⟨dź⟩, ⟨e⟩, ⟨f⟩, ⟨g⟩, ⟨h⟩, ⟨ch⟩, (⟨x⟩,) ⟨i⟩, ⟨j⟩, ⟨k⟩, ⟨kh⟩, ⟨l⟩, ⟨ł⟩, ⟨m⟩, ⟨n⟩, ⟨ń⟩, ⟨o⟩, ⟨p⟩, ⟨ph⟩, ⟨r⟩, ⟨s⟩, ⟨ś⟩, ⟨t⟩, ⟨th⟩, ⟨u⟩, ⟨w⟩, ⟨v⟩, ⟨y⟩, ⟨z⟩, ⟨ź⟩. Aspirated consonants ("[j]est to bowiem istotna cecha języka *romani*, którą w pisowni należy zachować"

---

[55] Adam Bartosz is not a Rom but speaks Romani fluently. He is a productive ethnographer and was director of the district museum in Tarnów until 2012. The museum houses the largest exhibition on Romani culture in Poland (https://pl.wikipedia.org/wiki/Adam_Bartosz).

['since this is an essential feature of Romani that must be preserved in writing'], Bartosz 2009: 164) are indicated with a following ⟨h⟩, e.g. ⟨ćhaj⟩ 'girl', ⟨kher⟩ 'house', ⟨phabaj⟩ 'apple', ⟨them⟩ 'place, country'. Uvular fricatives can be spelled ⟨ch⟩ or ⟨x⟩, however, Bartosz (2009: 163) emphasizes the difference between /x/ and /h/, which are separate phonemes. A special feature of the *Pisownia sulejowska* is the character ⟨ł⟩ for the labialized velar approximant [w], which unmistakably demonstrates Polish influence, for example in ⟨łoło⟩ ['wɔwɔ] 'rot' instead of ⟨lolo⟩ ['lɔlɔ], as in other Romani varieties (Bartosz 2009: 162). The orthography also reflects a more palatalized pronunciation of certain consonants – also under the influence of Polish –, which is visible in the characters ⟨ć⟩, ⟨ćh⟩, ⟨dź⟩, ⟨ń⟩, ⟨ś⟩, ⟨ź⟩ (Bartosz 2009: 163). However, different rules apply for them in the *Pisownia sulejowska* than do in Polish orthography: In the latter, these graphemes could never be followed by an ⟨i⟩, in the former this is absolutely possible; see Bartosz's examples ⟨ćaćipen⟩ 'truth' or ⟨podźi⟩ 'skirt' (Bartosz 2009: 161). This makes sense because Romani – in contrast to Polish – has words containing the phoneme combinations /si/, /ci/ etc. They are spelled ⟨si⟩, ⟨ci⟩ in the *Pisownia sulejowska*, thus ⟨sikaweł⟩ is pronounced [sikav'ɛw] instead of [ɕikav'ɛw], as would be expected for Polish. There is only one realization of /r/ in the Polish Romani varieties, so only one grapheme is necessary. To spell Polish loan words, it is also permitted to introduce other characters from the Polish alphabet, and Bartosz pleads for their unmodified adoption (Bartosz 2009: 164). The proposal has been received positively by the language community, and Mirga (2009) expressly uses it for his *Słownik romsko–polski* ['Romani–Polish dictionary'].

Serbia

After the publication of *Gramatika romskog jezika* ['Grammar of the Romani language'] (2005), Rajko Đurić[56] undertook the project *Pravopis romskoga jezika* ['Orthography of the Romani language'] in 2011. Although the book has *pravopis* 'orthography' in its title, it also includes detailed information on phonetics, morphology and syntax, explanations of linguistic terms and selected verbs in Romani. The author sees the orthographic development of Romani as an important opportunity to improve communication between Roma and non-Roma and to break down prejudices:

---

[56] Rajko Đurić, a Rom, was born in 1947 near Smederevo in former Yugoslavia. He studied at the Faculty of Philosophy at the University of Belgrade and received his doctorate in sociology in 1985 through research on Romani culture in Yugoslavia. He was president of the International Romani Union from 1990–2000 and has been secretary general of the International Roma PEN Center since 2001 (Đurić 2011: 217; https://de.wikipedia.org/wiki/Rajko_Đurić).

> Vrlo snažene predrasude prema Romima i anticiganizam, kao specifičan oblik rasizma, stvaraju i u ovoj oblasti mnoge prepreke i teškoće. S druge strane, analfabetizam, koji je veoma izražena pojava među Romima, ograničena i sužena komunikacija i, naročito, socijalna beda, sprečavaju da se napori i dostignuća ove vrste dublje i ukorene. (Đurić 2011: 7)

> ['The very strong prejudices against Roma and antigypsyism as a specific form of racism also create many obstacles and difficulties in this area. On the other hand, illiteracy, which is very pronounced among the Roma, limited and restricted communication and, especially, social poverty prevent efforts of this kind from deepening and taking root.']

In his preface, Đurić (2011: 6) refers to the International Commission for the Standardization of Romani and its valuable work since its founding in 1990, but does not explicitly make clear whether his orthographic proposal is intended for Roma worldwide, Roma in Serbia or for another target group, and on which variety it is based. The choice of the Latin alphabet could speak for a target group beyond Serbia, but since the book is written in Serbian, Roma in Serbia or the countries of former Yugoslavia are probably the main target group. Đurić deals with various orthographic principles and finally decides to use the phonematic one with some etymological elements. The alphabetic inventory is as follows: ⟨a⟩, ⟨b⟩, ⟨c⟩, ⟨č⟩, ⟨čh⟩, ⟨ć⟩, ⟨ćh⟩, ⟨d⟩, ⟨dj⟩, ⟨dž⟩, ⟨e⟩, ⟨f⟩, ⟨g⟩, ⟨h⟩, ⟨x⟩, ⟨i⟩, ⟨j⟩, ⟨k⟩, ⟨kh⟩, ⟨l⟩, ⟨lj⟩, ⟨m⟩, ⟨n⟩, ⟨nj⟩, ⟨o⟩, ⟨p⟩, ⟨ph⟩, ⟨r⟩, ⟨rr⟩, ⟨s⟩, ⟨š⟩, ⟨t⟩, ⟨th⟩, ⟨u⟩, ⟨v⟩, ⟨y⟩, ⟨z⟩, ⟨ž⟩ (Đurić 2011: 10). For the five aspirated consonants, aspiration is marked with an ⟨h⟩. It is also noteworthy that a distinction is made between alveolar ⟨r⟩ (also used syllabically as in ⟨brš⟩ 'year', ⟨krlo⟩ 'voice', cf. Đurić 2011: 15) and retroflex ⟨rr⟩, as well as between ⟨h⟩ and ⟨x⟩. The digraphs ⟨nj⟩ and ⟨lj⟩, as in ⟨phenja⟩ 'sisters' and ⟨xoljariko⟩ 'sharp', are considered mono-segmental, as in Serbian. The inclusion of the grapheme ⟨y⟩ is justified as follows:

> Glas **y** [. . .] koristi se iz etimoloških i istorijskih razloga, kao i zbog reči stranog porekla. Naime, u mnogim naučnim studijama o romskom jeziku koje su objavljene na nemačkom, engleskom, francuskom i drugim evropskim jezicima, slovo **y** koristilo se da bi označilo glas koji zvuči kao **j** ili **i**, glas koji leži između ta dva glasa. Citiranje tekstova u izvornom obliku zahteva da slovo **y** ima svoje mesto u romskom pismu. Osim toga, upotreba slova **y** je neophodna da bi se u pisanom obliku napravila jasna razlika izmedju **medijuma**, s jedne strane, i **aktiva** i **pasiva**, sa druge strane. (Đurić 2011: 28–29; emphasis in the original)

> ['The sound **y** [. . .] is used for etymological and historical reasons, as well as for words of foreign origin. Indeed, in many scientific studies on Romani published in English, French, German and other European languages, the letter **y** has been used to denote a sound that sounds like **j** or **i**, a sound that lies between these two sounds. Quoting texts in their original form requires that the letter **y** have its place in Romani spelling. Moreover, the use of the letter **y** is essential to make a clear distinction in writing between the **medium**, on the one hand, and the **active** and **passive**, on the other.']

Final devoicing is not reflected in writing. With respect to future development, Đurić (2011: 72) sees one of the central tasks in the elaboration of a complete orthographic terminology in Romani and an orthographic dictionary. It remains unclear whether this orthographic proposal has been taken up by persons other than Đurić himself.

8.3 Summary

The aim of this chapter was to identify all known projects for the creation of an alphabet and orthography for Romani in Slavophone countries and to compare them against the theoretical background of Smalley (1964) and Coulmas (1989). It cannot be ruled out that there are other projects beyond those mentioned here that have not been published or have not received significant dissemination.

In any case, the eleven examples from eight countries presented here illustrate that the trend towards regional or national rather than international approaches to codifying written Romani, as described by Matras (2005), has been going on for several decades in the Slavic countries. They differ on whether the authors propose a solution for (almost) all Romani varieties in their country (e.g. Poland) or only for the largest one(s) (e.g. North Macedonia), and on whether they make several different proposals for different varieties in the country (e.g. Russia).

It has been demonstrated that, in most cases, the proposals are based on the writing system of the majority language in the respective country, such that one can speak of an approximation rather than a demarcation in relation to the majority language. However, this approximation should be interpreted pragmatically rather than emotionally, because some authors emphasize the independence of their alphabet despite its close affinity to the writing system of the majority language. This is emphasized by the special characters and diacritics found in each alphabet. Interesting exceptions in this respect are North Macedonia and Bulgaria: Although, here, one would expect the Cyrillic script to be used as the basis, the authors opt for the Latin script in order to achieve a wider, even international, appeal for their alphabets. The dominant orthographic principle employed by the authors, among whom are Roma as well as non-Roma, is the phonematic one. They do, however, sometimes make concessions to other principles or are not completely consistent in its application.

To what extent the orthographic proposals have been adopted by the respective language communities is the most difficult question to answer. It can be demonstrated that most of them have found later use in publications such as dictionaries, grammars or textbooks, i.e. in an academic context. Yet, in order to be able to make judgements about how many Roma use them in their everyday

Tab. 10: Overview of the orthographic projects (R = Rom, NR = non-Rom).

Year	Country	Romani variety/-ies	Publication	Autor(s)	Alphabet(s)	Principle(s)	Aspirated consonants	Special characters	Application
1938	Soviet Union	North Russian Romani	*Cygansko-russkij slovar'*	M.V. Sergievskij (NR) & A.P. Barannikov (NR)	Cyrillic	phonematic	⟨чx⟩, ⟨кx⟩, ⟨пx⟩, ⟨тx⟩	⟨r⟩, combination ⟨шu⟩	yes
1969	Czecho-slovakia	Northern Central dialects	*Romano ľil nevo*	Andrej Pešta (R)	Latin	phonematic & morphological	⟨čh⟩, ⟨kh⟩, ⟨ph⟩, ⟨th⟩	acute for short future forms	yes
1980	Yugoslavia (Macedonia)	Arli (& Džambazi)	*Romani Gramatika*	Šaip Jusuf (R) & Krume Kepeski (NR)	Latin	mainly phonematic	Latin ⟨čh⟩ etc., Cyrillic ⟨x⟩ etc.	⟨ä⟩, ⟨kj⟩, ⟨gj⟩, mixing of ⟨h⟩ & ⟨x⟩	yes
1990	Russia	Kalderaš	*Cygansko-russkij i russko-cyganskij slovar' (Kəldərarskij dialekt)*	R.S. Demeter (R) & P.S. Demeter (R)	Cyrillic	phonematic	Latin ⟨čh⟩ etc., Cyrillic ⟨x⟩ etc.	⟨ŕ⟩, ⟨p⟩, ⟨pp⟩, ⟨ňa⟩ etc.	yes
1992	Macedonia	Arli	standardization conference	Friedman (1995)	Latin & Cyrillic	?	Latin ⟨čh⟩ etc., Cyrillic ⟨x'⟩ etc.	no letter for the schwa sound	?
1996	Bulgaria	in Bulgaria and beyond	*Romskijat păt. O Romano Drom*	Xristo Kjučukov (R) & Miroslav Yanak(i)ev (NR)	Latin (English influence)	?	⟨chh⟩, ⟨kh⟩, ⟨ph⟩, ⟨th⟩	⟨w⟩, ⟨ya⟩ etc., ⟨sh⟩ etc.	?
2000	Bulgaria	in Bulgaria and beyond	*Angluni vorba*	Ian Hancock (R) & Xristo Kjučukov (R)	Latin	?	⟨čh⟩, ⟨kh⟩, ⟨ph⟩, ⟨th⟩	reduction of the English influence	?

Year	Country	Title	Author	Script	Principle	Notable graphemes	Standard?
2006	Slovakia	*Pravidlá rómskeho pravopisu*	Milena Hübschmannová (NR) et al.	Latin	phonematic, morphological, etymological, 'interdialectal'	⟨čh⟩, ⟨kh⟩, ⟨ph⟩, ⟨th⟩	–
2009	Poland	*Propozycja zapisu języka romani – Pisownia sulejowska*	Adam Bartosz (NR) et al.	Latin	phonematic	⟨čh⟩, ⟨kh⟩, ⟨ph⟩, ⟨th⟩	⟨dż⟩, ⟨t⟩	yes
2011	Serbia	*Pravopis romskogo jezika (O čačolekhavno e rromane čhibako)*	Rajko Đurić (R)	Latin	phonematic & etymological	⟨čh⟩, ⟨čh⟩, ⟨kh⟩, ⟨ph⟩, ⟨th⟩	⟨čh⟩, ⟨y⟩, digraphs ⟨nj⟩, ⟨lj⟩	?
2013	Ukraine	*Opyt sostavlenija alfavita dlja zapisi ustnoj reči krymskyx cygan*	V.G. Toropov (NR) & P.B. Gumeroglyj (R)	Cyrillic	phonematic & etymological	⟨čh⟩, ⟨kh⟩, ⟨ph⟩, ⟨th⟩	–	?

private communication, in internet forums and blogs or in non-academic publications, a separate study would be necessary. Table 10 summarizes all the undertakings discussed in this chapter with their most important characteristics.

The process of finding an adequate orthography for Romani in Slavophone countries continues. A few years ago, the first Romani–Montenegrin dictionary was published in Podgorica (Demir, Durmiš and Demir 2015), and, in Slovenia, a project for regional standardization was launched as early as 2003 (Antauer, Živa and Peršak 2003), the results of which, however, are not known to us. In Croatia, there does not seem to be a proposal for the transcription of Romani, but considerations in this direction can be found in the *Romsko–hrvatski i hrvatsko–romski rječnik* ['Romani–Croatian and Croatian–Romani dictionary'] (Kajtazi 2008: 17). These efforts have not yet come to completion.

9 Conclusion

The aim of the present book was to show the diverse facets of language contact between the Slavic languages and Romani – on the structural and the lexical level, in the form of matter and pattern borrowing and in writing. To this end, four existing contributions on Slavic-Romani language contact (Meyer 2018, Meyer 2019, Meyer 2020a, Sonnemann 2022) were thoroughly revised, where relevant translated into English, embedded in a contemporary contact-linguistic framework and supplemented by a comprehensive investigation of Romisms in diastratic varieties of different Slavic languages.

A basic idea of the book is the assumption of a structural similarity between Romani and the Slavic languages, which is based on a critical evaluation of the Romani dialect classifications by Elšik and Beníšek (2020). To demonstrate how large the structural gap between Romani varieties can actually be, a comparison of Kalajdži (Bulgaria) and East Finnish Romani was undertaken in Chapter 2. It could be shown that these Romani varieties are comparable with the Slavic languages in terms of distance to one another, and it would therefore be justified to speak of Romani *languages* rather than *dialects* as well as of a Romani *language family* just as one does of a Slavic language family. Of course, it is also true that the individual Romani varieties enjoy a much lower degree of standardization than do the Slavic languages. This notwithstanding, on the structural level, we are in fact dealing with comparable phenomena. This book thus served as a unique opportunity to compare to what extent similar structures are borrowed between different pairs of languages from two language families.

Thereafter, Chapter 3 – with the goal of examining contact phenomena through a contemporary lens – provided an introduction to Matras' (2020) *pragmatic-functional approach to language contact*, the theoretical groundwork for this book. This contemporary, typologically oriented approach brings together synchronic and diachronic aspects of language contact and overcomes the understanding of languages as separate systems in the head of a multilingual speaker. To repeat Matras' own words, the idea was to create a framework

> that can allow us to approach language contact phenomena in a holistic way and to explain how communicative interaction in what we perceive to be multilingual settings can shape the choices that users make and the way they manage their repertoire of linguistic structures. (Matras 2020: 335)

Crucial in the context of this framework are the concepts of the linguistic repertoire and the bilingual mode, which were also introduced here, and from which links were drawn to (matter and pattern) borrowing, codeswitching, fusion and other basic concepts of contact linguistics.

Chapters 4 and 5 provided numerous examples of different outcomes of the language contact between Slavic and Romani. Examples of *pattern replication* are, among others, the reflexive dative ("dative of inner involvement"), the genitive periphrasis in Bulgarian Erli according to the Bulgarian model, the split between the marking of positive and negative possession as well as the omission of the copula according to the East Slavic model in Romani varieties in contact with Russian and Ukrainian and the formation of an analytic passive in the Balkans under Bulgarian (and Greek) influence. Pattern replication also includes the loss of certain features, for example of the definite article in contact with all Slavic languages except for Macedonian and Bulgarian, of genitive constructions in favor of ablative constructions in Arli and Prilep under Macedonian influence, of the opposition imperfect–aorist in North Russian Romani and of causatives in Slovak Romani. Higher cardinal numbers, aspect / aktionsart prefixes and discourse markers, by contrast, are classic examples of *fusion*. Instances of *contact-induced grammaticalization* are the development of an analytic perfect in Arli or the new infinitive in some Romani varieties in contact with West and East Slavic.

As for *matter borrowing*, inflectional endings from Slavic are rarely borrowed, with the few exceptions being plural endings for nouns, person-number markers from Slovene and / or Croatian in Slovene Romani and a Russian-type imperative plural in North Russian Romani. What is also quite rarely attested is the borrowing of interrogatives, possessives, personals and demonstratives. Derivational morphology is much more easily transferred than is inflectional morphology, especially diminutive suffixes and suffixes for abstract nouns, degree and indefinite markers.

Phonology was said to occupy an intermediary position between matter and pattern borrowing. In the contact-situation of Slavic–Romani, we witnessed the replication of Slavic phonemes in loanwords, the convergence of phoneme systems and the substitution of phonemes in loanwords through inherited sounds. In the domain of syntax, especially conjunctions and prepositions have been frequently borrowed from the Slavic contact languages into Romani. Contact-induced change in word order is rare; the only example that was presented here is the tendency of Romani varieties in contact with West Slavic languages to place the pronominal object before the verb. In principle, Slavic impact seems to be less strong on syntax than on other linguistic levels of Romani.

Many of the identified contact features can also be clustered into areal groups. The features that Romani in south eastern Europe shares with other Balkan languages have been described in many Balkan-linguistic works (e.g. Boretzky and Igla 1999; Friedman 2001a, 2021). Two exemplary contact phenomena in Romani in the Balkans are object doubling (which is, however, facultative and not grammaticalized) in contact with Macedonian and a structure modelled on the Bulgarian renarrative in some Romani varieties in Bulgaria. However, even beyond the Balkan linguistic area, we can find areal patterns: Concerning case use, the Northeastern group (especially Russian, Lithuanian and Latvian Romani) differs from other Romani varieties with respect to a whole range of constructions, e.g. in the instrumental construction, the promotion of state construction or pattern replication of different Russian genitive constructions. The Romani varieties under the influence of Slavic contact languages without an article – which are the vast majority of the Slavic languages – are in the process of losing their own definite article, notably those in Slovenia and the Northeastern dialect group. The Romani varieties in contact with the 'North Slavic' languages make massive use of Slavic aspect / aktionsart prefixes, and some of them have developed a "new infinitive".

As for borrowing hierarchies, Elšík and Matras (2006: 370–371) have identified two patterns related to two different motivations for borrowing on the basis of a large sample of 75 Romani dialects. The first ('marked') pattern consists of elements that require a greater effort in language processing and are thus more likely to be borrowed, e.g. higher cardinal numbers, comparative and superlative degree, expressions of contrast and separation and peripheral local relations. This set of borrowing hierarchies

> reflects the tendency of languages in the bilingual's repertoire to converge around those semantic-pragmatic functions that demand greater processing effort and around which it is more difficult to maintain control over the separation of subsets in the linguistic repertoire (Matras 2020: 171).

The elements in the second ('unmarked') set of hierarchies are more prone to borrowing, e.g. 3SG inflectional endings > other inflectional endings, nouns in the nominative > nouns in other case forms, inflected verb-forms in the realis > inflected verb-forms in the irrealis etc. "Here, more frequent, simplex, accessible, and transparent forms have an advantage in terms of ease of replication" (Matras 2020: 171). Within the pragmatic-functional framework, Matras (2020: 237–238) assumes

> that it is the functionality of categories, and not merely their structural representation, that motivates bilingual speakers to generalise a form in the repertoire and adopt it for use irrespective of the choice-language of the interaction context, thereby making it part of another 'language'. [. . .] In this perspective, we view borrowing not merely as a plain modification of an abstract 'system', but as an activity in which speakers engage, and which is goal-oriented. Several different goals of borrowing were described, which can be reduced essentially to two principal motivations: to modify patterns of social interaction, and to modify patterns of language processing during communicative interaction.

Romani is also well-known for massive lexical borrowing from its contact languages. Adamou et al. (2016) have shown that different minority languages can exhibit very different patterns of lexical borrowing, depending on which patterns prevail in their bilingual community. The variety of the Bergitka Roma in Poland investigated in Chapter 6 with 21.5% lexical borrowings from Polish is, for example, very close to Molise Slavic with 22.6% lexical borrowings from its current contact language, Italian. Both are therefore to be classified as 'high borrowers' according to Tadmor's (2009) loanword-based typology of the world's languages. An important insight from this typology is that no language in the world is free of loanwords; the average value is even 24.2% (Tadmor 2009: 56). At the top position on Tadmor's list is a variety of Romani, Selice Romani in southwestern Slovakia, intensively studied by Elšík (2009): It possesses 62.7% loanwords (of which only 7.2% are Slavic, the majority being Hungarian) due to its sociolinguistic circumstances: universal multilingualism, minority language status, socio-political marginalization, a relatively short history, long absence from the ancestral homeland, permissiveness towards borrowing and a lack of standard. To be taken into account is also a degree of scientific bias in that this language contact has been well studied and the donor languages are also well known (Tadmor 2009: 58). These factors apply to Romani in general and give rise to the assumption that the other Romani varieties also belong to the group of 'high borrowers', in which 50% or more of the lexicon is borrowed from contact languages.

However, Adamou et al. (2016: 536) show that proportions of borrowing vary considerably among individual communities, such that it would be worthwhile to investigate other Romani varieties along the lines of Selice Romani and provide numerical data to support the assumption stated above. Our counts of two Romani varieties in Poland do not concern the entirety of the borrowed vocabulary, rather only the loanwords from the current contact language Polish; they amount to 21.5% (Bergitka Roma) and 12.5% (Polska Roma) of the recorded vocabulary. The same applies to the 28.0% of Serbian loanwords in Gurbet (Mirić and Ćirković 2022: 109–110). The investigation of these varieties also confirms once more the very basic tendencies that nouns are more readily borrowed than verbs and content words more readily than function words (Tadmor 2009: 59). Interestingly, study of the semantic fields involved revealed that the field of nature (animals, plants, landscape features, natural materials etc.) is most prone to borrowing in Bergitka and Polska Romani. Only thereafter come those of abstract concepts, dwelling and the 'modern world' (politics, military, education, economy). The human body is relatively far up on the borrowing scale and religion further below, which deviates from Tadmor's (2009: 64) findings, where religion and belief were on top of the borrowing scale and the body at the bottom. Whatever the stratification in a given variety looks like, it reflects "the enduring compartmentalisation of the relevant linguistic expressions in the bilingual repertoire" (Matras 2020: 188). Last but not least, alongside the main bulk of matter borrowing, all Romani varieties also have lexical calques or loan translations, e.g. of the basic phrases 'How are you?' and 'What time is it?'.

9 Conclusion

> Within the pragmatic-functional approach, loanwords can be summed up as bilingual speakers' way of adjusting their overall repertoire of lexical words and the constraints on the selective use of words in certain settings, or with certain interlocutors. The insights [known to contact linguistics] into the hierarchical nature of lexical borrowing provide us with an excellent opportunity to explore how this process of renegotiating the bilingual repertoire is related to the conceptualisation of reality. (Matras 2020: 188)

In contrast to this, the non-standard Romisms used by monolingual speakers of Slavic languages can definitely be called established loanwords. It was shown in Chapter 7 that a particularly large number of Romisms exist in diastratic varieties (historical argots, contemporary youth slang and colloquial varieties) of Czech and the South Slavic languages, while very few Romisms are documented for Polish; Russian and Ukrainian are in between. The most widespread modern Romisms already existed, for the most part, in the argots; they have been preserved over many decades, have undergone formal and semantic extensions and have, at the same time, 'advanced socially' from the secret languages of socially marginalized groups into the modern diastratic varieties. In Russian, around a seventh, in Bosnian / Croatian / Serbian and Czech, around a fifth and, in Bulgarian, around a third of the Romani lexemes from the historical argots have 'survived' up to now.

The final chapter of this book dealt with writing in multilingual settings and the question of how alphabets and orthographies have been created for Romani varieties in different Slavophone countries. Investigation of eleven projects from eight countries has demonstrated that, in most cases, proposals are based on the writing system of the majority language in the respective country, i.e. either the Cyrillic or the Latin alphabet, with both elements of the respective grapheme inventory and orthographic rules. Thus, one can speak of an approximation rather than a demarcation in relation to the majority language which should, however, be interpreted pragmatically rather than emotionally. Individual, unsystematic solutions in writing and the principle of "trial and error" nevertheless continue to pervade.

It must be underlined once more that for the whole project, and especially for Chapters 4–6, the RMS Database has been an invaluable source without which a large part of the research done here would not have been possible. It is a unique tool not only for Romani linguistics, but for linguistics in general, because there is no comparable database for any other language (family) worldwide.

For future research, it would be desirable to investigate contact phenomena in the domain of syntax in more detail, e.g. in the domain of predicate valency, even if the Slavic influence there seems to be less significant than on other linguistic levels. In the domain of the lexicon, precise counts and calculations of the loanword inventory (not only from Slavic, but from all contact languages) could be made for individual varieties in order to further complete Tadmor's typology and to put the already existing results on Selice Romani in relation to other Romani varieties. As far as Romisms in Slavic are concerned, studies on Slovene, Slovak and Macedonian are still needed. This could be very promising especially for the diastratic varieties of Slovak and Macedonian, because of the size of the Roma population in the respective countries, which makes it likely that a relatively large number of Romisms may be observed. Presently, however, there is a lack of suitable (online) dictionaries and other sources to enable such a study. Furthermore, very little research has been done so far on the ethnolectal varieties of Slavic languages spoken by Roma in Slavophone countries; the only detailed study available is that of Bořkovcová (2006) on Czech. Overall, however, it can be said that Romani has now been very thoroughly investigated from a contact-linguistic perspective, and it is gratifying that it still meets with such great interest in linguistics even 150 years after Franz Miklosich.

Appendix 1 (chapter 6): Alphabetical list of analyzed words

Polska Roma
adaptacyjny (Mil1) 'adaptive'
afisz (Gier2) 'poster'
agresor (Gier1) 'aggressor'
akcento (Gier2) 'accent'
ale (PL-018, PL-019) 'but'
ani... ani... (PL-018) 'neither... nor...'
asfalto (Gier2) 'asphalt'
asystent (Mil1) 'assistant'
atako (Gier1) 'attack'
autobuso (PL-018, PL-019) 'bus'
bank (Mil1) 'bank'
barano (PL-018, PL-019) 'sheep, ram'
bardzo (PL-018, PL-019) 'very'
baro (PL-018, PL-019) 'bar'
te bawineł (PL-018), *bawineł pe* (PL-019) 'to play'
benzyna (PL-018, PL-019) 'petrol, gas'
bez (PL-019) 'without'
bezpośrednio (PL-018, PL-019) 'directly'
bi(e)da (PL-018, PL-019) 'poverty'
biodro (PL-018, PL-019) 'hip'
biskupo (Gier1) 'bishop'
biuro (Mil1) 'office'
bizneso (Mil1) 'business'
blizko (PL-018, PL-019) 'close'
bo (PL-019) 'because'
Boże narodzenie (PL-019) 'Christmas'
bransoletka (PL-018, PL-019) 'bracelet'
broda (PL-019) 'beard'
bunto (Gier1) 'rebellion'
butelka (PL-018, PL-019) 'bottle'
byko (PL-018, PL-019) 'bull'
ceło (Gier1, Gier2, PL-018, PL-019) 'whole'
chociaż (PL-018), *choć* (PL-019) 'although'
choć (Dęb) 'at least'
chrobro (Gier1) 'brave, courageous'

https://doi.org/10.1515/9783110756173-010

te chwalineł (PL-019) 'to praise'
chwila (PL-019) 'moment'
ciastko (PL-018) 'cake'
cicho (PL-018) 'silent'
co (PL-018, PL-019) 'every'
cukro (PL-019) 'sugar'
cybula (PL-019) 'onion'
czarownica (PL-018, PL-019) 'witch'
czerwiec (Mil1, PL-019), *czerwcos* (PL-018) 'june'
często (PL-018, PL-019) 'often'
czi (Gier1), *czy* (PL-018, PL-019) 'if, whether'; *interrogative particle*
te czołgineł pe (PL-019) 'to crawl'
czwartek (PL-019), *czwartko* (PL-018) 'Thursday'
daka chrzestna (PL-018) 'godmother'
te denerwineł pes (PL-018) 'to get upset'
dębo (Gier1) 'oak'
dialekt (Gier2) 'dialect'
długi (PL-019) 'debts'
długo (PL-018, PL-019) 'long'
dokładnio (PL-019) 'exact'
doktor (PL-018, PL-019) 'doctor'
dopóki (PL-018, PL-19) 'until'
te doprowadzineł (te dylinipen) (PL-019) 'to drive (so. crazy)'
drogo (PL-019) 'expensive'
drugo (PL-019) 'second'
dusza (PL-019) 'soul'
dyrektoro (PL-018, PL-019) 'director'
dziąsło (PL-018, PL-019) 'gum'
dzienny (PL-019) 'daily'
dziennikarzo (PL-018), *dziennikarka* (PL-019) 'journalist'
dziura (PL-018, PL-019) 'hole'
dziwno (PL-018) 'strange'
fabryka (PL-019) 'factory'
festiwalo (Gier2) 'festival'
figura (Mil1) 'figure, statue'
filiżanka (PL-019) 'cup'
filmo (Gier2) 'movie'
te fruwineł (PL-018) 'to fly'
gazowo (Gier2) 'gas' *adj.*
geometryczny (Mil1) 'geometrical'

gęś (PL-019) 'goose'
gimnazium (Mil1) 'junior high school'
gorszy (PL-018) 'worse'
gość (PL-018) 'guest'
gotowo (PL-018, PL-019) 'ready'
gruszka (PL-018, PL-019) 'pear'
grzyb (PL-019) 'mushroom'
gwóźdź (PL-018) 'nail'
herbata (PL-019) 'tea'
historia (Mil1, PL-019) 'story; history'
honoro (PL-018) 'honour'
i (PL-018) 'and'
instrument (PL-018, PL-019) 'instrument'
inteligentny (Mil1) 'intelligent'
intencja (Gier1) 'intention'
jajko (PL-019) 'egg'
jeszcze (PL-018, PL-019) 'still'
jeżo (PL-018), *jeżako* (PL-019) 'hedgehog'
te jeździneł (PL-019) 'to drive'
już (PL-018, PL-019) 'already'
kalejdoskopo (Gier2) 'kaleidoscope'
kampingo (Gier2) 'camping'
kapeluszos (PL-019) 'hat'
kapusta (PL-019) 'cabbage'
te kaszlineł (PL-018, PL-019) 'to cough'
katechizmo (Gier2) 'catechizm'
kawa (PL-018, PL-019) 'coffee'
kawałko (PL-019) 'piece'
każdo/-y (PL-018), *każo* (PL-019) 'every'
kiedy (PL-018, PL-019) 'when'
kiedykolwiek (PL-019) 'ever'
kiedyś (PL-019) 'someday, sometime'
kierunko (PL-019) 'direction'
kino (Mil1) 'cinema'
klasa (Mil1) 'class'
klucz (PL-019) 'key'
koc (PL-019) 'blanket'
kolano (PL-019) 'knee'
kolczuga (Gier1) 'armour'
kolega (Mil1, PL-018, PL-019), *koleżanka* (PL-018, PL-019) 'friend'

kolko (PL-018), *kolka* (PL-019) 'thorn' < *kolec*
kongreso (Gier2) 'congress'
końco (PL-018), *koniec* (PL-019) 'end'
koralo (PL-018) 'bead'
te krążyneł (PL-018, PL-019) 'to rotate'
królo (PL-018, PL-019) 'king'
króliko (PL-019) 'rabbit'
krótki (PL-019), *krótko* (PL-018, PL-019) 'short'
krzak (PL-018, PL-019) 'bush'
krzesło (PL-019) 'chair'
te krzyczyneł (PL-019) 'to scream'
krzyk (PL-018, PL-019) 'scream'
krzywda (PL-018) 'harm'
kuchnia (PL-019) 'kitchen'
księdzo (PL-018) 'priest'
księżyco (PL-018, PL-019) 'moon'
kultura (Mil1, Gier2) 'culture'
kurczako (PL-018, PL-019) 'chicken'
kurtka (PL-018, PL-019) 'jacket'
kurzo (PL-018, PL-019) 'dust'
kwadrato (Mil1) 'square'
kwiat(ko) (PL-018, PL-019) 'flower'
te latineł (PL-019) 'to fly'
latopiżo (Gier2) 'bat' < *nietoperz*
liceum (Mil1) 'high school'
lider (Mil1) 'leader'
te lidzieł (Gier1), *lidźel, lidzineł* (Mil1) 'to lead'
lipco (PL-018, PL-019) 'july'
listo (PL-018), *lista* (PL-019) 'letter'
liść (PL-018, PL-019) 'leaf'
litera (PL-018, PL-019, Gier2, Mil1) 'letter'
lodo (PL-018, PL-019) 'ice'
te lubineł (PL-018, PL-019) 'to like, to love'
lusterko (PL-019) 'mirror'
łańcucho (PL-019) 'chain'
łatwo (PL-019) 'easy'
ławka (PL-018, PL-019) 'bank'
łokcio (PL-018, PL-019) 'elbow'
łudka (PL-019), *łydka* (PL-018) 'boat'
te (po)malineł (PL-018, PL-019) 'to paint'

matematyka (Gier2) 'mathematics'
mebli (PL-018, PL-019) '(pieces of) furniture'
metalo (PL-019) 'metal'
męczkirdo (Gier1) 'martyr' < *męczennik*
mieczo (PL-018, PL-019) 'sword'
między (PL-019) 'between'
miło (Gier1, PL-018, PL-019) 'nice'
minuta (PL-018, PL-019) 'minute'
miódo (PL-018), *miodo* (PL-019) 'honey'
misjakro (Gier1) 'missionary' < *misjonarz*
młyno (PL-018, PL-019) 'mill'
te mogineł (Mil1, PL-018, PL-019) 'can, to be able to'
morzo (PL-018), *morze* (PL-019) 'sea'
mosto (PL-018, PL-019) 'bridge'
może (PL-018, PL-019) 'maybe'
możliwo (PL-018) 'possible'
możliwość (PL-019) 'possibility'
można (PL-019) 'one can'
mrówka (PL-018, PL-019) 'ant'
mucha (PL-018, PL-019) 'fly'
te musineł (Gier1, Gier2, PL-018, PL-019), *muśineł* (Mil1) 'must, have to'
muzyko (PL-018), *muzykant* (PL-019) 'musician'
te myślineł (Gier1, PL-018, PL-019) 'to think'
nadzieja (PL-019) 'hope'
nagle (PL-019) 'suddenly'
naokoło (PL-018) 'around'
napełniono (PL-019) 'filled (with)'
na pewno (PL-018, PL-019) 'for sure'
te naprawineł (PL-019) 'to repair'
naszyjnik (PL-018) 'collar'
nauczyciel(ka) (Mil1, PL-018, PL-019) 'teacher'
nerwowy (PL-018) 'nervous'
niebo (PL-019) 'sky'
niedziela (PL-018, PL-019) 'Sunday'
niektóry (PL-019) 'some'
te nienawidzineł (PL-019) 'to hate'
nieraz (PL-019) 'many a time'
nigdy (PL-018, PL-019) 'never'
nigdzie (PL-018, PL-019) 'nowhere'
niski (PL-018, PL-019) 'short'

niż (PL-018, PL-019) 'than'
obcy (PL-018) 'strange'
obiado (PL-019) 'lunch'
obojętnie (PL-018) 'no matter, -ever'
obok (PL-019) 'beside'
obozo (Gier1) 'camp'
obrazo (PL-018, PL-019) 'picture'
ocena (Mil1) 'grade'
od razu (PL-019) 'at once'
odważny (PL-018, PL-019) 'courageous'
te odwiedzineł (PL-018, PL-019) 'to visit'
o dziesiątej (PL-018, PL-019) 'at ten'
ogroda (PL-018), *ogrodo* (PL-019) 'garden'
okno (PL-018, PL-019) 'window'
okulary (PL-019) 'glasses'
olejo (PL-018, PL-019) 'oil'
ołtarzo (Gier1) 'altar'
opieka (Mil1) 'care'
oprócz (PL-018, PL-019) 'except for'
organizacja (Mil1) 'organization'
orło (Gier1) 'eagle'
orłoskro (Gier1) 'eagle' *adj.*
orzech(o) (PL-018, PL-019) 'nut'
osiedlenio (Gier2) 'settlement'
o siódmej (PL-018, PL-019) 'at seven'
ostatnio (PL-018, PL-019) 'last'
ostrożno (PL-019) 'careful'
te (za)oszczędzineł (PL-018, PL-019) 'to save'
te ożenineł (PL-019) 'to get married'
palco (PL-018, PL-019) 'finger'
panna młoda (PL-018) 'bride'
państwo (PL-018) 'state'
papieros (PL-019) 'cigarette'
papieżo (Gier1) 'pope'
paszporto (PL-018, PL-019) 'passport'
paznokcio (PL-018, PL-019) 'fingernail'
perła (PL-019) 'pearl'
pewno (PL-019) 'sure'
piacho (PL-018, PL-019) 'sand'
piątek (PL-018, PL-019) 'Friday'

pierwotno (PL-019) 'original'
pióro (Gier1) 'feather'
te pisyneł (PL-018, PL-019) 'to write'
piwo (PL-019) 'beer'
plan (PL-018) 'plan'
plastelinia (Mil1) 'modelling clay'
płaszczo (PL-018, PL-019) 'coat'
pływalnia (Mil1) 'swimming pool'
pocztówka (PL-019) 'postcard'
po drodze (PL-018) 'on the way'
pogoda (PL-019) 'weather'
pogrzebo (PL-018, PL-019) 'funeral'
te pojawineł pe (PL-019) 'to appear'
te poklepineł (PL-018) 'to tap'
pokojo (PL-018, PL-019) 'room'
polana (Gier1) 'glade'
policzko (PL-018, PL-019) 'cheek'
pol(i)o (PL-018, PL-019) 'field'
polsko (Mil1) 'Polish'
te pomogineł (Gier1, Mil1, PL-018, PL-019) 'to help'
poniedziałek (PL-019) 'Monday'
te poplamineł (PL-018) 'to stain'
te posprzątyneł (PL-019) 'to clean'
te potrafineł (PL-019) 'to be able to'
te potrzebineł (PL-018, PL-019) 'to need'
powieść (PL-018), *opowieść* (PL-019) 'story'
powinno (PL-018, PL-019) 'should'
powoli (PL-018) 'slow'
te pozwolineł (PL-019) 'to allow'
później (PL-019) 'later'
prawo (PL-018) 'right across' (sic)
te probineł (PL-019) 'to try'
problema (Mil1), *problemo* (Gier2) 'problem'
profesor (Mil1) 'professor'
prosto (PL-019) 'straight'
przedszkole (Mil1) 'kindergarten'
przejazdko (PL-019) 'drive'
te przekonineł (PL-018, PL-019) 'to convince'
przerażający (PL-019) 'terrifying'
te przestraszyneł (PL-019) 'to terrify'

przez (PL-019) 'through'
przeziębienie (PL-018, PL-019) 'cold'
te przeziębineł pe (PL-019) 'to catch a cold'
przyjacielo (PL-018) 'friend'
przyjazno (PL-019) 'friendly, nice'
przyjęcie (Mil1, PL-018, PL-019) 'reception'
przyszłość (PL-019) 'future'
pszenica (PL-018) 'wheat'
pudełko (PL-018), *pudło* (PL-019) 'box'
rachunek (Mil1) 'bill, check'
radio (PL-018, PL-019) 'radio'
ramię (PL-018, PL-019) 'arm'
rano (PL-018, PL-019) 'morning'
te ratyneł (Gier1) 'to rescue'
te reperyneł (PL-019) 'to repair'
rękaw (PL-018, PL-019) 'sleeve'
robako (PL-019) 'worm'
rodzajos (PL-019) 'type, kind'
rodzina (PL-018) 'family'
rogi (PL-018, PL-019) 'antlers'
rynko (PL-018, PL-019) 'market place'
rządo (PL-018, PL-019) 'government'
rzecz (PL-018, PL-019) 'thing'
rzeka (PL-018) 'river'
te sądzineł (PL-019) 'to judge'
sąsiad (PL-018, PL-019) 'neighbor'
sekret (PL-018) 'secret'
sierść (PL-018, PL-019) 'fur'
siostrzyczka (PL-018) 'little sister'
te siwineł (PL-018) 'to turn grey'
sklepo (PL-018, PL-019) 'shop'
te skończyneł (PL-018, PL-019) 'to finish'
te skręcineł (PL-018, PL-019) 'to turn'
skrzyżowanie (PL-018, PL-019) 'crossroads'
samotno (PL-018, PL-019) 'lonely'
słodycze (PL-019) 'sweets'
słowiański (Gier1) 'Slavic'
smalco (PL-018, PL-019) 'lard'
smutny (PL-018), *smutno* (PL-019) 'sad'
sobota (PL-019) 'Saturday'

socjalo (Mil1) 'social'
spacer (PL-018, PL-019) 'walk'
spisko (Gier1) 'conspiracy'
spokojny (PL-019) 'peaceful'
srogo (Gier1) 'severe'
stopa (PL-019) 'foot'
stos (PL-018, PL-019) 'pile'
te stracineł (PL-018, PL-019) 'to lose'
te straszineł (PL-018) 'to frighten'
te straszkereł (PL-018), *straszjakireł* (PL-019) 'to frighten'
te strzeżyneł (Gier1) 'to guard'
studia (Mil1) 'studies'
studnia (PL-018, PL-019) 'well'
stycznio (PL-018, PL-019) 'January'
stypendium (Mil1) 'scholarship'
sukienka (PL-019) 'dress'
swento (Gier1), *swanto* (Gier2) 'holy'
sytuacja (Mil1) 'situation'
szafa (PL-018, PL-019) 'wardrobe'
szczenię (PL-019) 'puppy'
szkoła (Mil1, Gier2) 'school'
sztandaro (Gier1) 'banner'
szuflada (PL-018, PL-019) 'drawer'
ściana (PL-018, PL-019) 'wall'
śliwka (PL-018, PL-019) 'plum'
ślub(o) (PL-018, PL-019) 'wedding'
śmiały (PL-018, PL-019) 'bold'
śniego (PL-018, PL-019) 'snow'
środa (PL-018, PL-019) 'Wednesday'
światło (PL-018) 'light'
święto (PL-018) 'celebration'
tajemnico (PL-019) 'mysterious'
taktyka (Gier1) 'tactic'
talerz (PL-018), *talerzo* (PL-019) 'plate'
targo (PL-019) 'market'
teatro (Mil1, Gier2) 'theater'
teści (PL-018), *teściowa* (PL-019) 'aunt'
też (PL-018, PL-019) 'also'
to (PL-018) 'this'
torba (PL-018) 'bag'

tradycja (Gier2) 'tradition'
tramwaj (Gier2) 'tram'
tretuaro (Gier2) 'pavement'
trójkąto (Mil1) 'triangle'
trybo (Mil1, Gier2) 'style'
tylko (PL-018, PL-019) 'only'
tytonjo (PL-019) 'tobacco'
ubezpieczenie (Mil1) 'protection'
udo (PL-018, PL-019) 'thigh'
uczeń (PL-018) 'pupil'
te uczineł (PL-019) 'to learn'
ukarano (PL-018, PL-019) 'punished'
ulica (PL-018, PL-019) 'street'
urodziny (PL-018, PL-019) 'birthday'
te używineł (PL-019) 'to use'
warga (PL-018) 'lip'
w ciągu (PL-019) 'during'
wełna (PL-018, PL-019) 'wool'
węglo (PL-018, PL-019) 'coal'
(nie)wiadomo (PL-019) '(un)known'
wiadomości (PL-018) 'news'
widoko (PL-019) 'sight'
wigilia (Gier2) 'Christmas Eve'
wilk(o) (PL-018, PL-019) 'wolf'
te (po)witineł (PL-018, PL-019) 'to greet'
własny (PL-019) 'own'
woj-[?] (Gier1) 'knight'
wojna (PL-018, PL-019) 'war'
wtedy (kiedy) (PL-019) 'anytime'
wtorko (PL-018, PL-019) 'Tuesday'
te wychowineł pe (PL-019) 'to grow up'
te wyglądineł (PL-019) 'to look'
wypadko (PL-019) 'accident'
te zaczineł (PL-018, PL-019) 'to begin'
zamiast (PL-018) 'instead of'
zamko (PL-018, PL-019) 'castle'
zanim (PL-018) 'before'
zaraz (PL-018) 'any minute'
zawsze (PL-018, PL-019) 'always'
te zdążyneł (Gier1) 'to manage to do'

zespoło (Mil1) 'team'
te zgadnineł (PL-018, PL-019) 'to guess'
zmęczono (PL-018, PL-019), *zmenćkirdo* (Dęb) 'tired'
te zmusineł (PL-018, PL-019) 'to force'
znać (PL-018) 'to know'
zupa (PL-018, PL-019) 'soup'
zwierzak (PL-018) 'animal'
żamba (Gier2) 'frog'
żelazo (PL-019) 'iron'
żołnierzo (PL-018), *żołnierz* (PL-019) 'soldier'
żołądko (PL-018), *żełądko* (PL-019) 'stomach'
żyd (PL-019) 'Jew'

Bergitka Roma
a (Bla, Gier3) 'and; but'
adaptacyjny (Mil2) 'adaptive'
administracja (Mil2) 'administration'
agresor (Bla) 'aggressor'
ale (Bla) 'but'
artysto (Gier3) 'artist'
asystent(ka) (Mil2) 'assistant'
atak (Bla) 'attack'
autobusis (PL-007) 'bus'
autos (PL-007) 'car'
aż (Bla) 'until'
baros (PL-007) 'bar'
te bawineł (Mil2), *bawineł pes* (PL-007) 'to play'
benzyna (PL-007) 'petrol, gas'
bezpośrednio (PL-007) 'direct'
bida (Mir) 'poverty'
biodros (PL-007) 'hip'
biskupo (Bla) 'bishop'
blizko (PL-007) 'close'
bo (Bla, Mir) 'because'
bogato (PL-007) 'rich'
te brakineł (Bla) 'to lack'
bransoletka (PL-007) 'bracelet'
broszura (Mil2) 'brochure'
bunto (Bla) 'rebellion'
bus (Gier3) 'bus'

bystry (Mil2) 'quick'
cało (Gier3, Mir), *ceło* (Bla) 'whole'
cerkwia (Gier3) 'church'
ciałos (PL-007) 'body'
te ciągnąć (PL-007) 'to tare'
cisto (Mir) 'clean'
chodnik (Gier3) 'pavement'
chrobry (Bla) 'brave'
chrystusoskro (Bla) 'Christian'
te chwalineł (PL-007) 'to praise'
ciastko (PL-007) 'cake'
ciekawy (Mil2) 'curious'
ciemno (PL-007) 'dark'
cukros (PL-007) 'sugar'
cybulja (PL-007) 'onion'
cyfra (Gier3) 'figure'
czapka (PL-007) 'cap'
czarownica (PL-007) 'witch'
czasos (PL-007), *ćaso* (Gier3), *ciasos* (Bla) 'time'
czerwcos (PL-007) 'June'
te czuineł (PL-007) 'to feel'
czwartkos (PL-007) 'Thursday'
czy (PL-007, Gier3), *ci* (Mir) 'if, whether'; *interrogative particle*
czysto (PL-007) 'clean'
te ćytyneł (Gier3), *(prze)ćitineł* (Mil2) 'to read'
ćwićisagos (Mil2) 'exercise' < *ćwiczenie*
dachos (Gier3) 'roof'
daleko (PL-007) 'far'
te decidyneł (Mil2) 'to decide'
dębo (Bla) 'oak'
doktoris (PL-007) 'doctor'
dom(os) (PL-007) 'house'
dopóki (PL-007) 'until'
te dotrzeineł (PL-007) 'to arrive, reach'
drewno (PL-007) 'wood'
drogeria (Gier3) 'chemistry'
drugo (PL-007) 'second'
drużyna (Bla) 'squad'
drzewo (PL-007) 'tree'
drzwi (PL-007) 'door'

dusza (PL-007) 'soul'
dyrektorija (Mil2) 'rectorate'
dyskryminacja (Mil2) 'discrimination'
dywanos (Gier3) 'carpet'
dziennikaro (PL-007) 'journalist'
te dźelineł (Gier3) 'to share'
edukacja (Mil2) 'education'
festiwalo (Gier3) 'festival'
figura (Mil2) 'figure, statue'
filiżanka (PL-007) 'cup'
fizyczny (Mil2) 'physical'
gardłos (PL-007) 'throat'
gazowo (Gier3) 'gas-'
geometryczny (Mil2) 'geometrical'
gęś (PL-007) 'goose'
te golineł pes (Gier3) 'to shave oneself'
gotowo (PL-007) 'ready'
granica (Bla) 'border'
groś (Mir) 'penny'
gród (Bla) 'stronghold'
grupa (Mil2) 'group'
grusza (PL-007) 'pear tree'
gruszka (PL-007) 'pear'
grzyb (PL-007) 'mushroom'
habitos (Bla) 'cowl'
historia (PL-007, Gier3) 'story; history'
honoris (PL-007) 'honour'
hufiec (Bla) 'detachment' *milit.*
i (Bla) 'and'
inny (PL-007) 'other'
inteligentny (Mil2) 'intelligent'
intencja (Bla) 'intention'
jeżos (PL-007) 'hedgehog'
kalejdoskopo (Gier3) 'kaleidoscope'
kamienios (PL-007) 'stone'
kampingos (Gier3) 'camping'
katechizmos (Gier3) 'catechizm'
kawa (PL-007) 'coffee'
każdo (Mil2) 'every'
kiedyś (PL-007) 'some day'

kieszeń (PL-007) 'pocket'
klasa (Mil2) 'class'
klęska (Bla) 'defeat'
klubos (Mil2) 'club'
te kładzineł (PL-007) 'to put'
kochać (PL-007) 'to love'
kolanos (PL-007) 'knee'
kolcos (PL-007) 'thorn'
kolczuga (Bla) 'armour'
kolega, koleżanka (PL-007) 'friend'
koleja (Gier3) 'train'
kolor (Mil2) 'colour'
konflikt (Mil2) 'conflict'
końcos (PL-007) 'end'
koralikos (PL-007) 'bead'
kotlaro (Gier3) 'boiler maker'
kotos (PL-007) 'cat'
kowaćis (Gier3) 'smith'
kresłos (Gier3), *krzesło(s)* (PL-007) 'chair'
te kroineł (PL-007) 'to cut'
królik (PL-007) 'rabbit'
króljos (PL-007) 'king'
krza(cz)ki (PL-007) 'bush'
księżycos (PL-007) 'moon'
kultura (Mil2, Gier3) 'culture'
kumpel (PL-007) 'friend'
kurzos (PL-007) 'dust'
księżyc (PL-007) 'moon'
kśano (Gier3) 'horse-radish' < *chrzan*
kwadratos (Mil2) 'square'
kwiatos (PL-007), kwetek (Mir) 'flower'
lampa (Gier3) 'lamp'
te latineł (PL-007) 'to fly'
te lepineł (Mil2) 'to glue'
lepszo (PL-007) 'better'
lider (Mil2) 'leader'
te lidzineł (Bla) 'to lead'
te liczyneł (PL-007) 'to count'
lipcos (PL-007) 'July'
liść (PL-007) 'leaf'

lodos (PL-007) 'ice'
lokalny (Mil2) 'local'
łańc[?] (Gier3) 'chain'
łatwones (Bla) 'easy'
łoktios (PL-007) 'elbow'
łódka (PL-007) 'boat'
luty (Gier3) 'February'
te malineł (Mil2), *(po)malineł* (PL-007) 'to paint'
maszyna (PL-007) 'machine'
matematyka (Gier3) 'mathematics'
mebli (PL-007) '(pieces of) furniture'
mećetos (Gier3) 'mosque'
metalis (PL-007) 'metal'
miastos (PL-007) 'town'
mieczo (Bla), *mieczos* (PL-007) 'sword'
te mierzyneł (Bla) 'to measure'
te mieszkineł (PL-007) 'to live'
miło (Bla) 'dear'
minuta (PL-007, Gier3) 'minute'
miodos (PL-007) 'honey'
misjakro (Bla) 'missionary'
miśliśagos (Mil2) 'thinking' < *myślenie*
młaka (Bla) 'swamp'
młynaris (Gier3) 'miller'
młynos (PL-007) 'mill'
te mogineł (Bla) 'can, to be able to'
mostos/-is (PL-007) 'bridge'
może (Bla, PL-007, Gier3) 'maybe'
możliwo (PL-007) 'possible'
mrówka (PL-007) 'ant'
mucha (PL-007) 'fly'
te musineł (Bla, PL-007, Mir), *muśineł* (Mil2, Gier3) 'must, have to'
muzykos (PL-007) 'musician'
te myślineł (Bla) 'to think'
myśos (Gier3) 'mouse'
nacja (Gier3) 'nation'
namiotis (PL-007) 'tent'
te namówineł (Mil2) 'to plot'
te napołnineł (PL-007) 'to fill'
nauczyćelka (Mil2) '(female) teacher'

nawet (PL-007) 'even'
na zewnątrz (PL-007) 'outside'
nazywinaw pes (PL-007) 'to be called'
te nażekineł (Bla) 'to complain'
niebo (Bla), *nebos* (PL-007), *niebos* (Mir) 'sky, heaven'
niedługo (PL-007) 'soon'
niemiecko (Bla) 'German'
nietopeżo (Gier3) 'bat'
nigda (Bla, Mir) 'never'
nitka (PL-007) 'thread'
niż (PL-007) 'than'
te nosineł (PL-007) 'to carry'
obejmować (PL-007) 'to embrace'
obowiunzek (Mil2) 'duty'
obozo (Bla) 'camp'
obraziz, obrazek (PL-007), obraz (Gier3) 'picture'
te ocalineł (Bla) 'to save'
od (Bla) 'from'
te odbiciaweł (Bla) 'to return'
te odbyineł pes (PL-007) 'to take place' < *odbywać się*
te odpoczineł (Bla) 'to relax'
te odwiedzineł (PL-007) 'to visit'
ogrodos (PL-007) 'garden'
okulary (PL-007) 'glasses'
olejis (PL-007) 'oil'
ołtarzo (Bla) 'altar'
opieka (Mil2) 'care'
opiekunos (Bla) 'carer'
organizacja (Mil2) 'organization'
orłos (Bla) 'eagle'
orzech (PL-007) 'nut'
ostatni (PL-007) 'last'
te ostrzeżyneł (Bla) 'to warn'
te otwierineł, otworzyneł (PL-007) 'to open'
oszukiwać (PL-007) 'to cheat'
pacha (PL-007) 'armpit'
pameca (Mil2) 'memory' < *pamięć*
państwo (PL-007) 'country'
państwowo (Mil2) 'state' *adj.*
papieżo (Bla) 'pope'

paszportos (PL-007) 'passport'
piaskos (PL-007) 'sand'
piątek (PL-007) 'Friday'
pierścionkos (PL-007) 'ring'
pięć (PL-007, Gier3) 'five'
te pilnineł (Mil2) 'to look after'
pirśo (Mil2) 'first'
te pisineł (PL-007, Gier3), *(na)pisineł* (Mil2) 'to write'
piwos (PL-007) 'beer'
plastelina (Mil2) 'modelling clay'
plemiona (Bla) 'tribe'
płaśćus (Gier3) 'coat'
te płatineł (PL-007) 'to pay'
płotos (PL-007) 'fence'
po (Gier3) 'each'
te pochodzineł (PL-007) 'to come'
te poddawać pes (Bla) 'to yield'
te podnosineł (PL-007) 'to lift'
podstawa (Mil2) 'basis'
podwórze (PL-007) 'yard'
pogańsko (Bla) 'pagan'
pogoda (Mil2, PL-007) 'weather'
pogrebis (PL-007) 'funeral'
pokois (PL-007) 'room'
polana (Bla) 'glade'
polsko (Mil2, Gier3) 'Polish'
pomoc (Mil2) 'help'
te pomożineł (Bla), *pomożineł* (Mil2), *pomagineł* (PL-007) 'to help'
poniedziałkos (PL-007) 'Monday'
pori berśrenge (Mil2) 'season'
te potrzebineł (PL-007) 'to need'
te pozwolineł (Bla) 'to allow'
późno (Bla) 'late'
prawo (Mil2) 'right'
prezes (Mil2) 'chairman'
profesjonalny (Gier3) 'professional'
prostokuntos (Mil2) 'rectangle'
te prowadzineł (Mil2, PL-007) 'to lead'
przedszkole (Mil2) 'kindergarten'
przedszkolny/-o (Mil2) 'kindergarten' *adj.*

przedział (Mil2) 'compartment'
te przestaineł (PL-007) 'to stop' < *przestać*
te przestraszineł (pes) (PL-007) 'to frighten'
przez (PL-007) 'through'
przyjacielis (PL-007) 'friend'
przyjęcios (PL-007) 'reception'
przykrość (Mil2) 'distress'
przyroda (Mil2) 'nature'
przyzwoliśagos (Mil2) 'consent' < *przyzwolenie*
przyszłość (PL-007) 'future'
pszewodnikos (Bla) 'guide'
pułapka (Bla) 'trap'
pszenica (PL-007) 'wheat'
pśćoła (Gier3) 'bee'
rada (Mir) 'advice'
rado (Mil2) 'with pleasure'
ramiono (PL-007) 'arm'
te ratineł (Bla) 'to rescue'
rękaw (PL-007) 'sleeve'
te risineł (Mil2) 'to draw'
robakos (PL-007) 'worm'
roślina (Mil2) 'plant'
te rozbineł (PL-007) 'to break' < *rozbić*
te rozumineł (PL-007) 'to understand'
rozumiśagos (Mil2) 'understanding'
te rozważineł (Bla) 'to consider'
te rozwiineł (Mil2) 'to develop'
różańcos (Mir) 'rosary'
rynkos (PL-007) 'market place'
rzecz (PL-007) 'thing'
rządis (PL-007) 'government'
rzeka (PL-007) 'river'
sala (Mil2) 'room'
samo (Mil2) 'the same'
sąsiedztwo (PL-007) 'neighborhood'
skarbos (Mil2) 'treasure'
sklepos (PL-007) 'shop'
te skończyneł (PL-007) 'to finish'
te skręcineł (PL-007) 'to turn'
skrzyżowanie (PL-007) 'crossroads'

sombato(s) (PL-007) 'Saturday'
specjalno (Mil2) 'special'
spotkanie (Mil2) 'meeting'
sprawa (Bla) 'issue'
słowiański (Bla) 'Slavic'
sługadzia (Bla) 'army'
sługadzis (Gier3) 'soldier'
smalcos (PL-007) 'lard'
smutno (PL-007) 'sad'
spisko (Bla) 'conspiracy'
społeczno (Mil2) 'social'
te spotkineł (PL-007) 'to meet'
sprawność (Mil2) 'fitness'
srogi (Bla) 'severe'
stać (Mil2) 'to afford'
start (Mil2) 'start'
stolikos (PL-007) 'table'
stołos (PL-007) 'bench'
stosis (PL-007) 'pile'
studnia (PL-007) 'well'
stycznios (PL-007) 'January'
swenti (Bla), *swento* (Gier3) 'holy'
sylwestr (PL-007) 'New Year's Eve'
synagoga (Gier3) 'synagogue'
sytuacja (Mil2) 'situation'
szafa (PL-007) 'wardrobe'
te szanineł (Mil2) 'to respect'
szansa (Bla) 'chance'
szkolno (Mil2) 'school' *adj.*
szkoła (Mil2, PL-007, Gier3) 'school'
szkoła podstawowa (Mil2) 'primary school'
szmaty (PL-007) 'clothes'
szufladka (PL-007) 'drawer'
ściana (PL-007) 'wall'
ślados (Gier3) 'trace'
śliwka (PL-007) 'plum'
ślubos (PL-007) 'wedding'
śpiąco (PL-007) 'sleepy'
środono (PL-007) 'Wednesday'
te śumineł (Gier3) 'to murmur'

te świćineł (Mir) 'to shine'
świnia (PL-007) 'pig'
targos (Gier3) 'market'
teatro (Gier3) 'theater'
temat (Mil2) 'topic'
tisz (Bla), *tiś* (Mir) 'also'
tradycja (Mil2, Gier3) 'tradition'
trewik (Gier3) 'shoe'
trójkuntos (Mil2) 'triangle'
ubrania (PL-007) 'clothes'
uczeń (PL-007) 'pupil'
uczynek (Bla) 'deed'
udos (PL-007) 'thigh'
te ukłonineł (PL-007) 'to bow down'
te ukończineł (Mil2) 'to finish'
umyslos (PL-007) 'mind'
upić pes (PL-007) 'to get drunk'
te uratineł (Bla) 'to rescue'
te urodzineł pes (PL-007) 'to be born'
urodziny (PL-007) 'birthday'
usta (PL-007) 'mouth'
warga (PL-007) 'lip'
warunek (Mil2) 'condition'
ważno (Mil2) 'important'
wbiegać (PL-007) 'to run (against, into)'
wełna (PL-007) 'wool'
te wędrineł (PL-007) 'to travel'
węglos (PL-007) 'coal'
te widzieł (PL-007) 'to see'
wierszyk (Mil2) '(little) poem'
wiećma (Bla) 'witch'
więzienie (PL-007) 'prison'
wilk(os) (PL-007) 'wolf'
winogrado (Gier3) 'grape'
wlewo (PL-007) 'left'
wojna (PL-007) 'war'
woj-[?] (Bla) 'knight'
wozos (PL-007) 'cart'
wroga (Bla) 'enemy'
wróżba (Bla) 'prophecy'

wtorkos (PL-007) 'Tuesday'
wymaganie (Mil2) 'requirement'
wyobraźnia (Mil2) 'imagination'
wypadkos (PL-007) 'accident'
wystarczająco (PL-007) 'enough'
wyznawca (Bla) 'confessor'
te wyzywineł (PL-007) 'to call'
zabawa (Mil2) 'game'
te zaćhineł (Mil2), *zacznineł* (PL-007) 'to begin'
te zaleźineł (Mil2) 'to depend'
zamkos (PL-007) 'castle'
te zapisineł (Mil2) 'to enrol'
zaproszenie (PL-007) 'invitation'
zasada (Mil2) 'rule'
te zasłużyneł (Bla) 'to deserve'
zawodos (Mil2) 'profession'
zawsze (Mil2, PL-007) 'always'
te zdążyneł (Bla) 'to manage to do'
te zebrineł (PL-007) 'to collect'
zegarkos (Gier3) 'watch'
zero (Gier3) 'zero'
zespoło (Gier3) 'team'
zęby (PL-007) 'teeth'
te zgadnineł (PL-007) 'to guess'
ziemia (PL-007) 'earth'
złodziej (PL-007) 'thief'
złoto (PL-007) 'gold'
złoty (Gier3) 'złoty (currency)'
zły (PL-007) 'bad'
te zmęczyneł (PL-007) 'to be tired'
te zminineł (Mil2) 'to change' < *zmienić*
te zmoczineł (Bla) 'to wet'
te znajdineł (PL-007) 'to find'
znakos (Bla) 'sign'
zostawić (PL-007) 'to leave'
te zostawineł (PL-007) 'to stay'
zupa (PL-007) 'soup'
zwierzę (PL-007) 'animal'
ża(m)ba (Gier3) 'frog'

te żebrineł (PL-007) 'to beg'
żelazos (PL-007) 'iron'
židos (PL-007) 'Jew'
żołądkos (PL-007) 'stomach'
żołneżis (PL-007) 'soldier'
żyto (PL-007) 'rye'
żywo (PL-007) 'alive'

Appendix 2 (chapter 7): Romani borrowings in diastratic varieties of Slavic

The word forms come from various Romani varieties, which are not specified here in detail. Note that not all possible forms in all possible varieties are given for each word, but only the form(s) from the relevant varietie(s) in the contact situation(s) in question. The given meanings are largely based on the dictionaries by Boretzky and Igla (1994a) for South-Eastern Europe, Hübschmannová et al. (1991) for the Czech Republic and Šapoval (2012) for Russia and Ukraine. The word accent is indicated if known. The words that can be found in the dictionaries but are not known to the consulted native speakers are marked with a ?. Some entries from the online dictionaries have to be classified as nonce creations, they are presented in square brackets.

Word (stem) and meaning	Historical argots	Present-day youth slangs and colloquial varieties
adaj 'here, hither'	**cz:** *adaj, adava* 'here, hither'	–
andre 'inside, into'	**bg:** *ándre* 'inside; prison' **cz:** *andre* 'there, in, into, to'	–
anel 'to bring'	**cz:** *an!* 'bring/give it to me!'	–
arakhel 'to find; to guard' etc.	**bg:** *araklarăm* 'to take, to steal' **cz:** *ara(k)!* 'attention!'	–
arno, jaro 'egg'	**bcs:** *arniška* 'eggs' **ru:** *jaró, javró, javrúška* 'egg'	–
aro 'flour'	**bcs:** *arina* 'flour' **ru:** *ravó* 'flour; rye'	–
[*aver* 'second, other']	[**bg:** *avér* 'companion; professional thief', dim. *avérče, alavér* 'friend']	[**bg:** *avér* 'friend; acquaintance; boy; man', dim. *avérče, avérka* 'woman', *avérski* 'amicable']
avralo 'crazy'	**bg:** *ávralo* 'stupid, crazy person'	–
avri 'outside, out'	**bg:** *ávrik* 'outside, out' **cz:** *avri* 'out; let's go!'	–
bakro 'sheep, ram'	**bcs:** *bakrinka* 'sheep' **cz:** *bakro* 'ram'	–
balavno, balamo 'non-Rom' etc.	**bcs:** *balavniška* 'policeman, lord' **bg:** *bá(a)lama* 'stupid person', *balamúr* 'Bulgarian; Christian; man'; *jalamúr* 'Greek'	**bg:** *balamúr(nik), bálama* 'fool, simple-minded person', dim. *bálamče*

(continued)

Word (stem) and meaning	Historical argots	Present-day youth slangs and colloquial varieties
balo 'pig' < balevas 'bacon'	**cz:** bále, bálo 'pig', bálecí 'pork', bálice 'pigs', bálátko 'piglet', balevas 'bacon' **ru:** balabás, balavás 'pig; pork', baljásina 'sausage, bacon'	**ru:** balabás 'food; delicacy; failure' **uk:** balabás 'head'
bango 'bent, crooked' etc.	**bcs:** bangav 'lame'; obangaviti 'to go lame' **bg:** píngo 'bent person'	–
bar 'stone'	**cz:** bar 'stone, rock'	–
barali 'pipe'	**bcs:** baralisati 'to smoke'[57]	–
baro 'big', baro paj 'sea', lit. 'big water'	**bg:** báro 'rich man; great man; lord; good'; báravec 'Rom', barávačka 'Romni'; bárovec, bárevec, bárevka 'boss, leader; fat person', dim. barevče **cz:** báro 'big', bárovný 'big'	**bg:** báro, bárovec 'rich, high-ranking, elegant man, snob', dim. bárovče, bárovka ‚rich, high-ranking, elegant woman, snobbish woman' **bcs:** bara 'sea, ocean; border', slana bara 'sea', preko bare 'across the borders', nabariti se 'to get drunk', nabaren 'drunk' **cz:** báre 'much, very'
barvalo 'rich'	**cz:** barvalo, barvalec 'rich man'	–
bašalel / bašavel 'to play (an instrument)'	**bcs:** bašalavisati 'to play (an instrument)', bašalaviška 'instrument'	**sk:** bašavel, bašálel 'excessive party'
bema 'penny'	**cz:** bémáček 'tenner'	–
beng 'devil'	**bcs:** bengiška 'devil' **cz:** beng, bink, penk 'devil; policeman'; bengík, bengoro 'policeman in a puppet show', bengóres 'evil'	**cz:** beng(o), bengoš 'policeman', benga, bengové, bengaboys 'policemen', bengokára 'police car', bengárna 'police station', benga v plechu 'policemen on patrol'

---

57 Uhlik suggests bar(r) 'stone' as the source word, which is not convincing.

Appendix 2 (chapter 7): Romani borrowings in diastratic varieties of Slavic — **195**

(continued)

Word (stem) and meaning	Historical argots	Present-day youth slangs and colloquial varieties
berš 'year'	**cz:** *berš* 'year'	–
bešel 'to sit; to live'	**bg:** *biščís, péčizot* 'house', *péčis* 'seat', *péčizet* 'shop', *pečífčija* 'somebody who sits' **cz:** *bešelit* 'to sit; to be in prison'	–
biboldo 'Jew; unchristened person'	**cz:** *biboldo, biboldák* 'Jew'	–
bijav 'wedding'	**bg:** *bíiav* 'wedding', *bíia* 'girl'	–
bokh 'hunger'	**bcs:** *bokališka* 'hungry being; to starve; hungry' **cz:** *bok* 'hunger', *bokalo* 'hungry'	–
bori 'bride; daughter-in-law'	**bg:** *bórija* 'bride'	–
bravinta 'liquor, brandy'	**cz:** *brávinta, brábinka* 'liquor, brandy' **ru:** *buravni* 'wine'	–
bul 'butt' etc.	**bcs:** *bulja, buljiška, bul(j)ina, buljahe(t), buljka* 'butt' **cz:** *bul, bulovnice* 'idem' **ru:** *buldá, bul'dá* 'pederasty'	**bcs:** *bulja, buljina* 'butt', *buljarenje, buljasker* 'eye-catching butt', *buljaš* 'person with a large butt', *buljiti* 'shit', *buljobris* 'toilet paper', *buljouvlakač* 'coward, scaredy-cat' **cz:** ?*bulovnice* 'butt' **sk:** *bulo, bulko* 'dull, uncouth person; villager; gadžo', fem. *bula*
bur 'bush, shrub'	**bg:** *búruci* 'mustache'	–
buti 'work'	**bg:** *búteš* 'work'	–
buzni 'goat'	**cz:** *guzně* 'goat'	–
cicni 'cat'	**bcs:** *cicnjajka* '(female) cat'	–
cidel 'to draw' etc.	**bcs:** *cidel* 'drinker; drunk; to drink'	–
ciral, kiral 'cheese'	**bcs:** *ćirališka, ćirina* 'cheese' **bg:** *kíral* 'idem'	–
čačo 'true' etc.	**cz:** *čáčo, čáčovný* 'nice, good'	–

(continued)

Word (stem) and meaning	Historical argots	Present-day youth slangs and colloquial varieties
čalavel 'to beat; to have sex; to cheat' etc.	**bcs:** čalavisati 'to take, to steal'; čalaviška, čalapiška 'prostitute', čalančur(l)ija 'neglected children' **bg:** čalástra, čalástrene 'drinking', čalástrim 'to drink'	**bg:** čálnat, čaldísan, čalnósen, čalbásen 'beaten (on the head), crazy'
čang 'leg'	**bcs:** čangale 'long legs', čangalast 'long-legged'	**cz:** ?čang 'thigh' **sk:** čongáľa, čungáľa, čongála '(long) leg'
či 'nothing'	**bg:** džíga 'there isn't/aren't any' **cz:** či 'nothing'	–
čiriklo 'bird'	**cz:** čirykle 'bird; weaker, subordinate prisoner'	–
čorel 'to steal'	**bcs:** čor(d)isati, čorlamisati, čornuti 'to steal', čorlama, čorisana 'theft; stolen goods', čordanović, čoriška 'thief' **bg:** čóris 'theft', čorizettísvam 'to steal' **cz:** čor, čór '(experienced) thief', čóres 'thief', čóri 'theft, robbery', čórka 'female thief', čórovat, čornout 'to steal', čórnutý 'stolen', čorok(h)ér 'prison', lit. 'thief house', vyčorovat, vyčornout 'to steal', čór na černo 'thief by night', čór na šaušprunk 'thief by day' **ru:** čardováť 'to steal', čardó 'stolen goods', čerdóvannyj 'stolen'	**bcs:** ćornuti, ćoriši, ćoriti, (u)ćorisati 'to steal', ćorisavanje, ćorisanje 'stealing', ćorka(na) 'prison', ćorkirati 'to imprison' **bg:** čor, čoradžija 'thief', čórav, čóra, čórja 'theft' **cz:** čórovat, čórnout 'to steal', čórovaný, čórlý, čórnutý 'stolen', čórkař, čóra, čórka, čóro, čórkař, čóresman 'thief', čór 'theft', čórkařský 'thievish', čórka 'pilferage; thief', [čoroděj 'very clever thief', čórkatlon 'thief triathlon (run to the swimming pool, swim, ride home on a stolen bike)', čórkatlonista 'thief triathlete'] **sk:** čór, čorkár 'thief'; čórka, čorka, čorkárstvo, čórovanie, čorkovanie 'theft', adj. čorkársky; čor(k)ovať, čor(k)nuť, čorznúť 'to steal'
čoro 'poor'	**cz:** čorok(h)ér 'poorhouse'	–
čuči 'chest, breast'	**bcs:** čuča 'breast'	–
čumidel 'to kiss'	**bg:** čúmis 'kissing'	–

(continued)

Word (stem) and meaning	Historical argots	Present-day youth slangs and colloquial varieties
čhaj '(Romani) girl; daughter'	**bg:** čaj 'girl; boy' čájče 'little girl' **cz:** čaja 'girl, sweetheart; woman' **ru:** č'chája 'girl'	**bg:** čaj 'girl, woman', čájka 'floozy', čájče 'young girl' **cz:** čajka, ?čajen 'girl', čaje! 'girl!' **sk:** čaja, čajka, čajočka '(pretty, hot) girl, young woman; girlfriend'
čhavo '(Romani) boy; son'	**bcs:** čaviška, čavić, čavče '(little) Rom' **bg:** čavo 'child' **cz:** čávo 'child', čávoro 'baby', čávalo 'stupid, childish' **ru:** č(j)ámoro 'litterbug'	**cz:** čávo 'boy, young man; gangster, cool guy' **sk:** čavo, čávo 'boy, guy; boyfriend; fool'; čavovať sa 'to show (off), to present oneself' **ru:** čav 'gopnik, pejorative name for a (criminal) youth from precarious backgrounds', čávyj, čavélla, čavél(a), čavėl(a) 'Rom, Gypsy'
čhib 'language; tongue'	**cz:** čib 'language'; číbalák, číbalo 'boss, leader'	–
čhinel 'to cut; to write'	**cz:** činelit 'to write', činiben 'letter' **ru:** čináva 'to stab', rasčendý 'proof, receipt'	–
čhor 'beard'	**bcs:** čorina 'beard'	–
čhorel, čhordarel 'to spill; to urinate' etc.	**bg:** čárajbe 'sperm'	**bcs:** (u)šórati, šórnuti 'to piss; to beat', zašórati 'to beat so. up', šórati se 'to come to blows', pošórati se 'to go to pee; to come to blows', šóranje, šóračka 'pissing', šóra(nje), šoraža, šórka 'punch-up', šoratorium 'toilet', šoravo 'shit, shitty', šoroskop 'interpretation of a urine analysis' **bg:** čórabe, čórajbe 'body secretions; sperm', šóram 'to pee; to drink alcohol', šóren 'peeing'

(continued)

Word (stem) and meaning	Historical argots	Present-day youth slangs and colloquial varieties
čhuri 'knife'	bcs: čurina, čuriška 'knife' bg: čúruk 'idem' cz: čurc, čúro, čúri, čúrek, čudl 'idem'	cz: čúro 'knife' sk: idem
dab 'strike; wound'	cz: dab, dap 'wound; gun'	–
dad 'father'	bg: dat 'father' cz: dat 'idem' ru: dat 'idem'	–
daj, dej 'mother'	bg: dája 'mother' cz: daje 'idem'; damradabuje, destradabuje vulgar curse[58] ru: dej 'mother'	–
dand 'tooth'	bcs: dandiška, danda 'tooth', dandara 'evil, sullen woman' cz: dand, gant 'tooth'	–
daral (pes) 'to be afraid'	cz: darák, dárel 'fear', dárelit (se) 'to be afraid'	–
das 'non-Rom; farmer; Serb; Christian; husband'	bcs: dasa, dasina 'Serb, Croat (male)', dasinka 'Serb, Croat (female)', dasulja 'old Serbian/Croatian woman', dasinski 'Serbian, Croatian'; in Bosnia desovan, desinka, desinče	bcs: dása '(handsome, elegant, respected) man; boyfriend'
degeš[59] 'riff-raff'	–	cz: degeš(ák) 'despicable person' sk: degeš 'fool; Rom, Gypsy', adj. degešský
del 'to give'	bcs: delisati 'to give', deliška 'giver'; lumajde![60] 'just give!'	–

---

58 Lit.: *dav mra da bule* 'I give my mother the butt', *des tra da bule* 'you give your mother the butt'.
59 Originally from Hungarian *dögös*.ADJ < *dög*.N 'carrion, carcass', borrowed into Czech via East Slovak Romani.
60 Blend of Romanian *numai* 'only' and Romani *de!* 'give!'.

(continued)

Word (stem) and meaning	Historical argots	Present-day youth slangs and colloquial varieties
denašel 'to run away, to escape'	cz: denášelit 'to run away, to escape'	–
deš 'ten'	cz: deš 'ten', dešengero 'tenner' ru: deš 'ten rubles', dešejék, dešenék '11', deš-dúj '12', deš-trýn '13', ënja-dyša '19'	–
Devel 'God'	cz: devel, devles, devlíček, devlínek, devlíneček 'God'	–
dikhel 'to see'	bcs: Dik jak! 'Pay attention!' (cf. also jakh) bg: díkis 'eyes; view', díkizi 'eyes', díkizik 'eye', dikízim, dikízja 'to look', dikizácija 'looking' cz: dykchelit 'to look, to see', dyk! 'look!'	sk: dig, dik, dyg, dyk expression of surprise, 'aha!, look!' uk: dik! exclamation of self-praise
dilino, delino 'crazy; stupid'	bcs: delina, deliniška, diliviška, daniluško 'fool, maniac' bg: diliníšta 'children' cz: dilina, diliňák, dylin 'fool, idiot (male)', dylina 'idiot (female)'	bcs: diléja, dildíka, dilájla 'fool, idiot' cz: dyliňák, dyliňak, dylina, dilina 'maniac, idiot, fool', dylina, dylinos 'stupid/crazy woman', dylinka 'stupid young woman fixated only on her looks', dylinec 'psychiatry', dylča 'idiot' sk: dilin(k)o, dilina 'fool, idiot'
drab 'drink; medicine; poison'	ru: vdrabadán, vdrebadán, vdrebedén', vdrebezén' 'person under the influence of alcohol or drugs'	uk: napytysja v drabadán 'to get very drunk'
drabarel 'to tell so.'s fortune'	ru: d(r)aberít' 'to play cards'	–
dranžuris 'plate'	cz: dranžůrek 'plate'	–
duj 'two'	cz: duj 'two' ru: duj, duék (duëk) 'two (rubles)' uk: du-dëkonnyj 'two-hryvna-'	bcs: dúja 'B (school mark)'

(continued)

Word (stem) and meaning	Historical argots	Present-day youth slangs and colloquial varieties
dukh 'pain, grief'[61]	**bg:** dúka, dúkaf 'penis'	**bg:** duduk 'penis'
džal 'to go' (1SG PERF geljom)	**bcs:** džal(d)isati, džalirati, džal 'to go, to walk'; džaldrma 'going', džališka 'pedestrian; fast; to go, to walk' etc., džalnuti 'to walk; to steal', dodžal(isati) 'to come; to bring', džaltara 'abhorrent woman', džavtara 'quarrelsome woman' etc., giljati, giljavati, gljavati, gljati 'to go (for a walk)'; dogljati 'to come', ugljati 'to go away', gljarnica, gljarka 'shoes', gljarnik 'street', gljavalica 'leg' **cz:** dža! 'go!', džahovat 'to go away' **ru:** ad'já 'go away', dži 'to go'	**bcs:** gíljati 'to go; to work; to fight; to run; to struggle', gílje 'shoes', gíljka 'shoe' **cz:** Jdi do dža! lit. 'Go to go!', euphemistic for 'Go to hell!' **sk:** džamore, Džamorák, džamorák 'Rom, Gypsy', fem. džamoráčka, Džamoráčka (cf. also more!)
džamutro 'groom; son-in-law'	**bg:** džámutro 'groom; son-in-law'	–
džanel 'to know, to be able to'	**bcs:** džanisati 'to know, to be able to', džaniška 'wise person' **cz:** džanelit 'to know'	–
džukel 'dog'	**bcs:** džukela, džuklija, džukac 'dog', džuk(l)a 'horse' **bg:** džúkel 'dog', džúkle 'doggy', džúkela 'Rom', džúkelsko 'poor', džukol'osam 'to steal' **cz:** čukl, žukl 'dog' **ru:** džukal, čúkel 'dog'	**bcs:** džúkac, džúkela 'dog, tyke'; derogatory name for a person, džúkački 'dog-', džúkelar 'dog breeder', džúki 'street dog' **bg:** džúkel dog' **cz:** čokl, čoklík, čoklíček 'dog, tyke', čoklař, čoklista 'dog owner', čoklbuřt 'cheap salami', čoklejno 'dog fouling', čoklovina 'strong smell of dog', čoklmafie 'group of irresponsible dog owners',

---

61 Argirov (1901: 32) mentions 'love' as another meaning of dukh, doubtful etymology.

(continued)

Word (stem) and meaning	Historical argots	Present-day youth slangs and colloquial varieties
		čoklovna 'playground or fitness-studio for dogs', čokložrout 'dog eater' (racist term for East Asian people), čoklsalon 'dog parlor', čoklvajler 'unspecified breed of dog' **sk:** čokel '(small) dog', dim. čoklík
džut 'Jew'	**bg:** džut 'Jew'	–
džuv 'louse'	**bcs:** džuva, džuvina, džuvija, dživulja 'louse', džuvalija 'money' **bg:** džúf(l)a, džúflinja 'louse' **cz:** džuvák, džúvalák 'beggar; policeman', džuvy 'lice' **ru:** čuvák 'boy, man, guy'	**cz:** ?džuva 'flea' **ru:** čuvák, čuvícha, čuvačók 'boy, man, guy' **uk:** čuvák, čuvílo 'idem', čuvícha, čuváčica, čuví, čuvýrdla 'female friend'
dživ 'wheat, grain'	**bcs:** đivina 'wheat, grain'	–
efta 'seven'	**cz:** efta 'seven' **ru:** éfto 'idem'	–
ek!, eki! 'here!, there!'	**bcs:** eki!, ek!, ekši! 'here!, there!'	–
enja 'nine'	**cz:** eňa 'nine'	–
gad 'shirt'	**cz:** gad, gat 'shirt'	–
gadžo 'non-Rom', gadži 'non-Romni'	**bcs:** gadžina 'Muslim, non-Rom', gadžovan 'idem' **bg:** gádža '(non-Roma-)woman; wife', gadžík 'Turk', gádže 'beloved, young, pretty girl', gádžeta 'beautiful girls' **cz:** gadžo 'non-Rom; man not belonging to the světští', gádže, gádži, gádžinka 'non-Romni; woman not belonging to the světští' **ru:** gažnjá 'woman'	**bcs:** gédžo, gédža, gedžován, gadžován 'farmer; uncouth person; Serb' **bg:** gádže 'girlfriend, beloved; girl, woman; boyfriend, lover' **cz:** gádžo 'non-Rom; Czech, Slovak', adj. gádžovský, gádžovka, gadžovka 'non-Romni; girlfriend', gádžovina 'invention by non-Roma', gadžův 'belonging to a non-Rom' **sk:** gadžo 'uneducated person; non-Rom', adj. gadžovský, noun gadžovstvo, gadžovka 'villager', Gadžograd 'Košice'
galbeno 'golden, yellow'	**bcs:** galben 'ducat'	–

(continued)

Word (stem) and meaning	Historical argots	Present-day youth slangs and colloquial varieties
gamo 'horse collar'	**ru:** *gámo* 'horse collar'	–
gav 'village'	**cz:** *gáv*, *gáva* 'village', *gávora* 'small village'	–
gero 'deceased person'	**cz:** *geróro* 'poor man'	–
gilabel 'to sing; to play (an instrument)'	**bg:** *gilíbija* 'song' **ru:** *lábat'*, *labát'* 'to make music, to play (an instrument)', *lábuch* 'musician'	**ru:** *lábuch* 'musician', *(s)labát'*, *lábuchat'* 'to make music, to play (an instrument)' **uk:** *(z)labáty* 'to make music, to play (an instrument); to play wrong (in music); to work', *pidlábuvaty*, *pidlabáty* 'to play along', *lába*, *labandžós* 'music', *lábuch* 'musician (general and in restaurants)', *pidlábka* 'background musician', *lábuda* 'nonsense, nuts'
giril 'pea'	**uk:** *geríl* 'pea'	–
gono 'sack'	**ru:** *gunó* 'sack'	–
graj, *gras(t)* 'horse', *grasni* 'mare'	**bcs:** *gras*, *gras(t)ina* 'horse' **bg:** *grasnéla* 'mare', *grasníe* 'mare; crock' **cz:** *graj*, *gráj* '(little) horse' **ru:** *gras*, *grasní*, *gra*, *grajá*, *graják* 'horse', *grajátnik* 'horse thief'	–
gudlo, *guglo* 'sweet; tasty; pleasant' etc.	**bcs:** *oguglati* 'to get used to sth.' **bg:** *gúdla* 'sweet milk' **ru:** *gugnó* 'sugar'	–
Gurbet 'Gurbet Rom(ni)'	–	**bcs:** *gurbet* 'ugly person'
gurumni, *guruvni* 'cow'	**bcs:** *gurumiška* 'cow' **ru:** *goruni*, *goroni* 'cow'	–
harangos 'bell'	**cz:** *haranges*, *harant* 'bell'	–
chal 'to eat'	**bcs:** *hal(d)isati*, *hal* 'to eat', *hališka*, *hapa* food', *(h)apiti* 'to eat; to understand', *hapica* 'food for children'	**bcs:** *has*, *hásanje* 'food', *hásati*, *hásnuti*, *halisati* 'to eat', *halap* 'greedy person', *halapljiv* 'greedy', *hapanje* 'theft', *hapati*, *hapnuti* 'to steal'

(continued)

Word (stem) and meaning	Historical argots	Present-day youth slangs and colloquial varieties
	bg: *(ch)abé, abénce, abizán* 'bread', *chabésărkaf* mouth', lit. 'food container', *abésărkaf* 'spoon', *abédžij(k)a* 'baker; innkeeper', *chas, abezétisvam* 'to eat' **cz:** *chaliben, chalovka* 'food', *chalovat* 'to eat' **ru:** *chávka* 'bread; money for food', *chávat', schávat', pochávat', chóvat'* 'to eat'	**bg:** *chabé* 'food; bread' **cz:** *chálo, chálka, chalka, chales, chalunk, chálec* 'food', *chálovat* 'to eat', *chálovač* 'insatiable eater' **sk:** *chales, cháles, chalo* 'food', *(s)chalovať, (s)chálovať* 'to eat'; *nachalovať sa, nachálovať sa* 'to eat one's fill' **ru:** *cháv(a), chavló* 'mouth; ivories; food', *chávka, chavanína* 'food', *chával'nik, chavélla, chával'nja, chávalo* 'mouth; face, puss', *chávčik* 'food; refectory, school canteen', *chavúl'nja, chávnja, chavélla* 'refectory, school canteen' *(za)chávat'* 'to eat; to understand; to believe', *schávat'* 'to eat; to accept reluctantly', *nachávat'sja* 'to eat one's fill' **uk:** *(po)chávaty* 'to eat, to chew', *(za)chávaty* 'to like', *(pro)chávaty* 'to understand', *chávalo, chávka, chávčik* 'food', *procházvanyj* 'experienced'
charo 'sword, saber'	**cz:** *charengero* 'policeman'	–
(c)harťas 'smith'	**cz:** *harťas* 'smith'	–
chas 'cough'	**bcs:** *hasališka, hasaluška* 'incurable lung disease in horses'	–
chev 'hole; vagina' etc.	**bcs:** *hevina, heviška, hevulja, hev* 'female genitals; whore; woman'	–
chindi 'butt'	**cz:** *chynďak, chynda* 'butt', *chynder* 'toilet', *chyndit* 'to shit'	**cz:** ?*chyndit* 'to shit', ?*chynd'ak* 'penis'
chochavel 'to lie, to cheat, to deceive'	**bcs:** *(ho)havisati, kokovelisati* 'to lie', *(ho)haviška, havička, hava* 'lie' **cz:** *chochvalec* 'liar, fraud'	–

(continued)

Word (stem) and meaning	Historical argots	Present-day youth slangs and colloquial varieties
cholov 'pants'	**cz:** *cholóva* 'pants'	–
chudel 'to take, to catch'	**cz:** *chudel* 'theft', *chudelit* 'to take, to catch; to steal'	–
ikhel 'to see, to look at' etc.	**bcs:** *ik(l)isati, ikišiti, ikel, ik* 'to see, to observe'	–
jag 'fire'	**bcs:** *jagiška* 'fire' **ru:** *jak* 'matches'	–
jakh 'eye'	**bcs:** *Dik jak!* 'Pay attention!' (cf. *dikhel*), *jakeška* 'eye' **cz:** *jaka, jakcha* 'eyes'	–
(j)ekh 'one'	**bg:** *ek* 'one' **cz:** *jek* 'one', *jeke* 'once' **ru:** *ėk* 'one'	–
kalo 'black'	**bcs:** *kalakurdija* 'gang', lit. 'black whore' **bg:** *kálopis* 'wine', lit. 'black drink'; *kalopísărkaf* 'vessel for wine' **cz:** *kálo, khálo* 'black; Rom', *kálovný* 'coal', *kálovná* 'chicory' **ru:** *ėkkalo* 'one ruble', cf. *(j)ekh*	**bg:** *kále* 'line drawn on the floor in a game', *kalen* 'malicious, dishonest'
kambana 'watch'	**cz:** *kambáně, gambáně, gambáňata* 'watch'	–
kamel 'to love; to want; to demand'	**bcs:** *kamiti* 'to demand'	–
kangli 'comb'	**cz:** *kanglík* 'comb'	–
kar 'penis'	**bcs:** *kariška, karaš, karina, kar* 'penis' **bg:** *mekaréste*[62] 'I don't care', *káiarto* 'sex', *káidisam* 'to have sex'[63] **cz:** *káro, kár* 'penis' **ru:** *kára, karuša* 'penis'	**bcs:** *kára* 'penis', *kárati* 'to have sex' **bg:** *karam na muskuli* 'narrowly, with a lot of effort', *keréste* 'penis', *kerestelija* 'man with a big penis', *mekaréste* 'I don't care', *kájdisvam* 'to cut, to chop' **cz:** *kar, kár* 'penis' **sk:** *kár* 'idem'

---

62 Composition: *me* 'I', *kar-es-te*.LOK 'on the penis'.
63 Doubtful etymology of *kaiarto, kaidisam, kajdisvam*.

(continued)

Word (stem) and meaning	Historical argots	Present-day youth slangs and colloquial varieties
karalo 'corn'	**bcs:** *karalić, karalija, karkalić* 'corn'	–
karialo 'meat'	**cz:** *karialo* 'meat'	–
karno 'thorn, sting'	**bcs:** *karnališka* 'policeman'	–
kaštrin 'wood'	**bcs:** *kaštrin, kaština* 'wood, tree'	–
katar o vuš 'at the mouth'	**bcs:** *katravoš* 'beard'	–
kereka 'wheel'	**cz:** *kérko* 'wheel'	–
kerel 'to do, to work' etc.	**bg:** *kerzija* 'theft', *kiriščija* 'thief', *kirízja, kirízim* 'to look'[64] **cz:** *k(h)érovat* 'to do, to work; to hurry; to be able, to understand', *vykérovat* 'to earn', *zk(h)érovat* 'to scold; to arrange; to get sth. done'	**bg:** *kirízja, kirízim* 'to look, to stare', *kirizčíja* 'gawker' **cz:** *kérovat* 'to tattoo; to meddle with', *vykérovat* 'to tattoo', *zkérovat* 'to arrange, to organize', *kérka, khérko, kérko* 'tattoo', *kérovaný, pokérovaný, zkérovaný* 'tattooed', *kérkař* 'tattooer (male)', *kérkarka* 'tattooer (female)', *kérkárna* 'tattoo studio', [*kérkonoš* 'tattooed person', *kérotoman* 'person obsessed with tattoos'] **sk:** *kéres, kerka, kérka* 'tattoo', *kerovať, kérovať, vykérovať, pokérovať* 'to tattoo'
kerki 'beer; liquor'	**bcs:** *kerkin(j)a, kerija* 'liquor'	–
kidel (drom) 'to set out, to go away'	**bcs:** *kidavelo*[65]	**bcs:** *kidati, kidnuti* 'to run away, to escape'
kinel 'to buy'	**cz:** *kynelit* 'to buy'	–
kofo 'profit'	**ru:** *kófa* 'money'	–
kokalo 'bone'	**bcs:** *kokalina* 'bone; meat'	–
kon 'who; somebody'	**ru:** *kónto* 'who', *nikónto, ni kónto, nikónda, nekóntyj* 'nothing'	–

---

64 Doubtful etymology of *kirizja, kirizim, kirizčija*.
65 Uhlik (1954: 20) paraphrases the word, but does not give an exact meaning.

(continued)

Word (stem) and meaning	Historical argots	Present-day youth slangs and colloquial varieties
koro 'blind'	bcs: korka, korela, koravica 'blind woman; old woman', koroviška, kuraviška, kuroha 'blind', koravac 'old man'	–
kotor 'piece'	cz: kotr 'piece'	–
kurel 'to have sex'	bcs: kurisati, kurel 'to have sex', kuriška 'sex', kalakurdija 'gang', cf. kalo	–
khabni 'pregnant'	bg: kábnija 'pregnant woman'	–
khandel 'to smell, to stink'	bcs: kandisati, kanjati 'to stink', kandilište, kandija 'toilet' cz: kanďas 'soldier', kandýna 'match'	bcs: kandísati 'to stink', kandija 'toilet' cz: kandel 'disgust, sth. disgusting' sk: kandel 'stench'
khangeri 'church'	cz: kanger, khanger, khangel, ganger, gangel 'church'	–
khanji, kahni 'chicken, hen'	bcs: kanjajka, kanička, kenjka 'chicken, hen' cz: kahně 'idem'	–
khapel 'to drink'	bcs: kaptisati 'to drink'	–
khelel 'to dance'	bg: kelávnija 'prostitute' cz: k(h)eliben 'performance, presentation', kelibnengero, kelibník 'comedian'	–
kher 'house'	bcs: kerin, kerna, kira, ćera 'house' cz: čorok(h)ér 'prison', lit. 'thief house', keher, kér 'house; flat; place where a burglary is committed', k(h)érař 'burglar', k(h)ére 'at home' ru: úker 'house'	cz: ?kér 'house; flat'
khul 'dung, dirt' etc.	bcs: kuliška, kul, kulina 'shit', kulana 'prison', kuletina 'pork' bg: kúla 'shit' cz: k(h)úlo 'shit'	cz: kulový 'shit, shitty; I don't give a shit', kulovka 'shit'

(continued)

Word (stem) and meaning	Historical argots	Present-day youth slangs and colloquial varieties
lačho 'good, nice, right'	**bcs:** lačo, lača, lače 'good', lačaran 'nice, pretty' **cz:** láčo, láčovný 'good' **ru:** lačó, lač, lač''ë 'good' **uk:** lačó 'good'	**bcs:** lačo, lačho, laćo 'super, sehr gut' **cz:** ?láčo(vný) 'gut'
ladž 'shame, disgrace'	**ru:** oblažát' 'to deceive', oblážnik 'fraud (male)', oblážnica 'fraud (female)'	**ru:** lažát' 'to make a mistake, to do sth. wrong (in general and while making music); to embarrass so.', lažanút'(sja), oblažát'sja 'to make a mistake, to be wrong, to suffer a failure', lažát'sja 'to make a fool of oneself', oblažát' 'to strongly criticize (unjustified)', láža 'nonsense, nuts; mistake while making music', lážnja 'nonsense, crap', lažók, lažúk, lažák, lažúčka, lažáčka 'bad pupil', lažóvščik 'fraud; botcher, dilettante', lažóvost' 'mess, both', lažëvyj, lažóvyj, lážnyj 'bad, deficient, unsuccessful' **uk:** láža 'unpleasant, embarrassing situation; mistake while making music', lažóvyj 'unpleasant, embarrassing; bad, inferior', (na)lažáty 'to do sth. wrong or embarrassing', lažonúty 'to deliberately do sth. bad to so.' lažonútysja 'to do stupid things', oblažáty 'to reject, to criticize', oblažátysja 'to be ashamed'
lav 'name; word'	**cz:** lav 'name'	**bg:** laf 'word; fairy tale; interesting conversation', lafja 'to have a conversation'

(continued)

Word (stem) and meaning	Historical argots	Present-day youth slangs and colloquial varieties
lel (1SG *lav*) 'to take'	**bcs:** *lavisati, leldisati, lel* 'to take, to steal', *laviška* 'theft; thief' **bg:** *lévam* 'to take', *lévkam, léfkam* 'theft', *lévkadžija, léfkač* 'thief'	**bg:** *lévam, lévkam* 'to take, to steal'
len 'river, stream'	**cz:** *len* 'river, stream', *lenórka* 'little stream'	–
lil 'leaf; book; letter; paper' etc.	**bcs:** *lil* 'pass(port), permit', *liliška, liljuška, liluša* 'letter' **cz:** *lil* 'permit, pass(port), letter'	–
lindiko 'clit'	**bcs:** *lindik* 'clit; female genitals'	**uk:** *lindík* 'clit'[66]
love 'money'	**bcs:** *lovine, lov, lova, love, loviška, lovuška* 'money' **cz:** *love, lóve, lováče, lováky, lovasy* 'money', *lovej* 'rich man' **ru:** *lavá, lav'é, posalov'e*[67] 'money', *posálovit'* 'to steal money', *posalóvščik* 'pickpocket'	**bcs:** *lóva, lóvica, loviška* 'money', *lovočuvar* 'scrooge', *lovostaj* 'lack of money', *lóvaš, lováš, lovátor, lovároš, lovan, lovaner, lovaran* 'rich man; greedy man', *lovatorica, lovanka* 'rich woman', *lovokradica* 'thief (female); woman who steals from men', *lovčuga, lovina, lovudža* 'big money' **cz:** *love, lóve, lováče, lováky, lovásky, lovky* 'money' **sk:** *lováče, love, lóve* 'money' **ru:** *lavė, lavé, lav'ë, lėvė, lovė, lové, lavėški, lavsán, lavándos, lavánda(s), lavóndos, labė* 'money', *lavánder* 'profit, earnings' **uk:** *lavé* 'money'

---

66 *Lindik* may also be a direct loan from Romanian (*lindic*), which is also the source of the Romani word (anonymous reviewer).

67 Stress unclear. Blend of Belarus. *póso* '(too) much' and Rom. *love* 'money'.

(continued)

Word (stem) and meaning	Historical argots	Present-day youth slangs and colloquial varieties
lovina 'beer'	**cz:** *lovina* 'beer'	–
lurdo 'soldier'	**cz:** *rulďák, ruldo* 'soldier'	–
mačho 'fish'	**bg:** *máče* 'fish'	–
maj particle, interjection	**bg:** *maj!, majder!* 'here you go!'	–
man 'me'	**ru:** *man, manëk* 'I'	–
mangel 'to ask for, to beg' etc.	**bcs:** *mangisati* 'to look for, to ask for', *mangiška* 'plea' **bg:** *ming'án, mángo* 'Rom' **cz:** *mangel* 'begging', *mangelář* 'beggar', *mangelit* 'to beg; to ask for', *mángo* 'Rom'	**bg:** *mángovec, mángo, mángal, mangasar, mangafa, mingjan(in)* 'Rom, Gypsy; fool; simple-minded person', dim. *mangovče, mangalče, mangasarče, mingjanče*; *mangalka, mangasarka, mingjanka* 'Romni; stupid, simple-minded woman', *mangalski, mangasarksi* 'Romani; stupid, simple-minded' **cz:** ?*(vy)mangelit* to beg'
mangin 'property, wealth' etc.	**bg:** *mángis, mangís, mangízi (mingí)* 'money', *mangízim, mangízja* 'theft'	**bg:** *mangízi, mángis, mángi, mángăr* 'money', *mangízlija* 'rich man', *mangízlijka* 'rich woman', *mangízja* 'to take money from so.; to steal', *omangízim* 'to get money'
mange 'ich.1SG.DAT'	**bcs:** *mango* 'friend'	–
manuš 'human, person; man'	**bcs:** *mánča* 'lord', *mánuk* 'human, person; man' **bg:** *mánuk* 'Turk; lord', *mánukoto, manče* 'lord, landlord', *mánuka* 'wife', *mánovka* 'girl', *manúčam (se)* 'to get married', *mánuče* 'child', *manúčinja* 'children', *mánufče* 'boy' **cz:** *manuš* 'man, husband', *manuše* 'wife'	–

(continued)

Word (stem) and meaning	Historical argots	Present-day youth slangs and colloquial varieties
marel 'to beat'	**bcs:** *marisati, marnuti* 'to beat', *mara* 'fight', *omarisan* 'beaten' **bg:** *máris, marís, maríz* 'fight', *marizím, marízja, marizlájsvam* 'to beat', *maríṣčija* 'policeman', *marízčija, marizčíja* 'policeman, soldier', *maríṣčísărkaf* 'uniform', *maríṣčica* 'wife of a policeman or soldier' **cz:** *márelit (se), márovat* 'to beat, to brawl', *márelka* 'row' **ru:** *marát', smarát', pomarát'* 'to kill, to slay'; *mordó* 'ruble'	**bcs:** *mára, marísanje* 'fight, row; theft', *marela, mariška* 'theft', *marísana* 'imprisonment', *márati, marísati, márnuti, marnjavati* 'to beat, to fight; to steal', *marísati se* 'to brawl', *izmárati* 'to beat up', *pomárati se* 'to get involved into a fight', *marica, mariola* 'police car', *marijaš* 'money' **bg:** *marís* 'beating', *marizím, marízja* 'to brawl', *marízčija* 'puncher' **cz:** *márovat* 'to beat' **sk:** *(z)márovať* 'to brawl', *(z)márovať sa* 'to do drugs, to smoke weed', noun *(z)márovanie*
maribe 'death'	**uk:** *maribé* 'death; skeleton', *maribyj* 'deadly'	–
ma(n)(d)ro 'bread'	**bcs:** *marina, marniška, manjiška* 'bread' **bg:** *maro, manur* 'bread' **cz:** *máro* bread; fasting' **ru:** *mandró* 'bread'	**bg:** *maro* 'bread', *maro nanaj, nanaj maro* 'sth. is not going to happen, cannot be done', lit. 'there is no bread'
mas 'meat'	**bcs:** *masina* 'meat' *masăro* 'meat', *masăradžija* 'butcher' **bg:** *másăro* 'meat', *masărádžija* 'butcher' **cz:** *masinger(ák), mostik* 'butcher'	–
mato 'drunk'	**bcs:** *matilo* 'drunkard; alcohol', *matiška* 'drunkards; drunk; binge drinking' **bg:** *mátis, mátizo* 'drunk', *matosúaše* 'binge drinking', *matósuam* 'to get drunk' **cz:** *máto* 'drunk', *mátora* 'drinker, drunkard'	**bg:** *máto* 'drunk; binge drinking'

(continued)

Word (stem) and meaning	Historical argots	Present-day youth slangs and colloquial varieties
melalї 'coffee'	**cz:** *melali, melalo, melardo* 'coffee'	–
men 'neck'	**cz:** *men* 'neck'	–
merel 'to die'	**bcs:** *merisa(va)ti* 'to die', *meriška* 'dead person; dead'	–
mindž 'vagina'	**bcs:** *mindža, mindžina, mindžuška, mindžulja* 'vagina' **bg:** *míndža* 'idem' **cz:** *minďoch, mindž, minč, minže* 'idem' **ru:** *minžá* 'idem', *menžá* 'fear', *menževát'sja* 'to be afraid; to be cowardly', *pomenževát'sja, pominževát'sja* 'to be afraid'	**bcs:** *míndža, mínđa* 'vagina' **bg:** *míndža, mindžuríja, mindžafara , mindžifurka* 'vagina', *mindžeka* 'whore', *mindžipljaktor* 'man who has sex with many women', *domindžos* 'miniskirt', *mindžoretka* 'cheerleader with a short skirt', *mindžipuj* 'lice in the pubic hair', *mindžakokar* 'oral sex' **cz:** *mindža, ?minda* 'vagina; cunt (invective); cat', *mindinka* 'attractive woman', [*mindžikvas* 'vaginal discharge'] **ru:** *menžá* 'frat', *menževát'sja* 'to be afraid, to hesitate'
mišto 'good'	**ru:** *mištó* 'good, OK'	–
mochto 'chest, coffin'	**cz:** *mochta* 'chest, coffin'	–
mol 'wine'	**bcs:** *mulina* 'wine'	–
more! 'hey! man! buddy!'	**bcs:** *more!* 'hey! friend! companion!' **cz:** *more!* 'idem'	**bcs:** *more!* 'hey! man! buddy!' **cz:** *more!* 'idem' **sk:** *more!, móre!* 'idem', *džamore, Džamorák, džamorák* 'Rom, Gypsy', fem. *džamoráčka, Džamoráčka*
morel 'to wash'	**cz:** *morelovat* 'to wash'	–
mothovel 'to say' etc.	**bcs:** *mamota, mamata!* 'silence!', *matovisati, motavisati* 'to talk, to speak', *motaviška* 'conversation'	–
muj 'mouth'	**cz:** *muj* 'mouth'	–
mukhel 'to let (go), to leave' etc.	**bg:** *múkles* 'silence; stupid, naive', *mukáv* 'to let' **cz:** *mukchelit* 'to let'	–

(continued)

Word (stem) and meaning	Historical argots	Present-day youth slangs and colloquial varieties
mulo 'dead; ghost of a dead person'	**cz:** *múla* 'corpse'; *mulák* 'ghost', *mulasit* 'to scare; to die', *múlo* 'dead'	–
muravel 'to shave' etc.	**bg:** *múrafes* 'shave', *muravaf* 'shaved'	–
murdalo 'dead'	**bg:** *murt* 'death', *muruplú* 'cleric'	–
mutrel 'to urinate'	**bcs:** *mutaravisati* 'to wet sth.'	–
naj, ninaj, nane, nanaj '(there is) not'	**bcs:** *naj, naje, naja, najel, najiška* 'not; it is not allowed; there is not', *najkan, najko* 'mischief' **bg:** *nanáj* 'not, nothing'	**bcs:** *naje* 'no, not', *šaje* 'no chance'[68] **bg:** *nanáj(si)* 'never' **ru:** *nané, nanė, naný* '(there is) not'
nakh 'nose'	**bcs:** *nakiška* 'nose'	–
nango 'naked'	**bg:** *nángo* 'poor; short man' **cz:** *nango* 'naked'	–
našavel 'to destroy; to lose'	**cz:** *našavelit* 'to kill'	–
našel 'to run away' etc.	**bcs:** *naštisati, naštel* 'to run away', *naštisanje* 'running'	–
ochto 'eight'	**cz:** *ochto* 'eight'	–
pandž 'five'	**cz:** *panč* 'five', *pančík* 'fiver', *pančka* 'five crowns' **ru:** *pinžá, pidžák, pjandž(a), pen'žá(k), beš-pán* 'five', *pendžátnica* 'Friday'	**sk:** *panšel* 'five hundred'
pani 'water'	**bcs:** *panina, panija, panjiška, panjajka, panja, pajiška* 'water' **bg:** *pánije* 'idem' **cz:** *páň, pháň* 'idem' **ru:** *chapan'e* 'blood'[69]	–

---

68 Blend of *šansa* and *naje*.
69 Deduced from *ho pani* 'the water'.

Appendix 2 (chapter 7): Romani borrowings in diastratic varieties of Slavic —— 213

(continued)

Word (stem) and meaning	Historical argots	Present-day youth slangs and colloquial varieties
parno 'white'	**bg:** *párniia* 'wite bear', *párnopis* 'liquor', lit. 'white drink', *parnopísărkaf* 'vessel for liquor' **ru:** *parn(j)ák, parnjága* '25-ruble-banknote'	**cz:** *parno* 'crystal meth' **ru:** *párno* 'idem'
patrin 'leaf'	**ru:** *potrým* 'registration card for horse owners'	–
pijel 'trinken'	**bcs:** *pijaviška* 'drunk; binge drinking; drink' etc. **bg:** *piizán* 'drunk', *kálopis* 'wine', lit. 'black drink', *kalopísărkaf* 'vessel for wine', *kápis, pijs* 'drinking', *pizaana* 'inn', *piís, píis* 'wine'	–
poli 'gold coin'	**bg:** *polúr, púgur* 'penny'	–
porjalo 'monkey; dog; horse; devil; policeman' etc.	**bcs:** *porijan* 'policeman'	–
pošumni 'wool'	**bcs:** *pušina* 'wool'	–
prno 'foot'	**bcs:** *prnjiška, pinjiška, pinjuška, prnališka* 'foot'	–
pusavel 'to sting, to pierce' etc.	**bcs:** *pusavisati* 'to stab'	–
phabarel 'to light; to smoke' etc.	**bcs:** *pabar(av)isati* 'to smoke, to light', *pabaraviška* 'smoking'	–
pustyn 'fur (coat)'	**ru:** *pastýn, postunënak, pastunjáty, postunjáty, pastunënok* 'jacket'	–
phagi 'punishment'	**cz:** *pág, phági* 'punishment'	–
phandel 'to close; to tie; to imprison' etc.	**bcs:** *pendupeh* 'prison' **bg:** *pandíz, pandís* 'prison; section', *pandízja* 'to imprison', *pandízčija* 'prisoner', *pandízim* 'to arrest' **cz:** *p(h)andelit, p(h)anglit* 'to close; to arrest; to tie' *p(h)andlo* 'closed; guard, policeman', *panglír* 'judge', *panglo* 'policeman' **ru:** *razphánda* 'told'	**bg:** *pandíz, pandís, pandíz palas* 'prison', *pandizčija* 'prisoner', dim. *pandizčijče, pandizčijka* 'prisoners', adj. *pandizčijski, pandízja, pandízim, opandizvam* 'to imprison', *pandizen* 'so. who was in prison' **sk:** *pangel* 'policeman', *pangelnica* 'police station'

(continued)

Word (stem) and meaning	Historical argots	Present-day youth slangs and colloquial varieties
phen 'sister'	**bg:** *pén'ja, pen* 'sister' **ru:** *pchen'* 'sister; brother'	–
phenel 'to speak, to talk, to say'	**bcs:** *pen(j)isati, pinjisati* 'to speak, to talk, to say' **bg:** *pénis* 'sermon', *penizettísvam* 'to say, to speak', *penizja* 'to talk, to tell', *pinis* 'attention', *pin(d)izim* 'to lool' **cz:** *p(h)enelit* 'to say'	**bg:** *péniz* 'trick', *píniz* 'joke'
phirel 'to go'	**bg:** *pirgo, pirgojc* 'Rom' **cz:** *pirel* 'way', *pirelit* 'to go'	–
phral 'brother'	**bg:** *pral* 'brother', *prăl, părăl* 'Rom', *părălka* 'Romni'	–
phukavel 'to complain'	**cz:** *pukavel* 'confession', *pukavelit* 'to confess', *pukaveleno* 'betrayed'	–
phuro 'old' (for animate beings)	**bg:** *púrija* 'grandmother', *púro* 'old man', *puríiata pečufčíiata* 'mother-in-law' **cz:** *púro, pchúro* 'old man'	–
raj 'lord'	**bcs:** *rajin(ac)* 'policeman' **cz:** *raj* 'lord; judge' **ru:** *raj* 'policeman'	**cz:** ?*raj* 'lord'
rakli '(non-Romani) girl', *raklo* '(non-Romani) boy'	**bcs:** *rakliška* 'girl' **cz:** *ráklo, ráklík* 'boy, adolescent', *rakle, raklička* 'girl' **ru:** *rakló, rakól* 'thief; tramp', *raklícha* 'female thief', *rykló, rychálo* 'liar, fraud' **uk:** *rakló* 'tramp', adj. *rakljác'kij, ráklyj* 'thievish'	**uk:** *rakló* 'cheeky, indecent person, lout; inapt person'
rašaj 'priest' etc.	**bcs:** *rašlije, riša* 'Priester' **bg:** *rášaj, raš(')le, rafle* 'idem'	–
rat 'night'	**cz:** *rat* 'night'	–
ratinel 'to rescue'	**cz:** *latyngr* 'lawyer', *ratengero, rateskero* 'doctor; lawyer'	–
rez 'vine, grape'	**bcs:** *rezno* 'wine'	–

(continued)

Word (stem) and meaning	Historical argots	Present-day youth slangs and colloquial varieties
roj 'spoon'	**cz:** *roj, rojka* 'spoon'	–
Rom, Romni, Romanes	**bcs:** *Romina, Romić* 'Rom', *Rominka, Rom(n)iška* 'Romni', *Roma* 'beautiful Romni' **cz:** *romános* 'Romani, Romanes', *romec, roms* 'one (person)', *romňe* 'Romni' **ru:** *runni* 'woman', *runni lubno* 'prostitute'	**bcs:** *Rom, Romaldinho* 'Romani boy who plays football very well', *Romun* 'Rom from Romania', *romanizacija* 'Romization', *romkinja* 'black coffee of bad quality' etc. **bg:** *romljanin* 'Rom', *romej* 'rich Rom' **cz:** *romofobie* 'fear of Roma', [*rombudsman* 'representative for national minorities', *romídek* 'Rom', *romokracie* 'situation in which Roma have more influence in certain areas of life', *romosvod* 'Romani community that serves as a scapegoat for all kinds of problems', *romotluk* 'skinhead', *romulet* 'Romani amulet' etc.] **sk:** *Romák, romák* 'Rom', *Romáčka, romáčka* 'Romni', *romácky* 'Romani, Gypsy-'
rovel 'to cry'	**cz:** *rovelit* 'to cry'	–
rup 'silver'	**cz:** *rup* 'silver' (noun), *rupun(o)* 'silver' (adj.)	–
sadik 'hat, cap, fez'	**bg:** *sádik* 'hat, cap, fez'	–
sap 'snake'	**ru:** *sápa* 'snake'	–
saster 'iron'	**cz:** *sastra* 'iron; bonds'	–
si 'there is'	**bcs:** *si, sija* 'there is' **ru:** *sin* 'idem'	**bcs:** *sijati* 'to have'
Sinto	**cz:** *sintej* 'free', *sinťák* 'Sinto'	–
solacharel 'to swear'	**cz:** *sovlechardo* 'married', *sovák* 'husband', *sovka* 'wife'	–
somnakaj 'gold'	**ru:** *su(m)nakuni, sanakuni* 'gold'	–
soske, sostyr 'why'	**ru:** *sósta, nasósta* 'what, why, what for', *nisósta* 'nothing'	–

(continued)

Word (stem) and meaning	Historical argots	Present-day youth slangs and colloquial varieties
sovel 'to sleep'	bcs: sovisati, sofkati 'to sleep', soviška, sovindos 'sleep; to sleep; well-rested' bg: sóvis 'sleep' cz: sovelit, suvelit, subelit 'to sleep'	–
stildo 'imprisoned'	cz: styldo 'prisoner', stylipen 'prison ward'	–
šargo[70] 'yellow'	cz: šargon 'chestnut (horse)'	–
šero 'head'	bcs: šera, šerina 'head' cz: šéra, šéro, šérice 'idem' ru: šeró 'idem'	–
šelengero 'policeman'	cz: šelengero, šelengerák, šilingere, šilingr, šilingrák 'policeman'	–
šinga 'horns; policeman'	bcs: šinga, šingać 'Polizist'	–
šošoj 'hare'	cz: šošoj 'hare, rabbit; cat, tomcat', šošoják 'tomcat', šošole 'cat'	–
šov 'six'	ru: šov 'six'	–
štar 'four'	ru: štar, štar', star 'four rubles'	–
šukar 'beautiful'	bcs: šukar 'beautiful' cz: šukárný 'idem' ru: šukírnyj 'good', pošukírnyj 'beautiful', nišukírnyj 'bad'	bg: šúkar 'beautiful', baš šúkar 'cool'
šunel 'to hear, to listen'	bcs: šunjisati 'to hear, to listen'	–
tato 'warm; homosexual'	bg: táto 'coffee; diarrhea', tatódžija 'café'	cz: tátoš 'homosexual' (noun)
tikno, cikno 'small'	bg: tíkno 'poor; small' cz: tikno, cikno, tykno 'small'	–
tradel 'to chase, to hunt'	cz: trádelit 'to hunt', trádelit dža 'to chase away'	–

---

[70] A borrowing from Hungarian sárga 'yellow'.

(continued)

Word (stem) and meaning	Historical argots	Present-day youth slangs and colloquial varieties
trasta 'bag, knapsack, sack'	**bcs:** *trašta* 'bag'	–
trin 'three'	**ru:** *trýn(ža)* 'three', *trín'ka* card game, *trynžák, trinžák, trýnka* 'three rubles'	–
thardi 'liquor'	**bg:** *tarí* 'liquor'	–
tavel 'to cook' etc.	**bcs:** *tavati, taviti* 'to cook'	–
thud 'milk'	**bcs:** *tudina* 'milk'	–
thuvalo 'tobacco'	**bcs:** *tumina, tuvina* 'tobacco' **bg:** *tújalo* 'idem' **cz:** *t(h)uválo* 'idem'	–
tirdel 'to smoke'	**ru:** *potýrdat', potýrit', ponyrdat'* 'to smoke'	–
upre 'up'	**bg:** *úpre* 'up'	–
vazdel 'to steal; to pick up' etc.	**bcs:** *vazdignuti, vozdignuti* 'to steal'[71]	–
vakerel 'to talk, to speak, to say'	**bcs:** *vrakel, vrakelisati, vakerisati* 'to speak, to say'	–
verdan 'cart'	**cz:** *vurdo, vurdýn* 'cart'	–
zoralo 'strong'	**cz:** *zuralo* 'strong'	–
zumin 'soup'	**cz:** *zumina, zuminka* 'soup'	–

---

71 Blend of *vazdel* and bcs. *dignuti*.

References

Ackerley, Frederick G. 1941. Bosnian Romani: Prolegomena. *Journal of the Gypsy Lore Society* 20. 78–84.
Ahmeti. 2003. O bašno [The rooster]. In Christiane Fennesz-Juhasz & Petra Cech (eds.), *Die schlaue Romni. Märchen und Lieder der Roma. E bengali Romni. So Roma phenen taj gilaben*, 88–93. Klagenfurt: Drava.
Ammon, Ulrich. 1995. *Die deutsche Sprache in Deutschland, Österreich und der Schweiz: das Problem der nationalen Varietäten*. Berlin/Boston: De Gruyter.
Angăčev, Ilija. 2008. *Kratka morfologija na ciganskija dialekt na Ljaskovec* [Short morphology of the Gypsy dialect of Ljaskovec]. Veliko Tărnovo: Faber.
Angelov, Angel G. 2014. Bulgarian Sociolects. In Karl Gutschmidt, Sebastian Kempgen, Tilman Berger & Peter Kosta (eds.), *The Slavic Languages. An International Handbook of their Structure, their History and their Investigation*, 2186–2201. (Handbooks of Linguistics and Communication Science 32.2). Berlin: De Gruyter Mouton.
Antauer, Živa, Janez Krek & Mateja Peršak. 2003. Projekt standardizacije jezika Romov v Sloveniji in vključevanje romske kulture v vzgojo in izobraževanje [A project of standardizing Romani in Slovenia and inclusion of Romani culture in upbringing and education]. In Vera Klopčič & Miroslav Polzer (eds.), *Evropa, Slovenija in Romi. Zbornik referatov na mednarodni konferenci v Ljubljani, 15. Februarja 2002* [Europe, Slovenia and the Roma. Collection of papers at the international conference in Ljubljana, February 15th, 2002], 131–141. Ljubljana: Inštitut za narodnostna vprašanja.
Anusiewicz, Janusz & Jacek Skawiński. 1996. *Słownik polszczyzny potocznej* [Dictionary of colloquial Polish]. Warszawa/Wrocław: Wydawnictwo Naukowe PWN.
Argirov, S. 1901. *Kămъ bălgarskitě tajni ezici (bracigovski meštrovski (djulgerski) i čălgădžijski taenъ ezikъ)* [On the Bulgarian secret languages (the secret languages bracigovski meštrovski (djulgerski) and čălgădžijski)]. Sofia: Dăržavna pečatnica.
Arkadiev, Peter. 2017. Borrowed preverbs and the limits of contact-induced change in aspectual systems. In Rosanna Benacchio, Alessio Muro & Svetlana Slavkova (eds.), *The Role of Prefixes in the Formation of Aspectuality. Issues of Grammaticalization*, 1–22. (Biblioteca di Studi Slavistici 39). Firenze: Firenze University Press.
Armjanov, Georgi. 2001. *Rečnik na bălgarskija žargon* [Dictionary of Bulgarian slang]. Sofija: Figura.
Ariste, Paul. 1969. Ein lettisches Ableitungssuffix im Zigeunerischen. *Baltistica* V(2). 179–181.
Ariste, Paul. 1973. Lettische Verbalpräfixe in einer Zigeunermundart. *Baltistica* IX(1). 79–81.
Bakker, Peter. 1999. The Northern branch of Romani: Mixed and non-mixed varieties. In Dieter W. Halwachs & Florian Menz (eds.), *Die Sprache der Roma: Perspektiven der Romani-Forschung in Österreich im interdisziplinären und internationalen Kontext*, 172–209. Klagenfurt: Drava.
Bakker, Peter & Yaron Matras. 1997. Introduction. In Yaron Matras, Peter Bakker and Hristo Kyuchukov (eds.), *The Typology and Dialectology of Romani*, vii–xxx. Amsterdam, Philadelphia: John Benjamins.
Barannikov, Aleksej P. 1931a. Songs of the Ukrainian Gypsies. *Journal of the Gypsy Lore Society* 10. 1–53.
Barannikov, Aleksej P. 1931b. Cyganskie ėlementy v russkom vorovskom argo [Gypsy elements in the Russian thieves' cant]. *Jazyk i literatura* 7. 139–158.

Barannikov, Aleksej P. 1933/34. *The Ukrainian and South Russian Gypsy dialects*. Leningrad: Izdatel'stvo Akademii Nauk SSSR.

Baro, Ondrej. 2003. So džalas o čhavo sune. Was der Knabe träumte. In Christiane Fennesz-Juhasz & Petra Cech (eds.), *Die schlaue Romni. Märchen und Lieder der Roma. E bengali Romni. So Roma phenen taj gilaben*, 194–221. Klagenfurt: Drava,

Bartosz, Adam. 2004. *Nie bój się Cygana. Na dara Romestar* [Don't be afraid of the Gypsy]. Sejny: Pogranicze.

Bartosz, Adam. 2009. Propozycja zapisu języka romani – Pisownia sulejowska [A proposal to write the Romani language – the Sulejów diction]. *Studia Romologica* 2. 153–166.

Beníšek, Michael. 2010. The quest for a Proto-Romani infinitive. *Romani studies* 20(1). 47–86.

Beníšek, Michael. 2013. Serednye Romani: A North Central Romani variety of Transcarpatian Ukraine. In Barbara Schrammel-Leber & Barbara Tiefenbacher (eds.), *Romani V. Papers from the Annual Meeting of the Gypsy Lore Society. Graz 2011*, 42–59 (Grazer Romani Publikationen 2). Graz: Universität Graz.

Beníšek, Michael. 2017. *The Eastern Uzh varieties of North Central Romani. Východoužské variety severocentrální romštiny*. Prague: Charles University dissertation. https://dspace.cuni.cz/handle/20.500.11956/87448. (accessed 28 June 2022)

Bertinetto, Pier M. & Denis Delfitto. 2000. Aspect vs. actionality: Why they should be kept apart. In Östen Dahl (ed.), *Tense and Aspect in the Languages of Europe*, 189–225. (Empirical Approaches to Language Typology 6). Berlin/New York: Mouton de Gruyter.

Bessonov, Nikolaj V. n.d. Kommentarii k stat'e A.P. Barannikova 'Cyganskie ėlementy v russkom vorovskom argo' [Comment on A.P. Barannikov's treatise 'Gypsy elements in Russian thieves' cant']. www.liloro.ru/romanes/bessonov9.htm. (accessed 20 April 2021)

Bierich, Alexander. 2008. Deutsche und jiddisch-hebräische Entlehnungen im polnischen, tschechischen und russischen Argot. In Sebastian Kempgen, Karl Gutschmidt, Ulrike Jekutsch & Ludger Udolph (eds.), *Deutsche Beiträge zum 14. Internationalen Slavistenkongress, Ohrid 2008*, 53–62. (Die Welt der Slaven. Sammelbände – Sborniki 32). München: Otto Sagner.

Bladycz, Robert. 2006. *Polsko historia. Perunoskro firba. Perun's tree* [Polish history. Perun's tree]. Wrocław: Stowarzyszenie ThESAURUS.

Blommaert, Jan & Ad Backus. 2013. Superdiverse repertoires and the individual. In Saint-Georges, Ingrid de & Jean-Jacques Weber (eds.), *Multilingualism and Multimodality. The Future of Education Research*, 11–32. Rotterdam: Sense Publishers.

Bodnárová, Zuzana & Jakob Wiedner. 2015. A comparative study of verbal particles in varieties of Vend Romani. *Romani Studies* 5, 25(2). 197–216.

Bondaletov, Vasilij D. 1967. Cyganizmy v sostave uslovnych jazykov [Gypsyisms in the inventory of conventional languages]. *Jazyk i obščestvo* 1. 235–243.

Boretzky, Norbert. 1986. Zur Sprache der Gurbet von Priština (Jugoslawien). *Giessener Hefte für Tsiganologie* 3(1–4). 195–217.

Boretzky, Norbert. 1989. Zum Interferenzverhalten des Romani (Verbreitete und ungewöhnliche Phänomene). *Zeitschrift für Phonetik, Sprachwissenschaft und Kommunikationsforschung* 42(3). 357–374.

Boretzky, Norbert. 1993. *Bugurdži. Deskriptiver und historischer Abriß eines Romani-Dialekts*. (Osteuropa-Institut der Freien Universität Berlin, Balkanologische Veröffentlichungen 21). Berlin: Harrassowitz.

Boretzky, Norbert. 1994. *Romani. Grammatik des Kalderaš-Dialekts mit Texten und Glossar.* (Osteuropa-Institut der Freien Universität Berlin, Balkanologische Veröffentlichungen 24). Berlin: Harrassowitz.
Boretzky, Norbert. 1996a. The 'new' infinitive in Romani. *Journal of the Gypsy Lore Society* 6(1). 1–51.
Boretzky, Norbert. 1996b. Arli. Materialien zu einem südbalkanischen Romani-Dialekt. *Grazer Linguistische Studien* 46. 1–30.
Boretzky, Norbert. 1996c. Entlehnte Wortstellungssyntax im Romani. In Norbert Boretzky, Werner Enninger & Thomas Stolz (eds.), *Areale, Kontakte, Dialekte. Sprache und ihre Dynamik in mehrsprachigen Situationen*, 95–121. Bochum: Universitätsverlag Dr. N. Brockmeyer.
Boretzky, Norbert. 1999. *Die Verwandtschaftsbeziehungen zwischen den südbalkanischen Romani-Dialekten. Mit einem Kartenanhang.* (Studien zur Tsiganologie und Folkloristik 27). Frankfurt am Main: Lang.
Boretzy, Norbert. 2002. Romani. In Miloš Okuka (ed.), *Lexikon der Sprachen des europäischen Ostens*, 927–939 (Wieser Enzyklopädie des europäischen Ostens 10). Klagenfurt: Wieser.
Boretzky, Norbert. 2013. Lexikalische Slavismen im Romani. *Zeitschrift für Balkanologie* 49(1). 10–46.
Boretzky, Norbert & Birgit Igla. 1994a. *Wörterbuch Romani-Deutsch-Englisch. Mit einer Grammatik der Dialektvarianten.* Wiesbaden: Harrassowitz.
Boretzky, Norbert & Birgit Igla. 1994b. Romani mixed dialects. In Peter Bakker & Maarten Mous (eds.), *Mixed Languages. 15 Case Studies in Language Intertwining*, 35–68. Amsterdam: Institute for Functional Research into Language and Language Use.
Boretzky, Norbert & Birgit Igla. 1999. Balkanische (südosteuropäische) Einflüsse im Romani. In Uwe Hinrichs (ed.), *Handbuch der Südosteuropa-Linguistik*, 709–731. Wiesbaden: Harrassowitz.
Boretzky, Norbert & Birgit Igla. 2004. *Kommentierter Dialektatlas des Romani*, vol. 1. Wiesbaden: Harrassowitz.
Boretzky, Norbert, Petra Cech & Birgit Igla. 2008. *Die südbalkanischen Dialekte (SB I) des Romani und ihre innere Gliederung. Analyse und Karten.* (Grazer Linguistische Monographien 26). Graz: Universität Graz.
Bořkovcová, Máša. 2006. *Romský etnolekt češtiny. Případová studie* [The Romani ethnolect of Czech. A case study]. Praha: Signeta.
Böthlingk, Otto von. 1852. Ueber die Sprache der Zigeuner in Russland. *Bulletin de la Classe Historico-Philologique de l'Académie Impériale des Sciences de St.-Pétersbourg* 10(1–3). 217–219.
Bredler, František. 1914. *Slovník české hantýrky (tajné řeči zlodějské)* [Dictionary of the Czech hantýrka (secret thieves' cant)]. Železný Brod: Ferd. Krompe.
Breu, Walter. 2000. Zur Position des Slavischen in einer Typologie des Verbalaspekts (Form, Funktion, Ebenenhierarchie und lexikalische Interaktion). In idem (ed.), *Probleme der Interaktion von Lexik und Aspekt (ILA)*, 21–54. (Linguistische Arbeiten 412). Tübingen: Niemeyer.
Breu, Walter. 2007. Der Verbalaspekt im Spannungsfeld zwischen Grammatik und Lexik. *Sprachwissenschaft* 32(2). 123–166.
Breu, Walter. 2009. Verbale Kategorien: Aspekt und Aktionsart. In Karl Gutschmidt, Sebastian Kempgen, Tilman Berger & Peter Kosta (eds.), *The Slavic Languages. An International Handbook of their Structure, their History and their Investigation*, 209–225. (Handbooks of Linguistics and Communication Science 32.2). Berlin: De Gruyter Mouton.

Budziszewska, Wanda. 1957. *Żargon ochweśnicki* [The cant of tradesmen and thieves]. Łódź: Łódzkie Towarzystwo Naukowe.

Bunčić, Daniel. 2008. Die (Re-)Nationalisierung der serbokroatischen Standards. In Sebastian Kempgen, Karl Gutschmidt, Ulrike Jekutsch & Ludger Udolph (eds.), *Deutsche Beiträge zum 14. Internationalen Slavistenkongress, Ohrid 2008*, 89–102. (Die Welt der Slaven. Sammelbände – Sborniki 32). München: Otto Sagner.

Bunčić, Daniel. 2015. 'Diastratische Diglossie' in Russland des 18. Jahrhunderts oder: Wann wurde Kirchenslavisch zur Fremdsprache? In Elena Dieser (ed.), *Linguistische Beiträge zur Slavistik. XX. JungslavistInnen-Treffen in Würzburg, 22.–24. September 2011*, 29–45. München (Specimina Philologiae Slavicae 186). München/Berlin/Leipzig/Washington D.C.: BiblionMedia.

Bunčić, Daniel. To appear. Sprachliche Variation. In Daniel Bunčić, Hagen Pitsch & Barbara Sonnenhauser (eds.), *Einführung in die Linguistik der slavischen Sprachen*.

Burridge, Kate & Keith Allan. 1998. The X-phemistic value of Romani in non-standard speech. In Yaron Matras (ed.), *The Romani Element in Non-Standard Speech*, 29–49. (Sondersprachenforschung 3). Wiesbaden: Harrassowitz.

Bussmann, Hadumod. 1996. Language family. In: Hadumod Bussmann (ed.), *Routledge Dictionary of Language and Linguistics*, 643–644. London: Routledge.

Casad, Eugene H. 1992. *Windows on Bilingualism. Dallas*: SIL.

Cech, Petra & Mozes Heinschink. 2001a. A dialect with seven names. *Romani Studies* 11. 137–184.

Cech, Petra & Mozes Heinschink. 2001b. Sinti Istriani, Lički Šijaci, Gopti und Cigani Brajdiči. Die Doljenski Roma in Slovenien. In Birgit Igla & Thomas Stolz (eds.), *„Was ich noch sagen wollte…": A multilingual Festschrift for Norbert Boretzky on occasion of his 65th birthday*, 341–368. Berlin: Akademie-Verlag.

Cech, Petra & Mozes Heinschink. 2002. Vokabular der Dolenjski Roma aus Novo Mesto und Bela Krajina, Slowenien. *Romani IV. Special Issue of Grazer Linguistische Studien* 58. 1–42.

Cech, Petra, Christiane Fennesz-Juhasz, Dieter W. Halwachs & Mozes Heinschink. 2004. *Die schlaue Romni. E bengali Romni. Märchen und Lieder der Roma. So Roma phenen taj gilaben*. Klagenfurt: Drava.

Clasmeier, Christina. 2015. *Die mentale Repräsentation von Aspektpartnerschaften russischer Verben*. (Slavolinguistica 21). Leipzig: BiblionMedia.

Comrie, Bernard & Greville G. Corbett. 1993. *The Slavonic languages*. 2nd edn. London: Routledge.

Coulmas, Florian. 1989. *The Writing Systems of the World*. Oxford/New York: Blackwell.

Cortiade, Marcel. 1991. Hauptarten der morphologischen Anpassung der Romani-Lexeme in der serbokroatischen Gaunersprache „Šatrovački" von Bosnien und Herzegowina. In Peter Bakker & Marcel Cortiade (eds.), *In the Margin of Romani. Gypsy languages in Contact*, 152–165. (Studies in Language Contact I). Amsterdam: Universiteit van Amsterdam.

Courthiade, Marcel. 2012. *„Alfabet odpowiedni dla języka cygańskiego oparty na naukowych podstawach" – o pisowni języka rromani* [„An alphabet appropriate for the Gypsy language, based on scientific foundations" – on spelling the Romani language]. Tarnów: Muzeum Okręgowe w Tarnowie.

Crystal, David. 2010. *The Cambridge Encyclopedia of Language*. 3rd edn. Cambridge: Cambridge University Press.

Cvetkov, Georgij N. (2001): *Romanė vorbi. Cygansko-russkij i russko-cyganskij slovar' (lovarskij dialekt). Okolo 4000 slov* [Romani words. Gypsy-Russian and Russian-Gypsy dictionary (dialect of the Lovara). Moskva: NIC "Apostrof".

Czeszewski, Maciej. 2001. *Słownik slangu młodzieżowego*. Piła: Ekolog.
Czeszewski, Maciej. 2006. *Słownik polszczyzny potocznej*. Warszawa: Wyd. Naukowe PWN.
Čarankaŭ, Leŭ N. 1974. Cyhanski dyjalekt u belaruskim moŭnym asjaroddzi. *Belaruskaja linhvistyka* 6. 34–40.
Čerenkov, Lev N. & Roman S. Demeter. 1990. Kratkij grammatičeskij očerk kėldėrarskogo dialekta cyganskogo jazyka. In Roman S. Demeter & Petr S. Demeter (eds.), *Cygansko-russkij i russko-cyganskij slovar' (kėldėrarskij dialekt). 5300 slov*. [Gypsy-Russian and Russian-Gypsy dictionary (dialect of the Kalderaš). 5300 words.]. 285–306. Moskva: Russkij jazyk.
Červenka, Jan. 2004. Některá specifika morfologie substantiv v subdialektech severocentrální romštiny ve slovenských regionech Kysuce, Turiec a Liptov [Some specifics of nominal morphology in the subdialects of Northern Central Romani in the Slovak regions Kysuce, Turiec and Liptov]. *Romano džaniben* 14 jevend [winter]. 177–185.
Dahl, Östen. 1985. *Tense and aspect systems*. New York/Oxford: Blackwell.
Demeter, Roman S. & Petr S. Demeter. 1990. *Cygansko-russkij i russko-cyganskij slovar' (kėldėrarskij dialekt). 5300 slov*. [Gypsy-Russian and Russian-Gypsy dictionary (dialect of the Kalderash). 5300 words.] Moskva: Russkij jazyk.
Demeter, Nadežda G., Nikolaj V. Bessonov & Vladimir K. Kutenkov. 2000. *Istorija cygan – novyj vzgljad* [History of the Gypsies – a new perspective]. Voronež: IPF "Voronež".
Demir, Ljatif, Nevsija Durmiš & Fatime Demir. 2015. *Crnogorsko-romski i Romsko-crnogorski rječnik* [Montenegrin-Romani and Romani-Montenegrin dictionary]. Podgorica: Zavod za udžbenike i nastavna sredstva.
Dębicki, Edward. 1993. *Teł nango boliben. Pod gołym niebem*. [Under the naked sky]. Szczecin: Wyd. Promocyjne "Albatros".
Dickey, Stephen M. 2000. *Parameters of Slavic Aspect: A Cognitive Approach*. Stanford: Cambridge University Press.
Djurić, Rajko. 1989. *Zigeunerische Elegien. Gedichte in Romani und Deutsch. Mit einer Einführung von Norbert Boretzky*. Hamburg: Helmut Buske.
Djurić, Rajko. 2002. *Die Literatur der Roma und Sinti*. Berlin: Ed. Parabolis.
Dobrovol'skij, Vladimir N. 1897. O dorogobužskich meščanach i ich šubrejskom ili kubrackom jazyke [About the Dorogobuž philistines and their secret languages]. *Izvestija ORJaS* 2(1). 320–352.
Dobrovol'skij, Vladimir N. 1908. *Kiselevskie cygane. Vyp. 1: Cyganskie teksty* [The Gypsies of Kiselev. Part 1: Gypsy texts]. Sankt-Peterburg: Tipografija Imperatorskoj Akademii Nauk.
Dobrovol'skij, Vladimir N. 1916. Nekotorye dannye uslovnogo jazyka dorogobužskich meščan, kalik perechožich, portnych i konovalov, stranstvujuščich po Smolenskoj zemle. Dannye jazyka Kubrackogo ili Šubrejskogo Dorogobužskich meščan [Some data about the secret languages of the Dorogobuž philistines, Kalik passers-by, tailors and horse-dressers, wandering the area of Smolensk]. *Smolenskaja starina* 3(2). 1–13.
Duličenko, Aleksandr D. 1981. *Slavjanskie literaturnye mikrojazyki. Voprosy formirovanija i razvitija* [Slavic microlanguages. Questions of their formation and development]. Tallinn: Valgus.
Duličenko, Aleksandr D. 2006. Sovremennoe slavjanskoe jazykoznanie i slavjanskie literaturnye mikrojazyki [Contemporary Slavic linguistics and Slavic microlanguages]. In Aleksandr D. Duličenko & Sven Gustavson (eds.), *Slavjanskie literaturnye mikrojazyki i jazykovye kontakty*, 22–46. Tartu: Tartu University Press.
Dunn, Jonathan. 2021. Representations of language varieties are reliable given corpus similarity measures. https://arxiv.org/abs/2104.01294. (accessed 31 January 2022)

D'jačok, M.T. & Viktor V. Šapoval. 1988. Russkie argotičeskie ètimologii [Russian argot etymologies]. In Aleksandr I. Fedorov (ed.), *Russkaja leksika v istoričeskom razvitii. Sbornik naučnych trudov.* 52–60. Novosibirsk: Unknown publisher.

Đurić, Rajko. 2005. *Gramatika romskog jezika. Gramatike e rromane čhibaki* [Grammar of the Romani language. Beograd: Otkrovenje.

Đurić, Rajko. 2011. *Pravopis romskoga jezika. O čačolekhavno e rromane čhibako* [Orthography of the Romani language]. Vršac: Visoka škola strukovnih studija za obrazovanje vaspitača "Mihailo Palov".

Eloeva, Fatima A. & Aleksandr Ju. Rusakov. 1990. *Problemy jazykovoj interferencii. Učebnoe posobie* [Problems of language interference. Tutorial]. Leningrad: Leningradskij universitet.

Elšík, Viktor. 2007. Review of Anna Rácová & Ján Horecký. Slovenská karpatská rómčina: opis systému. Bratislava: Veda 2000. *Slovo a slovesnost* 68(4). 311–314.

Elšík, Viktor. 2008. Grammatical borrowing in Hungarian Rumungro. In Yaron Matras & Jeanette Sakel (eds.), *Grammatical Borrowing in Cross-Linguistic Perspective*, 261–282. Berlin/New York: Mouton de Gruyter.

Elšík, Viktor. 2009. Loandwords in Selice Romani, an Indo-Aryan language of Slovakia. In Martin Haspelmath & Uri Tadmor (eds.), *Loanwords in the World's Languages. A Comparative Handbook*, 260–303. Berlin: De Gruyter Mouton.

Elšík, Viktor. 2017. Lexikální romismy v češtině. In Petr Karlík, Marek Nekula & Jana Pleskalová (eds.), *CzechEncy – Nový encyklopedický slovník češtiny* [CzechEncy – New encyclopedic dictionary of Czech]. https://www.czechency.org/slovnik/LEXIKÁLNÍ_ROMISMY_V_ČEŠTINĚ. (accessed 31 January 2022)

Elšík, Viktor, Milena Hübschmannová & Hana Šebková. 1999. The Southern Central (ahi-imperfect) Romani dialects of Slovakia and northern Hungary. In Dieter W. Halwachs & Florian Menz (eds.), *Die Sprache der Roma. Perspektiven der Romani-Forschung in Österreich im interdisziplinären und internationalen Kontext*, 277–390. Klagenfurt/Celovec: Drava.

Elšík, Viktor & Yaron Matras. 2006. *Markedness and Language Change: The Romani Sample*. Berlin/New York: Mouton de Gruyter.

Elšík, Viktor & Yaron Matras. 2009. Modality in Romani. In Björn Hansen & Ferdinand de Haan (eds.), *Modals in the Languages of Europe. A Reference Work*, 267–322. Berlin/New York: Mouton de Gruyter.

Elšík, Viktor & Michael Beníšek. 2020. Romani Dialectology. In Yaron Matras & Anton Tenser (eds.), *The Palgrave Handbook of Romani Language and Linguistics*, 389–427. London: Palgrave Macmillan.

Estreicher, Karol. [1903] 1979. *Szwargot więzienny*. Kraków: Nakł. Księgarni D.E. Friedleina.

Fałowski, Przemysław. 2013. Words of Romani origin in the Czech and Croatian languages. *Studia Linguistica Universitatis Iagellonicae Cracoviensis* 130. 95–115.

Ficowski, Jerzy. 1956. *Pieśni Papuszy (Papušakre gila). Wiersze w języku cygańskim* [Papusza's songs. Poems in the Gypsy language]. Wrocław: Ossolineum.

Friedman, Victor A. 1985. Problems in the codification of a standard Romani literary language. In Joanne Grumet (ed.), *Papers from the Fourth and Fifth Annual Meetings Gypsy Lore Society, North American Chapter*, 56–75. New York: Gypsy Lore Society, North American Chapter.

Friedman, Victor A. 1995. Romani standardization and status in the Republic of Macedonia. In Yaron Matras (ed.), *Romani in Contact. The History, Structure and Sociology of a Language*,

177–188. (Amsterdam Studies in the Theory and History if Linguistic Science 126, Series IV – Current Issues in Linguistic Theory). Amsterdam, Philadelphia: John Benjamins.

Friedman, Victor A. 1999. Evidentiality in the Balkans. In Uwe Hinrichs (ed.), *Handbuch der Südosteuropa-Linguistik*, 519–544. Wiesbaden: Harrassowitz.

Friedman, Victor A. 2001a. Romani Multilingualism in its Balkan Context. *Sprachtypologie und Universalienforschung* 54. 46–159.

Friedman, Victor A. 2001b. The Romani indefinite article in its historical and areal context. In Birgit Birgit & Thomas Stolz (eds.), *„Was ich noch sagen wollte...": A multilingual Festschrift for Norbert Boretzky on occasion of his 65th birthday*, 287–301. Berlin: Akademie-Verlag.

Friedman, Victor A. 2005. The Romani language in Macedonia in the third millennium: Progress and problems. In Barbara Schrammel, Dieter W. Halwachs & Gerd Ambrosch (eds.), *General and Applied Romani Linguistics. Proceedings from the 6th International Conference on Romani Linguistics*. München: LINCOM Europa.

Friedman, Victor A. 2019. Parallel Universes and Universal Parallels: Balkan Romani Evidential Strategies. In Iliyana Krapova & Brian Joseph (eds.), *Balkan Syntax and (Universal) Principles of Grammar*, 37–48. (Trends in Linguistics. Studies and Monographs 285). Berlin/Boston: De Gruyter Mouton.

Friedman, Victor A. 2021. The Balkans. In Evangelia Adamou & Yaron Matras (eds.), *The Routledge Handbook of Language Contact*, 385–403. London/New York: Routledge.

Gast, Volker & Johan van der Auwera. 2012. What is 'contact-induced grammaticalization'? Examples from Mayan and Mixe-Zoquean languages. In Björn Wiemer, Bernhard Wälchli & Björn Hansen (eds.), *Grammatical Replication and Borrowability in Language Contact*, 381–426. Berlin/Boston: De Gruyter.

Găbjuv, Petko. 1900. Prinos kăm bălgarskite tajni ezici [Contribution to the Bulgarian secret languages]. In *Sbornik za narodni umotvorenija, nauka i knižnina* XVI–XVII. 842–875. Sofia: Dăržavna pečatnica.

Gierliński, Karol P. 2006. *Historia Polskakri. Perunoskro rukh. Perun's tree* [Polish history. Perun's tree]. Wrocław: Stowarzyszenie ThESAURUS.

Gierliński, Karol P. 2007. *Miri szkoła. Romano elementaro* [My school. Romani primer]. Kostrzyn nad Odrą: Drukarnia H&M Ignaszak.

Gierliński, Karol P. 2008. *Miri szkoła. Romano elementaro* [My school. Romani primer]. Kostrzyn nad Odrą: Drukarnia H&M Ignaszak.

Gilliat-Smith, Bernard J. 1915–16. A report on the Gypsy tribes of North East Bulgaria. *Journal of the Gypsy Lore Society* 9(1). 1–55, 9(2), 65–109.

Gilliat-Smith, Bernard J. 1922. The language of the St. Petersbourg Gypsy singers I. *Journal of the Gypsy Lore Society* 1. 153–162.

Gilliat-Smith, Bernard J. 1932. The dialect of the Gypsies of Northern Russia (Being a Review of Professor M.V. Sergievski's Cyganski Jazyk). *Journal of the Gypsy Lore Society. Third Series* 11. 71–88.

Gjorgjević, Tihomir R. 1903. *Die Zigeuner in Serbien. Ethnologische Forschungen, I. Teil.* Budapest: Buchdruckerei Thalia.

Grant, Anthony. 1998. Romani words in non-standard British English and the development of Angloromani. In Yaron Matras (ed.), *The Romani lement in Non-Standard Speech*, 165–191. (Sondersprachenforschung 3). Wiesbaden: Harrassowitz.

Grosjean, François. 1989. Neurolinguists, beware! The bilingual is not two monolinguals in one person! *Brain and Language* 36. 3–15.

Grosjean, François. 2001. The bilingual's language modes. In Janet L. Nicol (ed.), *One Mind, two Languages. Bilingual Language Processing*, 1–22. Oxford: Blackwell.

Gumperz, John J. 1972. Introduction. In: John J. Gumperz & Dell Hymes (eds.), *Directions in sociolinguistics. The ethnography of communication*, 1–25. New York: Holt, Rinehart and Winston, Inc.

Gumperz, John J. 1982. *Discourse Strategies*. Cambridge: Cambridge University Press.

Gutknecht, Christoph. 2010. Mein Freund, der Haberer. Wie ein hebräischer Begriff in Österreich politische Karriere gemacht hat. *Jüdische Allgemeine* 25.11.2010. www.juedische-allgemeine.de/article/view/id/9144. (accessed 31 January 2022)

Halilović, Senahid, Ilijas Tanović & Amela Šehović. 2009. *Govor grada Sarajeva i razgovorni bosanski jezik*. Sarajevo: Slavistički komitet.

Haliti, Bajram. 2006. *Dukhavni upral o hramo merimasko e kosmetese rromendje. Tugovanka nad hramom smrti kosmetskim romima. A lament over the temple of death for Romanys of Kosovo*. Beograd: Vlast. izd.: Memorijalnuno maškripe e Rromenego e holokaust studijengo ane Srbija thaj Crna Gora.

Halwachs, Dieter W. 2002. Anmerkungen zur Romani-Variante der Prekmurje. In Dieter W. Halwachs & Gerd Ambrosch (eds.), *Romani IV. Special Issue of Grazer Linguistische Studien* 58. 43–54.

Halwachs, Dieter W., Simone Klinge & Barbara Schrammel-Leber. 2013. *Romani – Education, segregation and the European Charter for Regional or Minority Languages*. (Grazer Romani-Publikationen 1). Graz: Universität Graz.

Hancock, Ian. 1971. The acquisition of English by American Romani children. *WORD* 27(1–3). 353–362.

Hancock, Ian. 1980. The ethnolectal English of American Gypsies. In Joey L. Dillard (ed.), *Perspectives on Amerian English*, 257–264. (Contributions to the Sociology of Language 29). The Hague/Paris/New York: Mouton Publishers.

Hancock, Ian. 1983. Slavic influence on Texan Romani. *Southwest Journal of Linguistics* 6(2). 115–132.

Hancock, Ian. 1988. The development of Romani linguistics. In Mohammad A. Jazayery & Werner Winter (eds.), *Languages and Cultures. Studies in Honor of Edgar C. Polomé*, 183–223. Berlin/New York: Mouton de Gruyter.

Hancock, Ian & Hristo Kjučukov. 2000. *Angluni vorba. Atanasov-Ramar, Toško, Čhordo kamipe* [First words]. Austin: Romanistan Publ.

Hansen, Björn. 2011. Slavonic languages. In Bernd Kortmann & Johan van der Auwera (eds.), *The Languages and Linguistics of Europe. A Comprehensive Guide*, 97–123. (The World of Linguistics 1). Göttingen: De Gruyter Mouton.

Haugen, Einar. 1950. The analysis of linguistic borrowing. *Language* 26. 210–231.

Haugen, Einar. [1953] 1969. *The Norwegian Languages in the Americas: A Study in Bilingual Behaviour*. Bloomington: Indiana University Press.

Heine, Bernd & Tania Kuteva. 2003. On contact-induced grammaticalization. *Studies in Language* 27(3). 529–572.

Heine, Bernd & Tania Kuteva. 2005. *Language contact and grammatical change*. Cambridge: Cambridge University Press.

Heinschink, Mozes F. & Petra Cech. 2013. Die Sprache der Roma – Grundzüge der Romani Čhib und Perspektiven für den Unterricht. In Sabine Hornberg & Christian Brüggemann (eds.), *Die Bildungssituation von Roma in Europa*, 53–87. (Studien zur International und Interkulturell Vergleichenden Erziehungswissenschaft 16). Münster: Waxmann.

Hejkrlíková, Jana. 2019. O Z. Guži: Khatar slovačiko romano gav prekal e armada andre ROI [Z. Guži. From a Slovak Romani village over the army to the Roma Civic Initiative]. *Romano hangos* 21(18–19). 5.

Hinrichs, Uwe. 2014. Soziolekte (serbisch/kroatisch/bosnisch). In Karl Gutschmidt, Sebastian Kempgen, Tilman Berger & Peter Kosta (eds.), *The Slavic Languages. An International Handbook of their Structure, their History and their Investigation*, 2171–2185. (Handbooks of Linguistics and Communication Science 32.2). Berlin: De Gruyter Mouton.

Hochel, Braňo. 1993. *Slovník slovenského slangu* [Dictionary of Slovak slang]. Bratislava: Hevi.

Horbač, Oleksa. 2006. *Argo v Ukraïni* [Argot in Ukraine]. L'viv: Instytut ukraïnoznavstva im. I. Kryp'jakeviča NAN Ukraïny.

Horváth, Luboš. 2006. Me kamav kole manušen, so keren, so kampel, aver ňič. Mám rád lidi, kteří dělají, co je třeba, a víc nic [I like people who do what is necessary and not more]. *Romano džaniben* ňilaj [summer]. 228–235.

Horvátová, Agnesa. 2003. *Pal e bari rama the aver paramisa. O velké ramě a jiné příběhy* [About the great lord and other stories]. Praha: Signeta.

Hübschmannová, Milena. 1993. Hlavné zásady romského pravopisu [The main principles of a Romani orthography]. *Romano ľil nevo* 3. 88–99.

Hübschmannová, Milena. 1994. Poznámky ke knize Jiřiny van Leeuwen-Turnovcové [Comments on the book by Jiřina van Leeuwen-Turnovcová]. *Romano džaniben* 3. 55–58.

Hübschmannová, Milena. 1995. Trial and error in written Romani on the pages of Romani periodicals. In Yaron Matras (ed.), *Romani in Contact. The History, Structure and Sociology of a Language*, 189–205. (Amsterdam Studies in the Theory and History if Linguistic Science 126, Series IV – Current Issues in Linguistic Theory.) Amsterdam, Philadelphia: John Benjamins.

Hübschmannová, Milena, Hana Šebková & Anna Žigová. 1991. *Romsko-český a česko-romský kapesní slovník* [Romani-Czech and Czech-Romani pocket dictionary]. Praha: Státní Pedag. Nakl.

Hübschmannová, Milena & Jiří Neustupný. 1996. The Slovak-and-Czech dialect of Romani and its standardization. *International Journal of the Sociology of Language* 120. 85–109.

Hübschmannová, Milena & Vít Bubeník. 1997. Causatives in Slovak and Hungarian Romani. In Yaron Matras, Peter Bakker & Hristo Kyuchukov (eds.), *The typology and dialectology of Romani*, 133–145. (Current Issues in Linguistic Theory 156). Amsterdam: John Benjamins.

Hübschmannová, Milena, Jan Červenka, Anna Koptová & Eva Gašparová. 2006. *Pravidlá rómskeho pravopisu. S pravopisným a gramatickým slovníkom* [The rules of Romani orthography. With an orthographic and grammatical dictionary]. Bratislava: Štátny pedagogický ústav.

Hugo, Jan, Markéta Fidlerová, Kateřina Adámková & Zdeňka Juránková (eds.). 2006. *Slovník nespisovné češtiny. Argot, slangy a obecná mluva od nejstarších dob po současnost. Historie a původ slov* [Dictionary of unwritten Czech. Argot, slang and colloquial speech from the oldest times to the present. History and origin of words]. 2nd edn. Praha: Maxdorf.

Igla, Birgit. 1991a. Probleme der Standardisierung des Romani. In James R. Dow & Thomas Stolz (eds.), *Akten des 7. Essener Kolloquiums über „Minoritäten/Sprachminoritäten" vom 14.–17.6.1990 an der Universität Essen*, 75–90. (Bochum-Essener Beiträge zur Sprachwandelforschung 10). Bochum: Brockmeyer.

Igla, Birgit. 1991b. On the treatment of foreign verbs in Romani. In Peter Bakker & Marcel Cortiade (eds.), *In the Margin of Romani. Gypsy Languages in Contact*, 50–55. (Studies in Language Contact 1). Amsterdam: Universiteit van Amsterdam.

Igla, Birgit. 1992. Entlehnung und Lehnübersetzung deutscher Präfixverben im Sinti. In Jürgen Erfurt, Benedikt Jeßing & Matthias Perl (eds.), *Prinzipien des Sprachwandels. I. Vorbereitung. Beiträge zum Leipziger Symposium des Projektes ‚Prinzipien des Sprachwandels' (PROPRINS) vom 24.–26.10.1991 an der Universität Leipzig*, 38–56. Bochum (Bochum-Essener Beiträge zur Sprachwandelforschung XVI). Bochum: Brockmeyer.

Igla, Birgit. 1997. The Romani dialect of the Rhodopes. In: Yaron Matras, Peter Bakker & Hristo Kyuchukov (eds.), *The Typology and Dialectology of Romani*, 147–158. (Current Issues in Linguistic Theory 156). Amsterdam, Philadelphia: John Benjamins.

Igla, Birgit. 1998. Zum Verbalaspekt in bulgarischen Romani-Dialekten. *Grazer Linguistische Studien* 50. 65–79.

Igla, Birgit. 1999. Disturbances and innovations in the case system in Bulgarian Romani dialects. *Acta Linguistica Academiae Scientiarum Hungaricae* 46. 201–214.

Igla, Birgit. 2001. Zur Entwicklung der Diathese in bulgarischen Romani-Dialekten. In: Birgit Igla & Thomas Stolz (eds.), *„Was ich noch sagen wollte..."*: *A multilingual Festschrift for Norbert Boretzky on occasion of his 65th birthday*, 405–422. Berlin: Akademie-Verlag.

Igla, Birgit & Desislava Draganova. 2006. Romani dialects in Bulgaria. *International Journal of the sociology of language* 179. 53–63.

Igla, Birgit & Irene Sechidou. 2012. Romani in contact with Bulgarian and Greek: replication in verbal morphology. In Martine Vanhove, Thomas Stolz, Aina Urdze & Hitomi Otsuka (eds.), *Morphologies in Contact*, 163–176. (Studia typologica, Beihefte 10). Berlin: Akademie-Verlag.

Imami, Petrit. 2003. *Beogradski frajerski rečnik*. Beograd: NKK Internacional.

Isačenko, Aleksandr V. 1968. *Die russische Sprache der Gegenwart. Formenlehre*. München: Hueber.

Jagić, Vatroslav. 1895. *Die Geheimsprachen bei den Slaven. 1. Bibliographie des Gegenstandes und die slavischen Bestandtheile der Geheimsprachen*. Wien: Gerold in Komm.

Janda, Laura, Anna Endresen, Julia Kuznetsova, Olga Lyashevskaya, Anastasia Makarova, Tore Nesset & Svetlana Sokolova. 2013. *Why Russian Aspectual Prefixes aren't Empty. Prefixes as Verb Classifiers*. Bloomington: Slavica.

Jek Romni kata i Prizreno [A Romni from Prizren] (2003): Lond taj šekeri [Salt and sugar]. In Christiane Fennesz-Juhasz & Petra Cech (eds.), *Die schlaue Romni. Märchen und Lieder der Roma. E bengali Romni. So Roma phenen taj gilaben*, 74–87. Klagenfurt: Drava.

Ješina, Josef. 1886. *Romáňi čib oder die Zigeuner-Sprache. Grammatik, Wörterbuch, Chrestomathie*. Leipzig: List & Francke.

Johanson, Lars. 2002. *Structural factors in Turkic language contacts*. Richmond: Curzon.

Jovanović, Slobodanka. 2003. O trgovco [The merchant]. In Christiane Fennesz-Juhasz & Petra Cech (eds.), *Die schlaue Romni. Märchen und Lieder der Roma. E bengali Romni. So Roma phenen taj gilaben*, 94–99. Klagenfurt: Drava.

Jørgensen, Jens N. 2008. Polylingual languaging around and among children and adolescents. *International Journal of Multilingualism* 5(3). 161–176.

Juda, Karel. 1902. Tajna řeč ('hantýrka') zlodějů a šibalů [The secret language ('hantýrka') of the thieves and mischievous]. *Český lid* 11(3). 139–143.

Kačová, Veronika. 2019. Karačoňa pro burkos [Christmas at the castle]. *Romano hangos* 21(18–19). 6.

Kajtazi, Veljok. 2008. *Romano-kroacijako thaj kroacijako-romano alavari. Romsko-hrvatski i hrvatsko-romski rječnik* [Romani-Croatian and Croatian-Romani dictionary]. Zagreb: Hrvatsko filološko društvo, Odjel za orijentalisti.

Kalina, Antoine. 1882. *La langue des Tziganes slovaques*. Posen: Żupański.
Kania, Stanisław. 1995. *Słownik argotyzmów* [Dictionary of argotisms]. Warszawa: Wiedza Powszechna.
Kenrick, Donald S. 1969. *Morphology and lexicon of the Romany dialect of Kotel (Bulgaria)*. London: University of London.
Kenrick, Donald. 1981. The development of a standard alphabet for Romani. *The Bible translator* 32(2). 215–219.
Kepeski, Krume & Šaip Jusuf. 1980. *Romani Gramatika. Romska gramatika* [Romani grammar]. Skopje: OOZT Knigoizdatelstvo "Naša kniga".
Kiefer, Ferenc. 2010. Areal-typological aspects of word-formation. The case of aktionsart-formation in German, Hungarian, Slavic, Baltic, Romani and Yiddish. In Franz Rainer (ed.), *Variation and Change in Morphology: Selected papers from the 13th International Morphology Meeting, Vienna, February 2008*, 129–147. Amsterdam, Philadelphia: John Benjamins.
Kjučukov, Christo & Miroslav Yanakiev. 1996. *Romskijat păt. O Romano Drom. Christomatija po romski ezik za IV–VIII klas* [The way of the Roma. Chrestomathy of the Romani language for class IV–VIII]. Sofija: Tilia.
Klich, Edward. [1927] 2011. *O polszczyźnie i cygańszczyźnie. Wstęp i dobór tekstów Bogdan Walczak* [About the Polish and the Gypsy language. Introduction and text selection by Bogdan Walczak]. Poznań: Wyd. Poznańskiego Towarzystwa Przyjaciół Nauk.
Kloss, Heinz. 1976. Abstandsprachen und Ausbausprachen. In Joachim Göschel, Norbert Nail & Gaston van der Elst (eds.), *Zur Theorie des Dialekts. Aufsätze aus 100 Jahren Forschung mit biographischen Anmerkungen zu den Autoren*, 301–322. (Zeitschrift für Dialektologie und Linguistik 16). Wiesbaden: Steiner.
Kochanowski, Vania de Gila. 1995. Romani Language Standardization. *Journal of the Gypsy Lore Society* 5(2). 97–108.
Kopernicki, Isidore. 1889. Notes on the dialect of the Bosnian Gypsies. *Journal of the Gypsy Lore Society* 1(3). 125–131.
Kopernicki, Izydor. 1930. *Textes tsiganes: contes et poésies avec trad. française. Teksty cygańskie*. Warszawa: Gebethner i Wolff.
Kortmann, Bernd & Johan van der Auwera. 2011. Introduction. In idem (eds.), *The Languages and Linguistics of Europe. A Comprehensive Guide*, xv-xviii. (The World of Linguistics, vol. 1). Göttingen: De Gruyter Mouton.
Kostov, Kiril. 1956. Ciganski dumi v bulgarskite tajni govori [Gypsy words in Bulgarian secret languages]. *Izvestija na Instituta za Bălgarski Ezik* 4. 411–425.
Kostov, Kiril. 1963a. *Grammatik der Zigeunersprache Bulgariens: Phonetik und Morphologie*. Berlin: Humboldt University dissertation.
Kostov, Kiril. 1963b. Bulg. mundartliches *папйн* (*пáпиня*) „Dummkopf". *Zeitschrift für Slawistik* 8(1). 62–64.
Kostov, Kiril. 1966. Maked. dial. *šošorea* 'pri̇́kan, zajak' < cyg. dial. *šošoréa* 'lepuscule!' *Ėtimologija*. 107–110.
Kostov, Kiril. 1974. Semantisches und Etymologisches aus dem bulgarischen sondersprachlichen Wortschatz. In Ljubomir Andrejčin (ed.), *V pamet na profesor Stojko Stojkov (1912–1969). Ezikovedski izsledvanija* [In memory of professor Stojko Stojkov (1912–1969). Linguistic investigations]. Sofia: Izdatelstvo na Bălgarskata akademija na naukite.
Kostov, Kiril. 1975. Cyganskie č(h)ang 'noga' i č(h)angalo 's (dlinnymi) nogami' kak obščie zaimstvovanija v nekotorych evropejskich jazykach [The Gypsy expressions č(h)ang

'leg' i č(h)angalo 'with (long) legs' as common loanwords in some European languages]. *Ètimologija*. 164–168.
Kostov, Kiril. 1989. Zur Determination der a-stämmigen entlehnten Maskulina in der Zigeunersprache Bulgariens. *Balkansko ezikoznanie/Linguistique balkanique* 32(2). 119–122.
Kovačič, Jelenka. 1999. *Domislin pe pu mande. Pomisli name* [Think of us]. Novo mesto: Tiskarna Novo mesto.
Kovačič, Jožica. 2003a. Šest balora [Six pigs]. In Christiane Fennesz-Juhasz & Petra Cech (eds.), *Die schlaue Romni. Märchen und Lieder der Roma. E bengali Romni. So Roma phenen taj gilaben*, 170–171. Klagenfurt: Drava.
Kovačič, Jožica. 2003b. Sap du brekh [Snake on the chest]. In Christiane Fennesz-Juhasz & Petra Cech (eds.), *Die schlaue Romni. Märchen und Lieder der Roma. E bengali Romni. So Roma phenen taj gilaben*, 172–173. Klagenfurt: Drava.
Kožanov, Kiril A. 2011. Balto-slavjanskie glagol'nye prefiksy v baltijskich dialektach cyganskogo jazyka [Balto-Slavic verbal prefixes in Baltic dialects of the Gypsy language]. *Acta Linguistics Petropolitana. Trudy Instituta lingvističskich issledovanij RAN* VII(3). 311–315.
Kozhanov, Kirill & Peter Arkadiev. 2017. How much pattern-borrowing does matter-borrowing presuppose? A study of Slavic verbal prefixes in contact. Presentation at the Workshop *Matter borrowing vs pattern borrowing in morphology, 50th annual meeting of the Societas Linguistca Europaea, Zürich 10–13 September 2017*. www.academia.edu/ 34588320/ How_much_pattern-borrowing_does_matter-borrowing_presuppose_A_study _of_Slavic_ verbal_prefixes_in_contact. (accessed 31 January 2022)
Kralčák, L'ubomír. 1999. Slovenčina v kontakte s rómčinou. In Slavomír Ondrejovič (ed.), *Slovenčina v kontaktoch a konfliktoch s inými jazykmi. Special issue of Sociolinguistica Slovaca* 4. 178–185.
Kroll, Judith F., Susan C. Bobb, Maya M. Misra & Taomei Guo (2008): Language selection in bilingual speech: Evidence for inhibitory processes. *Acta Psychologica* 128. 416–430.
Kurka, Antoni. [1907] 1979. *Słownik mowy złodziejskiej*. Lwów: Nakładem autora.
Kurth, Gérald. 2008. *Identitäten zwischen Ethnos und Kosmos. Studien zur Literatur der Roma in Makedonien*. Wiesbaden: Harrassowitz.
Kyuchukov, Hristo. 1999. Acquisition of Romani morphology. *Grazer Linguistische Studien* 51. 83–94.
Kyuchukov, Hristo. 2009. Standardization of Romani in Bulgaria. In idem (ed.), *"A Language without Borders..." The International Romani Language Conference in Stockholm and Uppsala, 7–9 January 2007*. 2nd edn. 56–65. (Endangered languages and cultures 5). Uppsala: Uppsala University Press.
Kyuchukov, Hristo, Jill G. de Villiers & Andrea Takahesu Tabori. 2017. Why Roma children need language assessment in Romani. *Psychology of Language and Communication* 21(1). 215–243.
Lapov, Zoran (2005): The Romani groups and dialects in Croatia. In: Schrammel, Barbara & Dieter W. Halwachs & Gerd Ambrosch (Hgg.), *General and Applied Romani Linguistics. Proceedings from the 6th International Conference on Romani Linguistics*. München, 79–89.
Leeuwen-Turnovcová, Jiřina van. 2003. *Historisches Argot und neuer Gefängnisslang in Böhmen. 2. Materialanalyse und Lehnquellen*. Wiesbaden: Harrassowitz.
Leggio, Daniele V. 2011. The dialect of the Mitrovica Roma. *Romani Studies* 21(1). 57–113.
Leschber, Corinna. 2002. Semantische Vorgänge bei lexikalischen Übernahmen aus dem Romani in diastratische Varietäten des Bulgarischen. *Grazer Linguistische Studien* 58. 57–101.

Levačič, Ludvig. 2003. O Rom taj o mojakraši [The Rom and the innkeeper]. In Christiane Fennesz-Juhasz & Petra Cech (eds.), *Die schlaue Romni. Märchen und Lieder der Roma. E bengali Romni. So Roma phenen taj gilaben*, 174–177. Klagenfurt: Drava.

Li, Wei. 2018. Translanguaging as a practical theory of languages. *Applied Linguistics* 39(1). 9–30.

Lípa, Jiří. 1965. *Cikánština v jazykovém prostředí slovenském a českém: k otázkám starých a novejších složek v její gramatice a lexiku* [The Gypsy language in the Slovak and Czech language environment. Questions on old and new components in its grammar and lexicon]. Praha: Nakl. Československé akademie věd.

Loebell, Helga & Kathryn Bock (2003): Structural priming across languages. *Linguistics* 41. 791–824.

Lubaś, Władysław. 2001–2006. *Słownik polskich leksemów potocznych* [Dictionary of Polish colloquial lexemes]. Kraków: Wydawnictwo Naukowe DWN.

Ludwikowski, Wiktor & Henryk Walczak. [1922] 1979. *Żargon mowy przestępców "blatna muzyka". Ogólny zbiór słów gwary złodziejskiej* [Criminal slang "blatna muzyka". A general collection of words from the thieves' cant]. Warszawa: Typ. Szrajber.

Machotin, Džura. 1993. *Adžutipe prě romani čib. Posobie po jazyku romani* [Textbook on the Romani language]. Tver': Self-published.

Matras, Yaron. 1997. Probleme und Chancen der Verschriftung der Sprache der Roma und Sinti. In Heiko Balhorn & Heide Niemann (eds.), *Sprachen werden Schrift. Mündlichkeit – Schriftlichkeit – Mehrsprachigkeit*, 110–116. (Libelle: Wissenschaft lesen und schreiben 7). Lengwil am Bodensee: Libelle.

Matras, Yaron. 1998a. Utterance modifiers and universals of grammatical borrowing. *Linguistics* 36(2). 281–331.

Matras, Yaron. 1998b. The Romani element in German secret languages: Jenisch and Rotwelsch. In idem (ed.), *The Romani Element in Non-Standard Speech*. 193–230. (Sondersprachenforschung 3). Wiesbaden: Harrassowitz.

Matras, Yaron. 1999a. Writing Romani: The pragmatics of codification in a stateless language. *Applied Linguistics* 20(4). 481–502.

Matras, Yaron. 1999b. Sprachplanung und Spracheinstellung im Romanes. In: Halwachs, Dieter W. & Florian Menz (eds.), *Die Sprache der Roma. Perspektiven der Romani-Forschung in Österreich im interdisziplinären und internationalen Kontext*, 95–111. Klagenfurt: Drava.

Matras, Yaron. 1999c. The Speech of the Polska Roma: Some Highlighted Features and Their Implications for Romani Dialectology. *Journal of the Gypsy Lore Society* 9. 1–28.

Matras, Yaron. 1999d. Johann Rüdiger and the study of Romani in 18th century Germany. *Journal of the Gypsy Lore Society* 9. 89–116.

Matras, Yaron. 2001. Tense, aspect and modality categories in Romani. *Sprachtypologische Universitäre Forschung* 54(2). 162–180.

Matras, Yaron. 2002. *Romani. A Linguistic Introduction*. Cambridge: Cambridge University Press.

Matras, Yaron. 2005. The classification of Romani dialects: A geographic-historical perspective. In: Barbara Schrammel, Dieter W. Halwachs & Gerd Ambrosch (eds.), *General and Applied Romani Linguistics. Proceedings from the 6th International Conference on Romani Linguistics*, 7–22. München: LINCOM Europa.

Matras, Yaron. 2007. The borrowability of structural categories. In Yaron Matras & Jeanette Sakel (eds.), *Grammatical Borrowing in Cross-Linguistic Perspective*. 31–73. (Empirical Approached to Language Typology 38). Berlin/New York: Mouton de Gruyter.

Matras, Yaron. 2010. *Romani in Britain. The afterlife of a language*. Edinburgh: Edinburgh University Press.
Matras, Yaron. 2014. *I Met Lucky People. The Story of the Romani Gypsies*. London: Allen Lane.
Matras, Yaron. 2020. *Language contact*. 2nd edn. (Cambridge textbooks in linguistics). Cambridge: Cambridge University Press.
Matras, Yaron & Jeanette Sakel. 2007. Introduction. In idem (eds.): *Grammatical Borrowing in Cross-Linguistic Perspective*, 1–14. Berlin/New York: Mouton de Gruyter.
Matras, Yaron, Christopher White & Viktor Elšík. 2009. The Romani Morpho-Syntax (RMS) Database. In Martin Everaert, Simon Musgrave & Alexis Dimitriadis (eds.), *The Use of Databases in Cross-Linguistic Studies*, 329–362. Berlin/New York: Mouton de Gruyter.
Matras, Yaron & Evangelia Adamou. 2020. Romani and Contact Linguistics. In Yaron Matras & Anton Tenser (eds.), *The Palgrave Handbook of Romani Language and Linguistics*, 329–352. London: Palgrave Macmillan.
Matras, Yaron & Evangelia Adamou. 2021. Borrowing. In idem (eds.), *The Routledge Handbook of Language Contact*, 237–251. London/New York: Routledge.
Meyer, Anna-Maria. 2017. Wielojęzyczna Polska – język romski w kontakcie z polszczyzną. *Postscriptum polonistyczne* 2(18). 145–155.
Meyer, Anna-Maria. 2018. Lexical borrowings and one-word codeswitches: Polish-Romani and Romani-Polish. *Anzeiger für Slavische Philologie* XLVI. 157–198.
Meyer, Anna-Maria. 2019. The creation of orthographies by means of 'Slavic' alphabets. In Sebastian Kempgen & Vittorio S. Tomelleri (eds.), *Slavic Alphabets and Identities*, 129–160. (BABEL 19). Bamberg: University of Bamberg Press.
Meyer, Anna-Maria. 2020a. The impact of Slavic languages on Romani. In Yaron Matras & Anton Tenser (eds.), *The Palgrave Handbook of Romani Language and Linguistics*, 261–301. London: Palgrave Macmillan.
Meyer, Anna-Maria. 2020b. Was ist Armeeslavisch? In Ivana Lederer, Anna-Maria Meyer & Katrin Schlund (eds.), *Linguistische Beiträge zur Slavistik. XXVI. und XXVII. JungslavistInnen-Treffen, 6.–8. Dezember 2017 in Bamberg und 12.–14. September 2018 in Heidelberg*, 63–88. (Specimina philologiae Slavicae 201). Berlin: Peter Lang.
Miklosich, Franz. 1872–80. *Über die Mundarten und die Wanderungen der Zigeuner Europa's*. I–XII. Wien: Karl Gerold's Sohn.
Miklosich, Franz. 1874–1878. *Beiträge zur Kenntniss der Zigeunermundarten*. I–IV. Wien: Karl Gerold's Sohn.
Milewski, Jacek. 2012. *Edukacja dzieci romskich. Praktyczny informator dla rodziców. Broszura pe Romane Dada. Broszura perdało Romane Dada* [Education of Romani children. Practical information for parents]. Radom: Producent Reklamy "Vena".
Miltner, Vladimír. 1965. The morphologic structure of a New Indo-Aryan language in Czechoslovakia. *Indian Linguistics* 26. 106–131.
Minkov, Michael. 1997. A concise grammar of West Bulgarian Romani. *Journal of the Gypsy Lore Society* 7. 55–95.
Minova-Ǵurkova, Liljana. 2003. *Stilistika na sovremeniot makedonski jazik* [Stylistics of the contemporary Macedonian language]. Skopje: Magor.
Mirga, Jan. 2009. *Słownik romsko-polski* [Dictionary Romani-Polish]. Tarnów: Romskie Stowarzyszenie Oświatowe Harangos, Muzeum Okręgowe w Tarnowie.
Mirga, Teresa. 1994. *Czemu tak? Soske kawka?* [Why so?] Podkowa Leśna: Koło Podkowy – Spółka Poetów.
Mirga, Teresa. 2006. *Wiersze i pieśni*. Tarnów: Muzeum Okręgowe w Tarnowie.

Mirić, Mirjana & Svetlana Ćirković. 2022. *Gurbetski romski u kontaktu: analiza balkanizama i pozajmljenica iž srpskog jezika.* [Gurbet Romani in contact: an analysis of Balkanisms and Serbian borrowings]. Beograd: Balkanološki institut SANU.

Mišeska-Tomić, Olga. 2009. Clitic and non-clitic possessive pronouns in Macedonian and Bulgarian. In Olga Dimitrova-Vulchanova & Olga Mišeska-Tomić (eds.), *Investigations in the Bulgarian and Macedonian nominal expression.* Trondheim: Tapir Academic Press.

Mladenov, Stefan. 1930. Tarikatskijat ezikъ na bălgarskite učenici [The Tarikat language of the Bulgarian pupils]. *Rodna reč* 4. 65–66.

Mladenov, Stefan. 1940. Tarikatskijat ezik [Tarikat language]. *Zlatorog* 21. 175–179.

Mokienko, Valerij & Harry Walter. 2014. Soziolekte in der Slavia (Überblick). In Karl Gutschmidt, Sebastian Kempgen, Tilman Berger & Peter Kosta (eds.), *The Slavic languages. An International Handbook of their Structure, their History and their Investigation*, 2145–2169. (Handbooks of Linguistics and Communication Science 32.2). Berlin: De Gruyter Mouton.

Myers-Scotton, Carol. 1993. *Duelling languages. Grammatical structure in codeswitching.* Oxford: Oxford University Press.

Myers-Scotton, Carol. 2002. *Contact linguistics.* Oxford: Oxford University Press.

Myers-Scotton, Carol. 2006. *Multiple Voices: An Introduction to Bilingualism.* Oxford: Blackwell Publishing.

Neweklowsky, Gerhard. 2015. *Franz Miklosich (1813–1891). Begründer der österreichischen Slawistik.* (Österreichische Akademie der Wissenschaften, Philosophisch-historische Klasse, Sitzungsberichte 866). Wien: Verlag der österreichischen Akademie der Wissenschaften.

Nichols, Johanna. 1992. *Linguistic Diversity in Space and Time.* Chicago: The University of Chicago Press.

Nichols, Johanna. 1997. Modeling ancient population structures and movement in linguistics. *Annual Review of Anthropology* 26(1). 359–384.

Nováček, Otakar. 1929. *Brněnská plotna* [The slang of Brno]. Brno: Vlastním nákladem.

Oberpfalcer, František. 1934. Argot a slangy [Argot and slang]. In: Václav Dědina & Oldřich Hujer (eds.), *Československá vlastivěda. 3. Jazyk*, 311–375. Praha: Vrchni red. Václava Dědiny.

Odaloš, Pavol. 1990. Argot v sučasnej jazykovej situácii na Slovensku [Argot in the contemporary linguistic situation in Slovakia]. *Slovenská reč* 4. 233–238.

Ondrus, Pavel. 1978. Argot slovenských vandrovných remeslníkov [The argot of the Slovak wandering craftsmen]. In Samostatná Pedagogická Fakultá v Plzni (ed.), *Sborník přednášek z konference o slangu a argotu v Plzni v září 1977*, 56–58. Plzeň: Pedagogická fakulta v Plzni.

Ong, Walter J. 1982. *Orality and literacy. The Technologizing of the Word.* London/New York: Methuen.

Oravec, Peter. 2014. *Slovník slangu a hovorovej slovenčiny* [Dictionary of slang and colloquial Slovak]. Praha: Maxdorf.

Pančenko, Januš A. 2013. *Izučenie vlašskogo dialekta romskogo jazyka: poiski i nachodki* [Research on the Vlax dialect of the Romani language: questions and findings]. Kiev: Naučno-issledovatel'skij centr orientalistiki imeni Omel'jana Pricaka NaUKMA.

Paspati, Alexander G. 1870. *Études sur les Tchinghianés ou Bohémiens de l'Empire Ottoman.* Constantinople: Imprimerie Antoine Koromela.

Patkanov, Istomin P. (1900): *Cyganskij jazyk. Grammatika i rukovodstvo k praktičeskomu izučeniju reči sovremennych russkich cygan* [The Gypsy language. Grammar and

instruction for practical learning of the speech of the contemporary Russian Gypsies].
Moskva: Tipolitografija "Russkogo Tovariščestva pečatnogo i izdatel'skogo dela".
Pešta, Andrej. 2007. E Roza [Rose]. *Romano džaniben* ñilaj [summer]. 198–221.
Petrovski, Trajko & Bone Veličkovski. 1998. *Makedonsko-romski i Romsko-makedonski rečnik. Makedonsko-romano i Romano-makedonsko alavari* [Macedonian-Romani and Romani-Macedonian dictionary]. Skopje: Vorldbuk.
Petulengro. 1915. Report on the Gypsy tribes of North-East Bulgaria. *Journal of the Gypsy Lore Society* 9. 65–109.
Piasere, Leonardo. 1985. *Mare Roma. Catégories humaines et structure sociale. Une contribution à l'éthnologie tsigane.* Paris: Laboratoire d'Anthropologie Sociale.
Pobożniak, Tadeusz. 1964. *Grammar of the Lovari dialect*. (PAN Oddział w Krakowie, Prace Komisji Orientalistycznej, 3). Kraków: Państwowe Wydawnictwo Naukowe.
Podzimek, Jaroslav. 1937. *Slovníček "Světská hantýrka"*. [Small dictionary of the "Světská hantýrka"]. Praha: Bezpečnostní služba.
Polenakoviḱ, Charalampie. 1951a. Prilozi kon makedonskite tajni jazici [Contributions to the Macedonian secret languages]. *Makedonski jazik* 2(3–4). 49–56.
Polenakoviḱ, Charalampie. 1951b. Ušte dva priloga kon makedonskite tajni jazici [Two more contributions to the Macedonian secret languages]. *Makedonski jazik* 2(9–10). 209–211.
Polenakoviḱ, Charalampie. 1952. Nov prilog kon makedonskite tajni jazici [A new contribution to the Macedonian secret languages]. *Makedonski jazik* 3(3). 57–58.
Popov, Vsevolod M. 1912. *Slovar' vorovskogo i arestantskogo jazyka* [Dictionary of the criminal and prisoners' slang]. Kiev: T-vo "Pečatnja S.P. Jakovleva".
Potapov, S.M. 1927. *Slovar' žargona prestupnikov (blatnaja muzyka)* [Dictionary of the criminal slang (blatnaja muzyka)]. Moskva: Associacija BLIK.
Puchmajer, Antonin J. 1821. *Románi čib, das ist: Grammatik- und Wörterbuch der Zigeuner-Sprache nebst einigen Fabeln in derselben. Dazu als Anhang die Hantýrka oder čechische Diebessprach.* Prag: Fürst-erzbischöfliche Buchdruckerey.
Puscher, Wilfried. 2005. *Romani und Russisch in Kontakt. Novation und Tradition.* Graz: University of Graz diploma thesis.
Putincev, A.M. 1906. O govore v mestnosti Chvorostan', Voronežskoj gubernii [About the dialect of the locality Chvorostan]. *Živaja starina* XV/1(1). 94–128.
Pyrkalo, Svitlana. 1997. *Peršyj slovnyk ukraïns'koho molodižnoho slenhu* [First dictionary of Ukrainian youth slang]. https://chtyvo.org.ua/authors/Pyrkalo_Svitlana/Pershyi_slovnyk_ukrainskoho_molodizhnoho_slenhu/.
Rácová, Anna. 1995. The lexicon of "Slovak" Romani language. *Asian and African Studies* 4(1). 8–14.
Rácová, Anna. 1997. Romani in contact with Slovak language. In Viktor Krupa (ed.), *Intercultural contacts and communication between East and West*, 83–87. Bratislava: Slovak Academic Press.
Rácová, Anna. 1999. On the category of aspectuality in Slovak Romani. *Asian and African Studies* 8(1). 62–66.
Rácová, Anna. 2000. Rómske základy ako zdroj neologizácie v slovenskej karpatskej rómčine [Romani roots as a source of neologisms in Slovak Carpathian Romani]. In Klára Buzássyová (ed.), *Človek a jeho jazyk. 1. Jazyk ako fenomén kultúry*, 45–51. Bratislava: VEDA.
Rácová, Anna. 2007. Romany word-formation bases as a source of neologization in the Slovak Carpathian Romany language. *SKASE Journal of Theoretical Linguistics* 4(1). 127–131.

Rácová, Anna. 2015. Slovak language and Slovak Romani. In Hristo Kyuchukov, Łukasz Kwadrans & Ladislav Fizik (eds.), *Romani Studies: Contemporary trends*, 79–95. (Roma 02.) München: LINCOM.

Rácová, Anna & Jan Horecký. 2000. *Slovenská karpatská rómčina. Opis systému*. Bratislava: VEDA.

Rácová, Anna & Milan Samko. 2015. Structural patterns and functions of reduplicative constructions in Slovak Romani. *Asian and African Studies* 24(2). 165–189.

Rippl, Eugen. 1926. *Zum Wortschatz des tschechischen Rotwelsch. Versuch einer lexikographischen Darstellung auf Grund einer Sammlung rotwelscher Ausdrücke und Redewendungen, von den ältesten Belegen angefangen bis in unsere Zeit, mit besonderer Berücksichtigung der Prager Hantýrka*. Liberec: Stiepel.

Ross, Malcolm. 2006. Language Families and Linguistic Diversity. In Keith Brown (ed.) *Encyclopedia of Language and Linguistics*. 2nd edn., vol. 6. 499–507. Amsterdam: Elsevier.

Ross, Anette. 2016. Estonian Lotfitka Romani and its contact languages. *Philologia Estonica Tallinnensis* 1. 154–172.

Rosten, Leo. 2003. *Jiddisch. Eine kleine Enzyklopädie*. 3rd edn. München: Deutscher Taschenbuch-Verlag.

Rozwadowski, Jan M. 1936. *Wörterbuch des Zigeunerdialekts von Zakopane. Mit Einleitung, Ergänzungen und Anmerkungen von Edward Klich. Słownik Cyganów z Zakopanego. Z wstępem, uzupełnieniami i uwagami E. Klicha*. Kraków: Nakładem Polskiej Akademii Umiejętności.

Rüdiger, Johann Ch. [1782] 1990. *Von der Sprache und Herkunft der Zigeuner aus Indien. Nachdr. der Ausg. Leipzig 1782*. Hamburg: Buske.

Rusakov, Aleksandr Ju. 2000. Severnorusskij dialect cyganskogo jazyka: 'Zaimstvovanie' russkich prefiksov [The North Russian dialect of the Gypsy language: 'Борrowing' of Russian prefixes]. In *Materialy XXVIII mežvuzovskoj naučno-metodičeskoj konferencii prepodavatelej i aspirantov*, vol. 21, 16–25. (Balkanskie issledovanija 21). Sankt-Peterburg: Izdatel'stvo SPbGU.

Rusakov, Aleksandr Yu. 2001a. The North Russian Romani dialect. Interference and Code Switching. In: Östen Dahl & Maria Koptjevskaja-Tamm (eds.), *The Circum-Baltic Languages. Typology and Contact*, 313–337. Amsterdam, Philadelphia: John Benjamins.

Rusakov, Aleksandr Ju. 2001b. Imperative in North Russian Romani dialect. In Viktor S. Chrakovskij (ed.), *Typology of Imperative Constructions*, 287–299. München: LINCOM.

Rusakov, Aleksandr Ju. 2001c. Code switching phenomena in Roma children's narratives. In Birgit Igla & Thomas Stolz (eds.), *„Was ich noch sagen wollte...": A multilingual Festschrift for Norbert Boretzky on occasion of his 65th birthday*, 431–438. Berlin: Akademie-Verlag.

Rusakov, Aleksandr Ju. 2004. *Interferencija i pereključenie kodov (severnorusskij dialekt cyganskogo jazyka v kontaktologičeskoj perspektive)* [Interference and codeswitching (the North Russian dialect of the Gypsy language from a contact-linguistic perspective]. Doktorskaja dissertacija. Sankt-Peterburg: Rossijskaja Akademija Nauk, Institut lingvističeskich issledovanij.

Rusakov, Alexandre & Olga Abramenko. 1998. North Russian Romani Dialect: Interference in case system. *Grazer Linguistische Studien* 50. 109–133.

Salmons, Joe. 1990. Bilingual discourse marking: code switching, borrowing, and convergence in some German-American dialects. *Linguistics* 28. 453–480.

Sakel, Jeanette. 2007. Types of loan: Matter and pattern. In Yaron Matras & Jeanette Sakel (eds.), *Grammatical Borrowing in Cross-Linguistic Perspective*, 15–30. Berlin/New York: Mouton de Gruyter.

Schmalstieg, William R. 2014. Baltoslavic. In Karl Gutschmidt, Sebastian Kempgen, Tilman Berger & Peter Kosta (eds.), *The Slavic Languages. An International Handbook of their Structure, their History and their Investigation*, 1144–1153. (Handbooks of Linguistics and Communication Science 32.2). Berlin: De Gruyter Mouton.

Schrammel, Barbara. 2002. *Kerki fadšal o ciro. The borrowing and calquing of verbal prefixes and particles in Romani dialects in contact with Slavic and German*. Graz: University of Graz diploma thesis.

Schrammel, Barbara. 2005. Borrowed verbal particles and prefixes in Romani: a comparative approach. In: Barbara Schrammel, Dieter W. Halwachs & Gerd Ambrosch (eds.), *General and applied Romani linguistics. Proceedings from the 6th international conference on Romani linguistics*, 99–113. München: LINCOM.

Semiletko, V'jačeslav. 2008. Do pytannja pro leksyčni osoblyvosti sjervits'koho dialektu movy romiv Ukraïny [On the question of lexical peculiarities of the Servy dialect of the Ukrainian Roma]. In *Romy Ukraïny: Iz mynuloho v majbutnje (do Roms'koï Dekady Jevropy 2005–2015)*, 359–363. Kyïv: Ministerstvo kul'tury i turyzmu Ukraïny.

Sergievskij, Maksim V. 1931. *Cyganskij jazyk. Kratkoe rukovodstvo po grammatike i pravopisaniju* [The Gypsy language. Short instruction to its grammar and orthography]. Moskva: Centrizdat.

Sergievskij, Maksim V. & Aleksej P. Barannikov. 1938. *Cygansko-russkij slovar'* [Gypsy-Russian dictionary]. Moskva: Gos. izd-vo inostrannych i nacional'nych slovarej.

Smalley, William A. 1964. *Dialect and Orthography in Gipende*. In idem (eds.), *Orthography Studies: Articles on New Writing Systems*. London/Amsterdam: United Bible Societies.

Sonnemann, Anna-Maria. 2022. Slavische Verbalpräfixe im Romani. Formen und Funktionen. *Die Welt der Slaven* 67(1). 34–67.

Sowa, Rudolf von. 1887. *Die Mundart der slovakischen Zigeuner*. Göttingen: Vandenhoeck und Ruprecht.

Starhon, René. 2018. *Čávátka tachtěte suvel* aneb lexikální romismy ve "světském argotu" [Lexical Romisms in the argot of the "světští"]. *Studia ethnologica pragensia* 1. 72–85.

Stavic'ka, Lesja. 2005. *Argo, žargon, sleng. Socijal'na diferencijacija ukraïns'koï movy* [Argot, jargon, slang. The social differentiation of the Ukrainian language]. Kyïv: Kritika.

Sussex, Roland & Paul V. Cubberley. 2006. *The Slavic languages*. Cambridge: Cambridge University Press.

Swadesh, Morris. 1955. Towards greater accuracy in lexicostatic dating. *International Journal of American Linguistics* 21. 212–237.

Šapoval, Viktor V. 2001a. Istočnikovedenie i leksikografija žargona [Source studies and lexicography of slang]. In idem (ed.), *Tekst istočnika kak ob"ekt analiza dlja filologa i istorika*, 13–37. Moskva: Unknown publisher.

Šapoval, Viktor V. 2001b. Otkuda prišlo slovo *labuch*? [Where does the word *labuch* come from?] In *Russkoe slovo. Materialy i doklady mežvuzovskoj konferencii, posvjaščennoj 60-letiju Orechovo-Zuevskogo gospedinstituta*, 28–32. Orechovo-Zuevo: Unknown publisher.

Šapoval, Viktor V. 2004. Vlast' kak leksikograf (cyganskoe slovo v slovare blatnogo žargona) [The power as a lexicographer (a Gypsy word in the lexicon of thieves' cant)]. *Lingvistika: Bjulleten' Ural'skogo lingvističeskogo obščestva* 13. 115–131.

Šapoval, Viktor V. 2007a. *Samoučitel' cyganskogo jazyka (russka roma: severnorusskij dialekt). Učebnoe posobie.* [Tutorial of the Gypsy language (Russka roma: North-Russian dialect). School book.] Moskva: AST Astrel' Xranitel'.

Šapoval, Viktor V. 2007b. Cyganskie ėlementy v russkom vorovskom argo? (Razmyšlenija nad stat'ej akad. A.P. Barannikova 1921g.) [Gypsy elements in Russian criminal argot? (Considerations on the essay of A.P. Barannikov, 1921)]. *Voprosy jazykoznanija* 5. 108–125.

Šapoval, Viktor V. 2008a. *Kratkoe rukovodstvo po cyganskomu jazyku (kėldėrarskij dialekt)* [Short instruction to the Gypsy language (dialect of the Kalderaš)]. Sankt-Peterburg: "Anima".

Šapoval, Viktor V. 2008b. Novye 'cyganizmy' v russkich žargonnych slovarjach [New 'Gypsyisms' in Russian slang dictionaries]. *Voprosy jazykoznanija* 6. 49–77.

Šapoval, Viktor V. 2011a. *Cyganizmy v žargonnych slovarjach. Kriterii dostovernosti opisanija* [Gypsyisms in slang dictionaries. Criteria of the reliability of description]. Saarbrücken: LAP Lambert Academic Publishing.

Šapoval, Viktor V. 2011b. Cyganskie zaimstvovanija v russkoj reči [Gypsy borrowings in Russian]. *Russkij jazyk v škole: Naučno-metodičeskij žurnal* 2. 58–60.

Šapoval, Viktor V. 2012. *Kratkij slovar' cyganizmov v vostočnoslavjanskich jazykach. Opisanie leksičeskich zaimstvovanij iz dialektov cyganskogo jazyka v russkom, belorusskom i ukrainskom jazykach* [Short dictionary of Gypsyisms in East Slavic languages. Description of lexical borrowings from the Gypsy dialects in Russian, Belarusian and Ukrainian]. Saarbrücken: LAP Lambert Academic Publishing.

Šebková, Hana. 1999. *Romaňi čhib. Klíč k učebnici slovenské romštiny*. Praha: Fortuna.

Štrukelj, Pavla. 1980. *Romi na Slovenskem*. Ljubljana: Cankarjeva založba.

Tadmor, Uri. 2009. Loanwords in the world's languages: Findings and results. In Martin Haspelmath & Uri Tadmor (eds.), *Loanwords in the World's Languages. A Comparative Handbook*, 55–75. Berlin: De Gruyter Mouton.

Tahirović Sijerčić, Hedina. 2009. *Stare romske bajke i priče*. Tuzla: Bosanska riječ.

Tcherenkov, Lev N. 1999. Eine kurzgefasste Grammatik des russischen Kalderaš-Dialekts des Romani. *Grazer Linguistische Studien* 51. 131–166.

Tcherenkov, Lev & Stéphane Laederich. 2004. *The Rroma. Otherwise known as Gypsies, Gitanos, Γυφτοι, Tsiganes, Ţigani, Çingene, Zigeuner, Bohémiens, Travellers, Fahrende etc.* 2 vols. Basel: Schwabe.

Tenser, Anton. 2005. *Lithuanian Romani*. München: LINCOM.

Tenser, Anton. 2008. *Northeastern group of Romani dialects*. Manchester: University of Manchester dissertation.

Tenser, Anton. 2012. A report on Romani dialects in Ukraine: Reconciling linguistic and ethnographic data. *Romani Studies* 22(1). 35–47.

Tenser, Anton. 2016. Semantic map borrowing – Case representation in Northeastern Romani dialects. *Journal of Language Contact* 9(2). 211–245.

Tichanov, Pavlo N. 1899. Černigovskie starcy [The elders of Černigov]. *Trudy Černigovskoj učënoj archivnoj komissii* 2. 65–155.

Thieroff, Rolf. 1994. Inherent verb categories and categorizations in European languages. In Rolf Thieroff & Joachim Ballweg (eds.), *Tense systems in European languages I*, 3–45. Tübingen: Niemeyer.

Thieroff, Rolf. 1995. More on inherent verb categories in European languages. In idem (ed.), *Tense systems in European languages II*, 1–36. Tübingen: Niemeyer.

Thierry, Guillaume & Yan Jing Wu. 2007. Brain potentials reveal unconscious translation during foreign-language comprehension. *Proceedings of the National Academy of Sciences* 104. 12530–12535.

Thomason, Sarah G. 2001. *Language Contact. An Introduction.* Edinburgh: Edinburgh University Press.
Thomason, Sarah G. & Terrence Kaufman. 1988. *Language Contact, Creolization and Genetic Linguistics.* Berkeley: University of California Press.
Toninato, Paola. 2014. *Romani writing. Literacy, literature and identity politics.* New York/London: Routledge.
Toropov, Vadim G. 1999. Istorija izučenija cyganskogo jazyka v Rossii [The history of research on the Gypsy language in Russia]. In: A.M. Filippov (ed.), *Cygane. Sbornik statej*, 16–26. (Serija Novye issledovanija po ėtnologii i antropologii). Moskva: Institut ėtnologii i antropologii.
Toropov, Vadim G. 2003. *Slovar' jazyka krymskich cygan* [Dictionary of the language of the Crimean Gypsies]. Moskva: Rossijskaja Akademija Nauk.
Toropov, Vadim G. 2005. Cyganskie dialekty [Gypsy dialects]. *Jazyki Rossijskoj Federacii i sosednych gosudarstv*, vol. III, 354–365. Moskva: Nauka.
Toropov, Vadim G. & Pavel B. Gumeroglyj. 2013. Opyt sostavlenija alfavita dlja zapisi ustnoj reči krymskich cygan [Trial to create an alphabet for writing the speech of the Crimean Gypsies]. In: Kiril A. Kožanov, Sonja A. Oskol'skaja & Aleksandr Ju. Rusakov (eds.), *Cyganskij jazyk v Rossii. Sbornik materialov Rabočego soveščanija po cyganskomu jazyku v Rossii. Sankt-Peterburg, 5 oktjabrja 2012g*, 199–228. Sankt-Peterburg: Nestor-Istorija.
Trenevski, Tomislav. 1997. *Rečnik na žargonski zborovi i izrazi* [Dictionary of jargon words and expressions]. Skopje: T. Trenevski.
Trachtenberg, V.F. 1908. *Blatnaja muzyka: "žargon" tjurmy* [Blatnaja muzyja: prisoners' slang]. Sankt-Peterburg: Tip. A.G. Rozena.
Uhlik, Rade. 1951. *Prepozitivni i postpozitivni član u gurbetskom* [Prepositions and postpositions in Gurbet]. Sarajevo: Gradska štamparija.
Uhlik, Rade. 1954. *Ciganizmi u šatrovačkom argou i u sličnim govorima* [Gypsyisms in the šatrovački argot and similar secret languages]. Sarajevo: Zemaljski muzej.
Ułaszyn, Henryk. 1951. *Język złodziejski. La langue des voleurs.* (Łódzkie Towarzystwo Naukowe, Wydział Językoznawstwa, Nauki o Literaturze i Filozofii: Prace Wydziału I – Językoznawstwa, Nauki o Literaturze i Filozofii 11). Łódź: Łódzkie Towarzystwo Naukowe.
Vučković, Marija. 2017. Accomodation of Romani loan verbs in Czech and Serbo-Croatian. In Ilona Janyš ková, Helena Karloková & Vít Boček (eds.), *Etymological Research into Czech. Proceedings of the Etymological Symposium Brno 2017, 12–14 September 2017, Brno*, 441–454. Praha: Nakladatelství Lidové noviny.
Wagner, Peter. 2012. *A Grammar of North West Lovari Romani. Gramatika severozápadní olaštiny (lovárštiny).* Prague: Charles University dissertation. https://dspace.cuni.cz/handle/20.500.11956/43681. (accessed 23 May 2022)
Weinreich, Uriel. 1953. *Languages in contact. Findings and problems.* (Publications of the Linguistic Circle of New York 1). New York: Linguistic Circle of New York.
Wentzel, Tatjana W. 1980. *Die Zigeunersprache (Nordrussischer Dialekt).* Leipzig: Verlag Enzyklopädie.
Whitney, William D. 1881. On mixture in language. *Transactions of the American Philological Association (1869–1896)* 12. 1–26.
Wiemer, Björn & Ilja Seržant. 2017. Diachrony and typology of Slavic aspect: What does morphology tell us? In Walter Bisang & Andrej Malchukov (eds.), *Unity and Diversity in Grammaticalization Scenarios*, 239–307. Berlin: Language Science Press.

Wingender, Monika. 2003. Überlegungen zur Weiterentwicklung der Theorie der Standardsprache. In Wolfgang Gladrow (eds.), *Die slawischen Sprachen im aktuellen Funktionieren und historischen Kontakt: Beiträge zum XIII. internationalen Slavistenkongreß vom 15. bis 21. August 2003 in Ljubljana*, 133–152. Frankfurt am Main: Lang.

Wingender, Monika. 2013. Modell zur Beschreibung von Standardsprachentypen. In: Daniel Müller & Monika Wingender (eds.), *Typen slavischer Standardsprachen. Theoretische, methodische und empirische Zugänge*, 19–37. (Slavistische Studienbücher, Neue Folge 25). Wiesbaden: Harrassowitz.

Wingender, Monika. 2014. Typen slavischer Standardsprachen. In Karl Gutschmidt, Sebastian Kempgen, Tilman Berger & Peter Kosta (eds.), *The Slavic Languages. An International Handbook of their Structure, their History and their Investigation*, 1958–1972. (Handbooks of Linguistics and Communication Science 32.2). Berlin: De Gruyter Mouton.

Wlislocki, Heinrich von. 1994. *Zur Ethnographie der Zigeuner in Südosteuropa. Tsiganologische Aufsätze und Briefe aus dem Zeitraum 1880–1905*. Hg v. Joachim S. Hohmann. (Studien zur Tsiganologie und Folkloristik 12). Frankfurt am Main: Lang.

Wolf, Siegmund A. 1956. *Wörterbuch des Rotwelsch. Deutsche Gaunersprache*. Mannheim: Bibliographisches Institut.

Zaliznjak, Aleksej A. 1977. *Grammatičeskij slovar' russkogo jazyka* [Grammatical dictionary of the Russian language]. Moskva: Izdat. Russkij Jazyk.

Subject index

ability 52
ablative 41, 166
accent 114
accusative 60
acrolect 4
actionality 79, 82, 90
adjective 94, 96, 98, 100, 104, 105, 109, 113
adposition 55
adverb 79, 80, 97, 99, 100, 105, 109, 113
affix 37, 38, 46
aktionsart 66, 79, 81, 83, 88, 89, 90, 166, 167
alphabet 139, 140, 142, 143, 144, 145, 146, 147, 148, 149, 150, 151, 152, 153, 154, 158, 159, 160, 161, 169
aorist 47, 166
argot 117, 118, 120, 121, 122, 123, 124, 127, 129, 130, 131, 132, 133, 134, 135, 136, 137, 169
article 41, 42, 65, 95, 166, 167
aspect 47, 48, 66, 79, 80, 82, 83, 87, 89, 90, 91, 166, 167
aspiration 35, 146, 148, 153, 154, 158, 160
attitude 94, 129, 139, 141, 144
Ausbau 23

basilect 4, 129
bilingualism 2, 4, 26, 28, 29, 30, 31, 32, 33, 34, 35, 37, 63, 88, 92, 106, 114, 115, 153, 157, 165, 167, 168, 169
borrowing 29, 30, 31, 92, 103, 113, 114, 115, 165, 167

Čalgădžijski ezik 120
calque 58, 83, 84, 87, 88, 90, 100, 102, 103, 168
cardinal number 100, 101, 167
case 38, 39, 41, 65, 167
causative 51, 166
codeswitching 3, 30, 92, 106, 113, 165
colloquial language 116, 117, 118, 122, 123, 124, 125, 129, 130, 131, 133, 138, 169
comparative 42, 43, 65, 99, 167
conditional 53

conditional sentence 59, 65
conjunction 55, 56, 57, 58, 105, 106, 166
connector 57, 97
consonant 35, 36, 37, 143, 146, 148, 151, 153, 154, 158, 159, 160
content word 168
copula 62, 63, 166
core form 92, 107
cultural loan 92, 104, 107
Cyrillic script 139, 147, 148, 149, 150, 153, 154, 156, 157, 161, 169

dative 39, 41, 51, 65, 166
definiteness 41, 42, 65, 166, 167
deixis 42, 46
demonstrative pronoun 42, 46, 166
derivation 37, 100, 108, 125, 127, 166
desire 51
determiner 99
devoicing 35, 148, 150, 151, 153, 154, 161
diacritic 150
dialect 6, 16, 17, 18, 20, 21, 25, 111, 153, 165
dialect classification 165
diastratic variety 114, 115, 127, 129, 136, 137, 165, 169, 170
digraph 148, 157, 160
diminutive 37, 38, 166
diphthong 146
discourse marker 63, 64, 97, 106, 166
distance 21, 22, 23, 25
donor language 93, 114, 115, 122

elative 43
ending 37, 38, 95, 96, 166, 167
ethnolect 114, 170
etymology 119, 120, 129, 130, 135, 145, 150, 153, 160
evidentiality 53, 54, 65

feminine 37, 38, 95, 108
focus particle 98, 99
fossilization 115
function word 168

fusion 31, 63, 88, 100, 101, 165, 166
future 47, 60, 65, 66, 151

gender 95, 96, 108
genitive 38, 39, 40, 41, 60, 109, 166, 167
grammaticalization 13, 31, 84, 166
grapheme 143, 145, 146, 150, 154, 159, 160, 169

identity 2, 4, 29, 121, 140, 144
imperative 54, 60, 83, 166
imperfect 47, 151, 166
imperfective 80, 82, 89, 109
indefiniteness 41, 43, 44, 45, 99, 166
infinitive 48, 49, 65, 109, 166, 167
inflection 37, 41, 52, 53, 92, 96, 97, 166, 167
instrumental 40, 167
intelligibility 21, 22, 25
intensifier 99
interlanguage 115
intermediary language 93
interrogative 45, 61, 99, 166
iterativity 80, 90

jargon 117, 118, 122, 135
jussive 54

language 16, 17, 20, 21, 24, 25, 27, 28, 32, 165
language acquisition 2
language contact 26, 31, 32, 165, 166
language family 16, 17, 21, 25, 165
Latin script 139, 142, 143, 145, 152, 153, 154, 156, 157, 160, 161, 169
letter 145, 146, 151, 154
lexical borrowing 112, 119, 167, 168, 169
lexicon 77, 83, 90, 92, 93, 94, 102, 103, 104, 108, 109, 111, 113, 115, 116, 123, 145, 169
literacy 140, 141, 142, 145
local adverb 98
locative 40

majority language 2, 4, 7, 66, 93, 100, 114, 142, 143, 146, 161, 169
masculine 95, 108

matter 30, 31, 33, 37, 165, 166
medialis 51
mesolect 4
minority language 2, 4, 31, 115, 167, 168
modality 51, 52, 53, 65, 66, 106
monolingualism 27, 28, 29, 32, 115, 169
morphology 37, 46, 64, 65, 83, 92, 108, 115, 127, 145, 151, 153, 166
multilingualism 7, 26, 27, 28, 29, 30, 32, 33, 35, 92, 93, 114, 115, 165, 168, 169

necessity 52, 53
negation 60
negative pronoun 99
neuter 95, 108
nominative 40, 41, 167
noun 92, 94, 95, 104, 105, 106, 107, 108, 109, 113, 166, 167, 168
number 166
numeral 100, 101, 105, 133, 166

object 60, 61
object doubling 58, 59, 65, 166
oblique 40, 96
optative 54, 58
orality 139, 140, 141, 142
ordinal number 100, 101
orthographic principle 139, 160, 161
orthography 139, 142, 143, 144, 145, 147, 148, 149, 150, 151, 152, 153, 154, 156, 157, 158, 159, 160, 161, 164, 169

palatal 36
palatalization 36, 44, 65, 146, 148, 149, 151, 152, 153, 159
part of speech 92, 94, 104, 105, 107, 113
particle 97, 99
passive 50, 166
past 47, 48
pattern 30, 31, 33, 37, 42, 102, 165, 166, 167
perfect 47, 65, 166
perfective 48, 82, 83, 89, 109
person 48, 166
personal pronoun 46, 50, 166
phasal adverb 97, 98, 113

phoneme 34, 36, 145, 146, 149, 150, 152, 154, 159, 160, 161, 166
phonetics 33, 36, 64, 115, 145
phonology 33, 34, 35, 36, 37, 64, 65, 115, 139, 145, 166
plural 37, 46, 48, 96, 166
positive 42, 43
possession 39, 40, 53, 166
possessive pronoun 46, 166
prefix 38, 42, 43, 48, 76, 77, 78, 79, 80, 81, 82, 83, 84, 85, 86, 87, 88, 89, 90, 109, 166, 167
preposition 38, 39, 41, 42, 45, 55, 56, 105, 166
present 47
prestige 31, 115, 144, 147
preterite 48
pronoun 44, 45, 46, 51, 100

quantifier 100, 113

recipient language 106
reflexivity 50, 51, 65, 109
renarrative 53, 54, 65, 167
repertoire 26, 27, 28, 29, 31, 32, 33, 35, 165, 167, 168, 169
retroflex 146, 160

secret language 4, 116, 120, 121, 129, 169
semantic field 94, 96, 107, 108, 113, 117, 168
sign 141
similarity 22, 23, 24
slang 116, 117, 126, 128
sociolect 118, 120, 137
sociolinguistics 117, 168
sound 34, 35, 65, 145, 146, 148, 154, 160, 166

standard language 5, 17, 25, 35, 123, 168
standardization 25, 139, 142, 143, 144, 145, 148, 154, 156, 157, 164, 165
stem 84, 95, 109, 134
stress 35, 36, 37, 65
subject 60
subordinate clause 60
substandard variety 117, 119, 123, 169
suffix 37, 38, 48, 80, 90, 96, 100, 108, 166
superlative 42, 43, 167
Světská hantýrka 120
syllable 35
syntax 54, 64, 115, 145, 166, 169

tarikatski ezik 120
temporal adverb 97, 113
tense 47, 48, 65, 66, 82
transitivity 47, 50, 85, 90, 96

velarization 34
verb 76, 77, 78, 79, 82, 83, 84, 85, 88, 91, 92, 94, 96, 104, 105, 106, 109, 113, 167, 168
voice 50
vowel 34, 36, 37, 65, 146, 148, 149, 150, 151, 154, 156, 157
vowel length 35, 37, 146, 149, 151
vowel reduction 36

word formation 37, 95, 108, 109, 113
word order 60, 62, 166
writing system 139, 140, 144, 151, 152, 158, 161, 169

youth slang 116, 117, 118, 123, 124, 126, 130, 131, 134, 136, 138, 169

Language index

Abruzzo 20
Albanian 4, 34, 44, 51, 120
Angloromani 20, 93
Arli 19, 34, 35, 36, 39, 41, 43, 44, 45, 46,
 47, 53, 56, 58, 59, 60, 61, 63, 78, 96,
 153, 166
Arlija 119, 156

Bačkačjke 44
Balkan 19, 33, 42, 43, 45, 47, 50, 51, 55, 58,
 59, 61, 62, 96, 166
Balkan Slavic 41, 48, 51
Baltic 17, 84, 87, 91
Balto-Slavic 17
Bashkir 149
Belarusian 17, 36, 83
Bergitka 42, 56, 61, 80, 86, 92, 94, 99, 103,
 104, 105, 106, 107, 108, 109, 110, 111,
 113, 167, 168
Bohemian 20, 34, 37, 48, 80, 121
Bosnian 17, 117, 119, 124, 126
Bosnian / Croatian / Serbian 35, 44, 76, 93,
 94, 118, 119, 124, 125, 126, 129, 136, 137,
 154, 169
Bosnian Romani 60
British Romani 20
Bugurdži 19, 34, 39, 47, 52, 56, 94, 96, 99
Bulgarian 17, 34, 35, 37, 38, 39, 41, 42, 44,
 45, 46, 47, 50, 52, 53, 56, 60, 77, 78, 93,
 95, 96, 118, 120, 123, 127, 128, 129, 135,
 137, 157, 166, 167, 169
Bulgarian Romani 59, 60, 93, 95
Burgenland Croatian 17

Calabrian 20
Caló 20
Central 19, 20, 37, 45, 55, 56
Central Slovak 44, 101
Čergari 34
Church Slavonic 17
Crimean 19, 34, 99, 149, 150, 151
Croatian 17, 48, 51, 52, 55, 58, 93, 123, 124,
 125, 126, 164, 166
Croatian Romani 20

Čuchny 84
Čurarja Arlije 51
Czech 17, 22, 23, 34, 35, 43, 44, 48, 51, 52,
 76, 79, 80, 90, 96, 102, 115, 118, 120,
 121, 122, 123, 129, 130, 131, 135, 137, 151,
 152, 169, 170

Dasikano 56
Doljenski 46, 51, 52, 53, 58, 59, 60, 77, 93, 99
Drindari 19, 102
Džambazi 153, 156

Early Romani 37, 46, 50, 96, 146
East Bulgarian 77
East Finnish 23, 165
East Slavic 42, 43, 44, 49, 60, 61, 62,
 76, 80, 86, 90, 91, 118, 122, 133,
 149, 166
East Slovak 20, 35, 36, 38, 42, 44, 49, 50,
 52, 53, 56, 59, 62, 79, 80, 87, 88, 90, 94,
 96, 99, 100, 101, 102
Eastern Už 38, 43, 44, 45, 59, 60, 80, 83, 95,
 96, 100, 101, 103
English 114, 116, 157
Erli 19, 38, 44, 45, 77, 78, 101, 166
Estonian Romani 45

Finnish Romani 93
French 122

German 20, 89, 93, 114, 116, 120, 122, 129
Gimpeny 3, 39, 43, 62
Greek 6, 17, 19, 37, 41, 50, 52, 59, 95, 96, 101,
 108, 109, 120, 122, 166
Gurbet 20, 34, 35, 36, 42, 44, 52, 78, 94, 119,
 125, 127, 168

Hebrew 116, 129, 140
Hravati 46
Hungarian 20, 43, 77, 94, 96, 101, 108, 110,
 113, 168

Iberian 20
Indo-Aryan 17, 48, 146

Indo-European 16, 17
Iranian 17, 48

Judezmo 120, 129

Kalajdži 19, 23, 101, 165
Kalderaš 20, 37, 39, 41, 45, 56, 81, 94, 96, 99, 149
Kashubian 17
Kazakh 149
Kovački 78, 96
Kubanska 39
Kumanovo 46

Latin 17, 122
Latvian 84
Latvian Romani 39, 40, 167
Lithuanian 36, 84
Lithuanian Romani 39, 40, 45, 56, 84, 85, 87, 88, 90, 99, 100, 101, 167
Litovska 84, 85
Lotfitka 84, 85, 93
Lovari 20, 36, 37, 38, 149
Lovari Čokeši 36

Macedonian 17, 34, 35, 39, 41, 42, 45, 46, 47, 50, 52, 53, 56, 58, 59, 61, 78, 79, 114, 129, 137, 138, 153, 154, 166, 170
Macedonian Romani 102
Manuš 20
Manuša Čurjarja 34, 51
Molise Slavic 17, 168
Montenegrin 164
Muslimanje 52
Muzikantska 52

Nakhale 44
New Indo-Aryan 102
North Balkan 20
North Central 21, 37, 51, 59, 100
North Russian 20, 33, 34, 36, 38, 39, 40, 43, 44, 47, 49, 50, 52, 54, 59, 62, 81, 82, 83, 84, 85, 88, 89, 93, 94, 95, 96, 101, 102, 147, 148, 166
North Slavic 37, 91, 99, 167
North Vlax 20
Northeastern 39, 41, 55, 56, 85, 90, 100, 167

Northern 19, 20, 37
Northern Central 5, 20, 33, 49, 79, 80, 101, 152
Northwestern 5

Old Indo-Aryan 69

Para-Romani 4, 20
Plaščuny 39, 58
Polabian 17
Polish 17, 34, 35, 44, 45, 48, 52, 53, 56, 76, 80, 81, 83, 84, 90, 91, 93, 94, 100, 102, 103, 104, 105, 106, 107, 108, 109, 110, 111, 112, 113, 118, 122, 132, 133, 137, 158, 159, 168, 169
Polish Romani 45, 158, 159
Polska 41, 42, 44, 47, 81, 83, 84, 85, 87, 92, 94, 99, 101, 103, 104, 105, 106, 107, 108, 109, 111, 113, 168
Pomeranian 17
Prekmurski 20, 77
Prilep 19, 41, 44, 166
Prizren 19
Proto-Romani 17
Proto-Slavic 17

Rešitari 34
Romanian 5, 20, 35, 43, 51, 86, 120
Rumungro 20, 40, 55, 100
Russian 3, 5, 17, 34, 35, 36, 38, 39, 40, 43, 44, 45, 47, 52, 54, 56, 58, 62, 64, 81, 82, 83, 84, 86, 88, 93, 94, 95, 96, 98, 102, 111, 118, 122, 123, 133, 135, 136, 137, 148, 149, 150, 166, 167, 169
Russian Romani 39, 43, 167
Rusyn 43

Sanskrit 5, 17
Selice 112, 168, 170
Sepeči 47
Serbian 17, 34, 37, 41, 42, 44, 52, 56, 63, 97, 114, 124, 126, 160, 168
Serednye 36, 45, 52, 83
Servi 39, 43, 44
Servy 38, 44, 64
Sinti 20, 49, 89, 93, 114, 121
Sliven 60

Slovak 17, 22, 23, 35, 38, 43, 44, 48, 50, 51,
    52, 53, 56, 62, 64, 76, 79, 80, 83, 90, 94,
    95, 96, 99, 101, 102, 103, 118, 121, 131,
    137, 151, 152, 170
Slovak Romani 56, 94, 101, 151, 166
Slovene 17, 35, 41, 46, 48, 51, 76, 77, 93, 101,
    137, 138, 166
Slovene Romani 48, 55, 101, 166
Slovincian 17
Sorbian 17
South Balkan 20, 52
South Balkan I 5, 19
South Balkan II 19
Southern Central 5, 20, 21, 37
South Slavic 5, 37, 43, 44, 45, 53, 54, 58, 59,
    76, 79, 90, 93, 94, 96, 98, 105, 111, 118,
    137, 169
South Slovak 96

Texan Romani 5, 93
Torlak 41
Turkish 4, 19, 34, 77, 117, 120

Ukrainian 3, 17, 34, 36, 38, 48, 52, 62, 64,
    83, 86, 103, 118, 122, 135, 136, 137, 148,
    149, 166, 169
Ukrainian Romani 45, 47, 50, 60, 86
Ursari 19

Vend 20
Vlax 5, 18, 19, 20, 21, 37, 39, 43, 44,
    49, 55, 58, 60, 61, 62, 83, 86,
    93, 96, 114

Welsh Romani 49, 93
West Bulgarian 77, 78, 96
West Slavic 5, 42, 43, 49, 58, 61,
    118, 166
West Slovak 20, 35, 36, 47, 49

Xaladytka 20, 44, 62, 83, 85
Xandžari 39

Yerli 42, 43, 56, 78, 101
Yiddish 121, 122, 129

www.ingramcontent.com/pod-product-compliance
Lightning Source LLC
Chambersburg PA
CBHW050520170426
43201CB00013B/2029